MacARTHUR'S AIRMAN

MacARTHUR'S AIRMAN

GENERAL GEORGE C. KENNEY
and the War in the Southwest Pacific

Thomas E. Griffith Jr.

University Press of Kansas

© 1998 by the University Press of Kansas

Published by the University Press of Kansas (Lawrence, Kansas 66049), which was
organized by the Kansas Board of Regents and is operated and funded by Emporia State
University, Fort Hays State University, Kansas State University, Pittsburg State
University, the University of Kansas, and Wichita State University

Library of Congress Cataloging-in-Publication Data

Griffith, Thomas E., Jr.
    MacArthur's airman : General George C. Kenney and the war in the
Southwest Pacific / Thomas E. Griffith.
        p.   cm. — (Modern war studies)
    Includes bibliographical references and index.
    ISBN 0-7006-0909-1 (alk. paper)
    1. Kenney, George C. (George Churchill), 1889–1977.   2. World War,
1939–1945—Campaigns—Pacific Area.   3. World War, 1939–1945—Aerial
operations, American.   4. World War, 1939–1945—Personal narratives,
American.   5. United States. Army—Biography.   6. Generals—United
States—Biography.   I. Title.   II. Series.
D767.G75   1998
940.54'4973—dc21   98-15696
                                                                                CIP

British Library Cataloguing in Publication Data is available

Printed in the United States of America

10 9 8 7 6 5 4 3 2 1

The paper used in this publication meets the minimum requirements of the American
National Standard for Permanence of Paper for Printed Library Materials
Z39.48-1984.

TO MY FAMILY

CONTENTS

ACKNOWLEDGMENTS

Like any historian or writer who undertakes a project of this magnitude, I have incurred debts that I can never possibly repay except to offer my sincere and heartfelt thanks. I must begin by acknowledging the invaluable help and encouragement of Richard Kohn throughout the course of this work. He has been a patient mentor as well as an outstanding teacher, and he combines those two aspects of his life with being a committed citizen. I can think of no better role model. Gerhard Weinberg, Miles Fletcher, and Don Higginbotham all suggested excellent revisions, and the work is better for their contributions. My special thanks to Tami Davis Biddle for reading several drafts and offering her extensive insights into the history of air power. Phil Meilinger and the faculty at the School of Advanced Airpower Studies deserve recognition for having the confidence to send me to graduate school. Professor Dave Mets has earned special appreciation for his teaching ability and his willingness to read the manuscript. To the entire school, past, present, and future, my thanks; I hope you will find this valuable.

A grant from the United States Air Force Historical Research Agency allowed me to make several research trips to Maxwell Air Force Base to cull their archives, which proved very rewarding. The Air Force Institute of Technology sponsored travel to Washington, D.C., and Norfolk, Virginia. At other times I relied on the hospitality of friends and family. My thanks to everyone who opened their home to me.

For providing background information on George Kenney and the Kenney family I am indebted to James Kenney, who shared the considerable research he had done on the family history, and Dorothy Dodson, also kindly allowed me to search through a trunk full of family mementos of her uncle George Kenney.

Numerous librarians and archivists assisted in finding documents and providing leads for other sources, but a few deserve special recognition. Cindy Battis at the Brookline Public Library went out of her way to search for details about Kenney's youth. Special thanks for the assistance of Duane Reed at the United States Air Force Academy, Jim Zoebel at the MacArthur Memorial, and Evonee Kincaid at the Center for Air Force History.

I am especially grateful to the many scholars who took time out from their own work to patiently answer my questions. Herman Wolk at the Center for Air Force History provided invaluable assistance on the Kenney Papers and gladly shared insights into the general's career from his own research. An interview with Don Goldstein at the University of Pittsburgh was helpful in giving me a different perspective on Kenney, while Richard Watson at Duke University kindly answered my questions about his work on the official Air Force history. Pete Faber and DeWitt Copp answered questions about the Air Corps between the wars, and Jim Titus kindly provided access to Martha Byrd's manuscript on Ken Walker. Thanks to William Baldwin for leading me through the records of the Corps of Engineers and to Edward Drea and Stanley Falk for their comments on the manuscript. Two historians in Australia, David Horner and Alan Stephens, went above and beyond the call of duty in answering my inquires about sources "down under."

Last, but certainly not least, this book simply could not have been written without the support of my family. My parents provided my first role models and made certain that I had the background to carry this off, and I can never thank them enough. My brothers and their families have always been very supportive, but Bob and Greg deserve recognition for their special assistance in this project. Liz took time out from her own studies to read the manuscript and surely made it better. Dyanne, Megan, Kate, and Trey never became very interested in George Kenney, perhaps because he took so much of their father's time, but they patiently endured my nights and weekends at the computer. For their continued support I am grateful.

While I am thankful for all the help I have received, any errors must remain my responsibility alone. The views and opinions presented here are likewise mine and do not represent the position of the Department of Defense, the United States Air Force, or any of their subordinate agencies.

INTRODUCTION

The United States battleship *Missouri* sat peacefully at anchor in Tokyo Bay on the cloudy morning of September 2, 1945, a scene in sharp contrast to the bloody four years of warfare in the Pacific. General George C. Kenney stepped aboard the mighty warship shortly after eight o' clock that morning, taking his place in the front row of dignitaries gathered to witness the signing of the surrender documents that would officially end the war with Japan.[1] His presence there was well deserved. As General Douglas MacArthur's air commander in the Southwest Pacific theater since July 1942, George Kenney had contributed operational skill, intellectual flexibility, and technical innovations that had made air power a crucial part of the Allied victory.

Kenney's achievements have not gone unrecognized by historians. In his major study of America's war in the Pacific, *Eagle Against the Sun*, Ronald Spector reports that "General George C. Kenney found a dispirited and disillusioned air organization, which he quickly overhauled and beat into life."[2] D. Clayton James, best known for his three-volume biography of MacArthur, credits Kenney's influence in shaping MacArthur's strategic thinking during the war.[3] Geoffrey Perret, author of a recent popular narrative on the Army Air Forces in World War II, rates Kenney a "superb" commander.[4] Although Kenney generally receives high marks, at least one student of the war in the Pacific argues that Kenney's achievements have been overstated. In his study of Ennis C. Whitehead, Kenney's deputy, historian Donald Goldstein maintains that Whitehead, not Kenney, was the "driving force and genius behind the Allied Air Forces in the Southwest Pacific."[5]

These opinions about Kenney's contributions, however, are based on a very narrow range of sources. Since Kenney's performance has never been examined in depth, these authors must draw most of their conclusions about his accomplishments from the official Air Force histories of World War II and Kenney's own account of the war, published under the title *General Kenney Reports*.

Relying on this limited array of sources has some obvious shortcomings. Written at the conclusion of the war, the official Air Force histories provide a wealth of detail and are useful starting points for any research on air warfare in World War II, but they tend to focus on the tactical details of the air fighting and emphasize the decisiveness of air power in a given campaign. These studies downplay the limitations of air power and avoid detailed analysis or criticism of air commanders such as Kenney. In addition, some aspects of Kenney's operations were classified and hence unavailable when the official histories were written, most notably his reliance on signals intelligence.

Kenney's own work is lively and engaging, offering insight into his personality as well as his ideas on warfare, but badly flawed. There are a few omissions that distort the record, and Kenney sometimes exaggerates his own influence in the war. In addition, his account must be assessed in light of the heated interservice debates occurring when the book was published, a factor that led him to emphasize the effectiveness of air power over the contributions from the other services. As historian David Horner put it, an "assessment of [Kenney's] performance is both helped and hindered by his remarkable book."[6] No matter how interesting and useful the work is for its revelations into the nature of high command and the role of air power in the war, in the end it remains a memoir, exhibiting all the shortcomings and strengths of that genre. It should not be mistaken for a history of the war. The net result is an incomplete and often inaccurate picture of the effect of air power and of George Kenney's leadership in a theater where air power was, in Spector's assessment, "the dominant element."[7]

The lack of an in-depth biographical study of Kenney points out the paucity of detailed studies on air leaders in general.[8] Despite the importance of air power in warfare during the last half of the twentieth century and the amount of ink spilled by historians about the morality of air warfare and the motivations of air commanders, the number of studies about leading airmen remains surprisingly small.[9] In a comprehensive survey of the biographies of air leaders, historian Philip Meilinger found that the works tended to focus on the lives of the few very public figures and that few were scholarly studies.[10] A study of George Kenney covering his career both before and during World War II is one step toward understanding the perspective of airmen and the nature of leadership for an air commander. Moreover, focusing on Kenney provides one small corrective for understanding the complicated nature of air power, especially as it played out in the Southwest Pacific. Because of the many roles that airmen performed and the central position Kenney had in directing the air units, an analysis of his operations will provide a more complete picture of the war in the Southwest Pacific.

This work focuses on George Kenney as a theater air commander. The first section details his personal and military background, the source of many of his ideas about air warfare. The remainder of the study examines and evaluates his record of command in World War II, employing air power both in an independent role and in operations with ground and naval forces. While I examined a variety of sources, like other historians who cover this period, I used Kenney's own account both for the details it offers and for the glimpse it affords of how Kenney viewed the war. However, because of the problems with this memoir and a propensity for some writers to rely on it for more than Kenney's impressions, I have attempted to correct the record and point out where his account of events is at odds with other sources.

By virtue of his position, Kenney was involved primarily in planning future operations. His responsibility was the overall theater application of air power; this analysis will likewise attend to the theater level of operations. I have attempted to capture the many different aspects of command at that level, from combat operations and tactics to planning, intelligence, supply, and morale. Strategic decisions about the overall conduct of the war will be included both to provide the context for operations and to aid in determining Kenney's impact on those strategic decisions. Likewise, individual air engagements and bombing missions will be cited where appropriate, but not usually dissected in great detail. Readers hoping for a detailed discussion of air missions will have to look elsewhere.

Kenney's success in employing air power rested on his knowledge of modern warfare and a strong belief in the unique contribution of air power to military operations. The most important task for the air force, he believed, was to reduce, if not eliminate, the enemy's ability to interfere with friendly operations. The first aim of an air commander was to gain the unimpeded use of the air space: in short, to control the air. This would allow friendly air and surface forces to pursue actions free from interference from the enemy. With air superiority established, aircraft could attack enemy ground troops far behind the front lines and bomb supply areas, roads, or even factories, thereby reducing the enemy's ability to wage war. In Kenney's opinion, aircraft were misused if they were employed only as substitutes for artillery, dedicated to bombing the enemy forces on the front lines.

Although Kenney was dogmatic in his ideas about the purpose of air power, he was extremely flexible in their implementation. He was willing and able to change almost any aspect of his command in the pursuit of his aims. He junked unsuitable tactics, embraced innovative modifications to aircraft, and adapted his organization to the constraints and opportunities presented by a situation. The means, he believed, should always be adapted to the ends—whatever was necessary to get the job done. Indeed, flexibility and adaptation were the hallmarks of Kenney's leadership.

Another important factor in Kenney's success was his personal dealings with other commanders. When Kenney arrived in the Southwest Pacific he quickly established a close personal and professional relationship with Douglas MacArthur, the theater commander. Kenney related well to MacArthur on a personal level; he also brought to their relationship an impressive knowledge of air warfare, an area that MacArthur knew was important, but in which he had no real expertise. Likewise, Kenney recognized and took advantage of the talent and experience of his subordinates, especially Ennis Whitehead, Kenney's deputy commander and the commander of the forward operational headquarters that Kenney established.

During Kenney's apprenticeship in the Army he crossed paths with many of the ground and air officers whom he would later serve with during the war. While Kenney had no difficulty getting along with his fellow Army officers, he harbored a deep dislike for naval officers, ironic considering the geography of the Southwest Pacific theater. Despite the requirements to coordinate air, ground, and sea operations, relations between the Navy and Kenney were never very good, and he made few efforts to improve them.

In spite of antagonism and obstacles, including the constraints of weather, geography, strategy, and resources, Kenney succeeded in making air power contribute its maximum effectiveness in an environment that combined the fighting forces of different services and different nations. The story of George Kenney's role in World War II will not explain every aspect of air warfare in the Southwest Pacific, but it will expand our understanding of how one airman faced the challenge of commanding an air force in war.

THE EARLY YEARS

"From then on, I knew that was what I was going to do."

George Kenney was born on August 6, 1889, in Yarmouth, Nova Scotia, the first child of Joseph Atwood Kenney and Anne Louise Churchill, but the latest in a long line of Kenneys in America. The family traces their heritage, through marriage, back to two members of the original *Mayflower* company—Stephen Hopkins and William Brewster.[1] The first recorded evidence of the Kenney name in America came on September 24, 1662, when John Keayne, an innkeeper in Boston, bought a house and some land near the center of Quincy, Massachusetts.[2] The family of George Kenney's mother, Anna Louise Churchill, also included some of the earliest European settlers—the first Churchill came to New England in 1643.[3]

The Kenneys were primarily fishermen and merchants who remained in the Boston area until 1761, when the family migrated to Nova Scotia with a number of other English settlers. Although originally a French colony in North America, Nova Scotia was taken over by the British during the Seven Years' War between France and England. In a bid to ensure British control of the island, French settlers were deported and the British governor of Nova Scotia, Charles Lawrence, established a colonial assembly and began recruiting settlers from New England.[4] The favorable terms offered to the potential settlers, combined with the enthusiastic reports on the attractive conditions in Nova Scotia by agents sent from New England to investigate the territory in 1759, spurred interest in the area. Although individual motives for moving varied among the settlers, for fishing families, like the Kenneys, who frequently stopped in Nova Scotia on their expeditions to the fishing grounds in the North Atlantic, the move simply changed a temporary way station into a permanent home.[5] In 1761 Herman Kenney, a direct ancestor of George Kenney, settled in Barrington, Nova Scotia, and became the first magistrate of the town.[6] By 1763 at least 5000 people had moved from New England to Nova Scotia; despite an influx of immigrants from other nations, the area along the southern coast became, in the words of historian George Rawlyk, a "New New England."[7]

In spite of this similarity, Nova Scotia did not experience the political changes of the New England colonies and, consequently, did not join with the rebels during the American Revolution. The political separation of Nova Scotia from Massachusetts that occurred after the American Revolution did little, however, to disrupt the social, cultural, and economic ties between the residents of southern Nova Scotia and those of New England.[8]

Like many other families, the Kenneys remained in Nova Scotia after the Revolutionary War, but the family also maintained close ties to New England. George Kenney's father, Joseph Kenney, was born in Barrington, Nova Scotia, on November 25, 1862, the oldest child of James Colwell Kenney and Sarah Jane Crowell.[9] Joe, as he was called, was a handsome young man with a striking singing voice; Edith Porter, a cousin of George Kenney, thought Joe had "one of the most beautiful voices" in the world.[10] No doubt this singing talent helped attract the attention of Anne Louise Churchill, daughter of the famous sea captain George Washington Churchill. The two met in Yarmouth, Nova Scotia, where Joe had been hired as a singer for a church, and were married there on November 16, 1888.[11]

Although both Joe and Anne had long-standing family ties to Nova Scotia, Joe's parents had moved to Beverly, Massachusetts, in 1882; and sometime around 1900 Joe and Anne Kenney followed, settling in Brookline, Massachusetts.[12] Even after this move the couple traveled frequently between Massachusetts and Nova Scotia. Although George Kenney was born in Yarmouth, his sister Gertrude, Joe and Anne's second child, was born in Brookline, Massachusetts, in 1892; and the two youngest children in the family, Ruth and Arthur, were both born in Nova Scotia: Ruth in 1893, Arthur in 1894.[13]

Joe and Anne Kenney's decision to relocate was probably inspired by economic necessity. Prosperity in the Canadian Maritime Provinces depended on exporting lumber and fish to the United States, but in 1886 an American tariff on fish effectively closed this market for Nova Scotia fishermen, forcing many of them to emigrate to the United States and find work on American vessels. While economic opportunities in Nova Scotia were decreasing in the late nineteenth and early twentieth centuries, the opposite was true in the United States, where industrialization was expanding employment opportunities.[14] The result was high unemployment in Nova Scotia, but ample opportunities in the United States. Boston became the "goal of ambitious youth."[15]

Joe Kenney's move to Boston effectively completed the circle of migration back to the United States that had begun in 1761. The Kenneys were, at least according to political boundaries, Canadian citizens. Despite this formal definition of nationality, the Kenneys' perception, formed by the close ties to the United States and aided by the porous border between the United States and Canada, was that they were not Canadian.[16] George Kenney claimed throughout his life that he was the son of American citizens who were vacationing in Nova Scotia when he was born.[17] He was, in fact, very defensive about the circumstances of his birth. When a reporter who was curious about Kenney's nationality asked if he was Canadian, the general snapped, "If a cat has kittens in the oven, you don't call them biscuits."[18] A careful look at his family's history reveals that George Kenney was mistaken. His claim to American citizenship reflected more the belief he had in his nationality than a strict interpretation of the true circumstances of his birth.[19]

George Kenney's family moved to a working class section of Boston called Brookline, where his father worked as a carpenter and then as a driver for a plumbing company.[20] To help the family make ends meet financially, George's mother worked as a dressmaker in Boston and may have rented out rooms in their house at 10 Davis Avenue.[21] For several years she traveled back to Yarmouth, Nova Scotia, and managed a vacation house in the summer.[22] George Kenney attended Pierce Grammar School in Brookline, and he graduated from Brookline High School in 1907.[23] Although unmemorable as a scholar or athlete, he was nevertheless accepted by the Massachusetts Institute of Technology (MIT), where he studied civil engineering.[24] In addition to his studies at MIT, George discovered that he had some talent as a writer. He worked on the school newspaper, *The Tech,* and was a member of the paper's editorial board.[25] Kenney also earned money for school by writing for a commercial newspaper; he later developed a service that provided campus news to the *Boston Journal,* the *Boston Record,* and the *Boston Advertiser.*[26]

Sometime in 1909, during George's second year at MIT, Joe Kenney left the family, an event that forced George, as the male head of the household, into the role of the primary economic supporter.[27] The exact reasons for Joe Kenney's disappearance remain murky. According to one source, Joe and two other men were accused of embezzling $20,000 from a company and left the area to avoid prosecution.[28] Another relative, however, gave a more prosaic explanation: Joe left the family because he could no longer get along with his wife.[29] Based on the lack of any available news accounts about the crime and on Joe's job as a driver, it seems most likely that domestic strife was the reason he left home.

Whatever the exact explanation for Joe's disappearance, the episode undoubtedly left its mark on George Kenney, although he never revealed any of his feelings. An unpublished paper he wrote late in life, entitled "Personalities," provides a glimpse into the impact of the event. In the paper Kenney attempted to define the most important characteristics of the significant or memorable people of his lifetime. Most of the people in the essay were public figures: Theodore Roosevelt, Woodrow Wilson, Franklin and Eleanor Roosevelt, Henry Ford, and William Knudsen. Significantly, George Kenney made no mention of his father, but did write about his maternal grandfather as an exemplary "personality" and his childhood hero.[30]

Perhaps it is not surprising that George Kenney would have remembered his grandfather, George Churchill, so fondly. Not only was young Kenney his namesake, but following Joe Kenney's disappearance, George Churchill was probably the closest father figure to the family. Kenney was also undoubtedly drawn to his grandfather because of the sea captain's heroic exploits. Probably the most dramatic incident occurred on a voyage in 1886 from Quebec to Glasgow, Scotland. During the trip the ship's rudder was lost during a heavy storm, threatening to strand the boat in the North Atlantic. Churchill and his crew fashioned a makeshift rudder that allowed them to continue the voyage, but the heavy seas continued to tear at the ship. In the end, they created six replacement rudders and, after sixty-eight harrowing days at sea, finally made it to port, earning the captain the nickname "Seven-rudder" Churchill as well as praise on both sides of the Atlantic.[31] Given this standard, perhaps George Kenney tried, in some measure, to emulate his grandfather's exploits in his own life.

In the year following his father's disappearance, Kenney attended a flying competition sponsored by Harvard University and the city of Boston, an event that also had a profound impact on his life. The gathering, held in September 1910, was the first large air competition of its kind in the United States. The contest, then called an air meet, lasted ten days and involved twenty-two aviators flying thirteen different kinds of aircraft. During the event aviators competed for prizes in various categories, including highest altitude, fastest and slowest speeds, and landing accuracy. Among the airmen invited was Claude Grahame-White of England, one of the "five leading aviators in the world," according to the *New York Times,* and the aviator who would have the greatest impact on young George Kenney.[32]

Claude Grahame-White arrived in Boston already a well-known aeronaut. An upper-class Englishman who had helped build his own airplane and made his first flight with little or no instruction in 1909, Grahame-White also started the first flying school in England. He first attracted widespread public recognition during an attempt to capture the £10,000 prize offered by the *Daily Mail* for the first flight from London to Manchester. Although he was unsuccessful in this endeavor, his efforts during the flight, aided by laudatory news accounts from friendly reporters as well as Grahame-White's own instincts for self-promotion, made him an air hero and celebrity in Great Britain.[33] The Englishman quickly became a crowd favorite in Boston too. He flew every day during the competition, despite weather conditions that grounded other aviators, and won a number of prizes, including the award for the fastest speed around a designated course and the highest altitude reached during the meet. In addition, he was the only competitor who took the challenge offered by the *Boston Globe* to fly twice around the lighthouse in Boston harbor, a distance of thirty-three miles from the site of the meet in Cambridge.[34] The manager of the air meet lauded Grahame-White's participation, calling him "the savior of the meet," adding, "if it had not been for his willing and active work . . . the meet would have fallen below par."[35] To be sure, Grahame-White was handsomely rewarded for his efforts and earned over $31,000 during the meet, including $10,000 for his flight around the Boston Light.[36]

Not surprisingly, the air meet drew thousands of Boston residents, including twenty-one-year-old George Kenney, who, years later, would remember two details about the competition. The first was Graham-White's prize-winning flight out to the lighthouse in Boston Harbor.[37] The other was more personal. Kenney helped the famous aviator with some menial task and was rewarded for his efforts with a short flight.[38] He later recalled the experience as a monumental event in his life. "From then on," he recounted, "I knew that was what I was going to do."[39]

No doubt the widespread public fascination with aviation in this era helped fuel Kenney's interest in aviation; shortly after his first flight with Grahame-White, Kenney and a few friends built their own airplane.[40] They modeled their aircraft on the monoplane design used by the Frenchman Louis Blériot to fly across the English Channel in 1909 and flown by Grahame-White at the Boston air show in 1910. Apparently Kenney and the other young aviators had not quite mastered the knack of aircraft construction. The ten-horsepower 1903 Ford engine they used was not powerful enough to lift the airframe more than "four or five feet off the ground."[41] When Kenney tried to turn the aircraft it stalled, crashed, and sank into the Saugus River northeast of Boston, a humble beginning for a future combat pilot and Air Force general.[42] Several years would pass before Kenney was able to pursue his dream of flying.

Kenney would have graduated from MIT in 1911, but he left school that year, later claiming that he was "getting kind of bored."[43] While school may have seemed boring after the excitement of his first flights, family financial problems, resulting from his father's disappearance, were probably a greater consideration in his decision to drop out.[44] After leaving MIT George Kenney worked at a number of different jobs. He moved to Quebec, Canada, and found employment as a surveyor for the Quebec Saguenay Railroad. Then in 1913 he moved back to Boston, perhaps to be closer to his siblings after his mother's unexpected death from anesthesia administered during an operation.[45] He was hired by the Stone and Webster Engineering Corporation, one of the top construction firms in the country, to work on building the new MIT campus.[46] In 1914 he returned to the railroads as a civil engineer, building a new bridge at New London, Connecticut, for the New York, New Haven, and Hartford Railroad. After that project ended, Kenney and Gordon Glazier, a close friend from high school, began their own general contracting firm— the Beaver Contracting and Engineering Corporation. They built roads, office buildings, and houses, and even participated in such major projects as the construction of the seawall at Winthrop, Massachusetts, and the bridge over the Squannacock River.[47]

Although the engineering and design work appealed to Kenney, he most enjoyed solving the problems that came up once a project started. He found the special challenges involved with hydraulic engineering—constructing special pilings and foundations to support a structure in swamps or on the wet ground near rivers—especially appealing because of the need for innovative solutions. As far as he was concerned, once those problems were solved, "well, it was just simple—pouring concrete."[48]

Despite his being bitten by the aviation bug, there is no indication that Kenney did any more flying during this time. In addition to building up his own company, he supported his younger brother and sister after his father's departure and his mother's death, leaving him with little extra money for an expensive hobby such as flying. While missing out on flying, Kenney was gaining management and leadership experience as well as practical knowledge that helped augment his school work in engineering at MIT and gave him a background that was difficult to match. The construction work almost never went as planned, making improvisation and flexibility vital to completing the projects.[49] As the head of a small business, Kenney had to bring together the work of several different subcontractors, gaining an ability to react to current circumstances as well as to forecast for the future. His work experiences, and in particular owning his own company, in combination with the family responsibilities thrust on him at a relatively young age, gave Kenney a sense of maturity and knowledge of the practical world beyond many of his peers. Outside events, however, would soon bring big changes to Kenney's life and give him the opportunity to realize his desire to fly.

ARMY AVIATOR

World War I

"We lost a lot of people in that 91st Squadron."

Like many other Americans', George Kenney's life changed dramatically in the spring of 1917. On April 2 of that year President Woodrow Wilson asked Congress to declare war against Germany. Wilson's decision to enter the war provided Kenney with an opportunity to move from his career as a civil engineer and businessman into an aviation career in the military.

Perhaps inspired by his grandfather's heroic exploits as well as his own desire to fly, Kenney wrote to the War Department soon after the United States entered the war and inquired about aviation training. Although he was told there were no vacancies at the moment, he continued to look for an opportunity to fly. A short time later an enterprising recruiting sergeant in downtown Boston told Kenney that if he joined the Army that day he would be sent to France immediately and be "flying at the front" in a week. Kenney was sorely tempted by the offer, but wisely found it too good to believe. "Luckily," as he put it, a letter from the War Department arrived a few days later, advising him that if he passed a physical examination he would be admitted to an Army aviation ground school.[1]

Kenney's delay in entering flying training reflected the tumultuous mobilization of the United States Army as it prepared to enter World War I. The U.S. Army was small at the start of the war, but the Air Service can only be described as minuscule. In fact, no separate arm or branch for aviation existed in the United States Army prior to the war. Instead, responsibility for aviation matters rested with the Aviation Division of the U.S. Army Signal Corps. This division contained just 65 officers, only 26 of them aviators, and about 200 mostly out-of-date aircraft. With such limited numbers, the airmen in the United States Army were in no position to contribute to the air war over western Europe in the near future. The first step for the Aviation Division, as for the rest of the Army, was a vast expansion of people and resources.[2]

Kenney began his training by enlisting in the Signal Corps reserve and attending an eight-week ground school, essentially basic training for pilots.[3] Similar in many respects to the military training programs conducted by the European countries already at war, the American course provided an indoctrination to military service, furnished an academic introduction to the mysteries of flight, and eliminated those considered by the military unsuited for flying—approximately 25 percent of those who entered the ground school.[4]

Whatever the background of the individual, basic training was always something of a shock. Although they would not be ground soldiers, aviation cadets still had to learn the rudiments of military life: how to march, how to wear a uniform, and even how "to take down and reassemble a Lewis machine gun blindfolded."[5] In addition to their military studies, cadets also learned Morse code, air navigation, flight theory, engine repair, and meteorology while participating in rigorous physical fitness training.[6] The pace was frantic. Cadets were jolted awake for a morning run at 5:30. They attended classes until late afternoon and then practiced marching until dinner. A study period followed the evening meal, and at 9:30 the cadets went to bed.[7] One former cadet later quipped, "Ground school remains more of a nightmare than a dream."[8]

Kenney officially began his aviation training on June 2, 1917, when he returned to the Massachusetts Institute of Technology for ground school.[9] The school had opened for training only two weeks earlier; one of the first universities to begin ground school, MIT was a logical location for this instruction because it was one of the leading universities in the country for aeronautical engineering and had established an aerodynamics laboratory in 1914.[10]

Kenney spent June and July at MIT and completed his ground training with no difficulty. His prior academic experiences at MIT likely gave him an advantage over those who entered the training without any engineering background, while his work experience, both as an employee and as the owner of his own business, provided an added maturity that helped him overcome the difficulties that others experienced in the program.[11]

After successfully completing ground training, fledgling aviators were sent to an Army airfield for flight instruction in the Curtiss JN-4 "Jenny." After some detailed instruction on handling the aircraft and several flights with an instructor who taught basic procedures for getting airborne and back on the ground safely, cadets were sent out alone on a "solo" flight. A successful solo was a significant step in the airman's training—the first stage in becoming a pilot. Those who could not solo were quickly mustered out of the program. Cadets who successfully passed this test still had a long way to go; they soon moved on to more complicated aerial maneuvers, such as learning how to land if the engine cut out, how to handle the aircraft when it stalled and began to spin, and how to fly together with other aircraft in formation, a necessity for survival in the air combat arena on the western front.[12] This flying phase of training lasted between six to eight weeks; upon successful completion, cadets were rated as reserve military aviators and commissioned as first lieutenants in the Army.[13]

Kenney began his primary flight training at Hazelhurst Field in Mineola, New York, immediately after completing ground school. He trained there under the tutelage of Bert Acosta, a man who would later win the Pulitzer Silver Trophy for setting a world speed record, pilot Commander Richard E. Byrd on a transatlantic flight, and fly in the Spanish Civil War.[14] Kenney's most vivid memory of this training was making his first three landings without power. Although these early aircraft were notorious for having an engine conk out, performing an engine-out landing at this early stage of training was not routine nor authorized.[15] He shrugged off the violation and jokingly told Acosta, "Any dammed fool can land if the motor is running. I just wanted to see what would happen in case the motor quit."[16] In spite of Kenney's miscue he passed through his training without any other memorable incidents. By the middle of September he had successfully completed the flying tests for his rating as a reserve military aviator. In early November 1917, six months after he began training, he received his commission and soon afterwards sailed for France and the fighting on the western front.[17]

When the war in Europe had erupted in 1914, the impact that aviation would have on the fighting was still unclear; however, contrary to the popular myth, military leaders were not ignorant of the potential capabilities of aircraft. Even before the Wright brothers' first flight in 1903, balloons had been used for bombing and observation; in 1911 aircraft were flying in small conflicts, including Italy's use of airborne bombing against the Turks in Libya. By 1914 it was clear that aircraft would serve in the war—the uncertainty was over the size of their impact and the best methods for their use.[18]

The most obvious role for aircraft was as an observation platform. Gaining the high terrain had traditionally been important in land warfare for a variety of reasons. One of the most important was that it gave commanders the ability to observe enemy movements from a distance. Balloons were used for observation; but they proved vulnerable to gunfire and, tethered to the ground, were unable to keep up with a moving army. Aircraft, on the other hand, were more difficult to shoot down and could fly to different areas and return with a detailed report. Not surprisingly, during the early days of the war, when the opposing armies were moving rapidly, aircraft played their most important role in reporting on enemy troop movements. In August 1914 information from an observation aircraft about a gap in the lines of the German army gave French commanders the ability to mount a counter-attack and stop the German advance on Paris.[19]

The fighting rapidly spawned other uses of aviation. If observation aircraft gave one side an advantage, the obvious response was to try to eliminate that advantage, producing another class of aviation known as fighter, or pursuit, aircraft. Friendly fighters were sent aloft both to protect observation balloons and aircraft from enemy fighters and to destroy the enemy's observation craft. The struggle for control of the air had developed. Alongside the observation and fighter divisions of aviation came aircraft that were used to attack targets on the ground. By the end of the war the term "bomber" was being used to describe aircraft that struck targets in the enemy's homeland, while a fourth category of planes, called attack aircraft, had evolved to strike targets in support of the ground forces. [20]

Since Kenney's training in the United States provided him with only basic instruction, like all new American aviators he arrived in France sorely in need of training in his particular type of aircraft. Since he was classified as a pursuit, or fighter, pilot, Kenney was sent to the Third Aviation Instruction Center at Issoudun, France, the largest American training facility in France, with more than 1000 planes and a dozen separate flying fields. Here American pursuit pilots were introduced to the French aircraft they would be flying over the front lines and given further instruction in advanced aircraft maneuvers and formation flying, as well as tips on surviving air combat on the western front.[21]

Unfortunately, Kenney received little of this training. His arrival at the base in mid-December coincided with the worst weather of the year. In a report on the accomplishments of aviation during the war, the chief of the Air Service noted that fall rains transformed Issoudun into "a sea of mud."[22] When aircraft tried to take off, mud was thrown up from the wheels and broke the wooden propellers "almost as fast as they could be put on."[23] Even without the muddy landing fields, the low clouds and rain effectively canceled flying since these early aircraft were equipped with only rudimentary flight instruments. The poor conditions drastically limited Kenney's flying at the base. When he and eighteen other pilots were assigned in mid-February to the newly arrived 91st Aero Squadron, they left Issoudun before their training was complete.[24]

The reason for their departure was unclear, but Kenney and his fellow pilots were upset by the move. Kenney, and presumably others, felt the transfer was punishment for repeatedly breaking regulations at Issoudun.[25] Although that motivation cannot be ruled out, more likely they were sent to the 91st simply because the unit had recently arrived in France and needed pilots to provide an American presence in the war. Kenney and his compatriots may have been at Issoudun the longest and hence the best option for filling out the 91st. As Kenney's comments about being punished suggest, their displeasure and disappointment at the move was triggered only partly by leaving the base early. They were also agitated about being assigned to an observation squadron rather than a pursuit unit.

All flyers in World War I were regarded as heroic figures in the popular culture, but fighter pilots attracted special attention. Certainly the reasons for this attitude varied. Some people may have felt the skill of the fighter pilot exceeded that of other fliers, while other people focused on the courage needed for air-to-air combat. One important factor was the public perception that in an age of mass armies and machine warfare, fighter pilots were engaged in solo combat, the last of the lone warriors, the so-called knights of the air, which made them appear more heroic and also made them easier to single out for recognition.[26] Whatever the exact reason, the view of fighter pilots as the most elite group in the flying fraternity was widespread. Observation flying, on the other hand, was widely disparaged. Even the chief of training for the Air Service was forced to admit that airmen viewed observation as "a very unpopular branch of aviation."[27]

While airmen may have belittled the observation role, the reconnaissance reports had proven invaluable to the ground commanders. Two distinct types of observation aircraft developed over the course of the war. Some observation squadrons worked close to the front lines and were assigned to an Army corps commander. Other squadrons, such as the one Kenney was assigned to, were used by higher-level Army headquarters and flew missions much deeper into enemy territory (25 to 30 miles behind the lines) to photograph troop locations and detect movements that might betray the enemy's intentions and likely areas for impending combat operations.[28]

From February to May 1918, Kenney and the rest of the squadron prepared for combat operations in the Salmson 2A2, a French-built aircraft specifically designed as an observation plane and introduced into service in late 1917. Kenney found the Salmson a "nice, maneuverable job" and, with its 250-horsepower radial engine, faster at combat altitudes than most of the German fighters.[29] During this training Kenney was briefly sidelined by an accident. On March 22, 1918, his engine failed on takeoff; and despite his efforts at practicing such landings during his initial training, he crashed, breaking his ankle and hand. Apparently the injuries were not too severe. He was back on flying status two months later and flew his first combat mission on June 3.[30] According to the squadron history, the escapade earned him the nickname "Bust-em-up George."[31]

The 91st flew its first combat missions from Gondreville, an airfield three miles east of Toul, France, under the direction of the French 8th Army during the summer of 1918.[32] This sector proved ideal for introducing the squadron to combat. There were plenty of airfields in the area, which was helpful in case the novice crews got lost and ran short on fuel, and relatively less enemy activity than other parts of the front, which allowed the aircrews of the 91st the opportunity to perfect methods for deep reconnaissance and resolve problems in photographing enemy positions. Even in the Toul sector, however, the realities of warfare intruded, forcing the squadron to change some of the procedures developed in training. Heavy German antiaircraft fire caused them to hike the altitudes of their missions from 10,000 feet to a more survivable 15,000 feet. In addition, German fighter opposition made single-ship missions untenable, and the American aviators flew with three or four aircraft together in formation. One or two planes were designated as the primary reconnaissance aircraft, while the others guarded against attack by German fighters.[33] On August 22, 1917, in what was likely his first combat engagement, Kenney and his flight tangled with six German Pfalz Scouts. Kenney was confident that he had shot down one of the opposing aircraft, but was not credited with a victory.[34] Although the squadron was relatively inexperienced, French army officers felt that "no better work had been done at any time during the war by any observation squadron on the western front."[35]

In mid-August the 91st was assigned to the headquarters of the American 1st Army and moved from Toul to prepare for the first large-scale American ground combat operation.[36] The impending offensive was designed to reduce a "bulge" in the Allied lines near the French town of St. Mihiel. To coordinate air operations for this offensive, General John J. Pershing gave Brigadier General William "Billy" Mitchell, the chief of the Air Service for 1st Army, control over 1,481 Allied aircraft—the "largest aggregation of air forces" assembled to date on the western front.[37]

Mitchell turned to the 91st Aero Squadron for most of the deep reconnaissance missions aimed at obtaining exhaustive details of the German forces and the terrain in the area.[38] Prior to the ground attack the squadron had pinpointed the location of the German long-range artillery, enabling American artillery to reduce the effectiveness of the German guns. Photographs taken during the preparations for battle also provided ground commanders with excellent details about the ground over which they would move, key information for working out the complex timing and movement needed to carry out offensive operations. During the actual ground fighting, the squadron scouted for enemy reinforcements that might be rushed to the area—a contingency never fulfilled.[39]

It was during the fighting around St. Mihiel that Kenney was awarded his first official aerial victory. On the morning of September 15, 1918, the first day of good flying weather during the offensive, Kenney was part of a four-aircraft formation, flying at about 12,000 feet just southeast of Gorze, France. Shortly after crossing the front lines, the formation was jumped by six Pfalz Scouts, and three of the German aircraft converged on Kenney's plane. While Kenney maneuvered wildly to avoid being hit by the German attackers, his observer, William Badham, who had been taking pictures in the back seat, quickly dropped his camera and returned fire with the rear gun. His shots found their mark. One Pfalz went down in flames, apparently discouraging the other two attackers. Despite being "badly shot up," Kenney managed to bring the aircraft home. He had scored his first official victory.[40]

Kenney and the 91st Aero Squadron had little respite after the fighting at St. Mihiel. On September 26, 1918, American forces began the Meuse-Argonne offensive, the largest American operation of the war. The objective was to capture the main German defensive position known as the Kriemhilde Stellung. While the fighting near St. Mihiel lasted only four days, the Meuse-Argonne offensive continued until October 6 and included the heaviest American fighting of the war.[41]

Just prior to the offensive, the 91st moved to Vavincourt, an airfield closer to the area of American combat operations in the Meuse-Argonne.[42] Whatever advantages the higher-level commanders thought the move held, squadron members found the new airfield "left much to be desired."[43] In their opinion, the field was too far from the front lines (about 25 miles) and had a very uneven runway, which caused all sorts of accidents. Worst of all, it was located near the intersection of two main roads, making it a prominent bombing target.[44] Despite these drawbacks the squadron stayed at the field and, as in the St. Mihiel offensive, spent the time prior to the ground fighting in flying reconnaissance missions to locate and photograph railroad yards and other "important points," such as German artillery emplacements.[45]

During the fighting in the Meuse-Argonne, Kenney was credited with his second victory. On the afternoon of October 9 he was sent out with two other aircraft to photograph the German trenches near Jametz. The flyers knew beforehand that this would be a rough mission. Army commanders needed the photos badly, but poor weather, mechanical problems, and German fighter opposition had stymied previous efforts. On this occasion Kenney was flying the photo ship and had two wingmen in support when they were attacked by fifty German fighters. Kenney and his observer, Asa Duncan, were jumped by six of the Germans, but managed to shoot down one Pfalz Scout. After fending off this attack, they tried to continue the mission, but were shot up by more enemy aircraft and turned to fight off some of the attackers that had latched on to another aircraft in the flight. Although vastly outnumbered, each American aircraft was able to down a German; none of the American aircraft was lost in the melee, but all limped home badly damaged. Kenney's instruments on the front panel were completely shot out, and the German bullets came so close that they cut off the left sleeve of his coat. The left wing fell off after he landed, and the plane was eventually scrapped. For his efforts in continuing the mission in the face of stiff enemy opposition and coming to the aid of his wingman, Kenney was awarded the Distinguished Service Cross, the second-highest decoration in the United States Army.[46]

Kenney won high praise for his flying during the war. A report written by an Air Service historian noted: "One of the most outstanding figures in the 91st Squadron was Captain George C. Kenney, who performed some of the most perilous army command missions in this sector and had more than 100 hours over the line in combat service."[47] He was also well respected in his squadron. One observer who flew with him remembered Kenney as an "excellent flyer, courageous [who] . . . could size up the situation quickly."[48] S. Prescott Fay, another member of the 91st, thought Kenney was "one of the ablest, coolest, most courageous pilots in the squadron."[49] Not surprisingly, Kenney's actions in his seventy-five combat missions were recognized by the Army through promotions and decorations. In late September 1918, he was appointed a flight commander in the 91st, a position given only to experienced pilots and one that placed him in charge of the discipline and well-being of eleven other flying officers. Kenney's selection for this position was an indication of his leadership ability and his performance in combat. He was advanced to the rank of captain on March 18, 1919, and awarded the Distinguished Service Cross and the Silver Star.[50] The Distinguished Service Cross was presented on January 10, 1919, by Brigadier General William "Billy" Mitchell, the chief of the Air Service, 1st Army, widely regarded as the leading combat airman in the American army, and a man whose exploits would help shape the context of Kenney's experiences in the Air Service over the next twenty years.[51]

When the war ended on November 11, 1918, the 91st could point to a highly successful record. In addition to their photographic work, they accounted for 17 of the 26 German aircraft downed by the 1st Army Observation Group during the Meuse-Argonne offensive. The squadron was also awarded a number of service decorations and ended the war with four aces (pilots with five or more kills), the most of any observation squadron in the American Air Service.[52]

While Kenney was undoubtedly pleased with his own exploits, and the record of the squadron, he was distressed by the losses his squadron suffered in the war. The 91st lost about three-quarters of its original pilots—a mortality rate that Kenney blamed on the lack of sufficient, realistic training.[53] When he and the other members of the squadron entered combat, he recalled, "We just knew how to fly an airplane. The first time I ever fired a machine gun in the air was at a German."[54] Perhaps Kenney's arrival at Issoudun in December, during the worst flying weather of the year, and his premature departure from the training base made his situation worse than most, but he was not alone in his complaints. The lack of adequate and appropriate training was a criticism echoed by many other aviators.[55]

Although it is difficult to measure in any precise fashion the impact that Kenney's experiences during World War I had on his actions in World War II, it is clear that the ordeal made a lasting impression. One of his first perceptions when he became the air commander in the Southwest Pacific in World War II was that poorly trained airmen were again being sent to war. This time Kenney was in a position to do something about the situation. The danger of going to war without proper training was a lesson he had learned the hard way in World War I, and he "wasn't going to inflict it on these kids in World War II."[56] He yanked scarce bombing units from combat missions to practice navigation and bombing and, against the wishes of the headquarters in Washington, established training bases in Australia and later in New Guinea.[57] While Kenney's motives for additional training were partly humanitarian, there was also a practical side to these measures. Better training increased the morale of the aviators and led to better combat results. In addition, Kenney's emphasis on training translated into fewer losses on combat missions, thus preserving aircraft for future operations. In short, training was a prudent investment for the future.

Kenney's wartime experience also provided him with a sense of the difference between learning about combat operations in theory and the realities of war. The best example may be Kenney's attitude toward gaining control of the air. While this concept was commonplace during World War I, and the idea was retained in discussions about air power in the years afterwards, a variety of technological, political, and economic factors pushed strategic bombing to the forefront and led some airmen to downplay the importance of gaining control of the air. Some strategic-bombing zealots even went so far as to claim that it was no longer necessary to defeat the enemy air force and that a "well planned, well organized, well flown air attack will constitute an offensive that cannot be stopped."[58] Air superiority was more than an academic idea to Kenney. He had seen friends shot down and had tried to fly missions while worrying about being attacked himself. The impact of being jumped by fifty German planes and having the left sleeve of his coat shot off must have made him skeptical of theoretical claims; he was not seduced by promises of being able to accomplish any task, on the ground or in the air, without gaining air superiority. "I stick to one basic principle," he later wrote, "get control of the air before you try anything else."[59]

Kenney's service during the war also led him to realize the importance of leadership and morale, for both aviators and the people who worked on the ground at the airfields and in the hangars. As an air commander he faced some unique leadership challenges. He was prohibited from flying on combat missions with his pilots and did not spend all his time in the rugged conditions at the forward airfields. Yet he was able to connect with the troops and motivate them. His chief of staff in Australia guessed that Kenney did so well in this regard because he had "the greatest understanding of the 'kids' who are really doing the tough work . . . he can remember his reactions at the front in the last war."[60] Kenney also took away from his experience in the war a feeling that combat medals were important as a morale booster. In World War II he had a very liberal attitude toward awarding decorations. Kenney's 5th Air Force, although only a small portion of the combat air forces in the war (the giant 8th Air Force in England was four times the size), had ten Medal of Honor recipients, as compared to the seventeen awarded in the 8th Air Force.[61] He believed that in the long run it was "men and morale that wins wars—not machines."[62]

AMERICA'S ENTRY into the First World War gave Kenney an opportunity to measure himself against the heroic exploits of his grandfather and pursue his desire to fly—an opportunity he eagerly grasped. He had few problems in his training, likely testimony to the advantages his maturity and age gave him over many other candidates. Kenney did well as an aviator on the western front, downing two enemy aircraft and earning a distinguished reputation among his colleagues for coolness and courage under fire. The war taught Kenney some hard lessons he would not forget: the significance of training to survival in combat, the importance of air superiority for all combat operations, and the value of leadership in guaranteeing the contribution of everyone, not just pilots or aviators, by caring for their morale. When World War I ended, however, few people thought about applying the lessons of this war to the future. America rapidly demobilized and turned away from far-reaching military commitments. Kenney, however, had realized his dream of flying and had no desire to return home. He would remain part of the small band of airmen who made up the Army aviators in the post–World War I era.

THREE

PREPARATION FOR COMMAND

The Inter-War Years

"A well-educated officer with war experience"

When World War I ended, George Kenney was a highly decorated soldier and an accomplished aviator, but the massive reduction of American forces after the war forced Kenney to make a difficult decision. He had two choices: stay in what would undoubtedly be a very small peacetime Army and continue flying, or leave the military and return to the business world where he had known earlier success. The desire to fly must have exerted a powerful pull—Kenney opted to remain in the nation's service and never looked back.

In retrospect, Kenney's assignments between the wars provided him with a superb background for his position in World War II as MacArthur's air commander. During these years his career went through three distinct phases. His initial assignments concentrated on the technical side of aviation, the research and development of new aircraft, engines, machine guns, and bombs. The second phase was spent in military schools, as both a student and an instructor, studying the use of air power in combat. Finally, Kenney was a staff officer, and he learned what it took to organize and lead large air forces. Although Kenney had a broad range of assignments, it is important to note that he had very little command experience, something that is usually considered a prerequisite for promotion and higher-level command assignments. Nevertheless, when the United States entered World War II, Kenney was well prepared to fulfill the duties of an air commander and, with his judgment and aggressive personality, to convince others of the impact that air power could have on military operations.

Border Duty

After the armistice ended the First World War, George Kenney and his compatriots in the 91st Aero Squadron stayed briefly in Germany as part of the Army of Occupation. Their duties during the occupation were easy. The squadron did little more than take over airfields formerly used by the German Air Force. This prevented the Germans from flying and allowed the Americans to inspect the German facilities and aircraft.[1] Kenney returned to the United States in June 1919 and after a well-deserved thirty days of leave, began a new assignment at Fort Sam Houston, Texas.[2]

Kenney's transfer to Texas was part of the buildup of U.S. forces on the Mexican border in response to unrest in the state of Chihuahua, where the revolutionary leader Francisco (Pancho) Villa was trying to consolidate power. Villa had first gained notoriety in 1916 for his raid into Columbus, New Mexico, in the midst of the Mexican Revolution. Mexican authorities were unable or unwilling to take action against Villa, and President Wilson ordered Major General John Pershing and the so-called Punitive Expedition to the border. Although most of the expedition, including Pershing himself, was withdrawn in the spring of 1917 when the United States entered the war in Europe, some units remained behind to safeguard American lives and property.

Sporadic raids by Mexican bands continued during the American involvement in World War I; but in 1919 the situation in the city of Juarez, just across the border from El Paso, Texas, was threatening to get out of control. Juarez was controlled by the army of General Venustia Carranza, Villa's rival in the region; and in June 1919 Villa attempted to establish his authority over the city, a move that threatened the safety of American citizens in El Paso. Although this skirmish turned out to be the last major battle for Villa's army, the Mexican government could not establish firm control over the region. Roving bands of raiders continued to cross the border, menacing American citizens, a situation that required the continued presence of American forces to stop the banditry.[3]

The War Department ordered Army Air Service units to Texas in June 1919 to support cavalry operations against Villa and these roving bands. As part of this buildup, Kenney was ordered to Kelly Field near San Antonio, Texas, and then in October sent to McAllen, Texas, where he became the commander of the 8th Aero Squadron. The observation aircraft in the 8th Squadron assisted the cavalry units in patrolling the southern part of the border between Mexico and Texas against incursions by bandits, who stole cattle, horses, and other supplies from the American ranchers. Typically, the observation aircraft patrolled a certain sector; if the crew of the DH-4 aircraft located a suspected group of thieves they relayed the information to a cavalry outpost by sending a radio message or by dropping messages in white canvas bags trailed by six-foot-long red streamers to the waiting cavalry troops.[4]

Life for the servicemen along the border was difficult. There was little social life, the living conditions were primitive, and the high temperatures and constant wind combined to make the experience miserable.[5] All in all it must have been a challenging experience for the new squadron commander, but one that gave Kenney a valuable leadership experience. He had little to say about his life on the border, except to note that the squadron at McAllen "had no discipline,"[6] and that the mechanics knew little about caring for the aircraft. These two factors, combined with the unreliable equipment, harsh weather conditions, and primitive landing fields, contributed to the squadron's losing 22 out of 24 airplanes in a single year of service on the border—a record any commander would want to forget.[7]

In July 1920, after only nine months in command, Kenney left the squadron for new duties just shortly after receiving his regular commission, an important step in his military career. Like other officers who entered the army during the war, Kenney had been commissioned a reserve officer. In the National Defense Act of 1920, Congress directed that all officers without a regular commission be discharged by the end of the year. Reserve officers who wanted to stay in the service needed to gain a regular commission by taking an examination and being interviewed by a board of officers. The examinations were apparently quite rigorous and covered areas that most officers had not studied in a number of years, including history, geography, algebra, and science. Fear of the tests drove airmen in many squadrons to spend long hours in extensive remedial instruction. Kenney appeared before his examining board at Camp Travis, Texas, on July 7, 1920, earning his regular commission as a captain with no apparent difficulty.[8]

The National Defense Act of 1920 also officially separated aviation personnel from the Signal Corps by making the Air Service a full-fledged combat branch of the Army. Airmen, led by Brigadier General Billy Mitchell, who had gained notoriety for his work in France, had hoped that the United States would form a separate and independent air arm after the war. Mitchell argued that neither the Army nor the Navy understood the capabilities inherent in the air weapon and that the only way to exploit those advantages was through an independent air force commanded by airmen. Despite his impassioned arguments, Mitchell could not persuade Congress of the need for a separate service.[9]

Mitchell's push for an independent service caused tensions inside the armed services as well. Army generals reacted sharply to his ideas, and Navy admirals grew irritated with his claims that aircraft had made battleships obsolete. Mitchell's arguments were especially divisive in the early 1920s because the American public favored a reduction in military spending and a defensive foreign policy. If Mitchell proved that aircraft were capable of defending the coastline, there would be an increase in the size and budget of the Air Service and a concomitant decrease in the Navy's share of the national budget—a prospect sure to raise the hackles of every naval officer worth his salt. Mitchell took his campaign public and began agitating for a bombing test against ships. In June and July 1921, Mitchell got the chance to prove his point in a series of trials that climaxed in the sinking of the captured German battleship *Ostfriesland*. The Navy protested that Mitchell had violated the ground rules for the test and the results were not conclusive. No matter. In the mind of the public Mitchell had proved his point.[10] While Kenney took no direct part in any of these activities, he undoubtedly knew they were occurring. More importantly, the tensions between ground, naval, and air officers over how air power should be used and commanded were already apparent; these interservice rivalries would remain an enduring part of Kenney's experiences throughout his career.

In the summer of 1920, however, Kenney was more preoccupied with changes in his personal life. During his tour in Texas, he met Hazel Richardson, a nurse originally from Mobile, Alabama. The two met in a hospital where Kenney was recuperating from another flying mishap. They were married in Mobile, perhaps en route to Kenney's next assignment at Camp Knox, Kentucky, where he headed an aviation detachment charged with developing new procedures for adjusting artillery fire from aircraft. After a brief stay in Kentucky, the newlyweds moved to Dayton, Ohio, where Kenney would attend the Air Service Engineering School and began a new phase in his career.[11]

Technical Education

Kenney entered the Air Service Engineering School in November 1920, and found it "a hell of a stiff course." The work, he recalled, picked "up where I left off at MIT."[12] The school, established to give air officers a specialized education in the science of aviation, opened its doors to six students in 1919.[13] The courses covered a wide range of subjects, ranging from mechanical engineering and theoretical aeronautics to business administration, and prepared air officers for duty in acquiring and evaluating the technical requirements of aircraft. Kenney obviously had not forgotten much from his work at MIT—he graduated first in his class at the Engineering School.[14]

After leaving the school in July 1921, Kenney began a series of assignments that took advantage of his technical education. He went to Garden City, Long Island, as the Air Service representative responsible for accepting fifty NBS-1 bombers being built by the Curtiss aircraft company.[15] This aircraft, originally designed as the Martin MB-2, was the primary bomber of the Air Service in the early 1920s. Its two Liberty engines could carry a crew of four at a top speed of 99 mph and a maximum height of 10,000 feet.[16] As a government representative at the factory, Kenney inspected and test-flew the new aircraft before they were sent to the flying units, providing him with an opportunity to see firsthand the problems and challenges involved in producing large numbers of aircraft.

Kenney's time in Long Island was also marked by personal tragedy and transition. His wife Hazel died in September 1922, shortly after giving birth to a son, William Richardson Kenney. Hazel had previously been pregnant with twins, but suffered a miscarriage, and doctors warned her about the risks of another pregnancy. She was, however, determined to have a baby. "If I die having this baby, it will be worth it," she told her sister.[17] Kenney, devastated by the death of his wife, also faced the practical problems involved with caring for an infant son; and he prevailed on Alice Maxey, a nurse and neighbor on Long Island, for help. The two were married almost a year later on June 5, 1923, in her hometown of Gardner, Maine, shortly before Kenney's return to Dayton, Ohio.[18]

On Kenney's return to the Air Service Engineering Division he was assigned to several different offices, from establishing quality control criteria for aircraft to determining delivery schedules for future aircraft. At the same time he also dabbled in aircraft design and modification. Among other ideas, he experimented with moving the machine guns from near the nose of the aircraft (where they had been in World War I) to the wings. Although this shift would increase the number of forward-firing guns, it required better reliability of the machine guns along with an increase in the wings' strength. Ultimately, the shift toward wing-mounted guns would not be completed until World War II.[19]

Military Education

After two years at the Engineering Division, Kenney left Ohio in the spring of 1925 to attend the Air Service Tactical School at Langley Field, Virginia, a move that marked the start of a new phase in his career. While he had previously focused almost exclusively on the technical aspects of aviation, Kenney would now begin to broaden his horizons and concentrate on the application of air power in war.[20]

Kenney entered a three-tired Army education system designed to prepare officers of all ranks for war. In the branch schools, such as the Air Service Tactical School, junior officers learned tactics and the use of forces in their particular arm of the service. The Command and General Staff School at Fort Leavenworth, Kansas, exposed midlevel officers to military operations at the division level and the effort required to combine and orchestrate the branches of the Army in ground warfare. The top tier was the Army War College in Washington, D.C., an institution that trained field-grade officers in strategy, policy, and theater-level operations. Since the Army education system focused on preparing officers for tasks in some future war, students were given situations that it was hoped would approximate what they could expect in coming conflicts. As a result, the situations and problems they grappled with were actually two or three levels above the officer's current rank and position.[21]

When the Air Service became a separate combat arm, its director proposed establishing an Air Service School of Application. The purpose of the school would be to teach air officers about their duties and responsibilities, investigate the problems of high-level air commanders, and prepare the students for the next level of military education, the Command and General Staff School. In February 1920 the War Department approved the establishment of the Air Service Field Officer's School, renamed the Air Service Tactical School two years later. While the curriculum stressed the tactics of the various classes of aircraft (observation, pursuit, bombardment, and attack), the students were also introduced to combat tactics of the Army and Navy as well as the supply planning necessary for preparing combat orders. The material was generally presented through lectures, after which the students were given a tactical problem and the opportunity to apply what they had learned.[22]

After graduating from the Tactical School, Kenney moved on to the Command and General Staff School at Fort Leavenworth, Kansas.[23] At this school officers broadened their perspective of warfare and learned how to integrate the various ground combat forces (infantry, artillery, and cavalry) into a coherent whole, as if they were division or corps commanders or staff officers.[24] As at the Tactical School, the faculty at the Command and General Staff School presented students with the material through a lecture, and then asked them to apply what they had learned through map problems and exercises. Drafting actual combat orders and logistical plans reinforced the techniques presented in classes and stressed the problems involved in maneuvering and sustaining large combat units.[25]

Although attendance at the Command and General Staff School was imperative for promotion, airmen were harshly critical of the school, especially its treatment of aviation. The curriculum narrowly focused on how aviation could directly assist the division or corps commander, recalling the observation, long-range reconnaissance, and artillery-spotting work done during World War I. Students heard little or nothing about the benefits of using aircraft to gain control of the air, attack enemy forces, or conduct strategic bombing.[26] Even in situations where aircraft might work closely with ground forces, there was no serious attempt to develop and introduce procedures for integrating air and ground forces; presumably those would be worked out under combat conditions.[27]

Kenney's year at the Command and General Staff School reveals how little of the material touched on air power. Only two of the ninety-seven lectures and just sixteen of the three hundred three classroom problem sessions touched on the Air Service.[28] There was a single class devoted to the use of aircraft in supporting a ground attack, as compared to three on "Attack and Defense of a River Line," another three on historical research about the attack on Fort Donelson in the Civil War, and four on "Division Technical and Administrative Staff."[29] In addition to the slight coverage given to aviation, the airmen found themselves outnumbered: Kenney's class contained 204 officers, just 9 of them from the Air Corps.[30] Perhaps the lack of attention to air matters played a role in Kenney's poor performance at the school—he graduated in the bottom quarter of his class, 174 out of 201, with an 82 percent average.[31]

The irrelevance of the material at the school was a constant bone of contention among the aviators and contributed to their critical attitudes toward service education.[32] Henry H. "Hap" Arnold, who would be the commanding general of the Army Air Forces in World War II, attended the Command and General Staff School the year after Kenney. According to his biographer, Arnold "was appalled to find the school ignoring the possible uses of the airplane."[33] He was so anxious to leave the school that his wife and family were waiting in the packed car as Arnold attended the graduation ceremony. His wife told an inquiring officer that Hap "wanted to get out of this goddamned place just as fast as possible."[34] Carl Spaatz, 8th Air Force commander during World War II and the first chief of staff of the U.S. Air Force, avoided going to the school for as long as possible. When he did attend the Command and General Staff School, Spaatz graduated next to last in his class and the faculty board rated him very poorly on his efficiency report, yet the "comments did not seem to hurt Spaatz with the Air Corps establishment—they may, in fact, have helped."[35] Another historian remarks, "The school had little influence on [Spaatz] and he apparently learned almost nothing of value there."[36] Donald Wilson, who served as Kenney's chief of staff during the war, went only because it was necessary for promotion and he wanted a break from his current duties. He found the course "devoid of serious recognition of the airplane as an instrument of war" even in operations with the ground forces.[37] One airman wrote, "I wonder just how much difference it would make to me where Lt. X puts his machine gun squad when I am flying over his sector at 25,000 feet."[38] Laurence Kuter summed up the problem nicely, noting that the Command and General Staff School was "widely considered in the Air Corps as a waste of time in maneuvering companies and battalions on the Gettysburg maps, [but] it was also acknowledged as an important leg up on the promotion ladder in the Army."[39]

While Kenney's performance likely reflected this common view towards both the school and the Army, he was also known in the Air Corps for his outspokenness—a trait that surely meant he locked horns with the instructors at the school over the need for an independent air force, a topic of continuing disagreement between air and ground officers.[40] During his year at the school this topic would have received a great deal of attention, as airmen and their supporters continued to push for more independence. Billy Mitchell's very public crusade for an independent air force climaxed with what one historian terms a "calculated attempt to force a showdown with his superiors."[41] In September 1925, during Kenney's student year at the Tactical School, Mitchell released a statement to the press following two aviation mishaps, blaming the accidents on "the incompetency, criminal negligence, and almost treasonable administration of the National Defense by the Navy and War Departments."[42] Mitchell's intemperate remarks earned him a court-martial that he used as a forum to convince the American public of the importance of aviation.[43] Mitchell's trial overlapped with another in a series of Congressional investigations into the benefits and drawbacks of an independent air force, a study that resulted in the Air Corps Act of 1926. Although this legislation fell short of the airmen's goal of complete independence, it did provide greater autonomy from the control of the ground forces, signified in the name change from Air Service to Air Corps. In addition, the act authorized a position for an assistant secretary of war for air, required that all flying units be commanded by a flying officer, and approved a five-year expansion in the size of the Air Corps.[44]

Kenney's low grades may also have been affected by his personal life. His second child, Julia, was born on June 14, 1926, just prior to the beginning of his year at Leavenworth.[45] The combination of a four-year-old son and a newborn daughter must have had some effect on his study habits. Apparently it was not all work, however. During the year Kenney was caught violating one of the strictest rules on the Army post—the ban on alcohol. The commandant of the school, Brigadier General Edward L. King, who had been a judge on the court-martial of Billy Mitchell, was well known for being a strict disciplinarian and having a dislike of aviators. One student officer remembered that King "even had a regulation that said children were to be kept quiet and off the streets after six o'clock every evening."[46] Not surprisingly, King believed in strictly enforcing the national law against the consumption of alcohol. One night Kenney was stopped on post and six bottles of liquor were confiscated from his car. While he was probably not the only officer breaking the prohibition law, getting caught in violation of the regulation almost certainly would have doomed his career. The next morning, in accordance with Army regulations, Kenney reported to Major Robert Eichelberger, the post adjutant. To Kenney's relief, and no doubt eternal gratitude, Eichelberger, for reasons that remain unexplained, threw away the summons.[47]

After a stormy year at the Command and General Staff School, Kenney returned to more familiar territory, the Air Corps Tactical School (ACTS). His stint there as an instructor occurred during a time when institutional ideas about the employment of air power began to change.[48] In the years prior, concepts about the use of aircraft had been drawn largely from the experiences of the First World War. During Kenney's tenure, faculty members began thinking seriously about using aircraft independently in strategic missions against a wide variety of targets, including the enemy's capital and industrial centers, air force, lines of communication, and rear supply areas. They argued that strategic attacks could achieve victory without the need to defeat the enemy's army, avoiding the terrible slaughter of trench warfare seen during World War I.[49]

Although these ideas were being debated during Kenney's years at ACTS, he was not a central figure in their development. Instead, he concentrated on an area called attack aviation, a specialized air mission developed near the end of World War I when German and British airmen began attacking targets near the front lines.[50] Exactly how and when such attacks should be carried out was still being debated when the war ended in 1918.[51] The British, for example, distinguished between two types of attack mission: trench strafing, or attacks on the most forward enemy troops, and ground strafing, attacks a short distance behind the front lines.[52] What was clear, at least at the Tactical School of Kenney's time, was that aircraft had to be specially designed for these missions and the general profile of such attacks. The aircraft needed to be fast and maneuverable, equipped with both forward- and rear-firing guns, and able to carry (relatively) large numbers of bombs. Airmen envisioned attack aircraft approaching a target at low altitude, the crew firing the machine guns to destroy ground targets and reduce the ground fire from the enemy gunners, while simultaneously dropping small bombs. Since the aircraft would fly most of its missions at low altitude, and in close proximity to enemy ground forces, the aircraft needed to have some kind of armor protection against enemy antiaircraft guns.[53]

While the theoretical design of attack aircraft was evident, the issue of the targets they would strike was continually debated. The discussion centered on whether attack aviation was best used against the opposing front-line forces or targets further removed. During Kenney's time at the Tactical School he emphasized the latter, reasoning that the friendly ground forces should be able to defeat the enemy forces facing them while attack aircraft were used against reinforcements.[54] Forces in the rear also were not dug in and protected, nor did they have massed defenses. Kenney conceded that these attacks might not kill large numbers of enemy soldiers, but that was not an accurate measure of whether the attacks were successful. Their value should not be judged by simply counting "the number of casualties inflicted by airplanes on the ground force," he maintained.[55] The missions would force the enemy to either take defensive precautions while marching or restrict their movements to the hours of darkness when they could not be attacked from the air. In short, commanders needed to assess the effectiveness of the air attacks based on stopping the enemy from "arriving on the battlefield in time to influence the action."[56] Kenney was helping pioneer the use of aviation in what would later be labeled "interdiction." Although enemy troops, truck columns, antiaircraft guns, and rear supply areas were considered lucrative targets for attack aviation, during Kenney's tenure airmen also considered the destruction of aircraft on the ground an important step in gaining control of the air, a prerequisite for successful attack missions.[57]

Kenney put his journalism experience at MIT to good use writing new textbooks on attack aviation. In comparison to earlier efforts, Kenney's products were better written and contained an added twenty pages of material analyzing the use of attack aviation. The textbook produced during Kenney's final year at the school discussed the evolution of attack aviation in Europe by the French, Germans, and British during World War I and touched on air operations after the First World War, including Royal Air Force (RAF) experiences in the Middle East and Russia and the work done by the United States Marine Corps in Nicaragua.[58] In addition to teaching about attack aviation, Kenney was also a member of the attack board, a group of officers charged with determining the requirements for new attack aircraft, equipment, and munitions.[59] In later years Kenney remembered his work quite proudly. "I was the papa of attack aviation," he recalled. "I wrote the textbooks on it, taught it, and developed the tactics."[60] While there is no doubt that Kenney's work at the Tactical School was important, perhaps quite naturally he tended to overstate his influence. Other officers in the Air Corps, especially those flying with the 3rd Attack Group, were developing tactics for attack aviation; and the examples he used in his teaching point out that many different countries used this class of aviation.[61] Nonetheless, Kenney can rightly be considered the one responsible for developing principles for attack aviation by synthesizing different historical experiences and writing the textbooks.

Although helpful as a template for young officers on how to conduct attack operations, Kenney's teachings were not designed as a critical inquiry into the problems of attack aviation. The lack of any in-depth analysis about the validity of the tactics hid potential weaknesses, such as the emphasis on flying at low altitude as a way to avoid detection and attack from enemy aircraft and antiaircraft guns.[62] While attacking targets from low altitude did make it more difficult for enemy fighters to find and then shoot down the attackers, these tactics offered little protection from antiaircraft fire. In fact, low-altitude attacks made aircraft extremely vulnerable to losses from enemy gunfire, a fact borne out in some of the experiences on the western front in World War I. At the battle of Cambrai in 1917, for instance, the British lost 35 percent of the attack aircraft sent out on the first day.[63] Had Kenney better analyzed these experiences, he might have developed a better appreciation for the problems of low-altitude attacks. Clearly some in the Air Corps did realize the problems and reacted, in part, by exploring ways to increase the accuracy of high-altitude bombing.[64] The lethality of the low-altitude environment also played a role in moving the Air Corps away from the low-altitude attack aircraft to medium and light bombers. These bombers were bigger than the attack aircraft, flew longer distances at higher altitudes, and delivered more bombs. In addition, the light and medium bombers were seen as multipurpose weapons, in comparison to the dedicated attack aircraft. By the end of the 1930s attack aviation in the Air Corps had been transformed into light bombardment.[65]

The experiences in World War II would confirm ground fire's deadly effectiveness on aircraft, especially those flying at low altitude. Perhaps fortuitously, when Kenney went to war in the Southwest Pacific he faced an enemy that, for a variety of reasons, had not built and could not deploy antiaircraft weapons in large numbers. As a result, he was able to successfully employ the low-altitude attack methods he had taught throughout the war, and he never saw the same kinds of losses from ground fire that occurred in other theaters during the war.[66]

Kenney's reasoning in advocating low-altitude attacks was based in part on improving bombing accuracy. Simply put, the primitive aiming systems of aircraft at the time made such strikes more accurate than those from a higher altitude. But in addition to the heavier antiaircraft fire, bombing from low altitude posed several other problems. The first involved the time necessary for the bombs to arm after they left the aircraft. To ensure that the bombs did not explode while they were on the aircraft, or immediately after they were released, a delay, usually measured in tenths of a second, was built into the arming mechanism. If dropped too low the bombs would not fall long enough to arm and, consequently, would not explode. If the bombs did arm, a low-altitude delivery could result in damage to the bombing aircraft from the fragments from the explosion. Depending on the size of the bomb, these fragments (called the "frag" pattern) could go out to a distance of several thousand feet. Allowing the aircraft to get a safe distance away from the area before the bomb exploded eliminated the danger to the aircraft.[67] One way to solve these problems was through improved fuses, but in the late 1920s a suitable delayed-action fuse had not been developed.[68]

Still another difficulty in low-altitude bombing was the amount of damage caused by the small, light bombs envisioned for use by the attack aircraft. Bombs that exploded when they hit the ground attenuated much of their blast, reducing their effectiveness. What was needed was a method for exploding the bombs above the ground so that their projectiles would travel further.[69] In an effort to solve these problems Kenney installed a parachute in the tail of the bomb that would deploy after release from the aircraft. The parachute slowed the bomb's rate of fall, providing enough time to arm; allowed the aircraft to escape the area prior to detonation; and exploded the bomb before it hit the ground.[70] Bombs using this same concept, known as "high drag" bombs, remain in use today.

Kenney's work at the ACTS not only provided him with many of the ideas he carried with him into the war but also strengthened his reputation in the service. In November 1930 Davenport Johnson, commander of the 3rd Attack Group, wrote several letters to Major Frank Andrews, then serving in the Office of the Chief of the Air Corps, requesting Kenney for his group. Johnson was in need of a "good" group operations officer (second in command) and thought that Kenney would be the best officer for the position. Both of these men had known Kenney at the Tactical School; Johnson taught with Kenney in 1927, while Andrews was a student in the class of 1928. Andrews agreed with Johnson's assessment and thought Kenney would be an excellent choice for operations officer.[71] Not everyone, however, was as impressed with Kenney at the Tactical School. His outspokenness rubbed some people the wrong way. A fellow instructor later reflected that Kenney had a reputation as a "renowned . . . ad-lib artist and indefatigable talker on any subject."[72]

In the end Kenney did not get the assignment to Johnson's group, but not because of his personality faults; instead he had been selected to attend the Army War College, the capstone school for Army officers. Officers selected for the school had outstanding performance evaluations, were graduates of the Command and General Staff School, and had been judged as eligible for a general staff position. The typical class contained about one hundred officers, ninety from the Army and the remaining ten from the Navy or Marine Corps. In theory these officers were among the best in the service, and the work was designed to prepare them for the highest commands in wartime and for duty on the general staff of the War Department.[73]

The ten-month course Kenney entered was divided into two phases. The first, entitled "Preparation for War," lasted from September until April and educated officers in the various divisions of the general staff (personnel, intelligence, operations, and logistics—abbreviated as G-1, G-2, G-3, and G-4 respectively) and the capabilities of potential enemies, as well as providing an understanding of the process used for developing war plans. In the second part of the year, termed "The Conduct of War," students applied and refined their knowledge through a variety of methods, including map exercises, a mock war game, and, if possible, a battlefield tour. While most of the instruction was accomplished through lectures, students also completed small group analytic studies and wrote individual papers.[74]

Most of the problem-solving work in the school was done as part of a committee of ten to fifteen officers. After researching a question the committee arrived at a proposed answer and summarized their written report in an oral presentation of their findings to the faculty and class.[75] Although this style of learning broadened the officer's perspective and introduced him to the problems of working with other staff officers, the constant rearranging of committees frustrated some students; and the group solution was usually not the best choice, but the best compromise. Despite these drawbacks, one historian maintains that the value of the system was in the informal evaluations the students made of each other: assessments of intellectual strengths and weaknesses "that could be relied upon during the mobilizations and wars to come."[76]

Kenney began the War College in September 1932 with a class of eighty-seven students. Among them were four Air Corps officers, including a man who was Kenney's friend and mentor: Major Frank Andrews. While the air officers were a minority in the Army, they were sorely underrepresented at the War College—their number at the school was less than half the relative strength of airmen in the service.[77] During the "Preparation for War" phase of the course, Kenney worked on several different committees. His first project compared how the United States, England, France, and Germany planned to fight in a future conflict. The report analyzed the principles and methods each country advocated for integrating artillery, cavalry, and infantry in assaulting defensive positions, pursuing the enemy, and defending a location. Conspicuous by its absence in the report was any reference to how aviation would be used in a future conflict, a shortcoming that might be explained by the small number of airmen in the school or by the general attitude in the army towards the importance of air power in warfare.[78] Kenney also worked on committees that researched modifications to the officer personnel system; the industrial mobilization plan for the United States; and the geographical, political, and economic conditions in Argentina, Brazil, and Chile—a report that also included an analysis of the probable actions these countries would take in a war against the United States. Prophetically, perhaps, Kenney was also assigned to a group charged with studying and updating the "Orange Plan"—the code name for the war plan against Japan.[79]

Kenney's analytic studies focused on two World War I battles. The first contrasted the march of the German 1st Army during the invasion of France in 1914 with a contemporary American force. The aim of the research was to highlight the supply and maneuver problems commanders faced in using a force of this size. The second study, for which Kenney served as the chairman of the committee, was an in-depth examination of a battle between the German and Russian armies in February 1915, called the Winter, or Second Masurian Lakes, Battle. In an effort to explain the overwhelming tactical victory by the Germans, the report discussed the factors that went into the clash of arms: the strategic background, arrangement of the forces, terrain and weather, the morale and training of the troops, and plans made by the headquarters.[80]

At the War College, as in the lower-level Command and General Staff School, the study of air power in warfare was, at best, limited.[81] The one study Kenney participated in on tactical methods for a future conflict did not include any mention of aviation. During the end-of-year exercises Kenney's class was able to use aircraft for more than simply observing and attacking frontline enemy forces—an option unavailable to previous classes. In addition, at least one committee did write a report on the use of aviation with ground troops.[82]

Given the relative lack of attention given to air power, perhaps it is not surprising that Kenney focused on this topic in his individual paper. In "The Proper Composition of the Air Force," Kenney examined the use of air power as an instrument for meeting the nation's security goals. During Kenney's term at the war college, American foreign policy was based on staying out of the affairs of Europe, and military activities were primarily concerned with defending the homeland and territories of the United States. In keeping with this strategic guidance, the primary mission of the Air Corps was the defense of the United States, in particular, conducting air attacks against enemy invasion fleets.[83] Kenney maintained that the first step in defeating an invasion force was to gain "freedom of action in the air" while denying this freedom to a hostile air force. At the same time, aircraft would be used to locate and attack the hostile fleet, landing parties, troop and supply concentrations, and enemy lines of communication.[84] After analyzing the types of aircraft and the air organization currently possessed by the United States, Kenney concluded that the Air Corps of the United States in 1933 could not meet the demands of this mission. He calculated that the United States needed over 1100 combat aircraft, yet in February 1933 the authorized strength of assigned aircraft for this task was only 621. In reality, the number of aircraft actually available to combat units was even less—only half of the authorized strength.[85] Furthermore, the observation aircraft were "insufficient, unsuited, and unequipped" to patrol the seas and detect an invasion fleet. Even if the attack force was sighted, the bombers on hand were "insufficient in strength"; and the attack aircraft that would be used against the ground forces once they made it to shore were "deficient in equipment and strength."[86] In short, the Air Corps could not succeed in its current state.

Kenney's report on the condition of the Air Corps marked his last assignment at the War College and the end of his formal military education. Although airmen at the time invariably had negative attitudes about attending an Army service school, these experiences were probably more important and more valuable than they later admitted. For one, the airmen's comments imply a relatively narrow definition of utility. If the school did not conform to their ideas on air power, or pay enough attention to the subject, they considered the entire course meaningless. No doubt their knowledge of ground operations, foreign policy, and industrial mobilization would prove useful later in their careers, but at the time they attended the schools it seemed irrelevant. Given the tension between air and ground officers, service education was simply another bone of contention. As MacArthur's air commander, Kenney was heavily involved in the planning for numerous ground operations, and his knowledge of army doctrine no doubt contributed to his understanding of how air power could be used to affect the outcome of military operations.

An important by-product of the Army school environment was the informal connections airmen made with other members of the Army. One airman, in an attempt to convince his fellow officers about the importance of attending the Army War College, argued that attendance there could help an officer "establish his reputation and start those contacts which can go a long way towards making pleasant official relations in his future assignments."[87] Historian D. K. R. Croswell, although generally very critical of the Army schools, agrees with this assessment and concludes that these networks "proved to be an important complement to the traditional chain of command."[88] While these contacts were not always useful, occasionally they did prove valuable. In this regard, Kenney crossed paths with several officers he met at the various schools. Robert L. Eichelberger, later an important ground commander in the Southwest Pacific, was the officer who tore up Kenney's summons for alcohol at Fort Leavenworth. The chief of staff for MacArthur, Richard K. Sutherland, and the head of operations in MacArthur's headquarters, Stephen Chamberlin, were both members of Kenney's War College class and worked with him on separate committee reports.[89]

The common schooling of air and ground officers was important for another reason: the ability to communicate between two very different perspectives on warfare. Despite the shortcomings of the service education, both the Command and General Staff School and the War College provided officers with the ability to "speak the same language."[90] Obviously, the school taught officers more than the appropriate jargon to use in any given situation. Since even common and often-used words can have ambiguous meanings, teaching individuals to "speak the same language" meant providing a common vocabulary of ideas, metaphors, perspectives, problems, and approaches used in reaching a solution to a particular problem. In the military, just as in academic disciplines, business, or other professions, storytelling, metaphors, and analogies transmit ideas. During wartime, when officers were faced with tight deadlines and intense pressure, the common background and language they possessed was especially important because it allowed them to understand the assumptions, conditions, and compressed arguments behind proposed plans or orders without lengthy explanations.[91] Given Kenney's role with ground forces in World War II, the education was undoubtedly invaluable. Not only could he understand the implications of plans proposed by his ground counterparts, but he could also converse with them in their language, making him more effective in his explanations about the use of air power. The ability to phrase his thinking and proposals in ways his theater commander and ground counterparts would find reasonable and persuasive should not be dismissed lightly.

If a common language and interactions with ground officers increased Kenney's ability to communicate with them in the war, his education with naval officers was sorely lacking. Very little of his service education addressed operations between the ground and sea services, and his only opportunity to personally discuss ideas about air-sea operations with naval officers would have come from his year at the Army War College.[92] This lack of contact did little to increase Kenney's understanding of the capabilities and limitations of naval forces or the naval perspective of warfare, shortcomings that would be evident during World War II.

Staff Officer

After graduating from the War College, Kenney stayed in Washington to work in the Office of the Chief of the Air Corps, the highest headquarters staff in the Air Corps.[93] In late June 1933, Kenney reported to his new assignment in the Plans Division as an assistant to Major James Chaney. His duties included working with the War Department Section of the Joint Economy Committee and the Army's Chemical Warfare Technical Committee.[94]

The life of a staff officer was hardly glamorous, and Kenney found himself involved in a variety of projects of varying importance. One task involved gathering details about the runways and facilities at various airfields in the northeastern United States. This study was part of a larger effort to integrate the Air Corps into Army war plans, and Kenney's research provided data on airfields that could be used in case of war.[95] He gained some recognition within the service during his first year on the staff when he helped translate an article by the Italian air theorist Giulio Douhet that was disseminated throughout the Air Corps and to influential congressmen by the chief of the Air Corps, Major General Benjamin D. Foulois. While the actual translation from French was done by Dorothy Benedict, Kenney's journalistic experience and aviation background helped make Douhet's ideas accessible to the rank and file of the Army Air Corps.[96]

One of Kenney's duties in the Plans Division was preparing material for Congress about matters involving the Air Corps. In early 1934, he played a key role in drafting legislation for yet another attempt to gain an independent air organization. Although the Air Corps Act of 1926 afforded a measure of institutional independence, airmen continued to advance the idea of a service free from the control of ground or naval officers. While the Army General Staff struggled to control this bureaucratic insurgency, airmen enlisted the support of influential congressmen. One of the most important, and insistent, of those supporters was Democratic Congressman John J. McSwain of South Carolina, who became chairman of the House Military Affairs Committee in

February 1932. In January 1934, as he had every year, McSwain proposed
hearings on aviation and submitted a bill for an independent air force. At his
behest the Office of the Chief of the Air Corps prepared the legislation. Since
the Air Corps was still part of the Army, which opposed the move, air officers
had to undertake this project in secret.[97] As in any staff product, a number of
officers had a hand in preparing this legislation, but the majority credited Kenney with writing the final proposal.[98]

The members of the Army General Staff stubbornly resisted the legislation and were infuriated by the subterfuge involved in proposing it.[99] Members of the War Department, including the Army chief of staff, General
Douglas MacArthur, were also irritated because they had recently decided
to organize the air units of the Army under a single air commander, another
small step towards independence. MacArthur's move to consolidate control
over air units was part of a larger reorganization designed to improve the
combat readiness of the Army. A board of high-ranking officers had approved the concept of a new air organization, called General Headquarters
Air Force (or GHQ Air Force) in October 1933; but it was not publicly
announced until Congressman McSwain proposed his legislation in January
1934, leading some to believe that the Army would never have made the
move without congressional pressure.[100]

Despite the general recognition for the need to have a centralized air
headquarters, implementation of the plan was delayed by other events. On
February 9, 1934, President Franklin D. Roosevelt accused the commercial
airlines of improprieties in the methods they had used to gain the contracts
for air mail service and asked General Foulois and the Air Corps to take over
the air mail routes while new contracts were negotiated. With limited time
to prepare for the task, inadequate training and equipment for instrument
and night flying, and some of the worst winter weather in years, the operation strained the Air Corps beyond its capability. The service experienced
sixty-six crashes and twelve fatalities during the operation, while completing fewer flights than the commercial airlines during comparable periods, at
almost twice the cost.[101] In the aftermath of the debacle, President Roosevelt
appointed former secretary of war Newton D. Baker to investigate air mail
operations and the general condition of the Air Corps. The Baker Board
agreed with the concept of a GHQ Air Force and recommended that the
Army establish the headquarters, but undertake a one-year testing period
before deciding on the final organizational details.[102]

While the GHQ Air Force was not a fully independent air force, most
airmen considered it an important step in that direction. The GHQ Air Force
commander controlled aircraft designated by the Air Corps as "air force"

units, that is bombers, fighters, and attack aircraft. Observation squadrons, considered part of the "air service," would still fall directly under the Army field commanders. The GHQ Air Force commander reported directly to the theater commander during war and coordinated air operations over the entire theater. In peacetime the GHQ Air Force commander and his staff reported directly to the Army chief of staff.[103] Serious planning for GHQ Air Force began in October 1934, when Lieutenant Colonel Frank M. Andrews was transferred from command of the 1st Pursuit Group to the War Department. In December Andrews was named commander GHQ Air Force, effective March 1, 1935, when the one-year test of the organization would begin.[104]

As a planning officer in the headquarters of the Air Corps, Kenney found himself in the middle of this activity. He was deeply involved in developing the plans for the GHQ Air Force, and his experience as a member of a temporary GHQ staff formed during an exercise in the summer of 1934 gave him some insight into how the command should be organized.[105] In January 1935, Kenney was named to a group of officers charged with more detailed planning of the GHQ Air Force; later Andrews selected him to be the assistant chief of staff for operations and training when the command was officially established.[106] The position Kenney held was one of the most important on the staff because it focused on the day-to-day combat training for the flying units and would handle the responsibility for executing combat operations in the event of war. Kenney's selection for this position and elevation to lieutenant colonel (his first promotion in seventeen years) was merited by his professional stature in the Air Corps, his service education, and his performance of key duties at the War Department. No doubt Kenney's personal relationship with Andrews, first established at the Tactical School and then strengthened by their association at the Army War College, played a role as well in Andrew's choice of Kenney for his staff.[107]

As the officer charged with overseeing operations and training, Kenney stayed extremely busy during the first year of the GHQ Air Force, visiting units to discover the problems they had with equipment, doctrine, and training. Kenney's duties included overseeing day-to-day flying activities in the command, monitoring the number of flying hours for pilots, and preparing training instructions that dictated the missions necessary to attain flying proficiency.[108] In addition, his division planned exercises that mimicked anticipated combat scenarios. Since one of the goals of the GHQ Air Force was to improve the mobility of air units, these exercises forced units to pack up their equipment and supplies on short notice and move to an austere location for operations. In a further effort to improve the combat readiness of GHQ Air Force units, he planned war games that pitted units against each other to test combat tactics and planning procedures. At one exercise he used position reports given by the aircraft as a rudimentary air raid warning system that allowed fighters to intercept incoming bombers.[109] The pace was grueling. Kenney remembered being home "something like 39 days"[110] that first year, yet he reaped great benefits from the assignment. He had experienced the development of a combat air headquarters, a task that emphasized the importance of support facilities, training, and resources needed to maintain a high level of combat readiness. In addition, he had the opportunity to see firsthand the work and leadership needed to meld units into a coherent combat force.

At the end of an exhausting first year, GHQ Air Force prepared a report for the War Department that spelled out the record of the command and the lessons learned. Andrews and his staff, in no small way spurred on by the problems identified in the air mail fiasco, had pushed for better instrument-flying training to improve the ability of the Air Corps units to take off and hit targets in spite of poor weather. An increase in the number of flying hours each pilot flew per month and a "drive" for this type of training, pushed by the operations staff under Kenney's direction, jumped the number of qualified instrument pilots from 9 percent of the force to 67 percent in six months. Despite this improvement, the report cited numerous deficiencies that detracted from the combat readiness of GHQ Air Force, including the need for better navigation training, more precise weather information, and more bombing and gunnery ranges. In addition, there was still a shortage of aircraft and people to accomplish the missions assigned to GHQ Air Force, and the mobility of the squadrons needed improvement.[111]

The report also highlighted the problems with the command structure produced by the development of GHQ Air Force. Prior to this time the chief of the Air Corps wrote the training regulations and operational standards, but had little actual control over the day-to-day activities of the flying units. Now Andrews had responsibility for the combat employment and training of flying units. He was frustrated, however, by an inability to make modifications to their organizational structure in light of the results of the GHQ Air Force test or to transfer incompetent commanders. In short he did not have the authority to make the changes necessary to achieve a combat-ready force. The chief of the Air Corps retained responsibility for initial training of airmen when they entered the service, determined individual assignments, and purchased the equipment used by the units. Not surprisingly, the report written by General Andrews and his staff advocated increasing the authority of GHQ Air Force at the expense of the chief of the Air Corps. Naturally, the chief of the Air Corps, Major General Oscar Westover, disagreed, arguing that as the ranking airman, he should have all air units under his control.[112]

This dispute had some very real consequences for Kenney. In the summer of 1936, despite his close connection with Andrews and the fine work he was doing on the GHQ Air Force staff, he was sent to Fort Benning, Georgia, as an instructor at the Infantry School. The move banished Kenney from the Air Corps and meant a reduction from lieutenant colonel to his permanent rank of captain.[113]

Kenney's move was the result of two conflicts involving GHQ Air Force: one with the Army General Staff, the other with the chief of the Air Corps. Kenney placed most of the blame for his transfer on the dispute with the Army General Staff over the new Boeing B-17 bomber. The B-17 was being developed as a four-engine, long-range bomber of the future. The Air Corps saw it as a superb instrument for coastal defense, its primary mission at the time, as well as for strategic bombardment if that was needed. Naturally, the Air Corps was excited about the aircraft and had ordered experimental models, with the hope of going into full-scale production. The Army General Staff, and in particular the new Army chief of staff, General Malin Craig, on the other hand, disagreed with the thinking of the Air Corps and in June 1936 vetoed a request for additional B-17s.[114]

Before this decision Kenney had been dispatched to Washington to help explain why the aircraft was so important to the Air Corps. He faced a tough audience. One general told Kenney that the range of the B-17 was excessive and "a couple of hundred miles of range was enough to satisfy the interest of any Army commander."[115] Kenney bluntly replied in a way "they didn't like . . . because I was a temporary lieutenant colonel and a permanent captain and these were all major generals."[116] It is unclear exactly what it was that Kenney said, but his comment makes it clear that it was more his tone than the content of the remark. Although this run-in with the Army staff got Kenney into some hot water, it was only one factor in his transfer. In the spring of that same year he was also caught in the struggle between Westover and Andrews over control of the Air Corps.

As the service test of GHQ Air Force pointed out, Andrews was responsible for the performance of the units, but had no authority to move people between bases, remove officers who might not be performing adequately, or retain those he needed. Andrews argued that developing combat effectiveness depended upon GHQ Air Force's having more authority over air units. Westover, on the other hand, contended that GHQ Air Force should be placed under the chief of the Air Corps. The two airmen, and their respective organizations, were engaged in a bureaucratic battle for control of the Air Corps.[117]

Kenney later downplayed this conflict and simply stated, "There was a contest between the Chief of the Air Force [Westover] and the head of GHQ Air Force [Andrews]. I got caught in the middle of that argument."[118] In fact, it was Westover's irritation with the position of GHQ Air Force and Andrews that must have been the central factor in Kenney's reassignment. As the chief of operations and training, Kenney was an outspoken advocate of GHQ Air Force's need for more authority, and his previous associations and friendship with Andrews gave Kenney some added influence over his chief.[119] Kenney's first task after the formation of the new headquarters set the stage for his relations with Westover's office. In the aftermath of the air mail fiasco, the chief of the Air Corps planned to send a flight of ten bombers on a long-range trip from Washington to the Panama Canal. Since the actual flight would occur after March 1, 1935, the aircraft technically fell under Andrews's authority, and he sent Kenney to inspect the aircraft and crews for the mission. Kenney discovered that neither the planes nor the pilots were prepared and suggested canceling the trip. Based on Kenney's input and reports from other officers, Andrews scrubbed the flight. Westover protested, arguing that only he had the authority to cancel the mission, but the Army chief of staff upheld both Andrews's decision and his authority.[120]

Kenney's irreverent attitude towards the Army General Staff, most evident in his comments on the B-17 but probably shown on other occasions as well, was also antithetical to one of Westover's primary goals for the Air Corps—reducing friction between ground soldiers and airmen.[121] General Malin Craig, who named Westover as the chief of the Air Corps in December 1935, wanted "loyal support and hearty cooperation" from every member of the Air Corps, a directive that Westover promptly relayed to the force.[122] Disposing of Kenney not only removed an influential officer in the headquarters, but also sent a message about the kind of comments and attitude Westover considered inappropriate. Although Kenney tended to blame the General Staff, given Westover's control of Air Corps assignments it is likely that he was the one responsible for the move.

Andrews was deeply upset with the loss of Kenney because of both Kenney's professional abilities and their personal relationship. In an attempt to retain Kenney, Andrews wrote to General Malin Craig, the Army chief of staff. "Kenney," he pleaded, was "a loyal, efficient, well-educated officer with war experience that is a particular asset to this headquarters. . . . I cannot too urgently recommend his retention in his present position, not only in justice to the officer himself but in justice to this headquarters, and for the best interests of the service."[123] Despite his boss's fervent appeals Kenney found himself exiled from the Air Corps to the Infantry School at Fort Benning, Georgia, to teach young infantry officers the basics of ground combat.

As an airman at the Infantry School, Kenney was far removed from his element and unhappy with the situation from the beginning. He was a logical choice to teach air liaison with ground forces, but as a regular instructor on the faculty he also taught, among other things, the proper methods for defending and attacking river crossings and leading machine gun drills. Although he was promoted to major shortly after arriving at Fort Benning, this advancement did little to soften Kenney's disdain for the assignment.[124] After one year, and several previous attempts to leave, Kenney wrote to Frank Andrews, imploring his old commander for an assignment away from the Infantry School "as soon as possible."[125] Andrews fought hard to get Kenney back to his headquarters. In January 1937, Andrews reminded the Army chief of staff of his promise that Kenney could return to GHQ Air Force in a year, but found his efforts in vain.[126] The chief of staff would not allow Kenney to return to the headquarters and forced him to stay at Fort Benning for at least another year. Andrews not only was saddened by Craig's decision, but also felt "in some way responsible" for Kenney's move to Fort Benning.[127] While Craig made the final decision on Andrews's request, the chief of the Air Corps also had a part in the decision. The feud between Westover and Andrews continued, and Kenney was still being exiled because of his previous reputation.[128]

Although rebuffed in 1937, Kenney began maneuvering almost immediately afterwards to leave the Infantry School the next year.[129] Unable to engineer Kenney's return to the GHQ Air Force staff, Andrews wanted him to be the commander of the 7th Bombardment Group, but told Kenney to see General Craig about leaving Fort Benning. Andrews wanted to limit his role, afraid that "any further pressure I put on it will not only be useless, but may result in blocking the whole effort."[130] Kenney took the advice and flew to Washington. The meeting between Craig and Kenney turned out to be uneventful because Craig left the decision about Kenney's next assignment up to Westover. The chief of the Air Corps told Kenney that he could leave Fort Benning, but he could not go to any assignment, in any capacity, that fell under GHQ Air Force. This not only prevented Kenney from returning to Andrews's staff, but also stopped him from going to any flying unit in GHQ Air Force. Westover offered Major Kenney the command of an observation squadron, a position normally held by a first lieutenant. Kenney was obviously fed up with infantry soldiers. Any flying assignment, no matter how bad, was preferable to more time at Fort Benning; Kenney accepted command of the 89th Observation Squadron at Mitchel Field, New York, in the summer of 1938.[131]

At about this same time Kenney was involved in one of the many episodes during the interwar years that soured relations between airmen and

naval officers. During Kenney's stint at the Infantry School, the Air Corps
had received some of the B-17s he requested. The 1938 Air Corps maneuvers were designed to test these aircraft on reconnaissance missions against an
enemy fleet sailing towards the east coast of the United States. With no actual
"fleet" available, enterprising Air Corps officers suggested that intercepting
the Italian oceanliner *Rex* enroute to New York would not only provide good
training, but also afford a chance to score a publicity coup. Kenney managed
to wrangle his way onboard one of the three B-17s on the mission that located the *Rex* over 700 miles out to sea. The flight was broadcast coast-to-
coast on radio and made front-page headlines across the country the next
day.[132] While the event earned favorable public attention, naval officers were
incensed by the intrusion into their territory and demanded that henceforth
all Army aircraft be restricted to within 100 miles of the coast.[133]

Kenney's stint as an observation squadron commander was notable for several reasons. First, other than his brief stint on the border, it was his only operational command experience in the years after World War I. More important,
the assignment did not last long, and much of the time he was away from the
unit on special assignments. A factor that speeded his rehabilitation back into
the mainstream of the Air Corps was the untimely death of Westover in a plane
crash in September 1938. Westover's replacement, first temporarily and then
permanently, was Major General Hap Arnold, an officer who knew and
respected Kenney's abilities. Although Kenney and Arnold had never been stationed together, and Kenney certainly could not be considered Arnold's pro-
tégé, the two had met on occasion; given the small number of officers in the
Air Corps, it is likely that the two knew each other at least by reputation.[134]

The Road to War

Arnold would soon need all the help he could get. In November 1938,
shortly after Westover's death, President Roosevelt reacted to the Munich
Crisis and increasingly aggressive foreign policy of Nazi Germany by proposing an increase in aircraft production and the size of the Air Corps. The president hoped to present his plan to Congress in January, and Air Corps officers
spent the time between November and January feverishly planning this expansion. Arnold recalled Kenney and other officers to Washington to help
develop the plan to carry out the expansion.[135] By the summer of 1939, Congress had authorized an increase that would triple the number of aircraft in
the Air Corps, followed by even more increases after Hitler's invasion of
Poland in September 1939.[136]

Given Kenney's earlier background in aircraft production, it was only logical for Arnold to use this expertise. Kenney moved from his observation squadron to Wright Field near Dayton, Ohio, where he directed a staff wrestling with the myriad of details and problems that occurred as Roosevelt's expansion plans were turned into reality.

The big aircraft manufacturers, such as Boeing and Douglas, made only the airframes. Everything else, from engines and propellers to guns and tires, was bought by the Air Corps from other manufacturers and then sent to the airframe maker. Juggling the government-furnished equipment among the airframe manufacturers fell to Kenney, who became the point man for the Air Corps in ensuring that aircraft manufacturers met their production goals and that the aircraft were delivered to the correct units.[137] In retrospect, Kenney felt that Arnold saw him as a "troubleshooter," someone who could be counted on to straighten out a situation. If Arnold needed confirmation of Kenney's talents as a leader and organizer, his stint at the Materiel Command provided ample proof.[138]

Kenney's work in aircraft production was interrupted in early 1940, when he was sent to Europe as a military observer.[139] From February until April 1940, Kenney roamed all over France studying the aircraft, equipment, and organization of the French Air Force as well as German aircraft that had been either shot down or forced to land in France. Kenney was shocked by what he discovered in Europe. He found American technology woefully behind and returned eager to make the changes he saw, such as installing armored seats for pilots and leak-proof fuel tanks. He discovered that the oxygen masks and heated flying suits currently being produced in the United States were inferior to the ones he found in a German aircraft shot down near the Swiss border, and he suggested giving more attention to equipment for high-altitude flying.[140]

Before leaving Paris for the United States, Kenney raised a lot of eyebrows in the War Department when he bluntly told American journalist Clare Boothe, "I've got to get home and help undo a hell of a lot of mistakes we've been making in our plane construction. If we don't pull ourselves together and undo them fast, we might as well throw half our air force into the ash-can."[141] Although Kenney had a gregarious, friendly manner, Booth was also impressed by the intensity and forcefulness of his observations.[142] Kenney's reports, and those of other air observers, spurred immediate interest in the Air Corps and the War Department, but it proved difficult to implement all of the changes Kenney recommended. Any modification would invariably delay production; and in the summer of 1940, after the defeat of France, the pressure to produce large quantities of aircraft outweighed the demand for qualitative improvements.[143]

During his sojourn in France, Kenney was promoted to lieutenant colonel (again) and when he returned to Wright Field was made second in command of the Materiel Division of the Air Corps, the organization responsible for the design and construction of aircraft, as well as other supplies needed by the air arm.[144] Although technically second in command, Kenney actually functioned as the head of the division because the chief spent most of his time in Washington to supervise the overall direction of production and represent the Air Corps in negotiations with other agencies.[145] Kenney's position made him responsible for most of the internal production matters, such as negotiating contracts, as well as inspection and acceptance of new products.[146] In January 1941, Kenney was also named as the commander of the Air Corps Experimental Depot and Engineering School, which added testing and evaluating new aircraft and equipment to his duties.[147] Perhaps this position also allowed Kenney to indulge the new ideas he amassed during his trip to Europe. In February 1941, shortly after becoming the commander of the Air Corps Depot, Kenney was promoted from lieutenant colonel to brigadier general, skipping the rank of colonel altogether, a reflection of the vast expansion transforming the American armed forces in the two years prior to Pearl Harbor.[148]

Kenney remained with the Engineering Section until March 1942, when he was named commander of 4th Air Force in San Francisco and promoted to major general. This was his first operational command above a squadron and made him responsible for the air defense of the west coast of the United States and the combat training of fighter and bomber crews. Arnold evidently sent Kenney to California in part to reduce the high accident rates of the P-38 and the A-29, a tough problem considering the pressure to continue training new aircrews and defending the Pacific coast of the United States. An investigation headed by Brigadier General Barney Giles on the 4th Air Force staff revealed that most of the accidents were caused by problems in training procedures. He recommended the use of a two-seat model of the P-38 to give novice pilots instruction under the direct supervision and control of an instructor. The introduction of this change and revisions in the engine failure procedures resulted in a drastic reduction in the P-38 accident rate. After only four months in California, however, Kenney was ordered to Washington. He was going to war.[149]

The Sum of His Experiences

Kenney would take into his combat command a blend of technical expertise and an in-depth knowledge of air strategy and operations that provided the framework for his performance in the Southwest Pacific. While his combat experience gained in World War I gave him some credibility among the officers and soldiers when he assumed command, it also helped him understand what his people were experiencing, an important facet for any air leader. This insight also undoubtedly affected his judgment and decisions. Combat experience alone, however, was not enough to make a high-level commander.

Based on his education at MIT and the Air Service Engineering School, as well as his various assignments in the technical areas of the Air Corps, Kenney became very familiar with the technical capabilities of aircraft and knowledgeable about the science of aviation. Perhaps more than most airmen he was quite open to and comfortable with technical innovation and experimented in many different areas. His observations from Europe demonstrated the close attention he paid to the changes needed in U.S. aircraft. While the nature of flying required some scientific and technical knowledge, Kenney's scientific curiosity marked him as a rare officer.[150]

Besides his familiarity with aircraft design, Kenney's association with the aircraft industry also contributed to his success as an air commander. First as a service representative, and later in coordinating aircraft production, Kenney became aware of the methods and techniques of large-scale manufacturing and production, a background that enabled him to better organize the extensive repair and maintenance needs of his combat air force. Although he spent little time in command of operational flying units during these years, Kenney demonstrated his ability to lead people and manage resources through his work at Wright Field as the Air Corps's point man for the rapid expansion of aircraft production.

It was his professional military education, however, that furnished Kenney with a number of benefits. Attending the Command and General Staff School and the War College exposed Kenney to some of the ground commanders he would deal with during the war, provided an appreciation for how they intended to wage war, and equipped him with a common language to communicate with his ground counterparts. Despite its onerous nature, even his two-year stint at the Infantry School added to Kenney's understanding of the details involved in ground warfare. Kenney's years as an instructor at the Air Corps Tactical School were invaluable. The process of writing textbooks on attack aviation and teaching other topics forced him, like many other officers, to develop a true professional expertise in air power through a detailed analysis of air warfare.[151]

Finally, as a staff officer, first in the Office of the Chief of the Air Corps and later at GHQ Air Force, Kenney experienced the "unglamorous" side of aviation—the exhaustive planning necessary to move air units thousands of miles and provide them the logistical support needed for sustained combat operations. At GHQ Air Force, Kenney organized air units for combat employment, prescribed training requirements for aviators, and planned maneuvers. In short, he was engaged in many of the same activities that would occupy him in 1942.

Kenney entered the war with a firm background in the nature of modern warfare and a strong conviction that air power could make a unique contribution. Although Kenney was familiar with theories on strategic bombardment, and appreciated the potential impact of such attacks, he was not obsessed with this application of air power. Instead, he held a more expansive view of air power than many of the strategic-bombing advocates. His familiarity with the benefits of reconnaissance grew out of his flying in World War I. The teaching and research in attack aviation Kenney had done at the Tactical School had emphasized the use of aircraft against troops and supplies on the roads. At the same time he recognized that gaining control of the air was a necessary first step before any operation. By the late 1930s Kenney had also become familiar with other ideas, such as parachuting soldiers from aircraft to attack "sensitive points throughout our rear areas"; and he appreciated the use of air transports for moving forces and supplies, a role well suited to aircraft since they were "not dependent upon roads, railroads, bridges, or terrain."[152] Airlifting troops and supplies, he believed, was "definitely a part of modern warfare"; and as commander of 4th Air Force, he studied ways to use transports alongside fighters and bombers to move friendly troops into sparsely settled areas. This "Air Blitz Unit" would protect and supply the friendly ground forces from the air until they could be reinforced.[153] By comparison, Kenney's extensive knowledge of air warfare is impressive. A long-time instructor in strategic bombardment at the Tactical School, for example, was "surprised" by the use of paratroops in World War II.[154]

In the years before the war, Kenney prepared himself to be an air leader and commander by gaining insight into using the various capabilities of a combat air force to meet the nation's military objectives. The primary task of an air commander, Kenney believed, was to integrate and coordinate the various components of the organization. "An Air Force is not merely a collection of airplanes," he wrote in 1938, "anymore than . . . a certain number of men constitutes an army."[155] An effective air force, he argued, needed a variety of aircraft to accomplish a wide range of missions and "a well-organized and operating system of supply" to provide the bombs and equipment needed to fly the missions.[156] To be successful, Kenney added, the air commander also needed the ability to communicate to his units spread out over many airfields; a system to provide warning of impending enemy air attacks; the ability to forecast the weather conditions before missions were flown; a sufficient number of air and ground crews; and a trained staff to plan air operations.[157] In essence, Kenney defined the difficulties he would later wrestle with during his years as an air commander—building and maintaining the components of a combat air organization.

EXPERIENCED AS A COMBAT PILOT, well versed in the scientific and material aspects of aviation, and knowledgeable in both the academic and practical aspects of military operations, George Kenney was among the most qualified Air Corps officers to become a theater air commander. War, however, would present unique challenges that demanded the most of his talents.

FOUR

TAKING COMMAND

August 1942 to January 1943

"No matter what I accomplished, it would be an improvement."

On a cold Australian winter evening in late July 1942, Major General George C. Kenney landed at an airfield 20 miles west of Brisbane. As the new commander of the Allied Air Forces in the Southwest Pacific theater, he faced a number of daunting challenges. Kenney knew that he had been summoned to this command because his immediate superior, General Douglas MacArthur, was dissatisfied with the performance of the incumbent air commander and the air units under his control. The pilots and ground crews were tired, discouraged, and demoralized. Large numbers of aircraft had been dispatched to the Southwest Pacific, but the Japanese continued to bomb Australia; an invasion of that country seemed likely. Given MacArthur's dealings with the previous air commanders and the perilous nature of the situation, how long George Kenney would last as MacArthur's air commander was anyone's guess.[1]

Kenney himself probably had few doubts about his own abilities to handle his new assignment. He was fifty-three years old with a wealth of experience in military aviation, yet at five feet, five and a half inches tall, he hardly fit the stereotypical image of a dashing airman. He had blue eyes and graying hair, closely cut. A jagged scar cut across the right side of his chin, a souvenir of an aircraft accident, exaggerating his full lips.[2] Journalist Clare Boothe found him, "a bright, hard, scar-faced little bulldog of a man with clear, keen, blue . . . eyes."[3] He was confident—some said cocky—about his own abilities and knowledge of air warfare and was aggressive in expounding those views to whoever would listen.[4] Gregarious and outgoing, he had a friendly, informal nature that could win people over quickly; but this same attitude led some to question, and perhaps underestimate, his intelligence and drive. Those who did quickly found themselves surprised, for he was bright, curious, observant, and blessed with an excellent memory.[5]

This new assignment would demand all of his prior knowledge of air warfare plus a generous dose of skill in dealing with other officers. Kenney would spend his first months in the Southwest Pacific reorganizing his command, developing appropriate air plans, and acquiring competent commanders. At the same time, he battled the Japanese over the eastern half of New Guinea and used his aircraft to support the American landing on Guadalcanal. Importantly, the reorganization and other changes Kenney implemented not only increased the combat capability of his forces, but also helped him earn the trust of the theater commander, General Douglas MacArthur.

The Situation

When Kenney initially learned that he was leaving the United States for combat, General Arnold told him that he would be sent to Cairo to replace Major General Lewis Brereton as the air commander in the Middle East.[6] By the time Kenney arrived in Washington for briefings at the War Department a few days later, there had been a change of plans. The problems with Brereton had been cleared up. Kenney was now headed for Australia. The next few days were spent, as he put it, "absorbing all the dope" he could on the Southwest Pacific Area (SWPA).[7]

Kenney learned that he was headed for an area that was not, within the overall Allied strategy for World War II, the top priority. Although military planners did not totally dismiss the threat posed by Japan, the focus of offensive operations was on Europe, with a defensive holding strategy planned for the Pacific. Not even the Japanese attack on Pearl Harbor changed this decision. At a conference with the British in late December 1941, American policymakers reaffirmed their commitment to defeat Germany first.[8]

During the initial phase of this strategy the United States would expand war production while maintaining a defensive posture. American commanders would engage in combat only to hold potential base areas and ensure that the supply lines from the United States to the combat theaters remained open. Particularly important to the war effort during this period was support by the United States in the form of war materiel, strategic bombing, and naval blockades for Allies already engaged in combat. After American forces had been trained and equipped they would carry out an attack on Germany. Only after the victory in Europe would the United States prosecute the war against Japan with full force.[9] After hearing these details and absorbing the implications for his command, Kenney gloomily concluded, "No one is really interested in the Pacific."[10]

Although Kenney's assessment was somewhat exaggerated, the chief of the Army Air Forces made it clear that he would not spread air units all over the world. General Hap Arnold wanted to send the maximum number of air-craft against Germany in a strategic bombing campaign, telling Kenney that the 600 aircraft already in the Pacific were all he could expect.[11] Arnold acer-bically pointed out that Kenney's predecessor, Lieutenant General George H. Brett, "kept yelling for equipment all the time, although he should have enough already" and that despite the large numbers of aircraft that Arnold had sent, "there didn't seem to be much flying going on."[12] The message for Kenney was clear: make do with what you have. Although Arnold was not Kenney's direct boss in carrying out combat operations, he still played an important role because Kenney remained dependent on the Army Air Forces commander for the aircraft, supplies, and people that he needed to carry out the air war in the Southwest Pacific. Arnold's words carried a lot of weight, and Kenney would deal with him frequently throughout the war.

In Washington, Kenney learned that one of the most important challenges he would face in the Southwest Pacific was developing an effective working relationship with his superior in combat operations, the theater commander, General Douglas MacArthur, a man who had been unimpressed by the com-bat performance of the air units under his command.

When World War II erupted, MacArthur was the commander of Ameri-can Army forces in the Far East, headquartered in the Philippines, and he felt the full fury of the Japanese attack firsthand. MacArthur had at his disposal for the defense of the islands the Far East Air Force, the Army air compo-nent in the Pacific. By December 1941, this air force possessed over 300 air-craft. Unfortunately, only the 107 P-40s and the 35 B-17s in the islands were considered modern combat aircraft, and not all of them were actually ready for combat missions.[13] When Major General Lewis H. Brereton, named com-mander of the Far Eastern Air Force in early November 1941, arrived in the Philippines, he was dismayed by the conditions he found: pilots and mechan-ics were inadequately trained in flying or maintaining the aircraft; the air raid warning network was almost nonexistent; and there was a lack of spare parts for the aircraft.[14]

While Brereton made an effort to remedy the situation, the lack of prepa-rations for war became shockingly clear during the devastating Japanese attack nine and a half hours after the attack on Pearl Harbor. Half of the available aircraft in the Philippines were destroyed that day, including 18 of the 35 B-17s. The communications center and radar installation on Clark Field received direct hits and were almost totally destroyed, making it impossible to coordi-nate any defense against further Japanese attacks. The American pilots were, relative to the Japanese, poorly trained; in the end, American air power could not stop the Japanese air attacks or the eventual invasion of the Philippines.[15]

As fighter pilots desperately tried to intercept and defeat the continuing Japanese air raids, the surviving B-17s were moved to Darwin Field in northern Australia, and on December 24 MacArthur ordered Brereton to relocate his air headquarters to Australia. The airman soon found himself on his way to India and out of MacArthur's command altogether.[16] Whatever the exact causes for the loss of the aircraft in the Philippines—and there were a number—MacArthur refused to accept responsibility for the debacle. Neither did he blame his chief of staff, Major General Richard K. Sutherland.[17]

When Japan's imminent conquest of the Philippines became clear, President Roosevelt ordered MacArthur's evacuation to Australia to become the commander of the newly formed SWPA. This was a new command, not envisioned prior to the war but rather formed in reaction to the events following the Japanese offensive that swept through the Pacific.

The command was created out of President Roosevelt's suggestion to Prime Minister Winston Churchill that the United States and the United Kingdom divide the world into three regions for prosecuting the war. The United States would be primarily responsible for the development of strategy in the Pacific and Great Britain for that in the Middle and Far East, with both sharing responsibility for Europe.[18] After this plan was accepted, the American chiefs of staff further subdivided the Pacific into two major areas, naming Admiral Chester Nimitz commander of the Pacific Ocean Area and MacArthur commander of the Southwest Pacific[19] (Figure 1). Although this divided command was not an optimum solution, and was constantly decried during the war, given the number of ships, planes, and soldiers the United States eventually fielded, the decision actually created more problems for the Japanese because it allowed the United States to attack smaller numbers of enemy forces than would have been concentrated against a single thrust.[20] On April 18, 1942, shortly after arriving in Australia, MacArthur was officially named the commander of the newly established SWPA and organized his force into three Allied component commands: Allied Air Forces, under Lieutenant General George H. Brett; Allied Land Forces, led by Australian General Thomas Blamey; and Allied Naval Forces, commanded by U.S. Navy Vice Admiral Herbert F. Leary.[21]

Brett soon found that he had no better luck in his relationship with MacArthur than his predecessor had, but the problems between the two actually began prior to MacArthur's arrival in Australia. Brett had been sent to Australia to assume command of all U.S. forces and establish a supply base to support future combat operations. Army Chief of Staff George C. Marshall emphasized that MacArthur, who was then still battling in the Philippines, was the senior Army officer in the region and that Brett would be

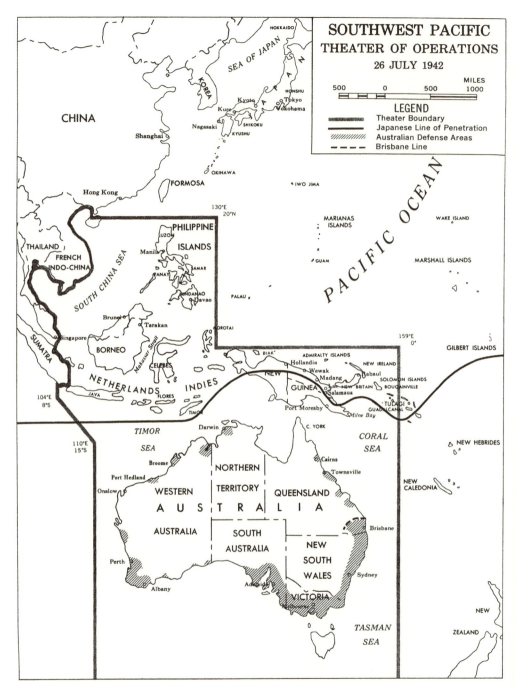

Figure 1. Southwest Pacific Area—Theater of Operations (Office of the Chief Engineer, General Headquarters Army Forces, Pacific, *Engineers of the Southwest Pacific*, vol. 6, *Airfield and Air Base Development* [Washington, D.C.: Government Printing Office], p. 12).

subordinate to MacArthur. Although placed under MacArthur's command, Brett was told by Marshall to submit a recommendation about what could be done to assist the American forces in the Philippines, instructions that put Brett in the awkward position of proposing actions that would affect his commander.[22]

Brett arrived in Australia on December 31, 1941, and after a quick orientation told Marshall that his ability to carry out or support combat operations was extremely limited and suggested stopping reinforcements to the Philippines. Brett's suggestion, along with similar recommendations already under consideration in the War Department, led to a review of the effort to reinforce the beleaguered forces on the Philippines.[23] Undoubtedly, MacArthur was aware of Brett's message and sensed disloyalty in the recommendation that the United States abandon the Philippines.

Brett's standing further diminished during MacArthur's departure from the Philippines. MacArthur's party left Corregidor in Navy patrol boats and traveled to the island of Mindanao in the southern Philippines, planning to transfer to B-17s for the flight to Australia. When MacArthur arrived there were no B-17s. Of the four planes dispatched, only one had made it to Mindanao, and it was in such poor condition that it was sent back to Australia. Four new B-17s were then flown to Mindanao, but two of these were forced to turn back because of mechanical problems. Although MacArthur was not altogether happy with the condition of the two that landed, he continued his journey to Australia. While Brett bore the brunt of MacArthur's criticism, he cannot be entirely blamed for the fiasco. Brett knew that most of his aircraft could not make this flight and had requested the use of new B-17s from Leary for the first mission. The Allied naval commander in Australia refused Brett's request, allowing the use of the new B-17s only after a message from MacArthur prompted intervention from Washington. Nevertheless, in MacArthur's mind Brett was responsible. Not surprisingly, when MacArthur arrived in Melbourne he repeatedly snubbed his air commander.[24]

It is also likely that MacArthur viewed Brett as a competitor for influence and position. While Brett was technically MacArthur's subordinate, he had been the ranking American officer in Australia for some time, a position that required him to work closely with the Australian prime minister, John Curtin, and his government. In early 1942, before MacArthur's arrival, Curtin had nominated Brett as commander in the region.[25] Curtin's offer of command, which Brett declined, established him as a rival in MacArthur's relationship with the prime minister and his role as the allied commander, something MacArthur feared.[26] While working closely with the incumbent prime minister, who represented the Labor Party, Brett also developed a cozy relationship with Australian politicians from the opposition party, who promised him the high command position should they be reelected. Despite Brett's later claim that he never wanted to be the theater commander, his previous time in Australia was the source of some friction.[27] Brett's relief was also the result of his "complete failure to accommodate" MacArthur's wishes.[28] In dealing with the Australian forces, Brett's actions were especially at odds with MacArthur's ideas. When Kenney arrived in Australia, he found a mix of Australian and American officers in the air headquarters. The chief of staff for the Allied Air Forces was Air Vice Marshall William D. Bostock of the Royal Australian Air Force (RAAF). Of the five directorates in the headquarters (operations, plans, intelligence, defense, and communications), Americans headed just two—operations and plans—while the remainder were under Australian officers.[29] Despite the balanced representation at the upper levels of the headquarters, most of the lower-ranking officers in the staff were Australians who had transferred directly from the RAAF headquarters, making the Australians numerically dominant in the headquarters.[30]

Although Brett made a conscious effort to forge a unified air command, and felt that the Australians were a "good bunch" who wanted "to be a very definite part of the war," the number of RAAF officers in the headquarters was indicative more of a lack of qualified American officers than of a concern for Allied relations.[31] In January Brett had asked the War Department for more qualified American staff officers, but his plea went unanswered, as did additional requests in the following months.[32] There was little help to give—the rapid and massive expansion of the United States military had made the small number of proven officers a commodity in high demand. The shortage of American officers had even forced Brett to use Australians, who had been trained differently and whose speech many Americans initially found confusing, as copilots in American aircraft.[33] This decision, and many others in a similar vein, were driven by necessity, not, as Kenney believed, by Brett's desire to improve Allied cooperation. In fact, Australians continued to fly with American units as pilots and crew members well after Brett's departure.[34]

Life out at the air bases further reflected Brett's dependence on Australians. The Australians divided the country into five military areas, giving the area commanders, all of whom were Australian ground officers, control over aircraft in that sector. In addition, the commanders of the individual aircraft bases were RAAF officers. Faced with a lack of officers for command and administrative positions and no established supply system, American airmen and soldiers had to use Australian administrative procedures, a situation that frustrated the Americans.[35] While Brett was not entirely comfortable with this situation, there was little he could do. In the words of one author, "no other arrangement was possible."[36] The views of American airmen at these bases about Australian control are not clear. While some Americans may have resented the situation, other reports indicate that there were good personal relations between Australians and Americans.[37]

The attitude of MacArthur and his staff toward the Australians was, however, unambiguous. As the commander of the Southwest Pacific theater, MacArthur was an Allied commander, yet he was supported by a headquarters staff made up almost entirely of extremely loyal U.S. Army officers who had left the Philippines with him. Army Chief of Staff General George Marshall once chided MacArthur on the composition of the staff, urging him to include Australian and Dutch officers. MacArthur claimed that he could not comply with Marshall's order; there was a dearth of qualified Dutch officers, and the best Australian officers were fully occupied in duties with the rapidly expanding Australian army.[38]

In reality, MacArthur was wary of the Australians and other allies from the beginning. Brett sensed that MacArthur's headquarters gave "little consideration to the Australians" and maintained that "there is every indication that the Australians are being side-stepped altogether."[39] The director of intelligence for the Allied Air Forces, an Australian officer, found the mixing of Americans and Australians "unpopular with MacArthur and the subject of diatribes by Sutherland who had no time for Australians."[40] When General Eichelberger arrived, MacArthur told him to pay his respects to the Australians "and then have nothing further to do with them."[41] Likewise, Lieutenant General Walter Krueger, who came to the Southwest Pacific in early 1943 as commander of 6th Army, learned upon his arrival that he would operate as the commander of an independent task force. Although never officially informed of the reason for this organization, Krueger suspected that MacArthur and his staff designed it to prevent General Blamey, the Australian in charge of the Allied Land Forces, from controlling American combat forces.[42]

Undoubtedly some of the tension between Americans and Australians grew out of ignorance. Reportedly, many American servicemen did not even know that Australians spoke English.[43] Donald Wilson, Kenney's chief of staff and a brigadier general in the Army, admitted that he arrived in Australia knowing little about the country despite having spent several years in the Philippines. "In my mind," Wilson remembered, "Australia was an insignificant island . . . on the 'under' side of the Earth."[44] No doubt this geographic and cultural ignorance exacerbated other differences that officers encountered over such fundamental issues as fighting methods, organization, and language.[45] Major General Robert C. Richardson, sent by Marshall to investigate conditions in Australia, provided added justification for MacArthur's feelings about the influence of the Australians in Brett's command: "The present organization of the American Air Forces, under which our pilots receive their combat missions from Australians, is resented throughout the entire command from top to bottom."[46]

MacArthur's feelings toward Brett might have been tempered by an outstanding combat performance from the air units, but their accomplishments since the start of the war had been remarkably poor. Whatever confidence MacArthur may have had in air power was badly shaken by the defeat in the Philippines. The loss of the American aircraft and the resulting inability to stop the Japanese invasion infuriated MacArthur: "There never was a time in the Philippines when I gave the air force a mission that was carried out successfully."[47]

MacArthur was further dismayed by the condition of the air units he found on his arrival in Australia. He estimated it would take several months and an "intensive effort to reach a satisfactory condition."[48] The Japanese bombing raids on the Australian mainland, in May, June, and July 1942, while not causing a great deal of physical damage, continued to demonstrate the Allies' inability to defend the Australian mainland against air attack.[49]

An episode that exemplified the combat problems of Brett's air units was the Battle of the Coral Sea in early May 1942. To defend their newly conquered territories in the Pacific, the Japanese hoped to develop a defensive perimeter of island garrisons that would enable them to control the sea and air. In late January 1942, Japanese commanders made plans to extend their defensive perimeter southward from Rabaul, a deepwater harbor located at the northeastern tip of New Britain, to the Solomon Islands and eastern New Guinea. If successful, the move would cut off the sea lanes between the United States and Australia, endangering the Allies' ability to carry out any operations in the South Pacific. A key objective in the thrust toward the eastern portion of New Guinea was the town of Port Moresby.[50] In early May 1942, MacArthur's headquarters received intelligence reports about the Japanese plans for a seaborne invasion of Port Moresby. Brett planned to use his long-range bombers as reconnaissance aircraft to find and attack the invasion force before it landed. Although some of his aircraft located the Japanese fleet on May 4 and 5, their sightings were not relayed to the Allied naval force in the Coral Sea, which eventually found the Japanese fleet on May 7. Brett's aircraft took part in the actual battle, but were notably unsuccessful: less than half of the bombers reached their targets, and those few that did inflicted only minimal damage. Particularly embarrassing was the mistaken attack on a group of cruisers and destroyers under the command of Admiral Sir John Crace of the Royal Australian Navy. Fortunately, none of the American and Australian ships were hit by the friendly bombers.[51]

Brett's problems with MacArthur intensified after the poor showing in the Coral Sea battle. In early June MacArthur issued a sharp rebuke to Brett for giving an interview without getting prior approval; two weeks later he reproached Brett for the recent promotions of four air officers to brigadier general without approval.[52] At the same time MacArthur queried Brett about the small number of B-17s available for missions (only 8 percent) and the failure to attack Japanese airfields.[53] Brett responded by noting that his troops could not do the impossible. There were not enough parts to fix the aircraft, and the long distances to the targets exhausted both the aviators and the aircraft.[54] Although these were legitimate problems, MacArthur and his staff were unsympathetic. On one memo from Brett explaining his difficulties, MacArthur's chief of staff wrote: "This letter does not cover the point raised by this [headquarters]: that no attack had been made against the assigned objective, i.e. airplanes and air installations."[55]

Brett's problems had also attracted attention in Washington. In late June the War Department asked MacArthur why he did not have more aircraft ready for combat missions, suggesting that the cause might be his excessive emphasis on offensive operations.[56] MacArthur argued that offensive air operations were, in fact, the only way to stop the buildup of Japanese offensive air power. The problems in maintaining the aircraft were, MacArthur believed, Brett's fault.[57] Arnold basically agreed with this assessment, maintaining that "the senior American officers who are there either have not [tried], or have not been able to correct many defects in supply and administration."[58]

Brett's organization, which had put American air units under Australian commanders, also raised concerns in Washington. Although Marshall had suggested that MacArthur include officers from other nations on his headquarters staff, that was far different from having Americans actually under the command of foreign officers. The War Department staff in Washington had been investigating the problems involved with mixing Australian and American forces, and Kenney was briefed on their ideas about a command reorganization before leaving for the Pacific.[59] According to Kenney, Marshall "didn't think much of mixing nationalities in the same organization."[60] General Arnold was especially critical of allowing Australian ground commanders control over American aircraft. "The Australians," Arnold maintained, "have been operating our combat units in accordance with their doctrines and no attempt has been made on our part to regain control."[61]

While many of the problems in Australia, such as the lack of supplies, a paucity of trained staff officers, and ill-equipped aircraft, were not entirely Brett's fault, as the commander of the American air units he bore the brunt of the blame. MacArthur's reports to Washington had made his unhappiness with Brett clear. In May 1942, President Roosevelt sent a three-man team to investigate conditions in Australia. When Lieutenant Colonel Samuel Anderson returned to Washington at the end of June, he told Marshall that Brett had to be relieved. "As long as Brett is there, you won't have any cooperation between ground and air," he told the chief of staff, and "I don't think you plan to relieve General MacArthur."[62] On June 29, 1942, shortly after receiving MacArthur's cable about Brett's inability to remedy the problems in maintaining aircraft, Marshall cabled MacArthur: "Desire your views and recommendations on possible replacement of Brett by [Lieutenant] General Frank Andrews."[63] MacArthur enthusiastically accepted the offer and felt the change "would strengthen the air component."[64] Andrews, then the commanding general in Panama, had no desire to work with MacArthur and, according to his aide, was incensed by the offer of a position that would have been, in effect, a demotion.[65]

Arnold had asked some of his staff about replacements for Brett; when one officer suggested Kenney, Arnold asked how MacArthur would "get along with sharp, gruff, and forceful George Kenney if he couldn't take smooth and capable George Brett."[66] Whatever the shortcomings of Kenney's personality, he seemed like the right man for the job. On July 6, Marshall told MacArthur that Andrews was unavailable, but offered either Brigadier General James H. Doolittle, "who has impressed all of us as an organizer, as a leader and as a dependable type," or Major General George Kenney, "who is rated tops by General DeWitt [Kenney's immediate superior officer]."[67] MacArthur opted for Kenney because, he said, "it would be difficult to convince the Australians of Doolittle's acceptability."[68]

Kenney Arrives

After his meetings in Washington, Kenney briefly returned to his old headquarters in San Francisco before departing for the Southwest Pacific on July 18, 1942.[69] When he arrived in Australia ten days later, Kenney met with MacArthur's chief of staff and listened to a host of complaints about the air units. In his initial meeting with MacArthur the next morning, Kenney heard much of the same. MacArthur lectured him about the airmen's poor bombing and their lack of discipline. As far as he was concerned, their accomplishments to date did not "justify all the boasting the Air Force had been indulging in for years."[70] MacArthur also sensed disloyalty among the airmen, to his mind the most damning indictment, for nothing was more important to MacArthur than loyalty. According to Kenney, MacArthur "would not stand for disloyalty. He demanded loyalty from me and everyone in the Air Force or he would get rid of them."[71]

Some of the hostility airmen felt towards MacArthur came from their perceptions about his opposition to air power. In 1925, MacArthur had been a judge on Billy Mitchell's court martial; according to Kenney, many airmen resented MacArthur for Mitchell's guilty verdict.[72] During MacArthur's tenure as the Army chief of staff, from 1930 to 1935, he clashed often and vigorously with airmen and their congressional supporters over the budgetary priorities for aircraft and the continuing quest for an independent air force. While MacArthur had sound reasons for his decision to limit spending on aircraft, airmen of the time believed that he neither appreciated nor understood the value of aviation.[73] Brett maintained that MacArthur's distrust of the air force stemmed from his "inability to understand it or operate it as he would ground troops."[74]

MacArthur may not have been as well versed in aviation as airmen would have liked, but he was aware of its potential contribution to warfare. In 1920, while superintendent at West Point, MacArthur had invited Mitchell to speak to the corps of cadets on the air war in France; and as the Army chief of staff, MacArthur had overseen the establishment of the first independent air headquarters.[75] More important, MacArthur's experiences in the first few months of the war had graphically demonstrated the importance of air power and the handicap of operating without a strong air force. Kenney could build on this foundation.

Undoubtedly, Kenney was also aware of Brett's poor personal relationship with MacArthur and hoped to repair that. General Arnold later wrote, "Brett should have done the 'getting along' since he was junior," an outlook he surely passed on to Kenney.[76] When Kenney arrived in the Southwest Pacific he realized the importance of getting along with MacArthur; if he did not, "his life would be very unhappy."[77] After listening to MacArthur vent his displeasure during their initial meeting, Kenney, never lacking in self-confidence, broke in and bluntly told MacArthur that he "knew how to run an air force as well or better than anyone else." He pledged his loyalty to MacArthur and with his backing promised to change things and "produce results."[78] It was abundantly clear to Kenney that there were "two important bits of salesmanship that had to be put over, if the Air Force was to play the role it was capable of. I had to sell myself to the General and I had to sell him to the kids."[79]

An important part of "selling himself" to MacArthur was proving his worth as an air commander. That started by improving the combat effectiveness of the air arm. Even before arriving in Australia, Kenney had a good idea of the things he needed to change to produce results. While increasing the number of working combat aircraft and improving the morale of the air and ground crews were both important, changes had to be made at the top. Kenney needed better officers and commanders—a situation he started working on before leaving Washington.[80] He told Army Chief of Staff General George Marshall and Army Air Forces Commanding General Hap Arnold that "no one could get anything done with the collection of generals" given to Brett and that he "intended to get rid of a lot of the Air Corps dead wood."[81] Although Kenney's demands angered Marshall and Arnold, they agreed to his requests, and Kenney made arrangements to have Brett's top commanders sent home.[82]

Brett was not unaware of the deficiencies of these men. He knew, for example, that one of his key officers had difficulty breaking away from peacetime routines, while another "should really be pulled out and put on an administrative job."[83] Commenting on a third general, Brett complained that this officer "had been sent here to get him out of the United States, in the same way as many other men had been sent to me."[84]

Brett's problems with his officers must have been noticeable, because some changes had started prior to Kenny's instigation. Two officers Kenney greatly respected, Brigadier General Ennis C. Whitehead and Brigadier General Kenneth L. Walker, had already been sent to the area.[85] Kenney had known both of them for over twenty years and believed that "if Brett had had them about three months earlier, his luck might have been better."[86]

Whitehead was, like Kenney, a long-time aviator; he entered the Army in 1917, completed pilot training, and sailed to France on the same day as George Kenney—November 14, 1917. Although they were at the advanced instruction center at Issoudun together, how well they knew each other during that time is unclear. After pursuit training Whitehead stayed at Issoudun testing French aircraft and teaching new students, a lengthy tour that caused him to miss out on combat in France. After a brief discharge from the Army upon his return to the United States, Whitehead returned to the service and had a number of interesting assignments in the years between the wars: he flew in the bombing tests with Billy Mitchell against the captured German battleship *Ostfriesland,* was selected to participate in a goodwill flight to South America, and worked in the intelligence division of the Army General Staff. Like Kenney, Whitehead attended the Air Service Engineering School, graduating first in his class in 1926. Kenney and Whitehead met again in 1930 at the Air Corps Tactical School and five years later on the staff of the GHQ Air Force.[87] Kenney had great respect for Whitehead, describing him as "a great leader and aviator . . . who planned every operation down to the last detail to insure success."[88]

While Kenney and Whitehead had similar backgrounds and ideas, Ken Walker was different. Walker had joined the Army Air Corps in 1917, too late to finish aviation training before the war ended. Kenney first met Walker at the Air Corps Tactical School in 1928, during Walker's student year. After graduation Walker stayed on as an instructor in the bombardment section.[89] Walker's interest in bombers and his work on improving bombing accuracy convinced him that high-altitude attacks would be more effective than bombing from low altitudes, a view that put him in direct opposition to Kenney's belief, honed as an attack instructor, in the efficacy of low-altitude bombing.[90] Walker was also wedded to the idea that superior speed and armament would protect bombers from attacking aircraft when they entered enemy airspace, so that there was little need to attack or eliminate the enemy air defenses. Walker believed that "a well organized, well planned, and well flown air force attack will constitute an offensive that cannot be stopped."[91]

Although Kenney respected Walker as an aviator and officer, and valued him as a combat leader, he never developed the same close relationship he had with Whitehead. It may have been Walker's belief in high-altitude attacks and Kenney's faith in low-altitude bombing that put the two at odds. Or the two may have had some long-standing personal differences and simply did not get along. Whatever the reason, the two men disagreed often during the first few months of the war. Kenney described Walker as a hard worker, but also found his subordinate "stubborn, oversensitive, and a prima donna" who was afraid to delegate authority.[92] Despite his shortcomings Walker was far better than the officers already there; and whatever the personal or professional disagreements, Kenney was glad to have him.

In addition to Walker and Whitehead, another member of Kenney's team was Brigadier General Donald Wilson, sent to Australia soon after Kenney's arrival to be chief of staff for the Allied Air Forces.[93] Wilson joined the Army as an infantry soldier, but later transferred to the Air Service and became a pilot. Much of Wilson's career, however, was spent at the ACTS. He was a student in the class of 1931 and then an instructor for seven out of the next nine years; he became known within the Air Corps for the work he did on strategic bombing theory.[94] Kenney first met Wilson during this period, and Wilson subsequently took over Kenney's role in teaching the course on observation aircraft.

These men typified the type of officer Kenney wanted in his command. He termed them "operators"—aggressive, energetic, and flexible individuals capable of leading and concerned foremost with getting on with the war.[95] Kenney expounded on his views in a letter he wrote to Arnold later in the war. Arnold had asked for Kenney's recommendations on which senior brigadier generals and colonels should be retired. Kenney based his assessment on the officers' ability to do an assigned task with enthusiasm, drive, and leadership, requirements he applied to himself as well as others. Perhaps unconsciously reflecting the lessons he had learned as a young entrepreneur, he believed that an important facet of leadership was the readiness to make decisions and accept the risk of being wrong. "The cry that the Army is full of red tape is a cry against the people in the Army who just don't seem to get results, who can't make decisions," Kenney wrote.[96] This type of individual was harmful to the organization no matter what position he held: "The mediocre man does not get ships sunk or planes shot down and unfortunately neither does he get air crews and ground crews trained on time nor supplies forwarded to the proper place on time. His depot does not produce results. Even as a staff man he bottlenecks studies and decisions that are vital to the operating forces."[97] Not surprisingly, any officer who fit this description quickly left the Southwest Pacific.

Kenney's hunch about the officers in the command was confirmed when he arrived in Australia. One, he felt, "will never realize that we are at war," while another had no idea what was going on during combat operations.[98] Kenney was ruthless in purging those who did not match his energy or sense of commitment. When a supply officer complained about combat units not completing their paperwork properly, he was quickly sent back to the United States.[99] Kenney later boasted that in addition to the general officers he dismissed, he also sent home "about forty colonels and lieutenant colonels and one captain."[100] His attitude toward the officers who failed to meet his standards was captured in an answer he gave to a request about suggestions for future assignments regarding a lieutenant colonel and major shipped back from Australia. Kenney replied, "Have no recommendation for assignment . . . unless you have vacancies for police and prison officers. Neither of them is of any use to the 5th Air Force."[101]

Organizational Changes

While good leaders were important, they could not do the job without the proper organizational structure or materials, and Kenney soon found that he needed to make other changes as well. After his initial meeting with MacArthur, Kenney made a rapid inspection trip of the air bases. He flew to the bomber field at Townsville, Australia, and then on to the most advanced Allied air base, at Port Moresby in New Guinea. After viewing the situation he concluded, "No matter what I accomplished, it would be an improvement. It couldn't be much worse."[102] As he set about reforming his organization, Kenney was a bundle of energy. He inspected and made changes in virtually every area in the command, from airdrome construction and maintenance procedures, to combat tactics and bomb loads.

Kenney's organizational changes reflected his efforts both to enhance the combat effectiveness of his new command and to conform with MacArthur's desire to reduce Australian control. He began at the top—the headquarters of the Allied Air Forces. The headquarters had been set up using the Australian directorate system, which permitted officers in charge of a section to issue orders under the commander's name—a system that not only was confusing to the troops in the field, but also reduced the commander's control over the staff. Combined with the large Australian presence in the headquarters, the directorate system added to the perception that Australians were commanding American forces. Although Kenney found the organizational setup "too complicated,"[103] he made no fundamental changes to it and continued Brett's policy of having both Australians and Americans in the headquarters. He did, however, reduce staff officers' ability to send out orders for the commander and strengthened his authority by making himself both the commander and the chief of staff until an American officer could take over that position.[104]

The power of the Allied Air Forces headquarters was also reduced by establishing a separate and distinct American air force. In early September Kenney divided the Allied Air Force into the American 5th Air Force, which he also headed, and the Australian RAAF Command headed by Air Vice Marshall William D. Bostock, Brett's former chief of staff. While these two organizations were divided along national lines, an important factor in earning MacArthur's trust, the retention of the Allied chain of command also allowed a geographical division of responsibilities, a move that helped improve the combat ability of the entire force. Fifth Air Force was designated the offensive arm, responsible for air operations in New Guinea and control of any air unit, American or Australian, assigned to the area. Likewise, the RAAF Command had charge of the air defense of Australia, antisubmarine duties, and bombing missions from northwestern Australia. This command could assign missions to all of the units in this area of operations, including an American fighter group and bombardment squadron at Darwin.[105] Although Kenney took credit for devising this separation, the War Department staff in Washington had been investigating the problems involved with mixing Australian and American forces, and Kenney was briefed on their ideas about the command reorganization before leaving for the Pacific.[106] Kenney's task was to implement this division without losing any combat effectiveness.

This reorganization clearly appealed to the American military, but it was not without its detractors, especially in the Australian Air Force, the most critical ally in the region. When Brett initially established the Allied Air Forces, his intent "was to have one Allied Air Force commander who would be completely in command of all Air Force tactical as well as maintenance and supply units."[107] His argument, however, held little sway with either the Australian prime minister, John Curtin, or his minster for air, A. S. Drakeford. Neither of these political leaders was overly enamored of arguments that rested solely on military efficiency. Rather, they were concerned that the effect of this organizational structure would be a total loss of control over the employment of their national forces. As a result, the Allied Air Forces commander was given control of RAAF units for combat operations, but no authority over maintenance of aircraft, supplies, or personnel.[108]

After learning of Kenney's intent to split the Allied Air Forces, the new chief of staff for the RAAF, Air Vice Marshal George Jones, argued that Kenney's new command structure abrogated any previous agreement concerning the Australian air force. Jones rightly claimed that the old Allied Air Forces structure had resulted in a division between combat operations and logistical support of RAAF units, a split that adversely affected the combat capability of the RAAF. In Jones's opinion, Kenney's reorganization afforded an opportunity to unify the Australian contribution by making one RAAF officer accountable; and, as the chief of staff, he should be given responsibility for combat operations.[109] Whatever the merits of Jones's argument, both Bostock and Kenney were reluctant to relinquish control over the Australian forces assigned for combat operations.

Although unable to resolve the organizational issue in his favor immediately, Jones was not deterred and continued his efforts throughout Kenney's first months in command. In November 1942, Jones wrote to Bostock, claiming that Kenney made the organizational changes without consulting Australian officials and reasserting his proposal to combine the RAAF Command under the headquarters of the RAAF.[110] Although Jones's charge about Kenney's unilateral action was correct, Bostock did not defend the action but replied by citing Jones's refusal to assign officers to the RAAF Command or recognize the new organization and the RAAF Command's resulting inability to carry out combat operations.[111] Bostock advanced his own solution of consolidating administrative and operational authority under RAAF Command, thereby limiting Jones's role. In January 1943 the chiefs of the Australian military met to resolve the dispute over the organization of the RAAF. They were, however, unable to come to a solution and only agreed to defer the decision pending a further review.[112]

While the controversy over the command of Australian air units was driven by differing ideas about how best to achieve military effectiveness, there was also a personal component to this battle. In fact, Kenney felt that personal feelings were, at bottom, the cause of the problems.[113] The feud between Bostock and Jones began in early 1942, when Jones was promoted over Bostock and eight other senior officers to be the chief of the Australian Air Staff.[114] The enmity between Jones and Bostock, and the debates over the control of the RAAF, would be a source of continuing strife throughout the war. Kenney termed these problems a "nuisance"; but since they did not affect combat operations and he was content with Bostock as the RAAF combat commander, Kenney never felt the need to change.[115]

As he was considering the needed organizational changes for the Allied Air Forces, Kenney's inspection trip revealed a number of other problems. Aircraft flying from the Allied air base at Port Moresby, New Guinea, were going on missions without being concentrated into combat formations. Crews had no idea of proper tactics, and they were given only a general target area rather than precise aiming points. Kenney also heard rumors that whenever the poorly trained bomber crews saw a Japanese fighter they jettisoned their bombs and returned to base.[116]

After viewing the problems in New Guinea, Kenney told Whitehead to stay in Port Moresby and take over control of the operation. Whitehead established a combat headquarters, later named 5th Advanced Echelon, and served as Kenney's commander in the forward area.[117] Forming this headquarters was an unusual step and had no precedent in prewar American air doctrine, yet Kenney made the move for a number of reasons. The lack of firm leadership was evident in the inept flying operations Kenney had witnessed, but in his role as the Allied Air Forces commander he had to stay in Brisbane to plan and coordinate operations with MacArthur and the land and naval commanders. Because of the difficulties in communicating from Australia, he needed someone at Port Moresby whom he could trust to oversee operations and provide American control of the missions. "Fifth Advon" under Ennis Whitehead was the answer.

This organizational structure allowed Whitehead to concentrate on combat missions and improvement of the air defenses at the New Guinea airfields. When aircraft arrived at Port Moresby, they were given fuel, some minor servicing, and whatever bombs or ammunition they needed before being sent on a combat mission. Any extensive repairs were left until the aircraft arrived back at its main base in Australia. Whitehead had the authority to change previously assigned missions based on weather, new intelligence, or the number of aircraft available. Furthermore, since Whitehead worked directly with the ground commanders in New Guinea, he could send flights to support the ground forces on short notice. In short, Whitehead's control over the day-to-day combat operations gave air units much needed flexibility to respond quickly to changing situations. The advanced headquarters also left Kenney free to concentrate on a myriad of other activities, such as finding ways to keep more aircraft flying and improving training and morale.[118]

To fulfill the combat requirements in the Southwest Pacific, Kenney had to devote a substantial amount of time, effort, and resources during this period to establishing an effective aircraft maintenance organization. While the number of aircraft sent to the theater in 1942 was impressive on paper, in reality Allied combat strength was woefully lacking—in Kenney's words, "appalling."[119] On his arrival, less than 50 percent of the total aircraft in the theater were available for combat operations, and in some categories the situation was even worse: of the 245 fighters in the American inventory, only 70 were combat-ready.[120] Keeping aircraft in good condition meant solving a host of problems. Most of the airfields did not have hard-surfaced runways and the fields were in poor condition, a combination that caused a great deal of damage to aircraft when they took off or landed. The weather conditions posed challenges too. High humidity in New Guinea corroded metal parts and wires, and aircraft mechanics discovered that the engine oil sent from the United States evaporated in the high temperatures of the tropics. The lack of supplies to make the necessary repairs exacerbated these problems.[121]

Kenney began a systematic effort to get more aircraft in the air. He discovered that the main supply area was located at Tocumwal depot, about 100 miles north of Melbourne, Australia, nearly 2500 miles away from where the supplies were needed at Port Moresby. This distance alone presented a challenge, but the rudimentary Australian transportation network aggravated the problem. As one of MacArthur's staff officers remarked, "The whole continent of Australia is as undeveloped as the central United States was before the Civil War."[122] While something of an overstatement, the observation points out the frustration the Americans felt. Each of the five states in Australia had built its own rail system, resulting in five different gauges of track. At each state border supplies had to be off-loaded and transferred to another train. In addition, many of the railroads were single track and equipped with antiquated engines.[123] On his way to a forward base in January 1943, Lieutenant Wayne Rothgeb quipped, "From the train's speed I don't think its wheels had turned in twenty-five years." After thirty-six hours the train had covered just thirty-six miles.[124] To overcome the maddeningly slow train travel and the lack of roads, large quantities of aviation fuel and supplies were sent by ship, but this too was a slow process. Air transportation was quicker; but the amount that could be moved was small, and the number of transport aircraft involved in ferrying supplies to combat operations prohibited their use on a regular basis.[125]

Kenney immediately instituted a number of changes. He began by shutting down the Tocumwal depot, an incredible facility with 71 miles of roads, a 900-foot railway platform, and a 300,000-gallon concrete water tank, built with considerable effort and expense (over $3.5 million), but too far from the front lines. Kenney sent the people and supplies north to the fighting. In addition, he established an advanced supply headquarters at Port Moresby and instituted around-the-clock work schedules at the rear-area repair facilities.[126] He sacked the head of the air force services organization and put an old acquaintance and former vice president of Douglas Aircraft, Major Victor E. Bertrandias, in charge of a new aircraft repair facility at Townsville.[127] Kenney also tightened units' reporting requirements about the status of aircraft. According to Kenney, Brett did not know how many aircraft he had to work with, making it impossible to plan future missions or understand the magnitude of the supply problem.[128] Henceforth, each evening flying units forwarded a report to Kenney's headquarters about the condition of their aircraft, giving him a baseline for planning.[129]

While changes at the upper levels of the command were important, Kenney understood that he also needed to motivate the people responsible for supplying and fixing the aircraft. This too was an important part of being an air commander. In many cases a military decoration and medal represented the only official recognition a person was likely to receive during the war. Previously it had been difficult to get approval for these awards, a policy that heightened the sense of isolation many airmen felt in Australia. Kenney pressed MacArthur for more decorations and medals, explaining, "I knew that little bits of pretty ribbon had helped in World War I, maybe they would help in this one, too."[130] When offered one hundred Bulova watches for the pilots, Kenney told watchmaker Arde Bulova that he would prefer to give them to the mechanics who worked on the aircraft instead.[131]

Kenney also made it a point to visit the various air bases in his command, both to discover for himself what was going on and to be seen by the troops.[132] He found the living and working conditions on the air bases in New Guinea intolerable and tried to improve conditions in the forward areas by flying in fresh food and refrigerators and installing screens and cement floors in the dining halls.[133] Technically, Kenney was not authorized to do this; the supply of food was regulated by another organization, but to his mind they were not doing an adequate job. Kenney felt it was his responsibility to take action: "Those kids of mine had to be fed properly."[134] While none of these things that Kenney did was out of the ordinary, each represented an improvement. One pilot felt Kenney boosted morale simply because he made people feel like what they were doing was important: "We started to get some true indication that people really knew we were even down in the Southwest Pacific and fighting."[135]

While Kenney boosted spirits among the members of his command, he also worked on getting more aircraft. Although warned not to expect any more, Kenney began pestering Arnold for more planes from the moment he saw conditions firsthand. Arnold remained convinced, however, that the European theater must have first priority and told Kenney that his forces would remain at a level of "sufficient strength to enable you to support yourself defensively and to carry out a limited offensive against the Japanese."[136]

Even when new or replacement aircraft arrived there were problems, and as the commander Kenney continually pushed for solutions. The first of the fifty P-38s, which Kenney had requested when he departed the United States, arrived in late August 1942. Kenney had contracted with the Australians to manufacture ten thousand 150-gallon droppable fuel tanks to increase the range of the aircraft; but before the aircraft could get into combat, maintenance crews discovered that the fuel tanks were leaking and had to be repaired.[137] The second group of P-38s arrived minus critical parts for their guns and later developed leaks in the engine cooling systems. Six replacement B-25s reached Australia without gun mounts, guns, or bombsights, making them almost useless in combat.[138] Similarly, defective parts kept the new B-24 aircraft out of combat operations for a month. The results of the first missions after the repairs, however, were disastrous: five planes and three crews were lost on the first eighteen flights. Kenney immediately pulled the group out of combat and began remedial training.[139]

MacArthur's Headquarters

As Kenney wrestled with a variety of operational and supply problems and reorganized the structure of the air command, he also worked to establish better relations with MacArthur and his headquarters. Before leaving for Australia, Kenney had been warned about the potential difficulties he might face in working with MacArthur's staff. General Marshall told him about "personality clashes that undoubtedly were causing a lot of trouble," a caution primarily directed at the struggles between the previous air commanders and MacArthur's chief of staff, Major General Richard K. Sutherland.[140] Sutherland, a Yale graduate who joined the Army in 1916, was a brilliant, though arrogant, officer noted both for his intense loyalty to MacArthur and for his ability to antagonize other individuals in the command with his vindictive and unscrupulous behavior.[141] He had served with MacArthur in the Philippines since 1938 and functioned as both the deputy commander and chief of staff, assuming many of the responsibilities that normally fell to MacArthur.[142]

Prior to Kenney's arrival, Sutherland had frequently interfered in air operations and kept Kenney's predecessors isolated. Lewis Brereton, the air commander in the Philippines, rarely spoke with MacArthur, dealing mostly with Sutherland instead.[143] Likewise, Brett warned Kenney that "he had so much trouble getting past Sutherland to see MacArthur that he hadn't seen the General for weeks and . . . just talked to Sutherland on the telephone when he had to."[144] In his parting words Brett described Sutherland as "an egotist with a smattering of knowledge pertaining to air matters" and "a bully, who, should he lose his ability to say 'by order of General MacArthur' would be practically a nobody." Brett recommended "a show-down early in the game with Sutherland."[145] Whatever the validity of their remarks, Kenney clearly faced a challenging situation with Sutherland.

Sutherland was more of a known quantity to Kenney than to his predecessors. Kenney and Sutherland met at the Army War College in 1933. They not only saw each other frequently, but even worked together for several weeks on a committee project, an experience that probably gave Kenney insight into Sutherland's personality and how best to deal with him.[146] Sutherland considered himself something of an air expert because of his flying experience, leading Kenney to conclude that he would have to remind the chief of staff "that I was the one that had the answers to questions dealing with the Air Force."[147] While Sutherland had not received an official pilot's rating from the Army, his flying experience was, in fact, fairly considerable. He been taught to fly in 1940 at the Philippine Army Training Center by U.S. Air Corps instructors following the standard guidelines for pilot training. In addition he had been awarded a private pilot's license by the Civil Aeronautics Administration and continued to fly regularly as a pilot or copilot during the war.[148]

At the very least these experiences boosted Sutherland's view of his own air prowess. An indication of his self-perception came in March 1943, when Sutherland asked to be formally recognized as an army pilot. He had 300 hours of flying time and wanted to be designated a "service pilot," a rating that restricted pilots to noncombat duties such as ferrying aircraft, giving flight instruction, and towing targets. Because Sutherland was over the age limit and not performing a duty commensurate with the rating, the request was denied. In his letter to Sutherland explaining the decision, General

Arnold graciously stated, "With full knowledge of the grand job you are doing I cannot but help feel that this rating would not materially alter your position." The officer writing the memorandum was more blunt: "The granting of the rating of service pilot to General Sutherland would not impress younger combat personnel. . . . The only advantage to be gained by granting General Sutherland the rating he requests would be those of a personal nature to General Sutherland."[149]

Besides Sutherland's knowledge of flying, his proximity to the air headquarters made it relatively easy for him to interfere with the air commanders. Mission orders were transmitted from the Allied Air Forces headquarters, located in the same building as MacArthur's headquarters, to the units at the outlying bases. Conversely, the ground commanders' dispositions were made far from headquarters, making it difficult for Sutherland to be as involved with them.

While Sutherland's personality played a large part in the airmen's complaints, there was also an institutional component to the dispute. The decades-long fight for organizational independence by Kenney and other airmen made them sensitive to any interference by ground officers in air matters. The fight within the service had been raging since 1918, and much of the controversy between ground and air officers centered on command and control of the aircraft. Airmen were convinced that aircraft should be put under the command of an air officer to realize the full impact of air power. Their reasoning was based, in part, on the realization that combat aircraft were limited resources, rendered less effective if dispensed in small numbers. To be sure, an independent mission, such as strategic bombardment, would also vindicate the importance of air power and the need for an independent service more than missions in support of ground units. Ground officers believed with equal certainty that air power should be distributed to each commander and used primarily to help support the ground forces in battle. This struggle produced friction in many commands early in the war over who "controlled" air power, a dispute resolved, by and large, in the airmen's favor. Kenney's own belief in an independent air arm, coupled with his combative personality and long experience with ground officers, made a confrontation with Sutherland all but inevitable. All the same, the vehement complaints about Sutherland's interference should be understood in the context of a long-standing feud over the institutional status of the air force.[150]

Kenney, armed with his knowledge of Sutherland's personality and forewarned about his practices, took to heart Brett's advice about an early confrontation. On August 4, 1942, the day Kenney officially took command, he received orders regarding air operations over the coming days. Rather than the broad mission guidance that Kenney felt was appropriate, he got detailed information on takeoff times, weapons, and even tactics. Kenney immediately challenged Sutherland, arguing, in typical Kenney fashion, that he was the "most competent airman in the Pacific" and that it was his responsibility to decide how the air force would support an operation. Kenney picked up a piece of blank paper and put a dot in one corner. The dot, he told Sutherland, was what the chief of staff knew about air power. The rest of the paper was what Kenney knew.[151] When Sutherland tried to argue, Kenney suggested that they "go in the next room, see General MacArthur, and get this thing straight. I want to find out who is supposed to run this Air Force."[152] According to Kenney, Sutherland "immediately calmed down and rescinded the orders that I had objected to," then apologized, saying that prior to Kenney's taking command he had been forced to write the orders.[153] While Kenney may have exaggerated the effect of this meeting (the two men would have other confrontations throughout the war), this was the last time that Sutherland directly interfered with Kenney's combat operations. Perhaps Kenney's confrontation vindicated Brett's analysis that Sutherland was a bully who backed down when someone stood up to him. More likely, Sutherland and Kenney both knew that as the chief of staff Sutherland should not have been issuing such detailed orders and that MacArthur would side with Kenney. In short, Sutherland "knew he was going to lose."[154]

Kenney also worked hard during the first few months to develop a close relationship with MacArthur. They both had their headquarters in the AMP insurance building on the corner of Queen and Edward Street in Brisbane. MacArthur's office was on the eighth floor and Kenney had his on the fifth, making it convenient for the airman to go up to MacArthur's office at almost any time.[155] Kenney took advantage of the proximity and made it a practice to see MacArthur at least once a day, often timing his visit so that the two could eat lunch together.[156] When MacArthur traveled to New Guinea to supervise operations, Kenney went along.[157] Since both men also lived in Lennon's Hotel, Kenney took to visiting MacArthur "quite often" in the evenings, further cultivating this personal relationship.[158] Whether the two men talked of personal or professional matters, or both, during these conversations is unclear and probably unimportant. It is clear that, at least in the first few months, Kenney focused on educating MacArthur about air power, spending two hours on his first day as air commander talking about air plans with MacArthur.[159] In addition to "selling" MacArthur on air power, Kenney's efforts also allowed him to break into MacArthur's circle of advisors, which heretofore had centered on the staff that accompanied him from the Philippines.[160] Kenney's personal dealings with MacArthur, according to one biographer, "introduced into the life of [MacArthur] an informal camaraderie which he had lacked."[161] In retrospect, Kenney felt that this relationship allowed him to get "away with murder because MacArthur would back me up"—an observation echoed by other officers in the command.[162] With this personal relationship came a high level of trust that allowed Kenney to use air power as he saw fit, usually with little interference from above. Kenney also became a close advisor to MacArthur on many matters, but outside of air issues this relationship was more uneven. MacArthur did not always follow Kenney's advice, often, in fact, choosing a course opposed to Kenney's thinking.

THE CHANGES KENNEY INSTITUTED during his first months in command established the tenor of his leadership. He immediately began working to establish both a professional and a personal relationship with the theater commander, General Douglas MacArthur, something neither previous air commander had been able to accomplish. Equally important in this relationship were the changes Kenney made in the air forces, creating a separate American air command and eliminating officers who were unfit for combat. Kenney also began educating MacArthur about the various capabilities and benefits of air power—attributes MacArthur desperately needed in the last half of 1942.

FIVE

THE PAPUAN CAMPAIGN

August 1942 to January 1943

"We learned a lot and the next one will be better."

At the same time that Kenney was wrestling with the changes within his organization, he also was overseeing combat operations. In early July 1942, just prior to Kenney's arrival in Australia, the American Joint Chiefs of Staff (JCS) approved a plan aimed at seizing the Japanese base at Rabaul, located in the northeastern corner of the island of New Britain, about 450 miles from Port Moresby. Carrying out the first part of these plans was Kenney's biggest task during his first months in command.

Plans

Rabaul was the key base in the Japanese defensive perimeter in the South Pacific. Its five airfields and deep harbor made it an excellent strategic location from which to attack and cut off the sea lines between the United States and Australia. Ample proof of the value of this base had come in May, when the Japanese used it as a jumping off point for their seaborne attack against Port Moresby, an effort foiled in the Battle of the Coral Sea. Capturing Rabaul would remove this threat to Australia, roll back the Japanese gains, and allow Allied forces to advance up the northern coast of New Guinea enroute to the Philippine Islands, and then on to Japan.

American planners laid out three phases, or what they termed tasks, for their offensive. Task One called for American forces to capture the Santa Cruz Islands and Tulagi in the Solomon Islands chain. This mission would be under the direction of Admiral Nimitz, the commander of the Pacific Ocean Area, based in Hawaii. The local, on-scene commander was Rear Admiral Robert L. Ghormley, head of the South Pacific command. Task Two would be to secure the northeastern coast of New Guinea, and Task Three was the capture of Rabaul. MacArthur would be in command of these two, but was ordered by the JCS to provide air and naval assistance to Ghormley during his campaign in the Solomons.[1]

MacArthur's plans for operations in New Guinea (code-named TULSA) depended on seizing airfields at Dobodura on the northern coast and building up the facilities at Milne Bay on the eastern end of the island. Once these areas were safely under Allied control, he would begin ground operations to eliminate Japanese forces on the rest of the island. The Japanese upset this design by striking first, staging another attack on Port Moresby. This operation was a two-pronged attack. The first group of Japanese troops landed on the north coast of New Guinea on July 21, near a native village called Buna, planning to march overland and capture Port Moresby. A second invasion force came ashore about a month later on the eastern coast of the island at Milne Bay (Figure 2).[2]

The Japanese attack committed American and Australian ground forces to fighting in an area described as "a military nightmare" by one historian.[3] New Guinea, the second-largest island in the world, lies just north of Australia and is best described as a mythological creature with a bird's head on the western end attached to a lizard's tail pointing east. Before World War II the western area, near the "head" of the bird, was controlled by the Dutch, while the eastern end, called Papua, was administered by the Australians. Papua was a land of swamps, oppressive heat, and seemingly unrelenting rainfall. The Owen Stanley mountain range, which divides the eastern half of New Guinea, has peaks rising up to 13,000 feet. With 150 to 200 inches of rain a year, Papua New Guinea was a land of jungles, rain forests, and swamps, with few towns and even fewer roads.[4]

While the mountains and weather created horrible conditions for infantry soldiers on the ground, they also had an important impact on air operations. Initially, the only Allied-controlled airfields were at Port Moresby, forcing aircrews to fly over the Owen Stanley mountains to attack Japanese airfields, shipping, or other targets. Typically, the weather in the morning would be clear, but during the day large thunderstorms would build up over the mountains. Flying through the storms was out of the question—the wicked updrafts and downdrafts would literally break airplanes apart. The tops of the thunderstorms were often higher than the aircraft could fly, but pilots who tried to duck under the clouds risked running into a mountain peak.[5]

Figure 2 (facing page). Papua and Northeast New Guinea (Office of the Chief Engineer, General Headquarters Army Forces, Pacific, *Engineers of the Southwest Pacific,* vol. 6, *Airfield and Air Base Development* [Washington, D.C.: Government Printing Office], p. 77).

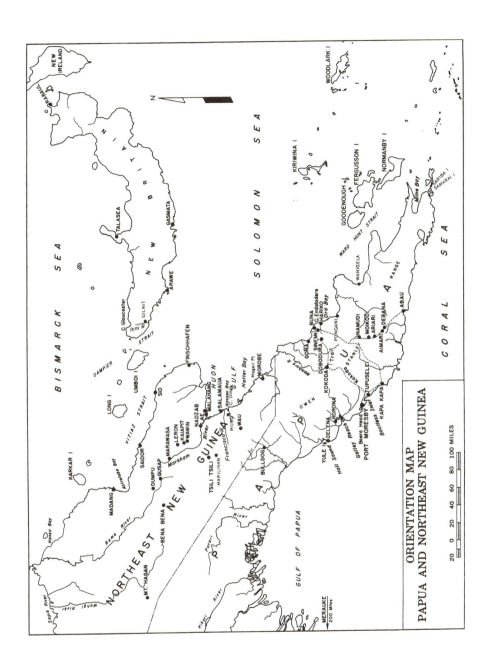

ORIENTATION MAP
PAPUA AND NORTHEAST NEW GUINEA

73

The fierce weather conditions, coupled with a lack of navigation aids, was a constant concern for pilots and crews trying to make their way back to their home bases. Flight instruments in the aircraft were of little help—one pilot recalled seeing compasses "30 or more degrees in error" and not having a reliable artificial horizon.[6] Fighter pilots, who relied on ground references for finding their way around, went on missions hoping the "weather did not close in as you returned."[7] The problems associated with the weather in the Southwest Pacific compounded enemy actions and created an added impediment to Kenney's efforts throughout the war.

Attacking Rabaul

The combination of the Japanese attack on New Guinea and the American offensive at Guadalcanal slated to begin on August 7, 1942, meant that Kenney's meager air units would be stretched thin, engaged in combat operations in both New Guinea and the Solomons, some 500 miles distant to the east.[8] Although there was no written air campaign plan prior to the operation, as Kenney's operation evolved it became clear that his forces would be involved in four separate tasks: removing the Japanese air threat, attacking Japanese shipping, striking Japanese ground forces, and airlifting troops and supplies to the battlefield. Kenney faced a constant challenge choosing which missions took priority and balancing the conflicting requirements.

To Kenney's mind, the "one primary mission" was to reduce the Japanese air strength and gain control of the air.[9] Since the source of Japanese air strength in the region was at Rabaul, he reasoned that attacks directed at Japanese air units there would also support Admiral Ghormley's offensive in the Solomons.[10] MacArthur, who had previously urged Brett to hit the enemy's airfields, enthusiastically approved Kenney's ideas, telling the airman he had "carte blanche" to do anything he wanted.[11]

In developing his plan for the use of air power, Kenney drew on his own knowledge of air warfare as well as established doctrine in the Army Air Corps. The elimination of the opposing air force, especially in support of surface operations, was well known to airmen.[12] Kenney had long believed that "freedom of action in the air and denial of the same to hostile air forces"[13] was the first objective of an air force and that "the denial to the enemy of freedom of air action is an essential preliminary to large-scale ground operations."[14] "The best way to combat hostile aviation," he postulated, was "to fight with the enemy in the air and to bomb his airdromes, air depots, and aircraft factories."[15] The distance from the Japanese home islands and the range of the aircraft at his disposal made it impossible for Kenney to attack aircraft factories or other strategic targets on the Japanese homeland, forcing him to concentrate on destroying "enemy aircraft on the ground and in the air."[16]

Kenney did not envision one giant air battle that would determine control of the skies. On the contrary, he realized that the effort against the Japanese needed to be "continuous,"[17] especially in light of their ability to send more aircraft into the area. Although Kenney's total air strength of 517 combat aircraft looked formidable on paper, only 150 were combat-ready, and most of the Australian aircraft were obsolete.[18] Kenney promised MacArthur that his first step towards air superiority would be a concentrated strike on an airfield near Rabaul on August 7, a mission timed to correspond with the start of Ghormley's landing on Guadalcanal. In preparation, Kenney stopped flying operations to ready 20 B-17s for a concentrated attack. Although small by later standards this force represented the largest Allied air strike in the theater to date.[19] While mechanics prepped the B-17s for Rabaul, shorter range A-20s, B-25s, and B-26s struck New Guinea airfields using the para-frag bombs Kenney had developed at the Tactical School and brought from storage in the United States.[20]

Kenney recorded the bombing of Rabaul on August 7 as a huge success. Eighteen B-17s took off from Port Moresby for the target, and the crews claimed the destruction of 75 of the 150 Japanese aircraft "lined up wing tip to wing tip on both sides of the runway."[21] The attack pleased MacArthur immensely, and he eagerly accepted Kenney's recommendation that a pilot who died in the raid be awarded the congressional Medal of Honor for his actions.[22] Notwithstanding the heroic actions of the B-17 crews, the raid was probably not as successful as Kenney presumed. Only 16 B-17s actually took off on the mission, and 13 of them made it to the target. Postwar reports from the Japanese indicated that the bombing inflicted only minor damage— far less than the results Kenney claimed.[23] The differences were undoubtedly caused by a number of factors. Confusion in the battle area and reports from the crews in the attack tended to inflate the successes, while the Japanese commander on the spot leaned towards minimizing the damage in reporting to his superiors. Kenney also misinterpreted an intercepted Japanese radio message as indicating better results than were actually achieved. The possibility that Kenney intentionally distorted the message cannot be dismissed, but it seems more likely that he was eager to grasp at any success, no matter how small, to boost the morale of his flying units.[24] The men in his command, and General MacArthur, probably needed some proof of Kenney's ability as an air commander. Knowing the limitations Kenney faced, MacArthur probably judged him on the effort in bringing off the attack, rather than precise damage estimates.

This comparatively large raid was a rare occurrence during Kenney's first months in command. Japanese control of the air in New Guinea made it dangerous for bombers to be based at Port Moresby permanently. Instead they flew from bases in Australia to Port Moresby for refueling, then continued on to Rabaul, requiring thirty-six to forty-eight hours to complete a single mission.[25] As a result, even with all of Kenney's changes there were few concentrated attacks on Rabaul during his first months in command. From the middle of September until the end of November, Kenney's support for Admiral Ghormley's efforts at Guadalcanal amounted to 180 B-17 flights and a handful of RAAF Catalinas on night bombing missions to Rabaul, plus a smattering of attacks on targets in the Solomon Islands.[26]

Kenney's plan to concentrate on Japanese air power was not without its critics. Throughout the fighting Admiral Ghormley asked that enemy shipping be given a higher priority.[27] The limited number of aircraft made it impossible for Kenney to support every request. He was convinced that hostile aircraft represented the greatest potential danger to both operations and should be attacked first. In September MacArthur's headquarters claimed that attacks on Rabaul had destroyed 93 planes and damaged 60 others, resulting in "a marked influence on operations in the south Pacific area."[28] Despite concerns from other quarters over the lack of attacks on Japanese ships, Kenney had apparently convinced MacArthur of the virtue in destroying Japanese air power first.[29]

Air Defense

While the flights against Rabaul were aimed at reducing the Japanese air strength in the entire area, the air defense of New Guinea remained a more immediate concern. The most important factor in Kenney's efforts to gain control of the air was improving the air warning network in New Guinea.[30]

In general, early warning gives the defender an important advantage in stopping an air attack. Simply put, the sooner the aircraft can be launched, the farther away from the target they can meet the incoming attackers. Intercepting an enemy formation 40 miles from the target, for example, was better than 10 miles, because defenders had more opportunities to disrupt the enemy formation and inflict losses. Early warning was especially important in light of the flying characteristics of the American P-39s and P-40s, the only fighter aircraft Kenney had available in large numbers. Both aircraft rapidly lost power above 12,000 feet, making it impossible for them to get to altitude and meet the incoming attackers on short notice. Furthermore, the aircraft were not as maneuverable as the Japanese Zeroes that escorted the attacking bombers.[31] In short, the P-39s and P-40s went into air combat with some significant performance disadvantages that could be overcome only through good tactics. The lack of maneuverability and power meant that engaging the Japanese fighters in a turning dogfight was a losing proposition. By using hit-and-run tactics though, American pilots could capitalize on the advantages of the American aircraft—heavier firepower and the ability to dive faster than the Zero—while minimizing the lack of power and maneuverability. These methods demanded prior warning so that the American fighters could climb high enough to meet the Japanese raiders. Dispersing aircraft on the ground and building protected parking areas would attenuate some of the damage; but with limited warning of the inbound attacks, Allied aircraft simply could not stop the Japanese bombing raids.[32]

On Kenney's first visit to Port Moresby, he witnessed an enemy air raid and estimated that the warning time had been "less than five minutes," a situation that demanded immediate attention.[33] The first, and perhaps most obvious, solution to the warning problem was the installation of additional radar sets in New Guinea. Although two radar stations were up and running near Port Moresby at the beginning of September, they provided only limited warning.[34] The radars operated by the RAAF could detect targets out to 75 miles, while the maximum range of the mobile American radar system, the SCR-270, was 150 miles, although in practice it turned out to be somewhat less, usually about 110 miles.[35] The SCR-270, however, could detect only the incoming aircraft's range and direction, not their altitude; the equipment also had numerous blind spots, such as finding aircraft at low altitude. To compensate for the inability to detect the target's height, a critical factor in intercepting enemy aircraft, it was sometimes paired with the SCR-268, which could compute the altitude of the aircraft but had a maximum range of only 25 miles.[36] In June, four SCR-270s had been installed in Australia, but only the short-range SCR-268s were actually in Port Moresby.[37] In addition to the technical limitations of the radar sets, there was a lack of spare parts, and few operators or mechanics in the theater had much experience with the equipment. Fewer than three hundred officers and men had graduated from radar training, and much of their knowledge was rudimentary at best.[38] The topography of the region posed additional problems. Since the radar could not see through the ground, the Owen Stanley mountains effectively shielded attacking aircraft until they were very close to Port Moresby.[39] Given all of these limitations, it was clear that Kenney needed some additional means of early warning.

A proven, albeit limited, method for providing longer warning times was the use of ground spotters to report incoming air raids. To help defend the vast, but lightly inhabited, tracts of territory in the South Pacific, the Royal Australian Navy set up a system of spotters, called coastwatchers, as early as 1919.

They were supervised initially by Australian Navy Lieutenant Eric Feldt; then MacArthur's headquarters absorbed the coastwatchers into the newly formed Allied Intelligence Bureau (AIB), an organization that managed the espionage, sabotage, and guerrilla activities in the Southwest Pacific. The coastwatchers, usually government administrators or plantation managers living in New Guinea and the Solomon Islands, were volunteers who had been given a radio and instructions on how to report enemy ship and air movements.[40]

The Australians had concentrated the original coastwatcher network in the Solomon Islands. Although many of these coastwatchers were caught after the Japanese invasion, others disappeared into the jungles and became a valuable part of the network in warning of Japanese air raids on Guadalcanal. In New Guinea and New Britain, on the other hand, the organization had to be started almost "from scratch."[41] Government officials and settlers on the islands who had been displaced by the Japanese invasion were recruited and trained, but the first coastwatcher was not put ashore in New Britain until July 1942; his task was to obtain intelligence on Rabaul, not set up an air raid warning system. Near the end of 1942, the AIB attempted to land several teams of coastwatchers in New Britain, but the large Japanese presence thwarted their efforts.[42] Newly trained coastwatchers were also dispatched to New Guinea, but the large numbers of Japanese forces caused problems there also. From most accounts these coastwatchers were useful in locating Japanese supply points, but actually provided little in the way of early warning about Japanese air raids.[43]

The most important source for warnings of Japanese air raids came from what was broadly termed signals intelligence, information derived from an enemy's use of electronic equipment. Although this intelligence can be obtained from many different sources, during World War II signals intelligence focused on intercepting and decoding enemy radio messages, widely known today by the code word ULTRA.[44] Intercepting Japanese communications and extracting usable information required a number of steps and organizations, all important to the final product. Actual collection of the data was accomplished by intercept sites located as far forward as possible in friendly territory. At these isolated outposts, teams of highly trained operators scanned known and suspected enemy radio frequencies, trying to find Japanese radio transmissions. The material they gathered was then sent to Central Bureau, an Allied intelligence organization formed in April 1942, shortly after MacArthur's arrival in Australia. Central Bureau transcribed the Japanese messages into clear text and translated them into English before delivering them to MacArthur's intelligence division, where they were integrated with other information for analysis.[45]

The Australian armed services, like the American military, had been working on intercepting and decoding Japanese radio messages even before World War II began, and many of the field sites that intercepted the Japanese radio messages were manned by the Australians. In addition to breaking the encryption codes used by the Japanese military, the Australians also became familiar with the radio codes used for routine communications. The Japanese used a special Morse code, called "kana" code, that had seventy-one symbols instead of the international code of twenty-six symbols, making it difficult to intercept and transcribe even if a message was sent in the clear.[46] Through intensive training and repetition, however, operators became proficient enough to read the "kana" code messages almost as soon as they were sent.[47]

The Japanese radio messages, sent either in code or in plain language, between aircraft and the ground stations gave the Allies reliable and accurate early warning of enemy air attacks.[48] A typical scenario unfolded as follows. Shortly after takeoff a Japanese bomber would send a message, typically "KA N" (roughly translated as "How do you read this transmission?"). The base would then reply back. These transmissions provided the initial indication of an impending attack, but provided little information on the size of the raid or its destination. Determining the intended target of the attack was the responsibility of the direction finding (D/F) radio intercept units. These units were immediately alerted after the first message and tracked any subsequent radio transmissions to determine the aircraft's position relative to the ground unit's location. This information was then transmitted to a command center for plotting and, if possible, correlated with other data, such as sightings from coastwatchers. The end product was an approximate track of the inbound bombers and their intended target.[49] The initial message that signaled an impending air raid was also sent to the appropriate air defense headquarters and used to formulate a plan for launching aircraft and positioning them to attack the incoming force. Weather reports proved easy to decipher because they followed a standard format and were taken as "a sure indication of a raid to follow." Even if an aircraft did not transmit in the air, on occasion warnings would be issued based on the radio activities heard on the ground. As early as July 1942, field units were able to provide seven hours of warning of a raid from Rabaul, a substantial increase over the thirty minutes available from radar.[50]

In addition to the early warning indications of air raids, these routine radio transmissions were useful in other ways. Ironically, the weather reports from the Japanese bases helped Allied commanders in planning air missions. If the Japanese weatherman reported heavy cloud cover over the base, there was no need to send a mission to that target.[51] Japanese aircraft escorting ship movements also tipped off the position, course, and speed of the convoys through radio transmissions, giving Allied commanders a clear picture of where the ships were going and when they could be intercepted.[52] Finally, when the Japanese sent additional aircraft into the area, ULTRA intercepts tracked their moves, giving Kenney a very accurate assessment of the enemy's air strength.[53]

The units that did the actual work of intercepting the radio messages, called wireless sections in the Australian Army and wireless units in the RAAF, got into action shortly after Kenney's arrival.[54] In September 1942, Number 55 Wireless Section of the Australian Army was sent to Port Moresby to provide early warning of enemy air raids. This section, along with a D/F unit, stayed until December, when they were replaced by a detachment from the RAAF's Number 1 Wireless Unit.[55]

Although this early warning information was available, the value and importance of signals intelligence was not immediately clear to everyone. In retrospect, it is easy to see the value of signals intelligence for air operations, but at the time its worth was more uncertain. This was, after all, a very new capability, and few officers had received any exposure to signals intelligence prior to the war. A signals officer based in the Philippines at the outbreak of the war asserted that his warnings of impending air raids were ignored and that a high-ranking air commander told him "to go somewhere else and peddle [his] dots and dashes."[56] In addition, the intelligence was not unambiguous; there was always the danger of a false alarm, which could lower the value commanders placed on this information.[57]

Kenney, on the contrary, quickly grasped the importance of signals intelligence and from the beginning did not hesitate in using it. His willingness may have stemmed from his technical background. He certainly would have understood the technical premise of radio waves and the possibility of intercepting the transmissions. According to his intelligence officer, Kenney enjoyed new ideas and was always eager to learn more about the capabilities and intentions of the Japanese.[58] Kenney's eagerness was also affected by his situation. He desperately needed an early warning system and information about the Japanese movements; signals intelligence provided an excellent means for filling this gap. Whatever his motivation, after several months of experience Kenney had learned the value of signals intelligence. In the fall of 1942, he requested five more RAAF wireless units. Although only two more were formed, Kenney continued to rely on them, as well as like units formed by the Army Air Forces, called radio squadrons (mobile), to provide early warning of enemy air raids and the rich intelligence they gleaned from Japanese radio messages.[59]

Stopping the Advance

At the same time that Kenney's forces were engaged in the protracted effort of gaining and maintaining control in the air, the Japanese troops who landed in New Guinea in late July 1942 continued their advance over the Owen Stanley mountains towards Port Moresby, a turn of events that forced Kenney to focus some of his force on striking the ships bringing supplies to the north coast of Papua, a role his airmen were ill prepared for.[60]

The established doctrine of Army Air Corps for sinking ships called for horizontal bombing runs from high altitude, but airmen had achieved few successes using these tactics in the Southwest Pacific. During the Battle of the Coral Sea, Brett's aircraft had done little damage against the Japanese ships. Under Kenney the aviators fared little better. They were unable to stop the initial landings in New Guinea, although they did manage to destroy some of the supplies put ashore near Buna and, on at least one occasion, turned back a ship bringing additional stores.[61] These limited successes made it clear to Kenney that he needed "something soon to stop Jap shipping."[62]

The harsh realities of war revealed numerous problems in applying the prewar thinking. One shortcoming was the number of aircraft needed to sink a ship. Air officers estimated they would need a formation of at least nine bombers to hit a maneuvering target.[63] Kenney, however, seldom had nine bombers available to fly on one mission. The small number of aircraft sent to the Southwest Pacific, combined with a lack of spare parts and trained technicians, limited the number of mission-ready aircraft.

In any event, the doctrine had paid little heed to what the nineteenth-century Prussian theorist Carl von Clausewitz called "the friction of war."[64] In Kenney's command this friction appeared in many forms. Tropical thunderstorms and a cloud deck at 1,200 to 2,000 feet made it impossible for nine aircraft to fly together and find the ships down below.[65] The reactions of the Japanese provided another source of friction. As one bombardier told Kenney, "When I'm bending over that bombsight trying to get lined up on one of those Jap ships and the bullets start coming through the windows in front of me, they take my mind off my work."[66] As a combat veteran Kenney knew the fear of battle and was sympathetic to the bombardier's complaint, but as the air commander he needed to find a way to accomplish his missions. Eliminating

Japanese air power would eventually solve this problem, but until that happened Kenney was not hesitant to junk the prevailing doctrine. The particular circumstances, he bluntly told Arnold, "have made it necessary to improvise and adapt our procedures to meet existing conditions."[67]

The first change Kenney made was to move to night bombing, which he believed would be more effective than daylight bombing. While he acknowledged the difficulty of finding the targets at night, he felt this drawback was balanced by other factors. "At night," he argued, "you don't have Zeros shooting through the bombardier's window and taking his mind off his work; a moving vessel does not see the bombs leave the plane . . . nor have time to dodge."[68]

Kenney's earlier work on attack aviation led him to look closely at low-altitude attacks against the ships as the best solution. "Low altitude will give more surprise, less trouble from fighters, and more bomb hits,"[69] he argued. Kenney championed a low-altitude technique termed "skip bombing," a tactic so-named because pilots flew at low altitudes and released their bombs 200 to 350 feet from the target. Ideally, each bomb would skip along the water like a rock until it hit the side of the vessel. The bombs would either explode on impact or sink and explode just under the bottom of the ship.[70] Although Kenney claimed credit for instituting this tactic, in fact low-altitude bombing against ships had been done by the British and the Germans. In addition, the Australian Air Force had already experimented with the technique in February 1942, months before Kenney's arrival. After hearing about the British efforts, General Arnold initiated testing in the United States of low-altitude bombing against ships; by July 1942, the Army Air Forces had officially published procedures for using this tactic.[71]

Regardless of the precise origins of the tactic, Kenney became an enthusiastic supporter of low-altitude attacks and they became a mainstay in the Southwest Pacific. Although the method was first tested by A-20 aircraft, it was the B-17 units that perfected the skip bombing technique. The big B-17s, however, proved too unmaneuverable, and hence vulnerable, unless the missions were flown at night or under "circumstances that warrant a high casualty rate."[72] The workhorse for low-altitude bombing in the Southwest Pacific became the Mitchell B-25 medium bombers. Aircrews flying the B-25 modified their attacks to hit the ships directly, rather than trying to skip bombs in front of the target. To distinguish these alternative low-altitude attacks from skip bombing, units termed the new tactic "masthead-height" bombing.[73]

What makes Kenney's shift to low-altitude attacks so noteworthy is that it represents both a dramatic change from established methods and a flexibility often missing in other air commanders. Insufficient numbers of aircraft and poor weather conditions plagued the adjacent South Pacific theater as well, but Army air commanders there did not demonstrate the same ability to break with prewar thinking. The ranking Army air officer, Lieutenant General Millard F. Harmon, blamed his problems in hitting enemy shipping on a lack of training for the aircrews, the extreme range at which he was forced to engage the naval forces, and trouble with the bombs. While all these problems existed and were found in some measure in Kenney's command as well, Harmon opted not to change tactics. He felt that "better results may be expected with more experience, operating in greater mass, and with [an] improved fuse [for the bombs]." Harmon also hoped to gain greater control over the decisions for using the aircraft.[74] Several months later, air commanders in the South Pacific were still counting on using a minimum of nine aircraft to attack shipping.[75]

The attitude of airmen in the South Pacific was not unique, but represents more the norm than Kenney's actions. During an assessment of bombing accuracy among the leaders of the Army Air Forces, General Arnold voiced his concern about poor bombing results and the inability of air commanders to adapt. Reports of aircraft bombing from high altitude "regardless of the target, opposition, weather, or other conditions" concerned Arnold. In a letter to all air commanders in late October, he begged for more flexibility, imploring them to "approach their problems with open minds and use methods which have the best chances of success."[76] He worried about a tendency to adopt a "certain rigidity of mind" that prevented airmen from employing their aircraft in the most effective manner.[77] At the same time Arnold also initiated measures to improve the methods for analyzing bombing errors and attempted to correct the problems in bombing accuracy through better training.[78]

For his part, Kenney needed no urging to adapt to new circumstances. He had started skip bombing trials shortly after taking command, and he took other measures that mark him as a creative and flexible commander. To afford some protection for the bombers while they were in the heavily defended target areas, Kenney began using escort fighters. Given the long distances in the Southwest Pacific and the short range of the American fighter aircraft, however, this option was not widely available in any theater in 1942. "Our . . . short-sightedness, mine included, didn't put the range in our fighters to do the job out here," Kenney admitted. "As soon as the P-38s get here with their extra range we'll add more [range] with droppable wing tanks."[79] His concern about escorting the bombers was driven partly out of concern for the men flying the mission, but also out of a hard-hearted assessment of the resources he had available. Based on the number of aircraft being delivered to the Southwest Pacific as replacements, Kenney figured that he could afford to lose only 2 percent of the aircraft sent out on a mission.[80] Hence, the struggle to increase the range of his fighter aircraft became a constant concern in Kenney's efforts throughout the war.

In addition to eliminating the Japanese air forces and sinking the ships supplying the landing at Buna, Allied aircraft were also used to hit targets along the Kokoda Trail. His teaching on attack aviation convinced Kenney that attacking the forward line of enemy troops should be left to the ground forces, while air attacks concentrated on reinforcements and supplies. After returning from a visit to Port Moresby during the Japanese advance, he met with MacArthur and discussed the problems in finding and bombing the enemy. Kenney insisted that the best contribution his air forces could make was "to sink ships and shoot down planes." MacArthur agreed and told Kenney to "keep right on doing what [he] was doing."[81] Kenney's airmen continued to harass Japanese construction efforts on an airfield near Buna while flying numerous sorties against the overland supply route, but found that hitting targets in the jungle proved difficult. Valuable assistance in finding and hitting supply targets came from Australian coastwatchers inserted into the Japanese territory in New Guinea to provide warnings of impending air attacks. The AIB inserted four teams of coastwatchers, mainly Australian Army officers, who found hidden supply dumps and the barges that the Japanese were using to move supplies and men. Their detailed knowledge of the area allowed them to give very precise instructions as to the location of the targets and resulted in the destruction of many of the supplies the Japanese were able to get ashore.[82]

The loss of supplies did little initially to slow the Japanese forces from pushing the Australian forces back along the Kokoda Trail, however; and by September 7, 1942, the Japanese were approaching Port Moresby.[83] Australian troops rushed into Port Moresby to defend against this main assault as MacArthur and his staff wrestled with options for defeating the Japanese.[84]

As Allied commanders grappled with the thrust over the Owen Stanley mountains, the Japanese staged another landing, this one on the southeastern tip of New Guinea at Milne Bay, threatening to outflank the Allied base at Port Moresby and extend their control over the entire area. Allied commanders, however, had also realized the benefits of Milne Bay and had positioned two Australian infantry brigades and two squadrons of RAAF P-40s to defend the engineers working on the airfields and dock.[85] Fortunately, Kenney had plenty of warning about the possibility of another Japanese move to New Guinea and wisely increased reconnaissance of the shipping routes to Milne Bay.[86] One Japanese convoy left Rabaul for Milne Bay on August 24; despite what Kenney termed a "heavy use of air," the Japanese forces, aided by bad weather, were able to land on the north side of the bay on the night of August 25.[87] Their plan was to move along the northern shore and advance westward to the coastal plain, where they would capture the airfield. The bad weather encountered during the attack on the convoy continued to plague air efforts; and throughout much of the fighting it was very rainy, with cloud heights around 2,000 feet and visibility of about half a mile.[88] Kenney, alerted by various intelligence sources, realized the seriousness of the situation and on August 26 charged Whitehead with putting every effort into stopping the Japanese.[89] Fortunately for the Allies, the weather abated somewhat the next day, allowing aircraft to attack the supplies on shore, the unloading transports in the bay, and the Japanese soldiers advancing to the airfield. Air strikes destroyed most of the food stockpiles and forced the Japanese to move only at night. Without supplies or reinforcements the Japanese troops ran out of momentum, and they were turned back near the airfield by the heroic efforts of the Australian defenders. The remaining Japanese evacuated on September 4; the threat to Port Moresby from the east had ended.[90]

While airmen helped stop the Japanese threat in the immediate vicinity of Milne Bay, they played a much bigger role far from the actual fighting. At the start of the Milne Bay attack, the Japanese dispatched seven barges carrying 350 troops critically needed to reinforce their landing. Coastwatchers tracked the barges on August 24 and the next day reported them stopped on nearby Goodenough Island. Nine P-40s swooped in and attacked the barges, sinking them all. Stranded on the island, the troops did not get to the fighting when they were needed, and later attempts to rescue them drained precious Japanese resources. Once again, timely intelligence had focused the use of air power at exactly the right spot at the right time. "In one air attack, an important part of the Japanese plan was dismantled," one historian argues.[91]

There was little doubt that Kenney's airmen had a critical impact in the fighting at Milne Bay. Although they failed to prevent the initial landing, they were able to effectively cut off the Japanese forces from any further reinforcements. The air efforts were aided by several factors. The location of Milne Bay in relation to Port Moresby allowed Allied aircraft to fly numerous missions without having to contend with the poor weather encountered over the Owen Stanley mountains. Airmen were also assisted by Australian army officers on the ground, who directed aircraft against enemy supply points. In addition, the Japanese could offer little resistance in the air. Their air bases in New Guinea were too far away, and most of the aircraft at Rabaul were supporting the attack on Guadalcanal.[92] An especially important factor in the Allied success was Kenney's ability to concentrate his forces at the most critical moment. Despite constant demands for aircraft, the Japanese advance on Milne Bay represented the most threatening move on Port Moresby. Recognizing the importance of the battle and having control of all the air assets allowed Kenney to throw everything he had into the contest.

With the Japanese advance at Milne Bay stymied, Kenney now turned his attention to defeating the Japanese advance on Port Moresby. MacArthur's options for outflanking and stopping the Japanese were limited. Although the Americans had little knowledge of New Guinea, it appeared that the jungle terrain would make an overland march nearly impossible, a fact confirmed after engineers surveyed the area in early September.[93] An attack from the sea against the Japanese positions near Buna was an attractive option, but several factors mitigated against such an assault: most important, Japanese control of the air and the sea on the northern coast of New Guinea, but also a lack of suitable landing craft and little information on the reefs in the area.[94] With few options at hand, MacArthur, with a little prompting, turned to air power to move his forces.

Air transports had already been used successfully in moving troops for a number of operations. In March the Air Transport Command airlifted a United States Army Coast Artillery battalion from Brisbane to Darwin, a distance of 1800 miles.[95] In late May a detachment of three hundred Australian soldiers, known as the Kanga force, was flown into the Buolo valley near the town of Wau in New Guinea to stem a Japanese advance into the interior. This force remained at Wau for several months and depended on aircraft for most of their supplies.[96]

With these successes in mind, Kenney conferred with Whitehead about the possibility of flying troops into Port Moresby. In addition to wanting to reinforce the Australians fighting on the Kokoda Trail, Kenney was worried that the Japanese would soon be threatening his airfields. MacArthur approved the plan to airlift the ground soldiers, but faced serious misgivings from his staff. Nevertheless, on September 15, elements of the 126th Infantry were flown into Port Moresby. Kenney's success in this first movement, plus his continuing worries about the airfields, prompted his offer to fly in another regiment, an operation that put him into a bind when he belatedly discovered that he did not have enough aircraft available. In the end, he succeeded only by borrowing transports from the Australian airlines and using some of his precious bombers as transports.[97]

To be sure, Kenney's use of aircraft in this manner was not new. It did, however, represent another example of his flexibility with regard to air warfare. The potential for using aircraft to carry ground troops had been clearly demonstrated even prior to America's entry into World War II. Kenney knew that German transports had been used to bring soldiers from Africa to Spain during the Spanish Civil War. Furthermore, he was convinced that the air movement of troops and supplies was "definitely a part of modern warfare."[98] By contrast, other air officers had very undeveloped ideas about air transportation and neglected this aspect of air power.[99] Of particular note: the production forecast for the number of aircraft required to defeat the Axis powers, while generally accurate, grossly underestimated the number of air transports that would be required. Planners predicated 2,560 air transports would be needed—only about a quarter of the total eventually reached by the Army Air Forces in World War II.[100]

Kenney's demonstration in airlifting ground forces opened another possibility for putting Allied forces on the northern coast of New Guinea. With Australians maintaining pressure on the main Japanese force on the Kokoda Trail, American troops could turn their flank through the air.[101] In mid-September Whitehead flew some reconnaissance missions and recommended moving a division by air to forward landing strips behind the Japanese advance.[102] Kenney also knew that the Australians had cleared an airstrip at a spot called Wanigela Mission in July in preparation for MacArthur's original plan to secure New Guinea, and a second airstrip was found nearby after a missionary told officials about a grass landing area at Fasari.[103] Although Wanigela offered a good forward location from which to attack the Japanese landing site at Buna, Kenney had difficulty convincing members of MacArthur's staff who worried about supply problems. They thought the plan was "reckless and irresponsible."[104]

Not all of the officers in the command were as stubborn as the headquarters staff. General Blamey, Allied Land Forces commander, and General Harding, commander of the 32nd Division, both appreciated the possibilities of using airlifted troops to defeat the Japanese force at Buna.[105] While many other officers might have supported the plan, Kenney's advocacy proved the most important in swaying MacArthur. With most of the staff against him, Kenney took the risk to convince MacArthur about the benefits of the airlift. If it failed MacArthur would look bad, but probably survive. It was Kenney who would take the blame. After several meetings, and no doubt many informal discussions, Kenney convinced MacArthur of the viability of the airlift option, and MacArthur approved the plan on September 24, 1942.[106] In early October the outflanking movement began when an infantry battalion was flown into Wanigela Mission, followed a week later by an infantry regiment.[107] Kenney oversaw the operation from Australia, again borrowing civil aircraft from the Australian airlines, while Whitehead managed the New Guinea end. Kenney took a risk, but took no chances with Japanese interference, telling Whitehead to provide fighter escort for the transports and bombing the nearby Japanese airfields to prevent them from taking off to attack the transports.[108] In the end, there was no Japanese resistance, and this initial portion of the airlift went smoothly.

Kenney's air movement of American forces to Wanigela came as the Japanese had already received orders to abandon their march on Port Moresby. The decision to forego the attack on Port Moresby grew out of an assessment by the Japanese Imperial General Headquarters in Tokyo of the overall course of the war in the South Pacific. The two-pronged attack on New Guinea and Guadalcanal to cut the sea lanes between the United States and Australia had seriously dissipated Japanese strength. The failure of the attack at Milne Bay and the airlift of Allied troops into New Guinea threatened the advance on Port Moresby. In addition, air attacks on supply lines had left the Japanese forces desperately short of rations and, according to their reports, "seriously diminished front-line combat strength."[109] With the battle on Guadalcanal also going badly, the Imperial Headquarters elected to concentrate on one spot and shifted reinforcements scheduled for New Guinea to Guadalcanal.[110] The Japanese retreated from Port Moresby to the northern coast of New Guinea around the villages of Buna and Gona, an area of swamps, jungles, torrential rain, and oppressive heat—hellish conditions for fighting. As one participant put it, "I don't think anyone ever picked a worse place to fight than the coast of Papua."[111] For the Japanese it was an ideal defensive location, setting the stage for several more months of brutal, bloody fighting.

The airlift of American forces and the Japanese retreat to the northern coast of New Guinea in October 1942 marked the beginning of siege warfare. American and Australian forces inched their way through rancid swamps and steaming jungles towards the Japanese positions at Buna and Gona. They faced an enemy hidden behind extensive defensive strongpoints and bunkers, from which they mowed down the advancing Allied troops. Although MacArthur was anxious to eliminate the Japanese presence, fighting in the area lasted until the end of January 1943.[112] During this phase of the fighting Kenney's missions remained much the same. His forces continued to bomb the Japanese airfields; these efforts, coupled with the fighting at Guadalcanal, gradually reduced the Japanese air activity.[113] The growing Allied supremacy in the skies and the feverish construction activity on the ground to build more airfields around Port Moresby allowed Kenney to bring seven fighter and two bomber squadrons forward by the beginning of November 1942.[114]

While Kenney's operations had a clear impact on the Japanese, it was also evident that he had gained MacArthur's confidence. In early September,

MacArthur wrote, "It has been little more than a month since you assumed command of the air component of this area. The improvement in its performance has been marked and is directly attributable to your splendid and effective leadership."[115] MacArthur was equally laudatory in a message he sent soon after to Army Chief of Staff General George C. Marshall: "General Kenney with splendid efficiency has vitalized the air force and with the energetic support of his two fine Field Commanders, Whitehead and Walker, is making remarkable progress."[116] "From unsatisfactory," he continued, "the air force has already progressed to very good and will soon be excellent. In comparatively few weeks I confidently expect it to be superior."[117] Not surprisingly, at the end of September MacArthur recommended that Kenney be promoted to lieutenant general, stating, "General Kenney has demonstrated superior qualities of leadership and professional ability."[118]

Kenney's impact was also noted by outside observers to the region. In late September, General Arnold arrived in Australia to observe conditions in the Pacific and explain Allied plans for the war. Arnold told Kenney that he could expect replacement aircraft and aircrews, but that no additional planes would be allocated to the Southwest Pacific. MacArthur debated Arnold about the need for more aircraft, but he also sang Kenney's praises.[119] Arnold needed little convincing of Kenney's value. "He is a real leader," Arnold wrote, "and has the finest bunch of pilots I have seen."[120] A member of the War Department staff who accompanied Arnold on the trip told Marshall that the "air team of Kenney, Whitehead, and Walker is obtaining results that boosted the morale of all except the Japanese. Coordination between GHQ and Air Forces leaves nothing to be desired."[121]

Airfields and Engineers

Although establishing a good relationship with MacArthur was of some satisfaction, an ongoing concern for Kenney was the need to rapidly build airfields in austere forward locations, a matter neither Kenney nor many of his fellow Army aviators had paid much attention to before the war. In World War I and throughout the 1920s and 1930s, airfields had been simply that—fields. All that a pilot needed to land and take off safely was a relatively flat surface with few obstructions to fly over. Parade fields and cow pastures became favorite landing spots for the early aviators.[122] The advent of faster, heavier, and more sophisticated aircraft meant a concomitant need for longer runways, stronger materials, and all-weather facilities—attributes engineers found in a natural setting "only under special conditions."[123] The potential problems posed by the new aircraft were highlighted on May 6, 1941, when the first XB-19, an experimental heavy bomber built by Douglas Aircraft, taxied out of its hangar in Santa Monica, California, and promptly sank into the pavement. The plane could not take off until the end of June, when a concrete runway was ready.[124] Clearly, engineers needed to do more research on the stress and strain these new aircraft would place on landing surfaces.

While there were numerous problems in building runways in the United States suited to the new aircraft, military engineers also struggled with the challenge of designing airfields that could be used on a temporary basis in wartime. Since the national military policy of the United States was almost purely defensive in the years after World War I, there was no need to develop expertise in rapidly building airfields in some distant area. As part of the response to events in Europe and the general buildup of the American military in the late 1930s, the Army Corps of Engineers and the Air Corps began studying the problems involved with building airfields in forward areas; they formed the first specialized aviation engineer unit in June 1940.[125] When Pearl Harbor was attacked in December 1941, there had been considerable effort expended in studying the requirements necessary for building air bases. Officers had examined the war in Europe and developed plans for building dispersed parking areas and earthen revetments. Likewise, the organization and equipment needed by the aviation engineers also received some attention. Planners realized that these units would require more and heavier equipment, such as tractors, rollers, and graders, than was found in a general engineering unit, yet at the same time needed to remain mobile. Wartime experiences would bring adjustments in almost every area, but the work prior to the war provided a valuable starting point for building airfields.[126]

Aviation engineers had played an important, indeed critical, role since the beginning of the war in the Pacific. Unlike the situation in Europe, where there was at least some existing infrastructure to support air operations, in the Southwest Pacific everything had to be built from scratch. MacArthur rightly saw the conflict as an "engineers' war."[127] Without the construction feats performed by the engineers, it would literally have been impossible to fight the war.

Concern over construction of the airfields was a continuing problem for the air commanders. Although Kenney and Whitehead were responsible for air operations and depended on the airfields, they exercised no control over the engineers in the theater. The responsibility for constructing the airfields fell to MacArthur's engineering officer, Major General Hugh "Pat" Casey, a member of MacArthur's staff in the Philippines.[128] Kenney made repeated efforts to gain control over the aviation engineers and often decried their being assigned to what were, in his opinion, nonessential projects. Casey was just as adamant about keeping control over the engineers, arguing that there were too few of them in the Southwest Pacific to risk parceling them out. It was better, he believed, to pool the equipment, manpower, and expertise of the engineers on whatever was the highest priority project, as defined by MacArthur, rather than waste their efforts in areas that were not absolutely essential to wartime operations. Casey was especially wary of letting Kenney get his hands on the aviation engineers and was convinced that once the aviation engineers had completed their work on the airfields, Kenney would use them for "building Air Force clubs" and permanent living facilities when they could have been employed on more worthwhile projects. The chief engineer also believed that Kenney's focus on airfield construction would slight the need for ports, pipelines, and roads, all essential to bringing supplies to the airfields.[129]

On the Offensive

Although the airfield construction program in New Guinea had made some progress during the fall of 1942, Kenney was still dissatisfied with the condition and number of the runways. In October he complained to MacArthur that he might have to send two fighter squadrons back to Australia because heavy rains had made their runways unusable.[130] Kenney needed more airstrips badly because, despite some Allied success, Japanese aircraft still hindered Allied operations. Japanese aircraft bombed ships bringing supplies to Allied ground forces, scoring their biggest success on November 16, 1942, when they sank four of the five supply ships assigned to the 32nd Division, delaying a planned advance by several weeks.[131] In December, the Japanese bombed American forward positions, including a field hospital and the airfield at Dobodura. In addition, the Japanese were able to air-drop supplies to their ground forces.[132] The battle over control of the air was far from over.

While Allied air attacks succeeded in stopping some Japanese resupply ships, other air missions were less successful. Over four days in mid-November, the Japanese used several destroyers to shuttle 2,300 troops from Rabaul to Buna. Although they were bombed by Allied aircraft, none of the strikes hit home; but the tide was beginning to turn.[133] Four destroyers left Rabaul on November 28, carrying a brigade of 720 soldiers to reinforce the Japanese positions near Buna. Bombers pounced on the convoy the day after it left port, damaging two destroyers and forcing the convoy back to Rabaul. After making repairs, the destroyers left Rabaul again on November 30, and arrived near Gona on December 1. Pressure from air attacks made it impossible to transfer the troops to shore, and the destroyers were forced to land the brigade 18 miles away from their intended destination. This landing site also came under attack, and only 425 of the soldiers were put ashore. The delays inflicted on the convoy at sea, combined with the inability to land troops, effectively eliminated these reinforcements from the fighting near Gona.[134] The last attempt by the Japanese occurred on December 7, when another convoy of destroyers left Rabaul. This effort was turned back once by air attacks; when the ships finally arrived near New Guinea, they were forced to land the soldiers 40 miles away from the action.[135]

A combination of factors contributed to the success of Allied aircraft after the middle of November, but the most important was the increased number of aircraft dispatched on the convoy missions. Although Kenney had not been able to greatly increase the overall percentage of aircraft available for missions, the total number of missions flown had doubled.[136] By increasing the rate at which the aircraft were used, at the end of November Kenney could send almost twice as many aircraft against convoys near New Guinea as he could two months prior, a factor that greatly increased the likelihood that the ships would be located and sunk.[137]

The Japanese retreat to the beachhead had effectively eliminated their supply lines on land, limiting air support for ground forces to bombing the opposing enemy forces directly; but Kenney was personally opposed to these missions. He felt strongly that aircraft should be used against large targets in the rear areas, where they would affect the overall objective of the campaign, and not be "frittered" away as artillery against dug-in and well-protected frontline soldiers.[138] Kenney realized that using aircraft in this manner might help win a battle, but argued that it could also "result in losing the war"[139] through attrition because missions in close support of the ground forces translated to higher loss rates, yet each plane destroyed less per mission. Despite these misgivings, he ordered attacks on the frontline Japanese forces during the months of siege warfare as the Allies tried to eject the Japanese from their positions near Buna.

The efforts in close air support missions were hampered by a variety of problems. The number of aircraft available was limited by the ongoing need to wrest control of the air from the Japanese.[140] The jungle foliage and terrain also made it difficult to find and hit targets, problems exacerbated by the lack of training in bombing close to friendly forces and established procedures for air-to-ground liaison or communication.[141] In addition, maps of the area were almost nonexistent, making it difficult for both pilots and soldiers to communicate their positions, let alone find and hit the enemy.[142] Some attempts were made to improve the results, such as establishing exact times for attacks, providing better methods for signaling the location of friendly ground forces, and, eventually, exchanging liaison officers between ground and air headquarters. Nevertheless, pilots still bombed at the wrong time, missed the target, or, worse, hit American soldiers.[143] General Robert Eichelberger, who took over command of the American ground forces in New Guinea in early December, understandably found "such lamentable incidents . . . dispiriting" to his troops.[144] Undeniably, Kenney's attitude also affected the priority and importance attached to this type of mission. He simply did not believe close air support was the most effective use of his aircraft. He likely felt compelled to use them in this role since the aircraft were available and American ground troops were fighting. One can only guess at the success that the missions in direct support of the ground forces might have achieved had Kenney chosen to be as innovative and flexible on this front as he was in other areas, such as airlifting supplies.

Flying men and materiel into airfields developed near the front lines at Buna and Dobodura soon became routine, and Kenney even accepted the challenge of flying in heavy equipment like 105mm howitzers, along with the associated equipment, to the forward positions.[145] The biggest handicap to aerial resupply operations remained the weather in New Guinea. Low clouds not only prevented aircraft from landing at the forward airfields, but also made dropping supplies from the air difficult since pilots needed to see the ground to determine the location of the drop area. Kenney sanctioned experiments with a system that used a radio signal to provide the location of the drop area; but by the end of November bad weather and an inadequate distribution system had reduced supplies at the front lines to a minimum. Fortunately, the weather broke and the supplies could be flown in.[146] Kenney, however, was determined to prevent the reoccurrence of such an episode and prevailed upon the Australians for air transports once again to build up supplies in the forward areas.[147]

Although the amount of cargo transported from Australia to New Guinea by sea throughout the fighting greatly exceeded the supplies flown in (2,450 tons by air versus 8,560 tons by ship), during the most critical period of fighting airlift was the most important source.[148] As General Eichelberger remarked, "Both Australian and American ground forces would have perished without 'George Kenney's Air.'"[149] By the beginning of December air transports were delivering two million pounds a week to locations all over New Guinea. The single most successful day for aerial resupply came on December 14, 1942, when seventy-four flights moved 178 tons of supplies from Port Moresby to Popondetta, near Buna.[150] The transports also evacuated the sick and wounded from the battlefields, moving over 100 soldiers a day during the heaviest fighting in December and early January. In the American 32nd Division, 2,530 sick and 991 wounded soldiers were able to leave the combat area in aircraft.[151] How many of these men were saved because they could be airlifted out rather than moved by other means is unclear, but at the very least it must have provided a morale boost to the soldiers fighting on the ground.

The fierce fighting on the ground in Papua New Guinea continued until the end of January 1943, when the last Japanese positions were overrun. The efforts of "Kenney's Air" against Japanese air forces and shipping might have been largely invisible to the infantryman and his company commander lying in the mud or slogging through the swamps trying to reduce these last Japanese strong points, but they were undeniably important in the overall scope of the fighting. In slowly gaining control over the skies of New Guinea and eroding the ability of the Japanese to resupply their combat forces, Kenney's flyers reduced the Japanese resistance. Driving away the Japanese air threat meant that more Allied aircraft could be devoted to ground support and ships could bring supplies forward, and conversely Japanese shipping could be stopped.

The effects of Kenney's efforts were readily apparent to the Japanese soldiers. By the end of December their normal daily ration of rice was cut from 28 to 10 ounces, and a few weeks later there was no rice left. Positions captured by American forces showed the undeniable impact of cutting off Japanese supplies—many of the Japanese soldiers were starving, and some had resorted to cannibalism. Allied air efforts had also kept the Japanese forces desperately short of weapons and medical supplies.[152] There is no doubt that it took hard, bloody fighting on the ground to clear the area of Japanese forces, but those same enemy forces adequately supplied and fed would have been a much more formidable foe and probably would have exacted a greater cost in American and Australian lives. Major Koiwai Mitsuo, a battalion commander in the Papuan campaign, summed it up best: "We lost at Buna because we could not retain air superiority, because we could not supply our troops, and because our navy and air force could not disrupt the enemy supply line."[153]

This disparaging view of Japanese air power was echoed by Kenney. Prior to the war he had read reports on the Japanese use of air power in China, concluding that "the Japanese have a lot of fairly good airplanes and considerable aeronautical equipment" but "they do not seem to have a clear conception of the proper role of the Air Force."[154] What he observed in the Papua campaign did little to change those views. He told Arnold that the Japanese army and navy "can hold their own in any league but he simply cannot train airmen to compare with ours in a hurry. His original highly trained crews were superb but they are dead."[155] Newly trained Japanese pilots could not fly at night or in bad weather, and, despite their previous successes against

American flyers, Kenney asserted that the Japanese victories were the result of courage, not skill—a statement more reflective of his prejudice, mirroring the racialist attitudes of the time, than of the reality of the situation.[156]

Although the experience and training levels of the Japanese pilots had started to diminish in 1942, for the most part they were still highly skilled pilots, and the number of flying hours they received in training was on par with their American counterparts. In addition, at the beginning of the war Japanese pilots possessed superior equipment and better tactics, which they used to great advantage. While most of this elite initial group was later lost, in late 1942 Kenney was underestimating his competition.[157]

Kenney had special contempt for the Japanese commanders and the way they used their aircraft, concluding they "did not know how to use . . . air decisively."[158] Kenney believed that the Japanese had squandered their opportunity to eliminate his aircraft from New Guinea. Instead of sending over repeated, large attacks that could wipe out Kenney's air fleet, the Japanese struck intermittently, in small groups, and never focused on a single target long enough to have any lasting impact.[159]

Although Kenney disparaged the Japanese air commanders, he had developed a grudging respect for their fighting ability in other areas. When he first arrived in Australia, Kenney had a low opinion of the Japanese soldiers; but after several months of fighting he had revised his view. He now believed that they were "the toughest fighters in the world" and that Americans, himself included, had underrated their fighting ability.[160] Expressing the attitude of many Americans at that time, he argued that their fighting ability rested on racial characteristics. The Japanese solder was "undoubtedly a low order of humanity," Kenney argued, "but he has the sense to use the weapons of war and do a good job at it." Japanese men joined the army, he asserted, to indulge their "liking for looting, arson, massacre, and rape." Kenney also used his observations to boost his own service and the importance of air power. The fanaticism and strength of the Japanese ground forces, in combination with the weaknesses he observed from their air force, led Kenney to conclude, "The Japanese weakness and our real hope for victory is in the air."[161]

Lessons Learned

Kenney felt that the Papuan campaign represented a model for future warfare in the Southwest Pacific: "The whole show has been a demonstration of how the war will be fought in this theater."[162] Although maps showed a large amount of territory under the Japanese flag, their hold rested on islands that were "nothing more or less than aerodromes . . . from which modern fire-power is launched."[163] While some of these locations were true islands, the jungle terrain and inaccessible interior of the large land masses in the Pacific, such as New Guinea, concentrated military forces into relatively small areas, making "all warfare . . . island warfare."[164] Kenney intended to fight future campaigns according to the following formula:

> (1) Get [air] control over the battle area. (2) Put an air blockade around the enemy forces in that area so that they get no more supplies or reinforcements. (3) Hammer the enemy positions, supply installations, and troops with constant air attack. (4) Cover and assist our own troops in destroying the enemy forces. Our own ground assault preferably should be from the rear or undefended flank. Frontal assaults only in case the air hammering has practically destroyed the enemy. (5) Occupy the territory, build airdromes on it and advance the bomber line some more.[165]

This formula would hold true during the coming months as MacArthur's forces advanced up the northern coast of New Guinea.

The success of Kenney's air units and his personality made MacArthur realize that he had undergone a "conversion" of sorts. In early December 1942, he told Eddie Rickenbacker, a World War I ace and then president of Eastern Air Lines, "I probably did the American Air Forces more harm than any man living when I was chief of staff by refusing to believe in the future of the airplane as a weapon of war. I am now doing everything I can to make amends for that great mistake."[166]

KENNEY COULD take great pride in his accomplishments. He had revitalized the air organization and infused it with capable, energetic officers. The fighting in Papua had confirmed many of his ideas about warfare. The next months would demonstrate the degree to which air power could contribute to MacArthur's advance.

SIX

MOVING WESTWARD

January 1943 to June 1943

"I am having an interesting time inventing new ways
to win a war on a shoe string."

The end of the fighting in Papua New Guinea marked the beginning of a new
stage in the war. The defeat of the Japanese at Buna and Guadalcanal shifted
the initiative for operations—the Allies would now dictate the pace and scope
of the war. The introduction of amphibious equipment and expertise during
the coming year meant an increase in the integration of air, land, and sea
forces. Still, the operational template that Kenney forecast at the end of 1942
held true: gain air control of the battle area, isolate the enemy ground forces,
and assist friendly ground forces during their assault against enemy positions. The aim of all these operations was the same—gain airfields from
which Kenney's airmen could move forward and begin the next round.

Strategic Context

Operations in the Southwest Pacific during 1943 were defined by the strategic guidance outlined during the Casablanca conference in January between
President Roosevelt and Prime Minister Churchill. Although most of that
meeting focused on the next moves in Europe, American military leaders
argued that forces in the Pacific could not simply stay on the defensive. They
proposed limited offensive operations to keep pressure on the Japanese,
including a continuation of the advances toward Rabaul already underway.
The British reluctantly agreed, although the two powers reached no consensus on the number of forces that should be sent to the Pacific.[1]

Rabaul, located on the northern end of the island of New Britain, continued to menace Allied military operations. The bay was a valuable natural
anchorage; just one of the many harbors inside the bay could hold at least
300,000 tons of shipping, making it an excellent naval base. Five Japanese

airfields surrounded the harbor, and the aircraft and 367 antiaircraft guns there provided a stout defense against air attacks.[2] The Japanese had already demonstrated the value of Rabaul in their attacks on Buna and Guadalcanal. Although temporarily in check, Japanese air, sea, and ground forces staging from Rabaul could easily threaten the sea lines between the United States and Australia. Defeating Japan, and recapturing the Philippines, would be possible only if Rabaul was eliminated as a Japanese stronghold.[3] Before reaching Rabaul, however, MacArthur's forces would have to secure positions further west in New Guinea.

Japanese commanders at Rabaul well understood the strategic value of their position—that was why they had captured it in the first place. After their setbacks in Papua and Guadalcanal, they made plans to reinforce their positions in New Guinea to thwart the Allied advance and protect the Rabaul stronghold.[4] The 18th Army under Lieutenant General Adachi Hatazo was assigned the task of defending Lae and Salamaua on the north coast of New Guinea and eliminating the Australian force operating near Wau. Stopping the buildup of the Japanese forces in New Guinea meant sinking the Japanese ships bringing troops and supplies from Rabaul. Kenney was convinced that he could do so and told MacArthur that his newest innovation was ready to stop the enemy's next move.[5]

Innovation

The relatively low priority assigned to the Southwest Pacific meant that Kenney and his commanders had to extract the most out of every aircraft on every mission. While excellent intelligence was helpful in this regard, another way Kenney magnified his combat power was by encouraging innovative combat methods and repairs. Salvaging every possible item from a wrecked aircraft, even if it was downed in Japanese territory, soon became routine.[6] Mechanics also learned to use anything on hand for repairs, successfully installing Australian sixpence coins in engine magnetos and substituting Kotex for air filters.[7] These efforts slowly paid dividends. Although the percentage of mission-capable aircraft and total number of aircraft in the theater grew very gradually, the number of missions flown jumped dramatically, from about 1,000 in September to over 4,000 in December 1942.[8]

Kenney also changed tactics and methods to adapt to the local conditions. He had shifted from high-altitude to low-altitude attacks on shipping, started using night attacks, and developed long-range fuel tanks to provide fighters the range to escort bombers. Kenney's flexibility was also evidenced by the technical changes made to aircraft in his command. To sink merchant shipping, mechanics modified B-25s into "commerce destroyers" by installing four 50-caliber guns in the nose and adding two 50-caliber guns to the upper turret.[9] Captain Paul "Pappy" Gunn, one of Kenney's most colorful and innovative officers, increased the combat capability of the Douglas A-20s by putting more powerful guns into the aircraft, adding two 450-gallon fuel tanks in the bomb bay, and building a bomb rack that allowed the A-20 to carry Kenney's parafrag bombs.[10] To better destroy the Japanese aircraft protected by earthen revetments, Kenney had local engineers develop a fuse that would explode bombs in the air, showering the area with bomb fragments. Other bombs were wrapped with heavy wire that could cut through the stout protective structures built by the Japanese.[11]

Some of these adaptations refined and updated ideas Kenney had been working with his entire career. For example, he knew from his teaching and research on attack aviation at the Tactical School that forward-firing guns would be extremely destructive at low altitude against a variety of targets. Likewise, his investigation into exploding bombs above the ground allowed him to understand the benefits of such a weapon. His experiences at the Engineering School and later assignments involving aircraft development provided insight into the advantages and disadvantages of various modifications. In short, he was primed to look for certain ideas and willing to make changes, an important combination for innovation to succeed.

Kenney relished the challenge of inventing new methods. "I am having an interesting time inventing new ways to win a war on a shoe string," he told a fellow officer.[12] "If I don't like the way a 'plane comes to me, or if I have a special job to do (and I have lots of them) I will fix the airplane myself and say nothing."[13] To be sure, Kenney did not invent every modification in his command, but as the commander he actively supported any change that promised to inflict more damage on the enemy. "I encourage personnel who have any ideas to go right ahead with them. It makes no difference what the man's rank or his previous experience. If he has an idea that sounds feasible he is told to go ahead and he is given every assistance."[14] Kenney gratefully acknowledged better methods no matter what their source, and on several occasions praised the Australians for their efforts in making changes to aircraft and equipment.[15] Likewise a sergeant in the 5th Air Service Command was singled out for a military decoration for "his remarkable ability to improvise equipment."[16] By his attitude Kenney energized the people who worked for him. As he put it, "Any time I can't think of something screwy enough I have a flock of people out here to help me."[17]

Undoubtedly, Kenney's efforts at instilling innovation were aided by the circumstances of the situation. The lack of spare parts in the Southwest Pacific and the unceasing demand for combat aircraft put a premium on innovation and flexibility, and, to be sure, Kenney's command was not the only one that saw enterprising individuals adapting to local conditions. But Kenney set a standard for accepting innovation that was unique.[18] Without his support, even in the broadest sense, many of these ideas would never have seen the light of day. In sum, Kenney established the organizational environment that allowed innovation to prosper.[19]

An example of the way innovation proceeded in Kenney's command can be seen in the development of the new nose gun turret for the B-24. The first production models of the B-24 proved extremely vulnerable to head-on attacks because they lacked an effective set of forward-firing guns. A member of Kenney's command, Colonel Arthur H. Rogers, hit on the idea of grafting the powered tail turret of the B-24 onto the nose section. Rogers first came up with the solution when he was going through B-24 training in July 1942, but the press of operations left him little time to work out all the details of his solution. In January 1943 he was able to flesh out his ideas and presented them to Brigadier General Carl Connell, commander of 5th Air Service Command. Connell, who had known Rogers previously, was eager to help and brought Rogers to see Kenney. Not surprisingly, Kenney enthusiastically endorsed the change. One aircraft was modified, christened "Connell's Special," and flown by the 90th Bomb Group on a trial basis. The new nose turret proved very effective, and the Air Service Command began converting most of the B-24s in the Southwest Pacific.[20] Kenney's role in this innovation, as it was in many others, was to encourage the process and support the efforts of the people who came up with new ideas. Eventually, B-24s were manufactured with a powered turret for a nose gun, making the field modifications unnecessary. These new aircraft, however, did not arrive in the Southwest Pacific until the summer of 1944, almost a year and a half after Roger's suggestion.[21]

Of course, not every innovation was a success, and some proved to be more problematic than others. The RAAF blamed the loss of three bombers on some of Kenney's parafrag bombs that exploded just after leaving the aircraft.[22] Since modifications usually meant removing the aircraft from flying status, Whitehead often complained that the changes had not been adequately studied beforehand or were taking too long. At one point he told Kenney, "I am convinced that there is too much experimental work being done and not enough thought given to production," later reminding Kenney, "we do not want . . . an installation which causes us a lot of grief later on."[23]

Even Kenney admitted that problems cropped up with new ideas; for example, a larger ammunition box proposed by one sergeant that increased the firing burst for a machine gun burned out the gun barrel at the same time. Kenney could have easily sided with Whitehead but knew that with his deputy focused so closely on daily operations that someone needed to protect and encourage the innovation process, despite the complaints. Kenney accepted the failures philosophically: "We have given ourselves lots of headaches, but we have also gotten some fine results."[24] Kenney's emphasis on innovation—tactical, technical, and organizational—produced just such "fine results" in March 1943, when his specially configured B-25s took part in an air-sea engagement known as the Battle of the Bismarck Sea.

Battle of the Bismarck Sea

The attack on the convoy steaming out of Rabaul in March 1943 was part of Kenney's continuing effort to stop Japanese reinforcements, but the success of the battle started far from the scene of the action. Prevailing in the air-sea engagements began with accurate and timely intelligence about the Japanese ship movements. Kenney's intelligence organization, which included a large number of Australian officers, spent a great deal of time carefully plotting the pattern of Japanese shipping and cataloging signs of an impending convoy. Generally these signals included sightings of additional Japanese aircraft on airfields near the convoy's expected route and an increase in the number of air raids on Allied airfields to stop any air interference. Japanese floatplanes would also be moved forward to hunt for Allied submarines, while the Japanese simultaneously increased their own submarine activity.[25] Although those were helpful indications in alerting commanders about a convoy, the final piece of the puzzle was pinpointing when the convoy would sail and what its destination was. For that information Kenney relied on analysis of the ULTRA information by MacArthur's Central Bureau. Reconnaissance flights remained important, but they served primarily to provide up-to-date information and offer a plausible explanation for how the convoy was spotted, rather than to find the ships on their own. Without this intelligence, searching for convoys would have required many more patrols and translated into fewer aircraft for other missions. The ability to read Japanese messages allowed Kenney to concentrate his forces at the appropriate place and optimum time to have the greatest impact. In modern terms, this intelligence was a "force multiplier."[26]

A convoy in early January 1943 highlighted both the use of signals intelligence and some of the shortcomings Kenney still faced. On New Year's Day aerial photographs revealed a massive amount of shipping in Rabaul Harbor. Two days later codebreakers intercepted a message indicating a convoy would depart sometime around January 6.[27] Kenney hoped he could stop part of the convoy before it left the harbor and ordered Kenneth Walker, the head of 5th Bomber Command, to make a dawn attack on January 5. Walker, a firm believer in the efficacy of strategic bombing and the self-defense capabilities of bombers, disagreed with Kenney's approach. Walker realized that a dawn attack meant that the bombers could not fly in formation and would have to bomb as single aircraft. Walker argued for an attack at noon, which would allow the aircraft to strike in formation, providing an opportunity to confirm Walker's beliefs in the defensive abilities of the B-17. Kenney, who feared the threat of Japanese air attacks and knew that he had no long-range fighters to accompany the bombers, was not persuaded and overruled Walker. The bombers would strike at dawn.[28]

Despite Kenney's clear ruling, Walker persisted in his plan; and twelve aircraft from his command attacked Rabaul around noon on January 5. Walker paid the price for his change, as he was flying in one of the two aircraft lost in the raid. Flying on the mission violated two of Kenney's orders: one, of course, was the time of the attack; the other was Kenney's standing prohibition against Walker flying in combat. Kenney, who himself had been blasted by MacArthur for flying over enemy territory, had previously admonished Walker for flying on combat missions, urging his bomber chief to apply his skills, talent, and training as an air commander so that "his outfit would take minimum losses," rather than fly on combat missions where he would just be "extra baggage."[29]

No good explanation has ever been offered for Walker's decision to go on the mission. He was acknowledged as a stubborn, driven man who fervently believed in unescorted, daylight bombing. This mission would have been his first real opportunity to test his method, and he probably could not resist the temptation to fly. Walker may have also felt that as a combat leader he had a responsibility to fly in harm's way and set the example for his aviators. Kenney obviously did not agree and felt there were other ways to display leadership. There may have been other factors that motivated Walker—the bad weather forecast for the mission, or even his feelings toward Kenney—but that would be speculation. In truth, no one knows why he made this fateful decision.[30]

Walker's actions infuriated Kenney. He told MacArthur that Walker would receive an official reprimand for disobeying orders on his return. MacArthur replied, "If he doesn't come back I'll put him in for a Medal of Honor."[31] The search for Walker continued for many days and consumed valuable combat sorties, but there was no sign of the missing crew. On January 11, 1943, the news of Walker's loss was released; in MacArthur's recommendation for the Medal of Honor, he cited Walker's "conspicuous leadership above and beyond the call of duty."[32]

Walker's mission succeeded in sinking one merchant ship, but little else. The remainder of the Japanese convoy, carrying the 102nd Infantry Regiment of the 51st Division, left Rabaul harbor on January 5, shortly after Walker's failed attack. The convoy of five transports and five destroyers proceeded towards Lae under heavy air cover provided by Japanese fighters flown into airfields on the western end of New Britain, as well as New Guinea. Problems in planning and communication prevented Kenney's units from mounting mass attacks on the convoy, and the piecemeal attacks allowed the Japanese fighters to mount a stiff defense against the Allied bombers. On January 7 one transport was struck, but 739 men of the 1,100 aboard were rescued.[33] The convoy began unloading troops and supplies near Lae, but heavy air attacks on January 8 crippled another transport and forced the rest of the convoy to depart. Although the ships were loaded with enough food to last 12,000 troops three months and half of the ammunition needed in a division-size engagement, only half of these supplies were transferred to land, forcing the Japanese commanders to cut rations in half immediately.[34] Even this limited success had extracted a heavy price, however. From Walker's attack until the convoy's return to Rabaul, Kenney dispatched fifty-six heavy bombers; ten of them were lost. In addition, of the ninety medium bombers sent out, eleven were destroyed.[35]

Although diminished in strength, the Japanese forces immediately moved inland toward a small detachment of Australian troops operating near the town of Wau. Kenney's air units quickly shifted away from the convoy attacks and focused on stopping this advance, which threatened to consolidate Japanese control of the area. Two thousand Australian soldiers, along with their ammunition, food, and weapons, were airlifted from Port Moresby to Wau in late January. The first Australians landed on January 29, 1943, and began fighting as soon as they left the aircraft. According to one report, "many of the Australian troops were wounded so soon following their landing that they were evacuated on the same planes that transported them to Wau."[36] Over a three-day period, 244 planeloads brought in over a million pounds of cargo. The reinforcements helped stop the advance, and by the end of January the Japanese had retreated to their positions along the coast near Salamaua and Lae.[37]

Although rebuffed in this advance, the Japanese began planning the movement of more reinforcements to Lae soon after the January convoy. General Imamura Hitoshi, the commander of 8th Area Army, and Lieutenant

General Adachi Hatazo, 18th Army commander, decided to bolster the forces in New Guinea by transferring the remainder of the 51st Division. This convoy would include eight transports carrying over 6,000 soldiers, twelve anti-aircraft guns, twenty-one artillery pieces, fuel, and ammunition. Japanese planners were not unaware of the risks they were taking. They expected heavy resistance and made extensive plans to defend the convoy from the sea and the air, sending along eight destroyers as escorts and providing an air umbrella from dawn to dusk. The Japanese also planned to attack the airfields at Port Moresby and Milne Bay in an effort to keep Allied aircraft on the ground. Even so, their staff officers speculated that half of the convoy would be lost before reaching its destination.[38]

A convoy of this magnitude represented a very severe threat to MacArthur's hope of continuing his advance toward the Philippines. With Australian and American ground troops worn out by the fighting near Buna and Gona and only limited naval forces available, the only way to stop the Japanese from consolidating their position in New Guinea was through air power. Realizing the importance of this convoy, Kenney planned to attack it ferociously with everything he had.[39]

Fortunately for the Allies, the Japanese obligingly continued the routine preparations for troop convoys the intelligence branch had noted earlier. On February 7, 1943, a Japanese floatplane was spotted twenty-five miles east of New Britain, and more Japanese aircraft were seen on the airfield at Lae—both signs, according to intelligence officers, that "a further attempt to reinforce Lae by sea may be intended."[40] Alerted by these indications, Kenney stepped up the reconnaissance flights over Rabaul and a mission on February 22 hit the jackpot: photos from the mission "showed a record concentration of merchant tonnage" (299,000 tons) in Rabaul Harbor.[41] Three days later Kenney received added confirmation—an ULTRA report of an intercepted Japanese radio message indicating that the convoy would leave Rabaul for Lae between March 5 and 12.[42]

With firm knowledge of the Japanese plans in hand, he immediately outlined a plan of action to Whitehead. Kenney reduced flying to a minimum so that the maximum number of aircraft would be available for the mission and sent as many aircraft as possible to the airfield north of the Owen Stanley mountains to prevent any weather interference. Kenney also wanted Whitehead to focus reconnaissance near the harbor so that the convoy could be located as quickly as possible after it sailed, since an early sighting would permit multiple attempts at sinking the convoy.[43] After briefing MacArthur on his intentions, Kenney left for Port Moresby for more detailed planning with Whitehead.[44]

Although the airmen had good information on when the convoy would depart (a later message updated the landing date to March 5, whi.h meant that the convoy would have to depart around February 28 or March 1), they remained uncertain about the route the convoy would take. At Port Moresby, Kenney and Whitehead pored over information gathered by intelligence officers about convoy routes over the past four months and weather forecasts for the first week in March. Although the intercepted messages pointed toward the convoy's landing at Lae, Kenney thought it was also possible that the convoy might land further west, at Madang or Wewak.[45] Based on weather forecasts and Allied efforts against previous convoys, Kenney guessed that the Japanese would sail along the northern coast of New Britain to keep out of range of Allied air attacks for as long as possible, then make a dash toward its destination. To cover all possible contingencies, Whitehead's staff developed three different options. If the convoy landed at Madang, only the longer-range bombers could be used—the distance precluded the use of other aircraft. If the convoy split up, with some ships sailing for Madang and some for Lae, then targets would be assigned on the basis of aircraft range. The best-case scenario for Kenney was a Japanese landing at Lae, which meant the Allies could attack in the Vitiaz Strait, a location that would allow him to use every aircraft at his disposal.[46]

Because the latter case was the most complicated, Whitehead and his staff meticulously planned out the details and scheduled a full-scale rehearsal for February 27. This training mission brought together all of the different aircraft scheduled for the actual attack and allowed the flight leaders a chance to straighten out any unforeseen problems. Some of the units involved in the attack had been perfecting their skills in low-level bombing over the past six weeks on a sunken boat near Port Moresby. Although the training resulted in the loss of one aircraft and damage to two others, the use of this realistic target gave pilots a much better idea of what they would see out of their windscreens in combat. As Kenney waited for the rehearsal, he visited some of the air units near Port Moresby, telling them a little about the plan and giving a pep talk on the importance of the mission. His meetings with the air and ground crews and observation of the practice attack led Kenney confidently to conclude, "The Japs are going to get the surprise of their lives."[47]

Despite the information about the convoy's departure, actually finding and attacking it turned out to be no easier than previous attempts and took three days of intense effort.[48] Number 81 convoy, consisting of eight destroyers and eight merchant vessels, was first spotted by Allied aircraft on the afternoon of March 1. Although B-17s attempted to bomb the convoy that night, the predicted bad weather along the northern coast of New Britain prevented them from finding the ships. Despite staying above the low clouds over the next two days, Allied aircraft managed to track the convoy, suggesting that radio transmissions from the Japanese aircraft providing air cover were also being used to track the position of the ships.[49] By the end of March 2, Kenney received reports that B-17 aircrews had sunk at least three cargo vessels, badly damaged two more, and set two others on fire.[50]

RAAF aircraft continued to harass and tail the convoy throughout the next night, relaying the enemy's current position to the attack force rendezvousing over Cape Ward Hunt the next morning.[51] About the same time, other Allied aircraft bombed the Japanese airfield at Lae to reduce interference from enemy fighters.[52] Just before 10:00 A.M. on March 3, the concentrated attacks began. B-17s bombing from 8,000 feet were in the lead, escorted by the P-38s and followed by two groups of B-25s flying at 5,000 feet. Immediately behind these aircraft came the low-altitude attackers: thirteen RAAF Beaufighters, twelve of Kenney's newly modified B-25 "commerce destroyers," and twelve A-20s.[53]

As the crews at low altitude spotted the convoy, formations split to attack individual ships. A violent, swirling melee ensued. Pilots dodged antiaircraft fire from the ships and maneuvered wildly to avoid hitting other aircraft. The scene from the sea was horrific. Flames engulfed merchant vessels and, as one sailor recalled, "whole ships blew up."[54] Kenney's airmen departed the scene leaving all of the transports on fire and sinking and three of the escorting destroyers sinking or badly damaged. A second attack in the afternoon followed, finishing off the stranded vessels.[55]

Airmen returned to the area for the next several days for what Kenney euphemistically termed "mopping up" operations, strafing the lifeboats and rafts carrying the Japanese soldiers.[56] Many airmen justified their actions as retribution for past Japanese atrocities, specifically the attack the day prior on crew members who had bailed out of their B-17. The incident occurred when four B-17s striking the convoy encountered fifteen Japanese fighters. A fire started in the wing of one B-17, and the aircraft pulled out of formation. Shortly afterwards, seven men were seen bailing out. One airman fell out of his parachute harness to his death, but the others "were followed down by enemy fighters, that strafed them as they fell."[57] Kenney's chief of staff, Donald Wilson, maintained that the Japanese shooting of the men in their parachutes "set the pace for the 'no-quarter' procedures from then on."[58] Aviator James Murphy was incensed by the Japanese actions. "I wanted to vent some of my anger," Murphy later recalled, "and kill every Japanese son of a bitch I could find."[59] He felt that his actions were acceptable because they would be blessed by the men who had been killed. "Somehow all of us knew that the crew [of the B-17] would be smiling at us for the things that we did."[60]

While some airmen were motivated by revenge, others felt that military necessity dictated the killing of the Japanese soldiers, believing that without the attacks many of the soldiers would have fought another day.[61] One officer summed up the attitude of many of the participants when he said, "The enemy is out to kill you and you are out to kill the enemy. You can't be sporting in a war."[62] The aviators took no pleasure in the acts, some even becoming sick; but most saw it as their duty. One squadron report summed it up well: "Although the necessity for strafing of undefended barges was completely understood, and the targets accordingly . . . strafed, the two missions were most distasteful for the crews involved."[63]

Kenney took no pleasure in the "mopping up" but believed that "the Jap asks no quarter and expects none. His psychology is win or perish and I believe that it is the national psychology."[64] He labeled the Japanese "tough fanatics with a queer psychology incomprehensible to us."[65]

Notwithstanding the grim nature of those missions, Kenney was exuberant about the overall results, claiming the destruction of between eleven and fourteen cargo vessels and sixty aircraft, as well as 15,000 soldiers. MacArthur's communiqué pushed the numbers even higher, claiming that the Japanese lost twenty-two ships, over one hundred aircraft, and 15,000 men. By comparison, Kenney's air units suffered only 25 casualties and lost just six aircraft.[66] Although it was a total Allied victory, in reality the Japanese losses were lower than the claims. All eight of the merchant vessels in the convoy went to the bottom, but only four of the escorting destroyers were sunk. At least 3,000 Japanese soldiers lost their lives in the Battle of the Bismarck Sea, far fewer than the number claimed.[67] In addition, the Allied air effort destroyed two-thirds of the Japanese aircraft at Rabaul that had been sent out to protect the convoy. One Japanese Army Air Force squadron was so badly mauled that it was sent back to Japan.[68]

As in any battle, several factors contributed to the overwhelming success of the convoy attack. Certainly the earlier experiences played a big role. In particular, the unsuccessful effort against the convoy to Lae in January had emphasized the need to concentrate aircraft to overcome the convoy's air defenses. Group Captain William H. (Bull) Garing, an RAAF pilot who had flown maritime operations for a number of years, convinced Kenney and Whitehead of the need for mass attacks; planning for the Bismarck Sea Battle was done with this aim in mind.[69]

Changes in tactics and armament also played a role. The low-level tactics and forward-firing guns on the modified B-25s surprised the Japanese.

They were not expecting attacks from that quarter and, consequently, kept their protective fighter cover at a higher altitude. The arrival of the first attackers and their escorts occupied the Japanese and forced the convoy to disperse and maneuver to avoid the bombs from above. These evasive maneuvers made it impossible for the ships to protect each other with their antiaircraft fire, making the low-level attacks easier. Modifying the firing pin of the bombing fuse shortly before the mission so that the pins would not bend when the bomb hit the water permitted the aircraft to skip their bombs toward the ships.[70] Kenney's and Whitehead's persistence at training also paid off. The six weeks of practice bombing on the wrecked ship off Port Moresby increased the pilots' accuracy immensely.[71]

The contribution of intelligence to this engagement was crucial and cannot be overestimated. The painstaking work of tracking and analyzing past movements provided Kenney with an accurate forecast of an imminent convoy and its probable sailing routes. Likewise, ULTRA information was invaluable for pinpointing when the convoy would depart, allowing Kenney to commit his forces when they would have the greatest impact. Without this information Kenney would have had to expend much more effort simply trying to locate important targets. The time and resources spent on these missions would have reduced the aircraft available for subsequent bombing missions. He would have been like a boxer swinging in the dark; if he landed a punch it would hurt, but striking a blow was difficult. With accurate and dependable intelligence the Japanese moves were largely transparent to Kenney, while the enemy had almost no knowledge of his plans. To Kenney's credit, he was willing and able to integrate the information into operations on very short notice.

Although Kenney tended to downplay the important role that intelligence played in his success, he saw the entire action as vindication of his efforts since arriving in the theater. "The Battle of the Bismarck Sea was not something that just happened," he later said. "We didn't just see the convoy coming and go out and hit it. It was planned and rehearsed. We prepared. We even picked the spot for the engagement."[72] Kenney was right. The results of the Battle of the Bismarck Sea represented decisions made many months before, weeks of training and work, all capped off by thorough planning and brave execution. Certainly Japanese errors and some luck were involved in the battle, but it was luck that rested on excellent preparation and sound tactics.[73]

Kenney was justifiably proud of the accomplishments of his airmen, and the battle garnered great public attention. A bold headline on the front page of the *New York Times* the next day screamed "M'ARTHUR FLIERS DESTROY 22 JAPANESE SHIPS; ENEMY LOSES 15,000 MEN IN CONVOY; 55 PLANES."[74] The newspaper called it "one of the greatest triumphs of the war."[75] The battle continued to focus public attention on the Southwest Pacific over the next several days; the *Times* ran articles detailing various aspects of the engagement, and pieces appeared in *Newsweek* and *Time*.[76]

There were several reasons the Battle of the Bismarck Sea received so much attention. First, few air battles during World War II occurred over the space of just a few days. While the results of most bombing missions could be tallied in terms of bomb tonnage or the number of aircraft destroyed, it was difficult to assess how one particular mission related to a larger campaign or to ending the war. The Battle of the Bismarck Sea, on the other hand, had more of the attributes of a naval or ground battle. It was tightly bounded in time and space, two factors that made the results easy for the average citizen to comprehend. In addition, the battle occurred when there was little competition for news. The fighting in New Guinea and Guadalcanal was over, and the conquest of North Africa had stalled. This was one of the few American exploits to write about. MacArthur's drive for recognition and headlines was also an important factor. The battle occurred as military planners were making strategic decisions about the future conduct of the war. No doubt MacArthur hoped that success in the Battle of the Bismarck Sea would translate into attention and support from Washington.

Despite the success achieved by Kenney's airmen, the claims put forth about the Japanese losses in the battle proved to be the most long-running and controversial part of the engagement. Kenney and MacArthur probably knew by the end of March that the first reports and the subsequent headline in the *New York Times* were exaggerated. Documents and diaries recovered from the wreckage on March 8 revealed the number of troops onboard, the loading schedules, and the sailing formation of the convoy.[77] A study by the intelligence division of the Air Staff in the summer of 1943 confirmed this information, and Kenney was ordered to issue a corrected version of the battle.[78] The chief of air intelligence told Kenney that the "results announced in the original communiqué must undergo a downward revision."[79] MacArthur, responding to the tone as well as the information in the request, refused to make any changes. He claimed that the intelligence analysis was faulty and threatened "action against those responsible" for questioning his reports.[80]

Kenney also responded vigorously in a letter to General Arnold that offers some justification for why Kenney would not change his report. Kenney believed that there were actually two different convoys that joined together just prior to the attack on March 3. Washington's version was faulty, he reasoned, because it dealt with only a portion of the force that was destroyed. Kenney also argued that there was no "particular value" to the public in releasing information about an event that had happened many months before.[81] More important, he was shrewd enough to realize that the numbers told only part of the story. "Had there been many more ships sunk, the immediate value of this operation could not have been greater," he maintained.[82] The battle had "caused a total disruption of Japanese plans and placed a burden on his system of supply and transportation that will continue to rest on him for some time to come."[83]

While Kenney's assessment accurately portrayed the effects of this air-sea battle on Japanese operations, Washington's analysis continued to nag him. Two years later, shortly after the Japanese surrender, he appointed a board of officers who had not been involved in the action to prepare a report on the Battle of the Bismarck Sea using Japanese sources. While Kenney claimed that the Japanese officers he talked to after the war told him their losses in the battle were even greater than he had claimed, the investigating board came to a different conclusion.[84] The officers interviewed Japanese officials about the convoy and the impact of the battle on the war plans. Their report confirmed the assessment of the intelligence survey completed in the summer of 1943, which judged that the convoy contained eight merchant vessels, all of which were sunk, and eight destroyers, of which four were destroyed. The investigating officers also concluded that the Japanese lost approximately 2,900 men, not the 15,000 mentioned in MacArthur's dispatch.[85] Although aware of this contrary evidence, Kenney was unswayed. Perhaps in an effort to convince people of the efficacy of air power, he stuck to his original version of events; and in his account of the war published in 1949, he used the figures that had first been reported, never commenting on the ensuing controversy.[86]

The results as they were first reported were typical of the confusing accounts that often occur after a swirling air combat engagement, but Kenney's and MacArthur's unwillingness to change was probably a combination of influences. One historian argues that the exaggerated reports on the Battle of the Bismarck Sea were "symptomatic of the publicity policy at GHQ," a policy based on boosting MacArthur's prowess and distrusting anyone, especially those in Washington, who might criticize his actions.[87] MacArthur's biographer claims that the reaction to the proposed revisions was consistent with other episodes that threatened his image or honor—MacArthur simply refused to back down.[88]

Although not as driven by the idea of personal honor as MacArthur, Kenney was sensitive to his image and had previously reacted critically to reports that questioned his claims. After being questioned about the number of enemy losses, he cabled Arnold, "I do not appreciate the implication of exaggeration or falsification by myself and members of my command and regard the questioning of the accuracy of an official report as a serious matter. . . . I can only speculate as to the motives involved."[89] No doubt the public recognition Kenney gained for the episode—among other things, he was on the cover of *Life* magazine in March 1943 and received an invitation to see the president—would have made any retraction personally embarrassing.[90]

Kenney's refusal to change his stance was likely linked to his relationship with MacArthur as well. MacArthur had stressed the requirement for loyalty from his officers in their first meeting, and since that time Kenney had drawn closer both personally and professionally to his commander. There was little point in being seen as disloyal to MacArthur over this issue.

As commander, Kenney also had to be sensitive to the morale of the men in his command, another reason to be cautious in revising claims. Although damage reports were useful for assessing the effectiveness of a mission, the information also provided a sense of accomplishment for the units. Kenney had trumpeted the claims from the first mass raid on Rabaul in part to help boost morale, and after the first P-38 engagements Kenney apparently "allowed a large number of claims to be confirmed for the sake of [morale] over statistical accuracy."[91] Since MacArthur, Kenney, and officials in Washington could rely on other sources of information for a more accurate assessment of the enemy's capabilities, it is unlikely that Kenney intended to deceive anyone. Given the access to better information than crew reports, he likely saw little harm in siding with MacArthur and being generous with the claims of his airmen for the sake of morale.

The contentious and acrimonious debate over the number of ships sunk has only served to obscure the real effects of this battle—the impact on Japanese operations, an outcome that was much greater than the figures alone suggested. Although the number of Japanese soldiers lost was less than the amount claimed, only about 800 ever made it to Lae; the rest were returned to Rabaul. Those who did survive lost all of their equipment, even their individual weapons.[92] Also lost in the attack were four months of supplies and enough ammunition for a division-sized battle.[93]

These impressive results were important, but the strategic impact was devastating. The events of March 3 sent a shock wave through the Japanese military. Japanese military leaders realized that they could not afford repeated losses on the scale they had just suffered. As a result, the Lae Transport Operation, as it was called by the Japanese, was their last attempt to send large numbers of reinforcements or supplies to Lae, critically weakening the soldiers already in the area. The commander of the Japanese 8th Fleet at Rabaul, Vice Admiral Gunichi Mikawa, maintained that the destruction of the convoy "opened the way" for the advance to the Philippines and "dealt a fatal blow to the South Pacific operations,"[94] an assessment echoed by other Japanese naval officers.[95] To be sure, the Japanese did not give up. They continued to send some troops to Lae; but they now had to land further west, at Madang and Wewak, and then trek through the jungle, subject to air attacks, heat, and disease, before getting to the combat area. Likewise, supplies were brought into western New Guinea; but it was difficult to move them forward to the combat forces, and the distance made it impossible to send heavy equipment. With large transports driven from the sea, barges and submarines were used to move troops and supplies, but both of these methods had disadvantages. The barges were not made for long-distance operations and broke down frequently. In addition, the boats proved easy targets for the American torpedo patrol (PT) boats that prowled the coasts at night. The submarines could not carry large amounts, and using them as transports diverted them from patrols for Allied ships. Since the convoy contained the aviation fuel and spare parts needed at the airfields, when these ships went to the bottom it effectively halted Japanese efforts to gain control of the air in New Guinea.[96] In short, Kenney's assessment that "had there been many more ships sunk, the immediate value of this operation could not have been greater" stands as the best testimony to this operation's value to the war in the Southwest Pacific.[97] It was a total victory.

Pacific Military Conference

Fresh from his success in the Battle of the Bismarck Sea, Kenney departed Australia for Washington, D.C., to take part in discussions about the future course of the war in the Pacific. The decisions made at the Casablanca Conference in January provided the general outline for operations during 1943 and established the goal in the South Pacific of continuing operations aimed at maintaining pressure on the Japanese, but the means to accomplish this end had not been spelled out. These details would be worked out at a meeting in Washington, D.C., in March 1943, known as the Pacific Military Conference. The discussants included members of MacArthur's command and Admiral Halsey's adjoining South Pacific command, officers from Admiral Nimitz's headquarters in Hawaii, and Washington planners.[98] Kenney attended the meeting along with the Southwest Pacific chief of staff, Richard Sutherland, and the head of operations and planning in MacArthur's headquarters, Stephen Chamberlin.[99] Although Sutherland would be the chief spokesman, MacArthur asked Kenney to go so that he could plead for more aircraft, hoping that Kenney could also keep Sutherland "out of trouble."[100]

One of the objectives of the Pacific Military Conference was to mesh MacArthur's plans with Admiral Halsey's efforts in the South Pacific. Properly coordinated, the two advances would form a pincer that could cut off and then destroy the Japanese stronghold at Rabaul.[101] Sutherland's presentation of MacArthur's plan immediately ran into difficulty: the needed forces exceeded the number that the JCS had planned on sending.[102] Kenney calculated that he would need thirty groups, or about 1,964 aircraft, but present plans allocated only half as many, eighteen groups totaling approximately 942 planes. Both Kenney and Sutherland were dejected over the differences.[103] Either the objective for the year would have to be changed or the number of forces increased. In the end, the theater planners and the JCS compromised, increasing the number of forces scheduled for the Pacific slightly while trimming the goals of the operations. There would be no direct invasion of Rabaul in 1943. Instead the directive issued by the JCS ordered MacArthur to eliminate the Japanese presence in New Guinea as far west as Madang and to establish Allied control over the western part of New Britain. In the South Pacific theater, forces under the command of Admiral Halsey would advance to the southeastern part of the island of Bougainville. This would put the two commands in a position to attack Rabaul directly, if ordered. Although Halsey continued to command the forces in his theater, MacArthur retained the strategic direction for determining the timing of the attacks.[104]

While in Washington, Kenney pressed everyone he met for more aircraft. Arnold was sympathetic, but his staff told Kenney that he was getting as many as were available. The news from the Battle of the Bismarck Sea was just being published during Kenney's visit and resulted in an invitation to the White House for a meeting with President Roosevelt to discuss the war in the Southwest Pacific, including the recent destruction of the Japanese convoy. Kenney seized the opportunity during their hour-long meeting to plead his case for more aircraft, an appeal that was instrumental in forcing the JCS to provide more aircraft to the Southwest Pacific than they had originally intended.[105]

Kenney also attended an unusual and somewhat unsettling meeting during this trip. Kenney, Sutherland, and their wives met with Representative Henry Luce and his wife, correspondent Clare Boothe Luce, for lunch at the Luces' apartment. Kenney had met Clare Booth briefly in Paris during 1940, but they did not meet to reminisce about old times. After lunch, Senator Arthur Vandenberg arrived to sound out the two men about recruiting MacArthur for the Republican nomination for president in 1944.[106] The "MacArthur Adventure," as Senator Vandenberg later termed it, began shortly afterwards when MacArthur indicated he would not resist efforts aimed at gaining the Republican nomination. Vandenberg's hopes rested on the convention becoming deadlocked between two other candidates and having MacArthur emerge as the consensus choice of the delegates. MacArthur never won enough votes to be a serious contender for the nomination, however, and in the spring of 1944 requested that efforts made on his behalf in the Republican primaries be stopped.[107]

What role Kenney played or counsel he offered during this period is unclear. He told Vandenberg that he did not want MacArthur to run for election and believed that MacArthur did not want anything to do with politics.[108] If Kenney actually advised MacArthur against running, and it is not clear that he ever did, his advice went unheeded. Others on MacArthur's staff, especially Sutherland and MacArthur's intelligence officer, Major General Charles Willoughby, were very heavily involved. Kenney certainly was aware of the efforts, and probably was not adverse to the idea that his commander might be president, but left no trace of his thoughts. More disturbing is the fact that he did not raise any concerns about the involvement of a high-ranking, serving commander in an election. The presidential campaign might also explain MacArthur's and Kenney's refusal to correct the loss figures from the Battle of the Bismarck Sea. An updated version of the story, released in the summer of 1943, would have seriously diminished one of MacArthur's most decisive victories to date and undermined support for his nomination.

Aside from this excursion into domestic politics, Kenney stuck to the task of pleading for more people, planes, and equipment. He was increasingly concerned about the number of engineering units allocated to the Southwest Pacific. Perhaps drawing on his own background of the problems in construction, as well as what he had witnessed to date in the war, he argued that Washington did not appreciate the need for all types of engineering units to build airfields and other facilities and the difficulties of carrying out combat operations in areas that had no modern infrastructure, remarking "in this type of warfare you need air force, engineers and infantry in about the same strength."[109]

The decisions at the Pacific Military Conference only outlined the general plans for the "Cartwheel" offensive in the South Pacific for 1943. When Kenney returned to Australia in late March his staff went to work, developing the details so that MacArthur's ground offensive in New Guinea and Halsey's efforts in the Solomons could succeed.

The Japanese Strike Back

The loss of the convoy in the Battle of the Bismarck Sea had made it clear to Japanese commanders that any hope they had of defending their positions in New Guinea and the Solomons rested on reducing the strength of the Allied air units. In April 1943, Admiral Yamamoto, the combined fleet commander, assumed command of air units at Rabaul with the goal of eliminating Allied air power in Operation I. Using aircraft flown into Rabaul from Truk, Yamamoto struck the Solomons from April 5 to 10 and then turned his attention on New Guinea. On April 11, 22 Japanese bombers, escorted by 72 fighters, hit Allied shipping in a harbor on the northern coast of New Guinea. The next day Port Moresby was on the receiving end of Japanese fighters and 43 bombers.[110] Buoyed by the exaggerated claims of his pilots that they had demolished 2 destroyers, 25 transports, and 175 planes, Yamamoto suspended the raids on April 16.[111] Yamamoto made plans to tour the area and visit the victorious pilots at their air bases. Allied cryptographers had broken the Japanese codes and knew his exact itinerary. On April 18, as his aircraft approached Buin, eighteen P-38s from Admiral Halsey's command arrived. Yamamoto's aircraft was shot down and crashed in the jungle, killing the man who had masterminded the attack on Pearl Harbor and was perhaps the best strategist the Japanese possessed.[112]

During the buildup of Japanese air strength at Rabaul, Kenney was in Port Moresby directing daily combat operations while Whitehead, who had been at the advanced headquarters almost continuously since the previous August, enjoyed a well-deserved break in Australia. Intercepted messages and photo reconnaissance missions revealed the influx of aircraft into the airfields at Rabaul, and intelligence officers predicted that the Japanese would soon begin large-scale air attacks against New Guinea.[113] Although forewarned about the possibility, Kenney sent the fighters east to protect Milne Bay, putting the fighters out of position when the Japanese arrived. Damage was light, and Kenney freely admitted, "I got badly fooled and was lucky to get out of it as well as I did."[114] The next day he did better. The RAAF Wireless Section at Port Moresby provided two and a half hours advance notice of the raid, and the Japanese lost one-third of the attacking force before reaching the northern coast of New Guinea.[115]

Though well-planned and executed, Yamamoto's air offensive only confirmed Kenney's existing low opinion of the Japanese. Their air commanders were "a disgrace to the airman's profession," unable to "understand air warfare."[116] They could not handle large numbers of aircraft and "made piecemeal attacks and didn't follow them up."[117] Kenney's assessment was certainly colored by his racialist attitudes, as the Japanese formations had been about the same size as his own. Yet in one area Kenney's analysis was correct. In Yamamoto's latest offensive the Japanese airmen had not persisted in their attacks, and they made little impact on Kenney's attempt to gain control of the air.

Organizing for Combat

Even during the press of combat operations, Kenney was continually seeking innovative solutions to a variety of problems. His changes were not limited to just technical and tactical matters. An example of an organizational innovation in response to the unique environmental and tactical situation that Kenney faced in the Southwest Pacific was the air task force. The 1st Air Task Force was activated at a forward airfield, across the Owen Stanley mountains from Port Moresby, called Dobodura, under the command of Colonel Frederick "Freddy" Smith on March 4, 1943.[118] As Kenney noted at the end of the Papuan campaign, the pace and pattern of operations in the Southwest Pacific would be closely tied to the range of the aircraft in the theater. Ground forces could not advance into an area until the Allies had gained control of the air and isolated the area. Ground troops would then invade and secure an airfield to support the next advance. Since the distance, environment, and equipment of the Southwest Pacific made it impossible for commanders to dependably communicate with the units at the forward airfields, the commander of an air task force, such as Smith, had "complete authority to handle any situation."[119]

In essence, the air task force was a miniature version of Whitehead's headquarters: an advanced headquarters that was flexible in size and assigned aircraft for a specific task. The air task force commander handled the problems at the forward field and provided liaison with the other forces, but had a minimum of administrative responsibilities for long-term care of the planes and people.[120] Although Kenney liked the organization, air task forces were never officially condoned in Washington. Without official standing it was difficult to get qualified officers to fill the positions in the organizations. Smith, for example, was officially the chief of staff for 5th Air Force at the same time that he was the commander of the 1st Air Task Force. Kenney brought the issue up with Arnold during Arnold's visit to the Southwest Pacific in the fall of 1942 and continued to press for more manpower during the Washington Planning Conference.[121]

Despite a shortage of qualified officers, Kenney continued to use the air task force because it offered several advantages. The most obvious benefit for the crews flying the missions was the ability to plan together. Having the headquarters of the 1st Air Task Force at Dobodura put it close to the flying units using the airfields in the same area. Since the air task force controlled all kinds of aircraft, planning for missions that used mixed aircraft types was relatively easy. Instead of trying to send messages to different units, the group operations and intelligence officers met at the headquarters and worked out the details and then returned to tell their own flyers about the plan.[122] The commander of 1st Air Task Force also worked out the details of operations with the RAAF in New Guinea through conversations with the RAAF equivalent to the air task force, Number 9 Group.[123]

From Kenney's perspective as a theater air commander, the air task force gave him a mechanism for centralizing control over aircraft in the theater and providing for flexible employment. The official American procedures for the air support of ground operations were codified in Field Manual 31-35 *Aviation in Support of Ground Forces,* a regulation based largely on maneuvers held in the Carolinas and Louisiana in 1941. This doctrine stated that air support would be provided by an air support command that functioned under the orders of the theater commander, not the air commander. In addition, the aircraft in the air support command would be allocated to corps or division commanders, who would establish the target priorities.[124] In short, the air support command would be under the control of the ground units, not the air commander.

Kenney viewed the idea of an air support command, and the concomitant dispersion of aircraft, as foolish and dangerous. He flatly stated, "The basic idea is wrong."[125] Kenney rejected a suggestion by one of his staff officers about forming an air support command, telling Whitehead that "supporting ground troops with an air effort is just another air operation" and that he saw no need for a separate organization.[126] Kenney also reasoned that the dispersion of aircraft to individual corps commanders would waste valuable and scarce resources. The air needs of each individual ground unit varied greatly in relation to whether they were actively engaged in an operation, whereas air operations could be carried out continually.[127] Centralizing control of the aircraft allowed them to be used more effectively because aircraft could be sent against different targets, depending on the current circumstances.[128] Whitehead agreed with this reasoning, affirming Kenney's belief that "there is no tactical reason for such a command."[129]

The idea of an air support command was squashed permanently when Kenney issued standard operating procedures for the Allied Air Forces flying in support of ground forces. In the opening section of the piece, published in July 1943, Kenney reiterated the ideas he had discussed with Whitehead about an air support command and his philosophy about the use of air power:

> The situation in SWPA does not permit the organisation [*sic*] and employ-
> ment of an Air Support Command as a separate element of the Air Force. The
> limited aviation forces available require that these forces be retained under
> centralised [*sic*] control for employment against objectives which are most
> important in furthering the plan of the Theater Commander. Whenever
> ground force action requires close support by aviation, all or a part of the Air
> Forces effort will be employed for this purpose. The proportion of Air Force
> effort to be devoted to close support is determined by the Air Force Com-
> mander in accordance with directives by the Theater Commander, and with
> consideration for all the objectives to be attained.[130]

MacArthur, convinced by prior performance of the value of Kenney's ideas
and his ability to use air power, apparently agreed with this formula. There
would be no air support command in the Southwest Pacific.

The method of dispersing the air units among different ground commanders proved unsound in other areas also. The commander of the North
African invasion, General Dwight D. Eisenhower, told Army Chief of Staff
General George Marshall, "Coordination in operations involving air units
has not been completely satisfactory. . . . I have come to the conclusion that
a single air commander is necessary."[131] Upon Eisenhower's recommendation
the command structure was reorganized and the idea of an air support command was dropped. By April 1943, the tenet of centralized control was codified in War Department Field Manual 100-20 *Command and Employment
of Air Power*, which stated: "CONTROL OF AVAILABLE AIR POWER MUST BE
CENTRALIZED AND COMMAND MUST BE EXERCISED THROUGH THE AIR FORCE
COMMANDER."[132]

While Kenney no doubt agreed with the idea of centralizing command
of the air forces, he disagreed with some aspects of the manual, such as the
division of air power. The manual divided the combat forces of an air command into a strategic air force, a tactical air force, and an air defense command.[133] Although Kenney's command had a bomber and a fighter command,
these were for administrative and logistical convenience, not combat operations. For combat he combined his aircraft in the air task forces according
to the mission. The task forces could be all of one kind of aircraft, or a mix
of fighters, bombers, and transports. The makeup depended on the requirements of the mission.[134] Like some other officers, Kenney did not believe that
an air command should be divided. An airplane should not be considered
either a tactical or a strategic airplane; one day it "may drop . . . on targets
ten miles away and the next day you may be working 5,000 miles away, and
to say that one is tactical and the other strategic really doesn't tell the story
and . . . uses these two ground terms which we should keep out."[135]

The progressive movement of airfields during MacArthur's planned advance through New Guinea also demanded flying units organized to move quickly. Kenney divided the flying squadrons into three echelons. The advanced echelon consisted of the men and equipment that preceded the aircraft, by either air or sea transport, to a new air base. They took with them enough supplies and equipment for ten days of operations and prepared the landing field for the air echelon, which arrived a few days later. The ground echelon, contained the remainder of the unit, which followed when transportation was available.[136] This organizational format, possibly inspired by Kenney's experiences in moving to different airfields in the First World War or the exercises he oversaw at GHQ Air Force, made it easier for squadrons to deploy quickly in response to changing situations, an ability that became more necessary as MacArthur went on the offensive.

The Toribands

The first operations in the Cartwheel offensive were scheduled to begin in June 1943. While the ground soldiers trained for the assault, Kenney's airmen continued to fly combat missions aimed at reducing Japanese air strength and isolating Salamaua, the strongest Japanese position in New Guinea, through an air blockade.

A new wrinkle in MacArthur's theater, and an increasingly important factor in the war, was amphibious landing operations requiring the close integration of air, land, and sea forces. Fortunately, the first attempt in this type of warfare in the Southwest Pacific came against the Toriband Islands, territory that was not occupied. These uncontested landings provided a good opportunity to develop and test procedures for the remainder of the war.

Planning for the first phase of the offensive movements in the Southwest Pacific began in early May. The invasion of the Woodlark and Kiriwina Islands would be accomplished by "Alamo Force," commanded by Lieutenant General Walter Krueger, the commander of 6th Army, who arrived in Australia in January 1943. To support the amphibious assaults on Woodlark and Kiriwina Islands, Kenney planned to use the RAAF Command to protect the eastern sea flank of the islands, while 1st Air Task force would provide direct support for the invasion.[137] One of the major sticking points in the planning involved air protection for the invasion. While the landing would be unopposed by Japanese ground forces, there was still the possibility of a stiff enemy reaction from the sea and air. MacArthur's intelligence rated the chance of air attacks involving over one hundred bombers as "probable."[138] Rear Admiral Daniel Barbey, the 7th Fleet Amphibious commander, had arrived in Brisbane in January 1943 and was the man responsible for training and organizing the amphibious landings. Barbey argued that aircraft should be constantly over the sailing force, providing an air umbrella. Kenney, on the other hand, felt that this would tie up too many of his aircraft, leaving them unavailable for other missions. In addition, since the attack was scheduled for dawn, Kenney's forces would have had to take off from the rough, unimproved jungle airfields in the dark, a sure recipe for disaster. He promised, instead, to pound the Japanese air strips prior to the attack and keep his aircraft ready on the ground to repulse any Japanese strikes. Barbey was "skeptical" of Kenney's plan and "looked with envy at . . . Admiral Halsey's force where carrier planes would provide continuous daylight cover."[139]

Kenney's reluctance to cooperate with Barbey was not just another example of a petty interservice rivalry, but rather evidence of sharply divergent views of how to wage war. ULTRA intercepts and other reports had given Kenney an accurate picture of the Japanese air strength and provided him with early warning of attacks from the Japanese air bases at Wewak and Rabaul, knowledge of the Japanese capabilities that Barbey may not have shared.[140] Barbey was also accustomed to planning with a nearby aircraft carrier dedicated to supporting the amphibious operation. Instead of gaining air superiority over the entire region, a carrier only needed to control the air over a small area for a limited time. In addition, naval carriers would be close enough to the landing area so that an air patrol could protect their "base," the carrier, as well as the invasion force. The proximity of the carriers also meant that even with a dawn invasion the carrier pilots could take off in daylight. Kenney, on the other hand, had many more tasks to perform than supporting this one operation, defended a much bigger area, and used very rough and unimproved airfields. Dedicating large numbers of his fighters to an air umbrella over the convoy required canceling or delaying other missions. In addition, the long distance from the air bases to the beachhead meant that Kenney's planes spent much of their time flying to and from the combat zone, with little time left to engage the enemy over the invasion area.[141] Kenney also argued that keeping an air umbrella over a sea convoy was a "losing game" because it gave the enemy the initiative for choosing the time and place of the attack and allowed them to overwhelm the defenders on patrol. It made more sense to defeat the enemy air force than provide a protective air umbrella.[142]

Another factor that affected Kenney's attitude was his general dislike and distrust of the Navy. Barbey commented on the interservice tension he perceived when he arrived at MacArthur's headquarters and thought Kenney was a major contributor to the problem. According to Barbey, "the Air Force usually prefaced their references to the Navy as the 'damn Navy.'"[143] Another naval officer on MacArthur's staff viewed Kenney as the "biggest anti-Navy agitator" in the headquarters.[144] Kenney had little patience for naval officers, especially when it came to running air operations, and he made few efforts to cooperate or get along with them. Kenney and the Allied naval commander, Vice Admiral Arthur S. Carpender, made an attempt to integrate aircraft and PT boats into the same area against Japanese barges, but the effort was short-lived, terminated when B-25s accidentally attacked a PT boat. Rather than investigate the incident and develop corrective measures, Kenney's first instinct was to blame the Navy for not disclosing the location of the ships. After this failed effort at cooperation, the commanders resorted to establishing separate areas for their forces.[145]

Kenney felt vindicated by the results of the attacks during the landings on Woodlark and Kiriwina. His plan was followed, and the Japanese, perhaps distracted by Halsey's landing on New Georgia, made no attempts to stop the invasion.[146] The landings did provide good training, and the airfields there proved useful later in Kenney's attacks against Rabaul and other targets in support of the offensive in the South Pacific theater.

WITH NEW GUINEA ISOLATED from large-sized reinforcements, MacArthur was ready to move westward, but needed an imaginative air campaign in the Markham Valley to eliminate the Japanese air threat before the ground forces could begin their amphibious assaults toward Rabaul.

SEVEN

ISOLATING RABAUL

June 1943 to January 1944

"I stick to one basic principle, get control of the
air situation before you try anything else."

The landings in the Toriband Islands were followed by operations under the
command of the Allied Land Forces commander, General Blamey, in the
Huon Peninsula of New Guinea aimed at the town of Lae. The harbor and
airfields around the town made it imperative that the Allies wrest control of
this area from the Japanese so that MacArthur could advance further west
in New Guinea. The allied plan called for an amphibious invasion of the
coast coupled with an assault on the interior Markham Valley by ground
forces airlifted into the combat zone. After eliminating the Japanese from
this area in New Guinea, MacArthur planned to jump across the straits onto
the island of New Britain, completing his half of the pincer movement around
Rabaul. The amphibious landings and massive airborne assault were the start
of complex, extensive combat operations in the Southwest Pacific.

Before any of these moves could take place, however, Kenney began for-
mulating the air campaign plan. He continued his efforts aimed at isolating
the Japanese garrisons in the Lae area, but knew his first job was "to defeat
the Jap Air Force."[1]

Air Superiority and Deception

The successful interdiction of the sea convoys by Kenney's airmen, most con-
vincingly demonstrated in the Battle of the Bismarck Sea, made it very difficult for the Japanese commanders to supply their forces, but they did not
give up the fight. Throughout May and June 1943, they had been building
up their air strength further west in New Guinea at bases near Wewak. They
used these airfields because they were out of range of Kenney's fighters, but
close enough to the Japanese frontlines to cause problems for the Allies. Ken-

ney's task was simple: he had to eliminate the threat posed by the Japanese aircraft before the attacks on Lae could commence.[2]

ULTRA information and air raid warnings from the wireless units kept Kenney well apprised of the buildup at Wewak and the activities of the Japanese units.[3] By flying in aircraft from as far away as Burma and the Netherlands East Indies, the Japanese had over 100 aircraft in New Guinea in May, twice as many as a month earlier. By the end of July the number of Japanese aircraft at Wewak had risen to 180.[4] In June, the 6th and 7th Air Divisions were activated at Wewak to control the growing numbers of aircraft, and in July the 4th Air Army Headquarters was established.[5]

Kenney's air strength was also increasing. Although the new P-47s he had been promised by Arnold were having developmental troubles, Kenney expected to receive an influx of other aircraft in the coming months. An additional group of P-38s was set to arrive in June, along with forty new P-40s and over one hundred B-25s, with more P-40s on the way.[6] Despite production delays and a myriad of other problems, Kenney had six more fighter squadrons and eight more bomber squadrons in July than he had in January.[7]

Kenney started air preparations well in advance of the landing date for the coming offensive. To prevent the Japanese from sending all their available air assets into New Guinea and to plant some degree of uncertainty in their minds about the location of future operations, Kenney assigned the RAAF Command the task of tying down the Japanese air units in the Netherlands East Indies. Kenney specifically ordered that large formations be used so that the Japanese would get the impression that air strength in the northwestern area of Australia was being built up in preparation for an Allied ground offensive in the Netherlands East Indies.[8] While RAAF Command kept the Japanese distracted, Kenney worked out a scheme to eliminate the aircraft at Wewak.

The Japanese airfields at Wewak were within range of Kenney's bombers operating out of the airfields near Port Moresby, but if the bombers were sent to the targets unescorted by friendly fighters, the Japanese could inflict huge losses. At one point, Kenney hoped to draw the Japanese into a trap by dropping insulting propaganda leaflets on the airfields and positioning aircraft nearby that would ambush the Japanese when they reacted by taking off to retaliate.[9] While this plan never materialized, and its validity remains doubtful, Kenney searched for other ways to "dominate the air over the Markham Valley."[10] What Kenney needed was an airdrome close enough to Wewak to allow fighters to escort the heavy bombers on their attacks.

The idea of carving out an airfield deep in enemy territory was not new. As commander of 4th Air Force in California, Kenney had proposed a test of an "Air Blitz Unit" for this purpose in early 1942. It was a bold proposal. The operation "will have no ground line, no highway, nor railroad, and no typewriter involved in the whole problem. It is entirely dependent upon air transportation and radio telephone communication."[11] Although Arnold turned down the request, citing a lack of aircraft, Kenney's thinking along these lines was already clear before he came to the Southwest Pacific.

The area in the Markham Valley seemed an ideal location for such an "air blitz," and a field at Bena Bena was already being used to insert coast-watchers deep into Japanese territory; but finding forward airfields for long-term operations and heavier aircraft was not a simple task.[12] Selecting potential airfields depended on good intelligence about the terrain, not always easy to obtain. Data on soil conditions, weather, and building materials could be collected from aerial photographs, interviews with prewar residents of an area, and reports from captured prisoners and documents, but were not always reliable. If possible, engineers tried to make a ground survey, which often proved the most helpful in determining possible landing fields.[13]

In selecting the location for an airfield, air commanders and engineers had to balance several competing criteria. Safe landings and takeoffs needed relatively flat areas, free from obstructions, aligned within 10 to 15 degrees of the prevailing winds in the area, and long enough to accommodate the aircraft using the field. Larger, heavier bombers obviously needed more runway to take off and land than did smaller, lighter planes.[14] Critically important for construction of an airfield was the composition of soil in the area. Some areas were simply too close to the water table to support the weight of any aircraft.[15]

Once the area for the airfield was agreed to, construction of the runways began. After the field was surveyed and the runway marked, the area was cleared and the top layer of soil was removed. Taking off the top layer of soil was especially important for laying runways in the jungles because that soil was usually a black loam that could not support much weight. An engineer who failed to remove that layer found it impossible to pile enough material on top to support the weight of heavier aircraft. The landing area was then leveled, and material such as gravel or coral, depending on the characteristics of the subsoil, was brought in to make the foundation of the field firmer. Usually the field was then covered with flexible pavements, such as asphalt, a thin coating of asphalt oil, or pierced steel planking, called PSP or Marston matting, which gave the fields a limited all-weather capability.[16]

With Kenney's support, Australian Air Force and American engineers, who had surveyed the Markham Valley earlier, began looking more closely for possible landing sites in 1943.[17] After extensive aerial reconnaissance of the area, engineers were sent out in early June to examine the area in the eastern part of the valley near a town called Marilinan. A hill at one end, requiring a steep landing approach, and the lack of room to disperse aircraft made it suitable only for transport aircraft. An area nearby, called Tsili-Tsili (pronounced Silly-Silly), was considered a better choice for both fighters and transports.[18] Kenney opted to use Tsili-Tsili but changed the name to Marilinan so as not to provide fodder for critics in case his plan failed—evidence of the large risk he was taking in the venture.[19] In any event, the installation was only a temporary expedient. Neither site could support aircraft when the September rains arrived, but it was hoped the Allies would be in control of Lae by that time and Marilinan could be abandoned.[20]

Building an airfield in the Markham Valley demanded that the engineers working there be protected from both ground and air attacks. Kenney asked the Australians for a battalion of infantry soldiers to defend against the enemy ground forces, opting for the Australian soldiers because he felt they would have no compunction about placing their soldiers under the command of an airman, an "unthinkable" situation for the American Army.[21] A more difficult problem was preventing an enemy air attack. Kenney could not attack the Japanese airfields and did not have enough aircraft to fly constant defensive patrols over Marilinan. Aircraft on ground alert at Port Moresby, however, were too far away to be of any real protection in case of a Japanese air raid. Kenney solved the problem through a clever deception plan. To draw attention away from the construction, Kenney flew a small number of engineers into two locations (Garoka and Bena Bena) further west in the Markham Valley, between the Japanese airfields at Wewak and the airdrome under construction at Marilinan. The engineers recruited natives to help them "raise dust" and create the impression of building a forward airfield. The hope was that the Japanese reconnaissance aircraft would focus on the "construction" at Garoka and Bena Bena before spotting the real airfield at Marilinan.[22]

At the same time, Kenney was pursuing another deception plan that involved the use of an aircraft carrier as bait to ambush Japanese aircraft. With construction of the airfields in the Markham Valley underway, Kenney asked General Arnold for two ships that could be painted to look like aircraft carriers. Kenney wanted to sail these ships off the northern coast of New Guinea. Since he knew that ULTRA intercepts would provide ample warning of a Japanese attack on the boats, he planned to position his fighters to ambush the Japanese as they attacked the "aircraft carriers." "This scheme will make him come to me," he boasted.[23] No doubt hoping to generate enthusiasm and support for his ideas, Kenney predicted, "With minimum losses to ourselves, we ought to be able to clean out his whole Air Force out of this theater and then, before he had a chance to replace it, mop up all the shipping within reach in broad daylight, land troops at will anywhere we pleased and really go places in this war."[24]

Although Arnold thought Kenney's idea was a good one, he had no way of supplying the ships; hoping to get support, he presented the plan to the rest of the JCS. While they also considered it worthwhile, shipping was the tightest constraint on Allied operations in the summer of 1943, and there was simply nothing available in the United States to help Kenney. Arnold and the rest of the JCS approved the project, giving it the code name "Horseplay," but told Kenney and MacArthur that they would have to obtain the ships locally.[25]

Kenney, who had not told MacArthur about his plan, had some fast explaining to do when the message from Washington arrived approving the project. Besides being embarrassed, Kenney was also "disgusted" by the way the matter was handled.[26] Arnold should have realized, he fumed, that if there had been ships available in Australia he would not have asked Washington for assistance.[27] MacArthur, who had grown used to Kenney's fertile mind during their association over the past year, was not alarmed by Kenney's initiative. MacArthur supported the scheme and suggested that a barge might serve as a suitable carrier decoy. Kenney doubted he could squeeze a barge out of MacArthur's supply chief and dejectedly concluded, "It was a good idea but it is dead now."[28] Still he did not give up; he began scrounging old barges and boats to build a fake invasion force. At the end of August he was still trying to sell others on his plan and get a few destroyers and other ships to make the invasion convoy look authentic. Neither the Allied land commander, General Blamey, nor the naval commander, Admiral Carpender, thought much of Kenney's plan, and he was ultimately forced to cancel this deception scheme.[29]

Kenney certainly deserves credit for his creativity and imagination in tackling the problem of gaining air control over New Guinea. Nonetheless he should have realized that getting a ship from the United States would be no easier than obtaining one locally. Many of the discussions at the Pacific Military Conference he had attended focused on the problems involved with the lack of shipping and its concomitant impact on combat operations in 1943.[30] In failing to consider this critical shortcoming in his deception plan, Kenney displayed a dismaying disregard for the strategic framework of the war.

Despite the failure of Kenney's carrier scheme, his ruse in the Markham Valley was still holding. As expected, the Japanese discovered the phony construction at Garoka and Bena Bena and made repeated, almost daily, attacks on the area to stop construction.[31] Kenney used an RAAF 1 Wireless Unit to track the Japanese flights and knew how far the patrols were flying, knowledge that allowed him to continue building up the real airfield for as long as possible.[32] On July 8, four P-38s, acting on a tip-off from an intercept site, caught ten Japanese aircraft over Bena Bena and shot down two of them.[33] Whitehead was ecstatic about the result and the use of signals intelligence. The results of this mission, he forecast, "will furnish further proof, if further proof is needed, of the urgent necessity of getting additional D/F units up here. If we can do this with what we have now, think of the possibilities with better equipment."[34]

In the meantime construction at the (new) Marilinan airfield continued at a frantic pace. The first three planeloads of infantry and a small group of engineers arrived on June 16, followed by four more planeloads the next day.[35] The 871st Airborne Aviation Engineers were flown in at the beginning of July, and construction on the main runways started on July 10, 1943. Augmented by native workers, the engineers worked on the field twenty-four hours a day.[36] On July 26 the first group of fighters landed, and by the beginning of August a radar warning unit had been established. Conditions at the field were still austere and supplies limited, but it was a start. To control operations at this forward location Kenney activated the 2nd Air Task Force on August 5 under the command of Lieutenant Colonel Malcom A. "Mike" Moore. By the middle of August, the airfield was fully ready for operations.[37]

Kenney's efforts at flexibility and innovation were abundantly clear during the building of the airfields in the Markham Valley. The 1,200 men there depended completely on transport aircraft for their supplies. The airfields were so close to the Japanese complex at Wewak that when large numbers of transport aircraft started flying in and out of Marilinan they needed fighter escorts. The fighters did not have the fuel to circle the airfield for very long, so Kenney's Air Transport Command developed specially trained teams to quickly load and unload the supplies from the transports. The Air Freight Forwarding Units practiced unloading and loading supplies into the body of a wrecked transport and cut their times dramatically.[38] Like pit crews at a stock car race, they could have an airplane unloaded and off the field in no time. The transports had already delivered jeeps to the forward areas, but the airfield construction project needed some big trucks. Kenney's troops devised a method for cutting two-and-a-half-ton trucks in half so that they could fit into the transports flown up to Marilinan, where they were welded back together.[39] The trucks were split behind the cab, and a one-wheel dolly was bolted on to the rear half of the cab. After removal of the fender, bumper, and windshield, this section was driven up a ramp and into one aircraft while the rear half was shoehorned into a second transport.[40]

Remarkably, the deception plan in the Markham Valley worked for almost two months, but on August 11 a Japanese reconnaissance flight was spotted over the new airfield. Kenney, appraised by ULTRA intercepts, realized that it was just a matter of time before the Japanese attacked, so he rushed two more squadrons up to the field.[41] The American fighters did not have long to wait: on August 15 the Japanese attacked with twelve bombers escorted by twenty to twenty-five fighters. Kenney's fighters, alerted by the radar and a wireless unit flown in several weeks prior, met the attackers and shot down six of the bombers and three fighters. The day was not without losses for Kenney's forces—two transports were hit on the ground, along with three fighters.[42] The next day the Japanese returned as a group of transports were landing. The American fighters flying above the transports managed to shoot down at least twelve Japanese fighters, and there were no losses on the ground.[43]

Though not fully stocked with supplies, the forward airfield was complete, and Kenney did not delay in moving against the airfields at Wewak. Whitehead and his staff had been busy working out plans for the attack; and on the morning of August 17, the air offensive against the Wewak airfields began. Despite their knowledge of the forward airfields, the first attack came as a complete surprise to the Japanese at Wewak; almost every one of their aircraft was on the ground, and the American attackers met little resistance. Whitehead and Kenney threw everything they had into the attacks. While the results were not as spectacular as Kenney claimed, they were still impressive: of the 120 Japanese aircraft on the fields, only 38 were still in flying condition two days later.[44] The number of aircraft destroyed does not alone convey the level of destruction the attacks inflicted or the impact on future operations. While the loss of aircraft was important, the raids also wiped out large quantities of gasoline and supplies that had been painstakingly brought into the base. Allied officers were uncertain as to the actual extent of the damage, but it was clear that the missions proved disastrous for the Japanese. Intercept operators soon picked up messages from the Japanese at Wewak, telling their headquarters that the base was low on gas.[45]

While Kenney's deception provided the method that allowed him to stage the air attacks on Wewak, the success was attributable to several factors. Foremost was the intelligence about the Japanese buildup, which allowed Kenney to concentrate his forces and make a mass attack at the most appropriate moment, literally when the Japanese airfields were full of aircraft. The Japanese 4th Air Army had built up the 6th Air Division over the past several months in anticipation of an Allied advance and reached its peak strength on August 15, just two days prior to Kenney's first raid.[46] Without this information Kenney would have been forced to make recurring attacks on the airfields, depleting his forces for later actions.

The Japanese, on the other hand, operated under a number of handicaps. Unlike Kenney, they had little detailed knowledge of their opponents' air strength or plans; although they did prove capable at times of analyzing message traffic and may have had some indications of the move, they could not react in time.[47] In addition, the airfields at Wewak had no radar for early warning, so the first indications of an attack were visual observations.[48] Finally, although Japanese commanders were aware of the dangers of putting aircraft in the open at an airfield, they had been unable to build additional airfields or dispersal areas because of a lack of heavy equipment. As Allied engineers had discovered, heavy construction equipment, such as bulldozers and graders, was absolutely essential for carving airfields out of the jungle. By one estimate the work that could be done with one bulldozer equaled 1,000 laborers working by hand.[49] Using this ratio, the 700 men and 220 pieces of heavy equipment (bulldozers, graders, trucks) in one American aviation engineer battalion could accomplish in 24 hours the same amount of work as 50,000 men with hand tools.[50] The Japanese did not have the people or the heavy equipment to match; only eight bulldozers were produced in Japan during 1943 and 1944, and there were only three road graders, none of them motorized, in Japan at the end of the war.[51] As a result of the construction problems the four airfields at Wewak were tightly packed with unprotected aircraft on the morning of August 14, making them easy targets for Kenney's airmen.[52] Despite their heavy losses, the Japanese continued to funnel aircraft from the Philippines and the Netherlands East Indies into New Guinea, but without supplies the planes were useless. Intercepted Japanese messages kept Kenney appraised of the Japanese actions, and he continued bombing Wewak through the rest of August; but by that time it was clear that the Japanese had little ability to seriously affect the upcoming Allied ground operations in Huon Peninsula.[53]

Preparations and Perspectives

Although Kenney devoted a great deal of attention to gaining air superiority, it was not his only concern; and his command continued to fly a variety of missions. Airmen bombed the airfields and shipping at Rabaul in support of Admiral Halsey's attacks in the Solomons, flew reconnaissance patrols, attacked convoys and barges, and brought supplies into all areas of New Guinea, while simultaneously softening up the Japanese ground positions around Lae and Salamaua. In short, despite the relative lull in ground combat, the pace of air operations continued unabated.[54]

As the theater air commander, Kenney was continually looking to the future and planning for upcoming operations. As a result, much of his time was focused on the toll the fighting was taking on the aircraft and airmen in his command. Frequently worried about not having the men or machines to carry out MacArthur's plans, Kenney wrote General Arnold in the hope of receiving some help in solving his problems. Although well aware that the national strategic priority was to defeat Germany first, at every occasion Kenney provided evidence about how well he was doing, in an attempt to get more of what he needed. Like MacArthur, Kenney was convinced that the people in Washington did not understand the demands of a combat theater, and his letters to Arnold reflected this attitude. Kenney argued that he needed to have some idea of when replacements would arrive so that he could plan combat operations that were scheduled three to six months in advance. Without knowing the forces he would have, he simply could not do the planning.[55] At times Kenney knew he must be exasperating Arnold, and at one point apologized for "continually crabbing about being short . . . but I am afraid it is about the only way I can present the picture as it confronts me." "I know that you are harassed to the point of exhaustion," he continued, "and that you are doing your damnedest to keep me quiet but I will trust to your continued good nature and keep on telling you my troubles."[56]

While Arnold was sympathetic and understanding of Kenney's needs, it was obvious from the beginning that the two saw the war through very different lenses. As a member of the JCS and as commanding general of the Army Air Forces, Arnold viewed the war in global terms. Based on the strategy and existing situation he had to balance the constant cry for people and planes between all the combat theaters, while also deciding on the tradeoffs between producing more aircraft and modifying existing ones. From the theater level the outlook was quite different. Kenney had little sympathy for the problems other air commanders might be facing and was primarily concerned with his problems in fighting the war. He cared relatively little about future development and simply wanted large numbers of aircraft.

This tension surfaced over many issues throughout the war, some important, others trivial. Kenney complained frequently about aircraft arriving with equipment that was not used in his area, such as heaters, or with unwanted modifications that he considered detrimental. He termed the installation of a gun turret on the bottom of the B-24 to defend against fighters attacking from below a mistake.[57] When he discovered that the copilot had been removed from one bomber he was incensed: "I emphatically want [the] provision for the copilot left in the airplane."[58] Kenney needed the long-range P-38s so desperately that he asked that no more changes to the aircraft be introduced so that production could be increased, and he fretted that the new aircraft were so different from previous models that they could not be fixed using similar procedures.[59]

Arnold, or more accurately his staff officers who drafted the suggested replies, responded to each of Kenney's complaints. Arnold pointed out that other flying commands needed heating equipment and it was impossible to build the planes without it; he likewise apologized for the gun turrets on the B-24s, but other areas of the world needed them too.[60] As to the elimination of the copilot's position, that had been thoroughly discussed and tested; the consensus was that the advantages outweighed the disadvantages. Arnold impatiently pointed out to Kenney that his command had raised no objection to this proposed modification at the beginning of 1943. Arnold also told Kenney that he had already taken steps to stop changes in the P-38.[61]

Kenney also displayed little appreciation for the tactical differences between his area of operations and others. Based on his experiences in the Southwest Pacific, as well as his previous leanings, Kenney believed that the low-altitude, high-speed tactics of attack aviation were still sound and "in evidence every day all over the world."[62] Arnold informed Kenney that his instincts were flat wrong: "Attack tactics have *definitely not* as you state proven sound 'every day all over the world.'"[63] When these tactics were attempted in Europe, the results were disastrous; on one mission, eleven out of eleven aircraft were lost. Arnold told Kenney that wartime experience demonstrated that their prewar ideas of different attack and fighter aircraft were being swept away by technological changes. While fighters had previously been built only for air-to-air combat, they were now being modified to carry bombs and were used successfully in low-altitude attacks. Arnold concluded that under present conditions there was no such thing as attack aviation. While some aircraft might use low-altitude tactics, the classes of aviation were bombers, fighters, and reconnaissance.[64] Despite Arnold's strong response, Kenney continued to badger the Army Air Forces commander. The problems encountered in Europe, Kenney argued, were the result of a lack of forward-firing guns that could suppress the enemy's antiaircraft fire. He pointed out that his tactics were being used by the Russians and had been used in North Africa with great success.[65] In reality Arnold's analysis of the situation was more correct than Kenney's. Because of the weakness of Japanese antiaircraft fire, especially on merchant ships and around the Japanese airfields, Kenney was unaware of the losses capable of being inflicted on large, low-flying aircraft by such weapons. Low-altitude attacks were being conducted, but they were done by aircraft far different from what Kenney was using.

Kenney's concerns about having enough aircraft for the upcoming operations and his frustrations with Washington were compounded by continuing supply problems. The P-47s finally arrived in Australia, but without droppable external fuel tanks to extend their range. Without those, they could not fly far enough to accomplish any missions in the theater. According to Kenney, "this airplane must have extra gas to go anywhere."[66] Although a drop tank had been developed in the United States, Kenney thought it "junk"; he ordered a prototype 200-gallon tank constructed locally and then contracted with Ford of Australia for mass production.[67] He also suggested moving the radio equipment from behind the pilot to another location and converting the compartment into a 40-gallon fuel tank.[68]

Problems also cropped up when new P-38s arrived outfitted with new very-high-frequency (VHF) radios, a change from earlier models that had been equipped with high-frequency radios (HF). Since all of the ground equipment and the other fighters in the area had the older HF equipment, the new P-38s were unable to communicate with anyone else. All of the updated ground equipment had gone to the other theaters, leaving Kenney's forces out in the cold. Kenney was irritated by the failure to properly supply his units, convinced that it showed a complete lack of concern for the conditions he faced in New Guinea.[69] Arnold promised to send a team of communication experts to the southwest Pacific to help out, an offer that apparently mollified Kenney.[70]

To add insult to injury, new A-20s came to Australia without any forward-firing guns, bomb racks or bomb-bay fuel tanks, making them virtually useless. Kenney's supply officers spent several weeks scrounging the necessary parts to make the aircraft combat-capable.[71] More time was wasted inspecting and cleaning the corrosion saltwater caused to the aircraft carried on the open decks of ships. In some cases the engines were so badly damaged they had to be removed.[72]

Aware of every detail, Kenney was also concerned with stockpiling consumables like fuel and ammunition. The gasoline and bombs his aircraft used had to compete for transportation with the supplies of every other combat organization. Hence, planning sessions often dissolved into negotiations over what should be given transportation priority for an operation. Prior to the attacks on Lae, Kenney warned Whitehead about the need to use fuel stocks from the main airfields at Port Moresby rather than from the forward airfield at Dobodura. Kenney feared that if Dobodura ran low on supplies, they might not be replenished in time for the operations in the Huon Peninsula in early September.[73]

At the end of July, Kenney told Whitehead to stop sending raids to Rabaul and begin concentrating on flying to the area around Lae. In addition to the operations against the Japanese airfields, bombers hunted down the barges now resupplying Lae. Intercepted radio messages again played a key role in pinpointing targets for the airmen. In late May Kenney received information about shipping between Wewak and Lae. Whitehead made arrangements to intercept the ships, but the results were disappointing. The barges were very small and the Japanese fighter cover extremely heavy.[74] In late July Kenney told Whitehead about a "tremendous amount of radio traffic" between two Japanese ground commanders signaling a major troop movement, an indication that barges would be moving between Madang and Finschhafen.[75] As he had in the past, Whitehead used the signals intelligence to reduce the time-consuming reconnaissance patrols and concentrate all of the available aircraft on attacking the proper targets.[76]

Invasion and Air Assault

As Whitehead worked on the air blockade of Lae, Kenney attended the final planning sessions for the amphibious invasion. As in the attacks on Woodlark and Kiriwana, the services disagreed on how air operations should be used in the attack. Kenney stuck to his preference for bombing the Japanese airfields beforehand and putting his aircraft on ground alert the day of the invasion; Barbey continued his insistence on a standing air patrol.[77] Barbey again argued in favor of a dawn attack because an assault in the early hours of the day would allow the convoy to sail under the protection of darkness and surprise the enemy. He felt that naval gunfire could be used to defeat any resistance that the ground forces might encounter. Kenney, on the other hand, promoted a slightly later attack time so that his aircraft could take off in daylight and bomb the defenders' beach positions.[78]

Adjudicating this dispute fell to MacArthur. Although General Blamey of the Australian Army was in command of the operation, he did not have the authority to "order" Kenney to provide an air umbrella or make the decision about the time of the attack; commanders had to cooperate and work around the problem or appeal to MacArthur for a decision.[79] This was the typical arrangement in the Southwest Pacific. Barbey found the system "unorthodox" and "contrary to the principle of unified command" observed in other combat areas. Still, he had to admit it worked.[80]

In the discussions about air operations for the Lae attack, MacArthur sided with Barbey and against his air commander on both counts. Why

MacArthur went against Kenney's advice is unclear. Perhaps he was not entirely comfortable with Kenney's solution and saw merit in Barbey's request. Or he might have been anxious not to cause trouble with the Navy. In any event, Kenney was forced to supply an air umbrella for a dawn attack. The number of aircraft deployed was not quite what Barbey had envisioned; he later complained that there was no standing air cover during the operation, although Kenney had assigned thirty-two aircraft over the convoy.[81] Barbey's victory with MacArthur on this occasion was by no means the end of the debate between him and Kenney over the proper conduct of air support.

While the clash between Barbey and Kenney centered on air plans for the amphibious landing, other factors also played into the animosity. Kenney was disturbed by the lack of cooperation from the Navy in a number of areas, but particularly bothered by the Navy's use, in their antiaircraft shells, of a proximity fuse that they refused to share with him. This fuse was so named because it allowed a bomb or shell to detonate within a certain distance of the target rather than on impact. Kenney hoped to use a proximity fuse to explode bombs above the ground, inflicting more damage on the Japanese bomb shelters. Kenney was aware of the principle behind an air burst and had advocated the development of such a device while at the Tactical School.[82] When he tried to get the naval officers in the Southwest Pacific to share the proximity fuse with him, however, he was rebuffed and assumed the worse. He tried to develop a proximity fuse locally, but with limited success, eventually writing to Arnold for help, commenting that the British seemed more like allies in the war than did the U.S. Navy.[83]

Kenney's distrust of the Navy in this instance was misplaced. The JCS had restricted the use of proximity fuses to situations where there was no possibility that enemy forces could recover the rounds that did not fire, such as over the open ocean.[84] The possibility of the Germans perfecting the proximity fuse, which could then be used against the American bomber formations over Europe, was especially worrisome to Arnold: "The enemy would have more to gain than we through the use of proximity fuses," he told Kenney.[85] While Kenney dropped his request, the explanation did little to dampen his animosity towards the Navy.

Despite interservice disputes and simmering animosity, planning for the invasion of Lae provided some examples of cooperation. While Kenney's land-based radars and the signals intercept sites provided warning about attacks from the west, there were significant gaps to the east and north that could delay warnings of a raid from Rabaul—a shortcoming that could prove particularly damaging in the amphibious invasion at Lae. Wing Commander H. A. Conaghan of the RAAF suggested using the Navy to fill the gap.

The destroyer *Reid* was assigned the task and placed off the coast of New Guinea near Finschhafen with Conaghan aboard to control the aircraft, an instance of using the various parts of each service to meet the overall goal of the operation.[86] The *Reid* turned out to play an important role in the upcoming fight.

The actual amphibious invasion of Lae took place on the morning of September 4, 1943, free, in the beginning, of a Japanese air response. As Allied weathermen had correctly predicted, the Japanese aircraft on New Britain were grounded by fog during the morning hours. While two of their number did find their way through the fog, the heaviest raid did not occur until the afternoon, and Conaghan's proposal paid off. Radar operators on the *Reid* picked up a large formation of aircraft headed toward the invasion force and sent the aircraft flying overhead, as well as those sitting on ground alert, against the attackers. The Japanese lost about a third of the force but managed to down two Allied fighters and damage two landing craft.[87]

Perhaps one of the reasons for Kenney's grudging support of air cover over the amphibious invasion of Lae was his belief that all MacArthur really needed to carry out his offensive in the Southwest Pacific was air power. He was frustrated, though, by the lack of support for his ideas, despite what had been done in the Papuan campaign. Kenney hoped to validate his vision for winning the war through air power with the airborne attack on Nadzab and the advance up the Markham Valley, set to accompany the amphibious attack on Lae.[88]

The original plan for the Nadzab assault had been to parachute a battalion of American troops prior to airlifting the Australian 7th Division in the next day. On further consideration, Whitehead decided that a battalion would not be large enough to capture the field, protect against any Japanese efforts to retake it, and clear away obstacles for the air transports to land the next day. Kenney, who was getting resistance from staff officers in the headquarters about the plan, gladly accepted Whitehead's recommendation to increase the size of the deployment; the 503rd Parachute Infantry Regiment was designated for the attack.[89]

The attack on Nadzab was a tribute to the ability of Whitehead and his staff to plan air operations thoroughly. As Kenney and MacArthur orbited over the landing area, an act that by itself illustrated the level of air dominance the Allies had achieved, six squadrons of B-25s swept through the area in good "attack aviation" fashion, strafing and dropping parafrag bombs to take care of any hidden Japanese defenders. Immediately behind the last B-25 came six A-20s flying line abreast, laying a smoke screen to hide the parachute drop. The ninety-six transport planes, escorted by three groups of fighters, released the entire parachute regiment of 1700 men in a little over two and a half minutes. One plane could not drop because of door problems and three soldiers died when their parachutes failed to open, but otherwise the drop was a success. Five B-17s loaded with supplies and equipment orbited the area, air-dropping fifteen tons throughout the day. Kenney termed the entire operation "a magnificent spectacle."[90]

The next day, transports began flying in the Australian 7th Infantry Division, which immediately marched towards the Japanese positions at Salamaua. Kenney's aircraft struck the Japanese ground forces that threatened the Australian advance towards the Salamaua airfield and the town itself. Sensing the closing trap, General Adachi ordered a withdrawal from Salamaua on September 8 and began moving his forces to the west to a new defensive perimeter.[91] The campaign for Lae was essentially over.

Finschhafen and the Markham Valley

The rapid fall of Lae and the capture of Nadzab assured Allied control of the lower portion of the Huon Gulf and opened up more options for follow-on attacks. Substantial Japanese forces remained in control of the Vitiaz Straits and points west. Allied commanders considered two options. One alternative was to continue inland through the Markham and Ramu river valleys in the interior of the peninsula. Another alternative was to conduct more amphibious assaults along the coast and capture Finschhafen, the next major Japanese outpost. Kenney favored the interior option for several reasons. Operating in the interior offered better locations for forward airfields that could be used to support future operations against Rabaul. The better flying weather in the valley would also allow more continuous air operations against Japanese bases. Just as important, Kenney argued that this option was quicker and would provide greater flexibility for future operations.[92] In short, operating in the interior would highlight the capability of Kenney's airmen to transport, supply, and defend the ground soldiers. That it concomitantly reduced the importance of the Navy and their amphibious craft would not have displeased Kenney.

While Kenney later intimated that he alone supported this move, the Allied Land Forces commander, General Blamey, actually presented the plan of an interior advance to MacArthur at a meeting on September 3, 1943. Undoubtedly Kenney and Blamey had discussed the plan before the formal presentation, because Kenney offered his immediate support and suggested airlifting the troops so they could move further and faster up the valley. Kenney's goal was to have an airfield near Dumpu, at the western end of the valley, in operation by the beginning of November. MacArthur supported Blamey's plan, with Kenney's additions, but also ordered an amphibious assault against Finschhafen to occur simultaneously with the inland advance.[93]

The planning for the amphibious attack on Finschhafen presented some of the recurring sticking points with the Navy. Barbey, upset about losing the two landing craft to a Japanese air attack during the landing at Lae, was adamant about having more aircraft on standing air patrol. He thought Kenney was humbled by his inability to totally protect the landing at Lae; and "after a bit of nudging by MacArthur," Kenney agreed to the request for continuous air patrols.[94] Another point of contention, as before, was the time of the landing. Kenney again argued for an attack after sunrise so that his aircraft could bomb and strafe the beaches prior to the amphibious assault, while Barbey preferred to use the surprise offered by darkness and rely on naval gunfire for protection. This point too was resolved in Barbey's favor. The Finschhafen landing occurred at 4:45 on the morning of September 21, 1943.[95]

As promised, Kenney sent large numbers of aircraft, and the *Reid* again provided the early warning radar coverage for the landing. On September 22, the Japanese threw seventy to one hundred aircraft against the landing. Their timing, however, could not have been worse. The aircraft already on patrol still had an hour's worth of fuel remaining, and their replacements had just taken off—over one hundred Allied fighters met the incoming raid. Allied pilots waded in, shooting down at least forty aircraft. Eight Japanese planes flying at low level were able to sneak in under the radar coverage and bomb the landing force, but fortunately no ships were struck.[96] Barbey believed the experience validated his views of how air power should be used for an amphibious landing, smugly noting, "There is nothing like an air cover of friendly planes to save a convoy from possible disaster."[97] Kenney never admitted that he was wrong and continued to argue against the need for a standing air patrol, but Barbey had made his point.

The invasion of Finschhafen was a violent but brief fight that ended with the capture of the town itself on October 2. This did not end the fighting along the northern shore of the Huon Peninsula, as Japanese ground forces withdrew westward to form a new defensive line in New Guinea. While the attack on Finschhafen was taking place, Kenney's forces continued their recurring missions against ships that might be sending reinforcements or supplies to the Japanese garrisons. The airfields at Wewak and Cape Gloucester in New Britain were also targeted for frequent raids. Although Kenney claimed to have "wiped out" Wewak at the end of August, he continued to send planes there throughout September. In a large attack on September 24, over 100 Allied bombers, escorted by 128 fighters, hit the airfields at Wewak.[98]

These continuing air operations were made possible by the construction of more airfields in the Markham Valley. The capture of Nadzab and the development of four airfields in the vicinity transformed the area into the most forward operating location in Kenny's command. Colonel David W. "Photo" Hutchinson and the staff of the 2nd Air Task Force moved from Marilinan to Nadzab to better control the air activities in the Markham Valley.[99] Hutchinson and the commander of the Australian 7th Infantry Division, General Vasey, headed a well-integrated air-ground team that cleared Japanese troops from the interior of the Huon Peninsula and advanced about 150 miles in just two weeks.

The plan for moving inland required close cooperation between air and ground forces as the transports moved Australian troops in before the Japanese could delay or stop the Allied advance. The plan was first tried with thirteen air transports flying 250 soldiers to Kaiapit, where they met and defeated a small Japanese patrol. The air movement surprised the Japanese and effectively blocked the Markham Valley from the garrison retreating from Lae, forcing them into the mountainous terrain. Trapped between the deadly mountains and Allied control of the valley, the Japanese lost 2,600 men and all of their heavy weapons during the trek.[100]

Laying claim to the rest of the interior valley followed the same general air-ground pattern as the move to Kaiapit. Infantry troops would be flown into an area by Hutchinson's transports, covered overhead by fighters, which could also be used to counter any threatening ground advances. As the infantry eliminated any enemy presence around the field, transports flew in additional troops, supplies, guns, and ammunition, while evacuating the sick and wounded. As this area was secured, a spot ahead was being scouted and a landing site selected for a repetition of the operation. Although the distances between landing sites was often not far, the use of aircraft allowed the Australians to advance faster than the opposing Japanese forces could build fortifications or defensive strongpoints. [101]

By the end of September, Australian ground forces had advanced as far as the intersection of the Gusap and Ramu rivers, beating Kenny's prediction by more than a month. This location was transformed into a large base complex, designated Gusap, and became home to Kenny's 3rd Air Task Force, commanded by Colonel Donald "Fighter" Hutchinson (so called to distinguish him from Colonel "Photo" Hutchinson, the commander of the 2nd Air Task Force).[102] The Australians were quite pleased with the operation and the work of the fighter and transport aircraft in the 2nd Air Task

Force. They felt that the close liaison between the air and ground units produced through this arrangement and the mobility afforded the ground forces served as a model for future operations.[103] Because the Australians relied on Kenney's air force for transportation as well as supplies and protection, in one sense this campaign depended on air power. In another sense, however, the airmen depended on the ground soldiers. Without them it would have been impossible to capture or protect the airfields and move forward. In truth it exhibited the best in using the strengths of two different forms of combat power. The result was that the operations moved Kenney's air bases, and the ability to provide air cover, closer to the western portion of New Guinea and New Britain, the areas of the next operation.[104]

Striking Rabaul

In keeping with the plan outlined by the JCS in March 1943, MacArthur's ground operations were temporarily halted after the invasion of Finschhafen and attention focused on Admiral Halsey's South Pacific command invasion of Bougainville. A prerequisite for this move was to significantly reduce the Japanese air strength in the region. Halsey, Kenney, and their respective planners met in September 1943 to work out the details for a series of combined air attacks on the Japanese air strength.

Rather than concentrate on Rabaul, the source of the Japanese strength, Halsey and his staff suggested that Kenney's forces hit all of the Japanese bases in the area during the last two weeks of October. Kenney argued for a more concentrated approach, unifying both commands on Rabaul. Since he knew that any Japanese air strike would raise havoc with the Navy landings on Bougainville scheduled for the end of October, he also agreed to begin bombing Buka to prevent any large air buildup there and told Whitehead to "keep an eye on Kavieng" but not to bomb it unless absolutely necessary.[105]

Although the majority of the previous strikes on Rabaul had been done at night or in the early morning (with the exception of General Walker's ill-fated flight), Whitehead had convinced Kenney that they should shift to daytime attacks. Whitehead based his recommendation on the increasing night loss rate and the decreasing impact of the bombing. Searchlights and anti-aircraft guns installed at Rabaul had turned it into "a very difficult night target."[106] By July Whitehead was losing "almost 5 percent" of the aircraft on night missions, and termed the almost 7 percent loss rate at night of the specially modified B-25s "expensive."[107] He attributed the losses to both accidents and the Japanese defenses, telling Kenney that he would prefer daylight missions that could bring some significant results even at the risk of heavier losses.[108] Whitehead also argued that the capture of Woodlark and Kiriwana Islands, and the subsequent construction of airstrips, made it possible for him to use one hundred fighters to escort the bombers to Rabaul during daytime, which would reduce the risk from Japanese fighters.[109] Kenney was overwhelmed by the logic of Whitehead's arguments. The situation had clearly changed, something that Whitehead grasped faster than Kenney. Kenney was not one to stick with something for the sake of ego, so he decided that the change to daylight bombing was in order.[110]

ULTRA intercepts were again a key factor in determining the timing of the move against Rabaul. As Kenney focused on the Japanese air strength at Wewak during the fighting in New Guinea, intercepted messages kept him apprised of the Japanese strength at Rabaul. The increase in the number of aircraft at Rabaul was linked to plans for a Japanese air offensive, called the "E" operation, against the Allies.[111] A photo reconnaissance flight on October 11 confirmed the presence of 294 Japanese planes on the airfields around Rabaul.[112] Although not scheduled to begin his attacks on Rabaul until later in the month, Kenney moved against the airfields the next day. Intelligence, together with the presence of Halsey's forces, made it possible for Kenney to ignore this target for months at a time and then return when it was most advantageous. If he had not amassed his aircraft for an attack on October 12, the Japanese might well have wreaked havoc during the landings at Bougainville.

The strike on October 12 was one of the largest and most complicated in the air war in the Southwest Pacific: 70 B-24s, 107 B-25s, and 12 Australian Beaufighters flew from New Guinea to Rabaul, escorted by 117 P-38s, which were serviced and refueled by the RAAF on the newly prepared airfield on Kiriwana Island. Although it was an enormous attack force by the standards of the theater, the detailed planning was done not at Kenney's headquarters but at the 1st Air Task Force, causing one War Department observer to comment on the "flexibility" of this kind of organization.[113] The low-altitude attack at Rabaul caught the Japanese by surprise. With comparatively few losses, Allied airmen claimed 3 large ships and 43 smaller ships sunk, 26 planes shot down in the air, and at least 100 aircraft destroyed on the ground.[114] As usual, Japanese reports tended to minimize the damage and listed considerably lower totals: 3 ships sunk or burning, 29 ships damaged, 15 aircraft destroyed, and 11 damaged.[115] Despite the disparity in the damage reports, Japanese officers interviewed after the war agreed that this was one of the most effective attacks on Rabaul and that large numbers of aircraft were heavily damaged on the ground at the Vuankanau airfield.[116]

Kenney continued the strikes on Rabaul through the rest of October, but bad weather after the initial raid on October 12 frustrated the efforts. Although many of his aircraft had moved to the northern coast of New Guinea, thunderstorms along the route, particularly over the Solomon Sea, hampered efforts to hit Rabaul. If aircraft tried to fly through the storms, they encountered vicious turbulence that disoriented the pilots and caused structural damage to the aircraft. Whitehead himself had encountered such problems once with an experienced bomber crew and issued strict guidelines to avoid flights through thunderstorms.[117] Although shut out of Rabaul, aircraft continued to fly to other areas, though still hindered by problems with the weather. On October 16, eight aircraft covering a group of naval ships in the Finschhafen area were unable to get back to their bases in the Markham Valley due to weather. All the aircraft and about half of the pilots were lost, causing Whitehead to emphasize a point he had repeatedly made: "Weather is still our greatest enemy."[118] By the end of the war Kenney's command had lost almost as many aircraft to accidents, caused largely by the weather, as to enemy action.[119]

The weather between New Guinea and Rabaul finally cleared near the end of October, and Kenney's flyers returned to the various targets at Rabaul.[120] Despite this sustained effort, and strikes from Admiral Halsey, the Japanese air strength at Rabaul continued to grow. Admiral Koga, Yamamoto's successor as commander of the combined fleet, dispatched 250 to 300 aircraft from Truk to stop the landings at Bougainville; and on November 1 the Japanese made three separate raids against the landing force, slowing the unloading of the men and equipment.[121] On November 2, Allied Air Forces returned to Rabaul, but with grim results. Despite thorough tactical planning for the mission, which included the use of phosphorous bombs to create a smoke screen from the antiaircraft guns, the Japanese met the raiders with fierce opposition. Kenney lost 9 of 75 B-25s sent to Rabaul and 9 of the accompanying 57 P-38s. In addition, 4 more aircraft crashed before they could make it back to their bases.[122] He later termed it "the toughest fight Fifth Air Force encountered in the whole war," and Whitehead characterized it as "a real brawl."[123] Some of the losses were the result of the low-altitude attacks that Kenney had so ardently championed. On this occasion the heavy gunfire from the ships at anchor proved deadly and accounted for all the B-25 losses. Kenney had also seriously underestimated the number of fighters the Japanese had moved into Rabaul, and the P-38s met about twice their number in the sky.[124] All in all, it was a rough day for Kenney's airmen.

Perhaps to compensate for the heavy losses and build up morale, Kenney boasted of the results claimed by the aviators: 114,000 tons of Japanese shipping destroyed or damaged, 85 airplanes out of commission, and 300,000 tons of supplies lost. "Never in the history of warfare," Kenney later wrote, "had so much destruction been wrought upon the forces of a belligerent nation so swiftly and at such little cost to the victor."[125] In truth, the results, at least numerically, belie these optimistic reports: the Japanese lost about 20 aircraft and 5,000 tons of shipping, while Kenney's losses were considerable.[126] In the end the most important outcome of the attacks was not the numbers Kenney cited, but the fact that the mission forced the Japanese aircraft around Rabaul to remain there to defend against Kenney's raiders. Anchored at Rabaul, they could not interfere with Halsey's landing force at Bougainville.[127]

Kenney's forces returned to Rabaul on November 5 for a combined raid with Halsey's carrier fleet that illustrated the limits of combining forces.[128] Halsey's aircraft hit the airfields at 11:30 in the morning, and Kenney's bombers appeared an hour later and bombed the town of Rabaul itself. The intense reaction put up three days earlier had taken its toll—Kenney could put up only twenty-five bombers. Halsey's raid had drawn off most of the Japanese defenders, and Kenney only lost one aircraft.[129] Halsey, who may not have known of Kenney's earlier losses, was incensed by the lack of effort and "resented the feebleness of his [Kenney's] support at this critical time."[130] Weather continued to play havoc with the attacks on Rabaul and forced the cancellation of many missions. Fittingly, the last effort at a combined operation with Halsey's forces to Rabaul on November 11 was hampered by bad flying conditions.[131]

Despite his claims, Kenney's attacks most assuredly did not "wipe out" Rabaul, but by the end of November Allied dominance in the sky and on the sea ended Rabaul's effectiveness as a barrier to the Allied advance. The Japanese made small attempts to send matériel to the garrison, and the Allies continued their bombing attacks, but by March 1944 there were few ships and no fighter aircraft left to defend the once mighty bastion of Rabaul.[132]

Arnold and Kenney

Kenney's successes in the fall of 1943 against New Guinea and Rabaul were welcome news to General Arnold in Washington. Kenney's complaints and the disagreements between the two men in certain areas to the contrary, Arnold still had great respect for Kenney's ideas.[133] "Your letters are always a great help, George," Arnold told him. "You are doing great things."[134] Perhaps the strongest evidence of Arnold's esteem for Kenney came in a personal letter Arnold wrote in October 1943, asking for Kenney's suggestions about the use of air power in the cross-channel invasion of Europe. Arnold turned to Kenney for advice, he said, because "there has probably been more ingenuity displayed in your operations than those in any other theater."[135]

After outlining the general situation in Europe, Arnold asked Kenney to consider how the aircraft in England should "be employed in order to get their full effectiveness in the Trans-Channel operations."[136] While Arnold may have been prompted to write because of the successes in the Southwest Pacific, he was also influenced by events in Europe occurring at the same time. In August 1943, the American bomber force in Europe began their first large raids into the heart of Germany. On August 17, 315 bombers, flying without escorting fighters, struck the aircraft plants at Regensburg and Schweinfurt. The results were disastrous: 60 bombers and 600 men, almost 20 percent of the attacking force, were lost. Throughout the summer bombers made several more raids deep into Germany, again with heavy losses. The worst mission of that year occurred on October 14, just three days after Arnold's letter to Kenney requesting advice on the air war in Europe. On that day, 26 percent of the bombers were lost.[137] In comparison, Kenney's heavy losses on November 2 amounted to just over 10 percent of the attack force.

Kenney's reply to Arnold's request was straightforward and provided insight into his view of air warfare. "I stick to one basic principle," he admitted, "get control of the air situation before you try anything else."[138] Kenney suggested that the best way to accomplish that goal was to attack aircraft on the ground and "entice the enemy fighters into combat and destroy them in the air."[139] Kenney recited the recipe he had found successful in the Pacific: attacking airfields at low altitude by strafing targets and dropping the parafrag bomb. Kenney stressed that the bombers should be accompanied by sufficient fighter protection, as a rule of thumb at least twice the number of suspected enemy aircraft. He stressed that bombers should attack targets that the opposing air force would be forced to defend, something that was not yet being done in Europe. The primary objectives of these attacks were not so much the bomber's target, although that too might be important, but the hostile enemy fighters. Kenney admitted that his plan sounded simple, and it restated many of the common ideas in the service, but in reality he found it a "long and difficult job."[140] Kenney closed with a comment about how he viewed the situation in the fall of 1943: "I realize that I am advocating a different scheme of air operation than that now going on in Europe. I realize too that the thesis that Germany may be crushed and forced to capitulate by massed bombing of her industrial homeland may prove to be the correct one by the close of 1943. Frankly I do not believe it but then I do not know the situation in Germany."[141]

It is tempting to say that Kenney's suggestions had an immediate impact on air operations in Europe, but that assertion is difficult to prove. Arnold was grateful for Kenney's comments and passed parts of the letter on to officers on his staff as well as to Army Chief of Staff General George Marshall and the chief British planner for the cross-channel operation.[142] In addition, he sent portions of Kenney's plan to Major General Lewis Brereton, who was in England developing the air plan for the invasion.[143] Kenney later met with Eisenhower and explained his ideas further. When Eisenhower asked for one of Kenney's airmen to go to Europe to take part in the air operations, Kenney sent Brigadier General Freddie Smith, the commander of the 1st Air Task Force.[144]

Still, the ultimate impact of these messages remains difficult to determine. Certainly Kenney was not the only airman to think along these lines, and it would be easy to exaggerate his influence on events in other theaters. But it is interesting to note that the tactics used in Europe in early 1944 to gain air superiority closely paralleled Kenney's ideas. By that time American fighters had enough range to escort bombers deep inside Germany; bombers attacked targets such as Berlin, sure to draw a reaction from the German defenders. A recent study of the air offensive in Europe concludes, "The major contribution of strategic bombing by June 1944 was its role in bringing about the weakening of the Luftwaffe's fighter arm, especially day fighters, through attrition."[145] Kenney was probably not the least bit surprised.

Cape Gloucester

Although Kenney committed most of his force to the attacks on Rabaul in October and November, missions in New Guinea continued unabated, stretching the force thin. Whitehead stressed the efforts he was committed to: naval forces around Finschhafen would "squawk to high heaven" at any reduction in the air patrols, and transports were still flying supplies to units in the Markham valley. In addition, they needed to guard against Japanese air attacks from Wewak.[146] Although weakened by the previous strikes, the Japanese continued to bring aircraft forward. In the middle of October, Kenney and Whitehead began to receive warnings about the Japanese buildup. By October 18, just after they started their sustained attacks on Rabaul, they knew an attack on New Guinea was imminent.[147] On November 6, the Japanese struck, destroying four P-39s and damaging twenty-one others at

Nadzab and strafing the airfield at Bena Bena.[148] Despite the addition of more signal intercept sites in New Guinea, there was no warning prior to this raid, and the Japanese escaped unmolested.[149] As Whitehead pointed out, having intelligence about the enemy's actions was only part of the equation; one also needed the forces to dedicate to the mission. "We knew that Wewak was building up but were unable to do anything about it."[150]

As Whitehead wrestled with the problems in New Guinea, Kenney started working on plans for invasions aimed at securing the western half of New Britain and taking control of the Admiralty Islands, completing the encirclement of Rabaul. In the summer of 1943, however, a study by the JCS concluded that the Allies' ability to control the sea and the sky made an invasion of Rabaul unnecessary. The JCS recommended simply neutralizing the base by taking all of the positions around it, a proposal approved by President Roosevelt and Prime Minister Churchill at the Quebec strategy conference in August 1943.[151]

Based on the original guidance, MacArthur's scheme had been to invade the western end of New Britain at Cape Gloucester and conduct another landing at Gasmata. The cancellation of the Rabaul invasion and the ability to control the straits without a ground attack made it possible to reexamine the need for these landings. Kenney argued strongly against sticking with the plans and urged MacArthur to cancel the attacks.[152] Other members of MacArthur's staff, as well as the naval and ground force commanders, all disagreed with Kenney's assessment and felt that controlling Cape Gloucester was necessary. Ultimately, MacArthur rejected Kenney's counsel. In the end an attack at Arawe, closer to the western end of the island, was substituted for one on Gasmata, and American troops landed there on December 15. The landing at Cape Gloucester followed shortly afterwards, on December 26, 1943.[153]

In addition to his concerns about the necessity of the invasions, Kenney faced more problems with the Navy in planning the air operations. Barbey continued to worry about the lack of air cover for the amphibious ships. Although by now Kenney had acquiesced to supplying an air umbrella for the invasion force, it was not enough to satisfy Barbey, who wanted control of even more aircraft.[154] For his part, Kenney was aggravated because his airmen were taking fire from American ships every time they flew one of these air cover missions. Brigadier General Freddie Smith, the commander of 1st Air Task Force and Kenney's planning representative, suggested that the ships not fire at any aircraft over the convoy at daybreak during the invasion *unless* the aircraft was positively identified as an enemy, but Barbey refused to go along with the suggestion. Kenney agreed with Smith's idea, and the problem was resolved after a meeting between Kenney and Vice Admiral Thomas C. Kinkaid, the new Allied Naval Forces commander. Kinkaid, who had seen action in the Battles of the Coral Sea and Midway and recently served as the commander of the North Pacific Force in the Aleutian Islands, arrived in Australia in late November 1943 as the replacement for Vice Admiral Arthur S. Carpender.[155] Together, Kenney and Kinkaid managed to solve the problem. Kenney promised to fly enough air cover missions and Kinkaid instituted a more restrictive firing policy for naval gunners.[156]

The usual efforts preceded the invasion at Cape Gloucester: bombing the Japanese airfields at Wewak and flying dozens of sorties against the barges forwarding supplies from Rabaul. From November 19 to December 25, Kenney's forces focused on the defensive positions around Cape Gloucester, flying 1,845 sorties and dropping 3,926 tons of bombs, an effort that even the perennially skeptical Admiral Barbey termed the "most extensive of any planned to date."[157]

Despite heavy bombing of the Japanese airfields and the early warning afforded by the coastwatchers and the radio interception sites, the Japanese managed to put up stiff resistance to the invasions. Coastwatchers provided warnings of an air raid against the invasion of Arawe on December 16 of at least forty aircraft, followed by thirty more the next day. During the landing on Cape Gloucester on December 25, coastwatchers provided about forty-five minutes of critical warning before the Japanese attacks.[158] Despite the alerts and the Allied air cover, the Japanese were still able to inflict heavy damage. The first raid arrived overhead at about 2:30 in the afternoon. The twenty bombers, escorted by fifty to sixty fighters, sank one destroyer and damaged three others, as well as two landing craft.[159] Later that same day the Japanese were much less successful; of the eighteen torpedo bombers they sent out, all were shot down.[160]

Kenney was elated about the effects of the Allied bombing on the landing and later boasted that the Marines walked ashore with their rifles on their backs.[161] In this instance his claim rang true. The massive and sustained bombardment, coupled with the air blockade around the area, had seriously weakened the Japanese defenders, who retreated inland.[162] While Kenney was naturally delighted with the pre-invasion bombing, he downplayed the less successful aspects of the operation, especially the losses that the Navy suffered. He commented that the loss of one destroyer led Kinkaid to consider the invasion a "flop," an uncharitable comment by Kenney about the Navy's complaint, but a view perhaps prompted by the two B-25s shot down by antiaircraft fire from American forces near the landing beach.[163]

B-29s in the Southwest Pacific

After the landings on Cape Gloucester Kenney returned to Washington for another round of meetings on the future course of the war. MacArthur's portion of the isolation of Rabaul would soon be complete; after Halsey captured Kavieng, Rabaul would be isolated. Kenney arrived in Washington as Army and Navy planners discussed how to dispose of the forces assigned to Halsey's South Pacific theater. Kenney suggested that the 13th Air Force, the name given to the Army Air Force units in Halsey's theater, be transferred to his control and used in MacArthur's drive through western New Guinea and into the Philippines. Arnold agreed in principle to Kenney's idea, but the shift needed the approval of the Joint Chiefs of Staff.[164] Just prior to leaving Washington, Kenney made a return visit to the White House, where he spent two hours with the president, talking about operations in the Southwest Pacific, and presented the president with a book commemorating the November 2 air attack on Rabaul. Kenney found that Roosevelt had a "surprising knowledge" about the area.[165]

During the visit to Washington, Kenney also spent time lobbying Arnold about getting some of the new Boeing B-29 Superfortresses assigned to the Southwest Pacific. The idea for a very-long-range bomber actually preceded American entry into World War II, and the design for the B-29 was submitted in late June 1940. Although the first experimental model of the aircraft did not fly until September 1942, the decision to begin full-scale production of the aircraft had already been made in May 1941.[166] The new plane was a giant for its time, almost 100 feet long and 28 feet high, boasting a wingspan of 141 feet, and promising to deliver heavy firepower. The most impressive aspect of the aircraft, especially from Kenney's perspective, was its range. Engineers initially estimated that it could fly 3,500 miles carrying 8,000 pounds of bombs.[167] The best performance Kenney could coax from the B-24s, with less than half that payload, was a 2,400-mile trip from Darwin, Australia, to the oil refineries at Balikpapan in Borneo, a group of targets he longed to strike.[168]

Kenney's assignment at Materiel Command from 1939 until 1942 exposed him to the specifications and development of the B-29, and during his time in the Pacific he kept abreast of the aircraft's development through his meetings in Washington and correspondence with General Arnold, as well as associates at Materiel Command.[169] A few months after his arrival in Australia, Kenney began campaigning for the new bomber, arguing that the key to victory over Japan was eliminating or neutralizing their ability to use the natural resources found in Borneo, Sumatra, and the Philippines. The best way to accomplish that goal, Kenney concluded, was through air power.[170]

While Kenney presented Arnold with a strategic rationale for assigning B-29s to the Southwest Pacific, he also dropped hints about more mundane matters in the hope that these would help sway Arnold. In late 1942 Kenney had received the first squadron of B-24s and discovered that their wheelbase was four feet wider than the B-17s, forcing engineers to widen all of the taxiways on the airfields in New Guinea. This difficulty prompted Kenney to suggest, "I have no idea what the tread on the B-29 is and suppose that it will be some time before I see one of them, but that will be another thing to remember for airdrome construction."[171]

In the summer of 1943 Kenney queried Army Air Forces headquarters again about the aircraft. In late July, perhaps prompted by reports about the B-29 test flights, he told Arnold, "I assume that I am still to get the first B-29 unit," and requested more details about the aircraft to properly plan for its arrival.[172] In reply, Arnold cautioned Kenney against placing too much emphasis on getting the aircraft: "No units are scheduled for your theater prior to June of next year [1944]." All the same, Arnold intimated that the B-29s might be sent to Australia after that date.[173]

Arnold's answer was a bit deceptive. In reality, he had no plans to send the aircraft to the Southwest Pacific: he intended to use them against the home islands of Japan. As early as March 1943, Arnold had initiated studies in Washington to find bases for the aircraft in the Pacific. Based on assumptions about the date when the aircraft would be ready for combat, the current rate of advance in the Pacific, and the desire to end the war against Japan one year after victory in Europe, air planners concluded that there would not be any Allied-held islands close enough to Japan by the fall of 1944. The other option was to base the aircraft in China. Placing them there would not only bring the Japanese homeland into bombing range, but also improve the morale of the Chinese and, it was hoped, keep them in the war—both important political goals for President Roosevelt.[174] On August 20, 1943, during the Quadrant strategy conference in Quebec, Arnold submitted a proposal to the Combined British and American Chiefs of Staff on basing the B-29s in China for raids against Japan.[175]

Although the initial proposal underestimated the supplies required, the concept of using the aircraft from bases in China had the political support of the president and seemed to offer another avenue for quickly defeating Japan. At the Sextant strategy conference in November, Roosevelt formally approved the idea; on November 10, 1943, he asked Prime Minister Winston Churchill and China's president, Generalissimo Chiang Kai-shek, for assistance. The Combined Chiefs of Staff agreed to supply construction units for building the air bases and begin bombing operations by May 1, 1944. The Chinese bases, however, offered only an interim solution; capturing the Marianas Islands in the Central Pacific was the preferred option, and the Combined Chiefs of Staff estimated that the B-29s would be flying from there by the end of 1944.[176]

Although Kenney was in the dark about many of the exact details, he knew enough people to receive hints that Australia was out of the running for the new bombers. In October 1943 he complained, "I have been hearing a lot of rumors recently about the destination of the B-29s . . . I understood that the first B-29s were coming to me."[177] Perhaps in an effort to avoid a confrontation with both Kenney and MacArthur, Arnold did not answer the question directly, but instead asked Kenney how he intended to use the aircraft. Kenney replied swiftly, outlining his ideas on shutting down the Japanese oil production centers at Palembang and Balikpapan, as well as using the bombers against shipping. Kenney promised that disrupting the flow of oil, in combination with the recapture of the Philippines, would end the war quickly.[178] Kenney also highlighted the problems Arnold would encounter in using the aircraft in other areas. Supply problems in China would hamper operations, he prophesied, and it would prove difficult to build air bases in the Marianas.[179]

Kenney obviously thought that his letter would be convincing, as he pushed preparations to receive the aircraft. Engineers received detailed information on the B-29, including its weight and turning radius and the desired airfield dimensions.[180] Kenney began his own investigation of airfields and areas for supply and repair depots to handle the mammoth aircraft, telling one officer that although the decision to send the aircraft to Australia had not yet been made, it was possible that they might have thirty-five B-29s as early as March 1944.[181]

Soon afterwards, however, Kenney received word that none of the aircraft would be headed to the Southwest Pacific. Major General Barney Giles, currently serving as Arnold's chief of staff, sent Kenney the news in November 1943. Giles had known Kenney from their days at 4th Air Force in early 1942, when Kenney had recommended Giles as his successor. With Arnold away at the Sextant conference, it fell to Giles to tell Kenney about the decision and offer some conciliation. "Your letter," Giles told him, "constituted a very strong case for your theater," but "after weighing all of the factors involved, allocation of the B-29s to the Fifth Air Force is not contemplated."[182] Despite the seemingly firm rejection, Giles added a postscript to the letter, urging Kenney to continue planning for the aircraft. "There is always the chance the decision may be changed," Giles counseled, and he felt confident that Kenney would eventually get some B-29s.[183] While Giles's comment was intended to mollify Kenney, the rejection was clear. Undaunted, Kenney pressed ahead.

During his trip to Washington a month later Kenney must have been hoping for a reprieve on the B-29s. On January 14 he met with Arnold and discussed, among other items, the issue of sending B-29s to Australia. An observer at one meeting noted: "General Arnold could not commit himself on routing any B-29s via Australia. He will think about it."[184] Kenney, however, took a more optimistic view of Arnold's comments, somehow getting the impression that fifty B-29s were bound for Australia.[185] He returned upbeat about the prospect of obtaining the aircraft, asking the engineers to give immediate priority to building an air depot and lengthening the runways at Darwin to handle the new bombers, a feat they estimated would take eight to nine months to complete.[186]

Not long after his return to the Southwest Pacific, Kenney, along with Sutherland and Chamberlin, attended a conference at Pearl Harbor to discuss operations in the Pacific for the next year. The offensive through the Central Pacific, commanded by Nimitz, was slated to attack the Marianas Islands and Formosa enroute to Tokyo, while MacArthur would continue his advance through New Guinea, then move north and liberate the Philippines before invading Japan. Although both routes would defeat the Japanese, the end would come much more quickly if the forces were concentrated along one axis. One of the key arguments for invading the Marianas was to provide a base for the B-29s. Kenney firmly disagreed, telling the gathering that missions by the B-29s from the Marianas Islands would simply be a "series of costly stunts."[187] The two staffs started out favoring their different plans, but by the end of the meeting they both favored combining their forces and recapturing the Philippines.[188] Kenney termed the last meeting a "regular love fest" and felt that their recommendations would force the JCS to consolidate forces under MacArthur.[189] While Kenney's opinion was just one factor in the outcome, coming from MacArthur's air commander the words certainly carried a lot of weight. It is not hard to imagine that his remarks were not well received by General Arnold or other members of air staff in Washington.

At the conclusion of the meetings in Hawaii, Sutherland flew to Washington to sell the JCS on the revised plan.[190] Despite the unanimity reached by the planners in the Pacific, Sutherland faced a tough sales job in Washington. Chief of Naval Operations Ernest King strongly supported the central Pacific thrust, as did Arnold.[191] Conceivably, Kenney's hopes for the B-29 could have received a boost from a study done by the Joint War Plans Committee about this time that concluded that prior to capturing the Marianas Islands, the bombers would be better employed in the Southwest Pacific and not China; but their recommendation came to naught. The president had already committed the airplanes to China.[192]

Reconnaissance in Force

As Sutherland winged his way to Washington, Kenney returned to the Southwest Pacific for the invasion of the Admiralty Islands scheduled for late April 1944. The Admiralties are a collection of islands about 200 miles northeast of Wewak. The two most important islands in the chain are Manus and Los Negros. Capturing Manus Island would completely sever the air and sea lanes to Rabaul and provide a deep harbor necessary for future operations. In addition, the Admiralty Islands had two airfields that could prove useful: Lorengau airfield on Manus and Momote on Los Negros, with a 5,000-foot runway.[193] MacArthur originally planned on invading Manus in April, and Whitehead had already started the standard pattern of preinvasion bombing. On February 6, 1944, a postflight report from a mission over the island mentioned that there had been no enemy antiaircraft firing. Other missions soon reported the same. On February 23 Whitehead sent three B-25s to the island with orders to circle at low altitude, trying to draw fire. After ninety minutes at low altitude the crews reported seeing no signs of life and concluded that the island had been deserted. In reality it was a clever bit of deception—the Japanese commander had ordered his men to stop firing and stay out of sight.[194]

Kenney saw this as a golden opportunity with comparatively few risks. From his most recent visit to Washington he knew that General Marshall was anxious to put more pressure on Japan and wanted to quicken the pace of the war.[195] A swift grab of the Admiralties would speed up the course of the war and might eliminate other landings. Equally important, an impressive success in the Admiralties might pay dividends with the planners in Washington and swing the ongoing debate towards defeating Japan by invading the Philippines. At the same time Kenney saw relatively few risks for such a bold move. His reports indicated the island was deserted and could be invaded immediately. To prevent any embarrassment in case things went wrong, Kenney suggested calling the invasion a "reconnaissance in force" or a raid.[196] Even if there were Japanese troops present, he was confident that Allied domination of the sea and sky made it possible to take the chance of the invasion. The ground troops could be evacuated in case anything went wrong, and Kenney's faith in air power gave him great confidence in the ability of his aviators to forestall any problems. As soon as possible after gaining control of the airfield he wanted to fly in engineers "to put the strip in shape for transport operations for . . . bringing in supplies or reinforcing troops in an emergency,"[197] a contingency he did not think very likely "as the Navy seems willing to consider the Bismarck Sea our own private lake."[198] MacArthur, who quickly grasped the implications of the move, did not need much prompting. On February 25 he issued the orders for a reconnaissance in force, and four days later the first troops landed.

Despite the flight reports of no enemy activity, other evidence indicated a large Japanese presence on the islands. Reports from advance parties and ULTRA had indicated that Kenney's assessment was wrong and the place was, as one report put it, "lousy with Japs."[199] Kenney, however, was committed to the plan and downplayed the contrary evidence, arguing that "the report meant nothing" and "if there are 25 Nips in those woods at night, the place would be 'lousy with Japs.'" He rationalized that the "scouts landed right where the Japs should have been to keep away from the airdrome area and where they have been bombed."[200] Although usually a ready consumer of ULTRA, on this occasion he trusted his instincts about the benefits and risks of the attacks rather than intelligence indications that provided a contrary view.

Kenney was certain that there would be no interference from Japanese aircraft. The bombing of the Japanese airfields at Wewak had turned it into little more than a staging base, and there were no working aircraft on either Los Negros or Manus. Just to be sure, he asked Whitehead to put some P-38s over the landing area the morning of the attack and to bomb the airfields at Wewak.[201] As added protection Kenney also had available the services of the RAAF's 1st Wireless Unit, which had moved to Nadzab in early February to monitor the Japanese radio frequencies and provide early warning of any Japanese air move against the landing.[202] Kenney's hunch about a possible air reaction was confirmed the next day. Analysis of signals intelligence confirmed that there had been no movement of Japanese aircraft from Hollandia to Wewak.[203]

In many ways Kenney's recommendation was fortuitous. Although the Japanese had not abandoned the island, the commander had moved his forces on to the large island of Manus to defend Seeadler Harbor, the most likely site for an American amphibious landing. Instead, MacArthur's reconnaissance in force sailed through Hyane Harbor on Los Negros and quickly surrounded the airfield at Momote. The smaller "reconnaissance in force" surprised the Japanese, who were awaiting the usual massive seaborne invasion force.[204] Although it took until the end of March to clear Los Negros and fighting did not officially end on Manus until the middle of May, the main objective, the Mamote airfield, was ready for use in March. In short, Kenney's suggestion was extremely risky, but it outflanked the Japanese main force and, most important, conformed to MacArthur's desires to speed up his advance.[205]

THE CAPTURE of the Admiralties and Halsey's operations in Kaveing completed the encirclement of Rabaul. Although the base still held almost 100,000 troops, without control of the sea and air they could do little to affect operations. They were left to "wither on the vine." Kenney anticipated that the stepping-stone pattern of operations that had gotten MacArthur's forces this far would remain the same throughout the drive westward in New Guinea and into the Philippines.

The future would present Kenney with some new problems. His forces would grow, but he would continue to encounter difficulty getting adequate numbers of aircraft into combat. More important, the next operations would require Kenney to mesh his operations more closely with the Navy, a situation that brought new challenges.

EIGHT

WESTWARD TO HOLLANDIA

January 1944 to October 1944

"I consider it unwise to rely on carrier units completely."

Capturing the Admiralty Islands marked the end of MacArthur's efforts to isolate Rabaul. With his right flank secure, he could now move westward in New Guinea and on to the Philippines. Based on the previous pattern of MacArthur's operations, dictated largely by the range of Kenney's aircraft, the next move would occur someplace around Hansa Bay in New Guinea. The gamble to take the Admiralties actually marked the beginning of a new phase in MacArthur's fighting, one that placed an increased emphasis on the speed of the advance. Although Kenney continued to advocate the same plan for air operations, MacArthur opted for a more aggressive approach that would depend on carrier-based aircraft and introduce new problems for air planners.

Planning for Hollandia

The predictable pattern of MacArthur's operations changed dramatically in early March, when he announced that he would bypass the strong enemy force defending Hansa Bay in favor of a two-division assault at Hollandia sometime between April 15 and 24, 1944.[1] Hollandia, located in an area known as the Netherlands New Guinea, was lightly garrisoned by the Japanese and seemed an ideal location for building a large base capable of supporting future operations. The area of Hollandia contained two deep bays, Humboldt Bay to the east, the only natural anchorage in the vicinity, and Tanahmerah Bay to the west. The two bodies of water were separated by the Cyclops mountains, a range that had peaks up to 7,000 feet. To the south of the mountain range was a flat plain leading to Lake Sentani and continuing into the rolling hills and jungles of New Guinea. Although there were few combat ground troops in the Hollandia area, the Japanese were using it as a rear supply base and hacked four airfields out of the jungle on the Lake Sentani plain to defend their defensive perimeter in western New Guinea (Figure 3).[2]

On March 5, about a week after the initial landing in the Admiralties, MacArthur radioed the JCS about his change of plans. At the time, MacArthur's chief of staff, Major General Richard Sutherland, was in Washington trying to sell the JCS on the plan agreed to by the Pacific planners in January to consolidate the Allied advance through the Philippines. Although the JCS approved MacArthur's plan to skip Hansa Bay, they maintained the two-pronged approach to defeating Japan; MacArthur would advance through New Guinea to the Philippines while Nimitz went into the Marianas Islands. Kenney was "dumbfounded" by a decision that rejected the option that he and the other planners in the Pacific considered sound.[3] Kenney was also upset because the verdict meant an end to his hopes for B-29s. Throughout Sutherland's visit Kenney continued to attack the idea of basing B-29s in the Marianas for raids on Japan. He thought that the problems involved with supplying the giant aircraft made the plan "absurd" and that the attacks would prove to be little more than "nuisance raids."[4] Ironically, the day prior to this decision by the JCS, Kenney sent a message to Washington reporting that the airfield at Darwin would be ready for the B-29s on May 1, 1944.[5] Despite this seemingly clear rejection of his plans, Kenney did not give up hope and continued preparations for the big bomber. At the moment, however, most of Kenney's attention was focused on the upcoming invasion of Hollandia.

Despite the isolation of Rabaul, the Japanese remained determined to hold their defensive perimeter in western New Guinea. The commander of the Japanese 18th Army, Lieutenant General Adachi, anticipated that MacArthur's next move would take place under the cover of Kenney's air and concentrated his forces near Hansa Bay.[6] The Japanese also redoubled their efforts at reestablishing control of the air in New Guinea. They set a goal in 1944 of producing 40,000 planes and increasing the number of airfields in western New Guinea from 27 to 120. In reality, both plans suffered from shortages in material and manpower. Aircraft production in the first four months of 1944 lagged behind the forecast, and airfield construction got nowhere as shortages in heavy equipment, materials, and transportation continued to plague the Japanese air war efforts. Of the 35 new airfields slated for construction in the first part of the year, only 9 were completed by April 1944.[7] The continuing inability of the Japanese to build new airfields helped simplify

Kenney's operational decisions. The limited number of targets meant that he could afford to hit every one, often several times. Since the Japanese were forced to pack their aircraft onto relatively few fields, they were extremely vulnerable to an Allied air attack.

MacArthur gave the impression that his move to bypass Hansa Bay for Hollandia was a bold stroke of genius, and he emphasized that fact by calling the main task force "Reckless." In truth the decision was based on extensive knowledge about the Japanese plans and the disposition of their forces. Despite the continuing efforts by Central Bureau to collect and decode Japanese radio communications, during 1943 they had been able to exploit, to any great extent, only the codes and ciphers used by the Japanese Navy. In April 1943 Central Bureau broke the Japanese Army Water Transport Code, an important break in pinpointing shipments sent over water. The codes used by the Japanese Army had proven impossible to crack until the Allies obtained a trunk full of Japanese Army code books in January 1944. Soon Central Bureau was reading almost every important message sent to the Japanese forces in New Guinea. When MacArthur made his decision to bypass Hansa Bay and attack Hollandia, he did so knowing the bulk of the Japanese 18th Army was waiting for him at Hansa Bay, while Hollandia was only lightly garrisoned.[8]

While Kenney supported the idea of speeding up MacArthur's advance, and had planned on proposing that MacArthur bypass Hansa Bay, he did not envision leaping beyond the range of his aircraft all the way to Hollandia.[9] The new proposal would give Kenney responsibility for eliminating the Japanese air strength at Wewak and Hollandia, but only a limited role in the amphibious assault—naval aircraft carriers would cover the invasion. Neither Kenney nor his deputy, Whitehead, was happy about this turn of events. Although many of their concerns about relying on the carriers could be dismissed as simply professional jealousy or bureaucratic bickering, factors that certainly had some impact, both men also had legitimate worries about the plan. Kenney argued that carrier-based aircraft, in comparison to his land-based bombers, could spend only a short time over the targets, had limited range, and carried small bomb loads, which did not provide enough firepower during the bombardment preceding an amphibious attack.[10] In addition, the carriers themselves had to periodically stop flying operations to refuel, rearm, and replace lost or damaged aircraft. "Carrier based aircraft,"

Figure 3 (facing page). Netherlands New Guinea (Office of the Chief Engineer, General Headquarters Army Forces, Pacific, *Engineers of the Southwest Pacific,* vol. 6, *Airfield and Air Base Development* [Washington, D.C.: Government Printing Office], p. 210).

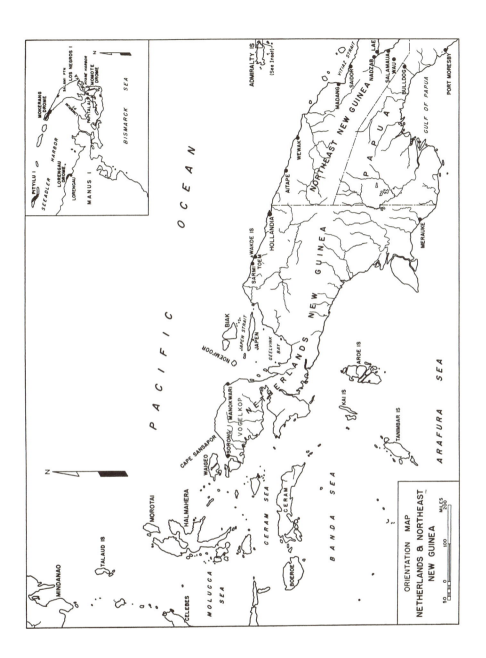

ORIENTATION MAP
NETHERLANDS & NORTHEAST
NEW GUINEA

157

Kenney later remarked, do "not have . . . staying power and therefore do not have the dependability of land-based aircraft."[11]

Although Kenney's assessment contained valid points, he also overlooked some of the benefits involved with the carriers. The carriers could move where they were needed, making the range of the aircraft onboard less important than for aircraft limited to land-based runways. In addition, naval gunfire from other ships in the task force compensated for the small bomb loads Kenney mentioned. The need to temporarily stop operations was, however, an important consideration. Kenney warned that the carriers would not be able to "remain in the Hollandia area for more than a few days."[12] If the airfields in the area were not ready for Kenney's aircraft quickly and the carriers had to leave, a situation he thought likely, then the ground forces would be sitting ducks for Japanese air attacks. To preclude such a fiasco, Kenney asked Whitehead to investigate the possibility of developing airfields at locations short of Hollandia.[13]

Whitehead agreed completely with Kenney's assessment and provided a detailed explanation of the problems involved with the operation; at the same time he investigated two other methods for supporting MacArthur's plan. Whitehead dismissed the engineers' optimistic reports about getting the airfields ready for operations and argued that it would be three weeks after the invasion before the airfields at Hollandia were ready for one fighter group. "We should have no illusions about speedy airdrome construction," he cautioned Kenney. The carriers, however, would have to leave three days after the invasion.[14] To neutralize all of the enemy air bases, cover the invasion force after the carriers departed, and support the ground attack, Whitehead suggested using the airfield at Tadji, 120 miles southeast of the invasion area.[15] Another possibility was to develop an airfield at Manim Island, Wharibe Island, or Wuvulu Island, all just off the north coast of New Guinea and within range of Hollandia for Kenney's planes; but none of these had terrain suitable for an airfield.[16]

Despite Kenney's misgivings, the general outline of the Hollandia plan was accepted in early March, and more detailed planning continued throughout the month. Many of the discussions focused on how to integrate the carriers with Kenney's land-based air. There was no possibility of appointing a single air commander for the invasion. First, such an arrangement would have exceeded the communications capability available at the time. Even within Kenney's own organization there was no way for him to control daily operations at airfields in New Guinea from his headquarters in Brisbane; the distance, weather, and radios simply did not permit that level of centralized control. Instead, he supplied the overall guidance for operations over several days and relied on Whitehead and the air task force commanders to conduct daily flight operations. Perhaps a more insurmountable obstacle to having a single air commander was the attitude of the participants. It is hard to imagine Kenney, with his virulent anti-Navy sentiments, giving Halsey control over the land-based aircraft. Likewise, the Navy would have been loath to surrender control of the carrier aircraft to either MacArthur or Kenney. Apparently neither side gave much thought to the idea of a single air commander; instead the planners concentrated on working out ways to support the invasion without integrating naval and land-based aircraft.[17]

The primary objectives for the Hollandia landings were three airfields located about 15 miles from the coast, just behind the Cyclops Mountains and north of Sentani Lake. Command of the Reckless Task Force was given to Lieutenant General Robert L. Eichelberger, who planned on making a two-pronged pincer attack. The 41st Division would land at Humboldt Bay, on the east side of the Cyclops Mountains, and drive west toward the airfields. Simultaneously, the 24th Division would be put ashore at Tanahmerah Bay and envelop the airfields from the opposite direction. Eichelberger planned the Tanahmerah Bay landing as the main effort, while the task of the 41st Division at Humboldt Bay was to distract and hold any enemy force that might interfere with the drive from the west. As Whitehead had suggested earlier, part of the invasion force would also attack at Aitape and quickly capture the airfield at Tadji. This force, called the Persecution Task force, consisting of two regimental combat teams, would also be in position to block any attempt by the Japanese 18th Army to move westward from Hansa Bay.[18]

Three different groups of aircraft had to be managed for this operation, and the final details for managing their part in the amphibious assault were resolved at a conference on March 23 and 24.[19] One group contained Kenney's Allied Air Forces, the second were aircraft from the 5th Fleet carrier task forces commanded by Vice Admiral Marc A. Mitscher, and the last was the smaller escort carriers normally assigned to Admiral Nimitz's command, but loaned to Admiral Kinkaid, the Allied Naval Forces commander.[20] Since the carriers would not arrive until the day prior to the invasion, Kenney did not have to make any changes to his operations before then. His units would be responsible for reducing the Japanese air threat at Wewak and Hollandia, destroying shipping along the northern coast of New Guinea, and reducing the enemy ground defenses in the Hollandia area. At the same time the 5th Fleet carriers (Task Force 58) would bomb the Japanese air bases in the Caroline Islands. Beginning at 4:30 AM on the day prior to the invasion, 5th Fleet carriers would take over responsibility for operations from just west of Aitape to the main landing areas at Humboldt and Tanahmerah Bay. The aircraft from the escort carriers would remain east of Aitape and cover the landing for the airfield at Tadji. After two days the 5th Fleet carriers would leave the area, and the escort carriers would shift westward and cover the ground forces in the Hollandia area for the next three weeks.[21]

During the time the carriers were in the area, Kenney's units were restricted east of Aitape, unless on missions to areas in western New Guinea far away from the Hollandia area. To keep from being mistaken for enemy aircraft, his aircrews were instructed to remain over land during the hours of darkness. The commanders also agreed that in an emergency the boundary line could be disregarded by common agreement, an arrangement assisted by putting liaison officers on the carriers and in Whitehead's headquarters.[22] This geographical separation of forces might have been the only arrangement possible given the communications ability of the time and the attitude of the participants, but the arrangement codified a tacit agreement not to combine the air units except under extraordinary circumstances.

The Leap West to Hollandia

As planning for the attack continued throughout March, Kenney started air operations aimed at isolating the Japanese. He told Whitehead that his first task was "to take out the air from Wewak to Hollandia and keep it beaten down so that aircraft from the carriers escorting the expedition can handle any Jap attempt to bust up the convoy."[23] The strength of the Japanese air bases in western New Guinea represented a significant threat to the success of the operation, and naval officers were skittish about operating their carriers for an extended period of time in close proximity to enemy air bases.[24] During a meeting in late March, Nimitz reiterated his concerns about the Japanese air threat; Kenney flatly assured the naval officers that he would have the Japanese aircraft "rubbed out" by April 5, a claim that many of the participants in the meeting found difficult to believe.[25]

Kenney assigned specific missions to the various air components he commanded to meet the demand of eliminating the Japanese air threat. A real concern was preventing the Japanese from bringing any more aircraft into the area. Kenney wanted to pin down Japanese air reinforcements that might be flown into Hollandia from further west in New Guinea, the Arafua Sea area, and the Netherlands East Indies; he ordered Bostock and the RAAF to take on that role.[26]

Additional aircraft that had been flying in the South Pacific area under Admiral Halsey helped make Kenney's job easier. During his trip to Washington in January 1944, Kenney lobbied for control of these air units when they finished operations against Rabaul. In March the JCS approved the transfer of 13th Air Force and other Army units from Halsey to the Southwest Pacific.[27] Kenney needed some of the flying units for the attacks against Hollandia and set up 13th Air Task Force as a headquarters. Admiral Halsey agreed to release the 5th and 307th bomber groups in April. Kenney planned on sending them to attack targets in the Admiralty Islands and airfields on Woleai Island to the north, as well as to assist the ground forces in New Britain and to conduct air searches north of the Admiralty Islands.[28] Kenney also convinced Halsey of the need for more long-range reconnaissance aircraft in MacArthur's area, and a squadron of PBY4s (naval B-24s) was moved to the Admiralty Islands. Although these aircraft belonged to the Navy, because they were land-based they followed Kenney's directions for operations, something he had insisted on with all of the land-based naval aircraft.[29] The actions of RAAF Command and 13th Air Task Force were primarily aimed at keeping the Japanese forces to the north and south of New Guinea occupied, while 5th Air Force concentrated on eliminating the Japanese air units along the north coast of New Guinea.

Before tackling the air complex at Hollandia, Kenney first needed to eliminate the Japanese aircraft at Wewak.[30] While Allied domination in the air prevented the Japanese from basing aircraft at Wewak for any period of time, they continued to use the field as a staging base.[31] Kenney was determined to eliminate this option, and throughout March his flyers pounded Wewak with 1,362 sorties and 2,434 tons of bombs. The Japanese put up some feeble resistance, but by the middle of March had abandoned any efforts at maintaining their presence there and retreated westward to Hollandia.[32]

As the flyers bombarded the airfields at Wewak, Kenney began focusing on eliminating the Japanese air bases near Hollandia. His planning was made easier by the exceptionally clear picture obtained through signals intelligence, which kept Kenney apprised of the Japanese buildup of forces in western New Guinea.[33] By the beginning of March the new aircraft flown into Hollandia pushed the total there over 250, but at any one time only about half of those aircraft were available for combat.[34] Kenney relayed the information to Whitehead, who proved more pessimistic about the intelligence, telling Kenney that they were facing twice that number of aircraft.[35] Even if the Japanese were able to concentrate the force as Whitehead feared, the Allies still had a numerical edge over the Japanese. At the end of February there were 803 fighters and 780 bombers in 5th Air Force. While only three-quarters of them were in condition for combat operations at any one time, this amount exceed what the Japanese could muster. Together with the RAAF's contribution—probably about 150 aircraft—Kenney had clear numerical superiority over the Japanese.[36]

In some ways, however, the number of aircraft was misleading. Most of the Japanese aircraft could fly from bases closer to the invasion area at Hollandia than Kenney's. Although his bombers could reach Hollandia, none of the fighters had enough range to accompany them that distance, and Kenney intended to stick with his policy of using the fighters to accompany the bombers and prevent unacceptable losses.[37] Although the search for airfields closer to Hollandia came to naught, newer model P-38Js had arrived, which obviated the need for finding a new airfield. The larger fuel tanks gave this model of the twin-tailed fighter a combat range of 570 miles, enough to escort the bombers all the way to Hollandia and back.[38] Unfortunately, there were too few of them for Kenney's taste, and he pushed the Air Service Command into manufacturing large external tanks for older model fighters. At the same time, Kenney hoped to lull the Japanese into a false sense of security and told Whitehead to restrict the range of the P-38s for the time being.[39]

The original air plan for the attacks on Hollandia was based on small night harassment attacks starting in the middle of March, with larger raids beginning about March 28, 29, and 30.[40] These plans changed dramatically on March 29, when Central Bureau intercepted a message from the Japanese 4th Air Army commander, Lieutenant General Teramoto Noriichi. Afraid that his aircraft were in danger of being destroyed, he ordered the airplanes flown out of Hollandia to Noemfoor and Biak—a move that would have been disastrous for MacArthur's plans.[41] Operating from Biak the Japanese aircraft could attack the aircraft carriers and amphibious craft bringing troops to Hollandia, but they would have been beyond the reach of Kenney's aircraft. Fortunately, the officers working in Central Bureau quickly grasped the importance of the message and passed it to their chief, Major General Spencer Akin, who handed it off to Kenney. Kenney flashed the information to Whitehead and told him to attack the airfields as soon as possible.[42]

Allied aircraft roared over Hollandia at noon the next day, completely surprising the Japanese, who never expected that the force would be so large or that fighters would arrive escorting the bombers.[43] Kenney's flyers returned to Hollandia over the next few days, bombing aircraft, shooting them down in the air, and destroying fuel, supplies, and repair facilities on the ground. Because the Allies planned to use the same airfields that the Japanese were now occupying, most of the bombers had been loaded with small fragmentation bombs in the hope that they would damage the aircraft on the ground, but not dig deep holes in the runway. In addition, aircrews were specifically told to concentrate on destroying the aircraft and do a minimum amount of damage to the runways.[44] That the attacks destroyed large numbers of aircraft on the ground is certain, but the precise number is difficult to determine. There is no doubt that the raids eliminated the Japanese air threat to the attack at Hollandia.[45]

Excellent intelligence combined with sound planning and execution explain a large part of the successful attacks on the airfields, but Japanese weaknesses also played a role. Continually handicapped by a lack of heavy equipment, construction engineers were never able to clear enough ground to disperse the aircraft, leaving them extremely vulnerable to air attacks. In addition, the Japanese had a very rudimentary network for providing warning about the air raids and no central command center to consolidate the information and make decisions, a weakness exacerbated by the loss of a convoy carrying a radar warning unit to Hollandia earlier in the month.[46] When Kenney's airmen arrived overhead, the Japanese were refueling some of the aircraft sent up earlier in the day. The eighteen minutes' warning they had of the Allied attack was not enough to flush the aircraft into the air or send up a strong force of defensive aircraft.[47]

Even though Whitehead was wary of the large numbers of Japanese aircraft flown into Hollandia, it was, in retrospect, a hollow force. By March 1944 the Japanese Army and Navy lacked trained pilots, the result of delaying the expansion of the pilot-training programs and a shortage of aviation fuel, which limited the amount of training that could be done.[48] Pilots could ferry the aircraft into Hollandia, but they did not remain there. The units at Hollandia simply did not have enough pilots to fly all the planes in combat.[49] In addition, the Japanese were plagued by maintenance problems, some of them self-induced, but others inflicted by the warfare against Japanese shipping routes. The air units lacked trained workers and spare parts to fix the aircraft, and they could not bring in the heavy equipment necessary for tasks such as swapping out aircraft engines or other repairs. One Japanese supply officer estimated that at the time of Kenney's attack on Hollandia only about a quarter of the aircraft were capable of combat flying: the rest had been grounded for a lack of spare parts.[50] At the time, however, Kenney and Whitehead had to respect the potential power of the Japanese air threat to the invasion. The deadly attacks in late March, in combination with Japanese problems, eliminated the air threat from Hollandia—Nimitz could bring in the carriers.

While Kenney's attacks on Hollandia may have tipped off the actual invasion site, the Japanese were also subjected to a clever, thorough deception plan that completely fooled them. A key component in this deception was the continued heavy air strikes by Kenney's bombers on Wewak and Hansa Bay. Since this was the usual precursor to a MacArthur attack, the missions reinforced perceptions about where the amphibious assault would take place.[51] While the aerial efforts helped convince the Japanese that they had guessed right, signals intelligence assured MacArthur and his commanders that their ruse was holding.[52]

Kenney's aviators also continued to carry out a variety of other missions, such as attacks on shipping to isolate the forces at Hollandia and Hansa Bay from any reinforcements. Kenney's aircraft were augmented by the arrival of radar-equipped B-24s. Called LABs or "Snoopers," these airplanes prowled the coast of New Guinea at night, a period that had previously provided some protection from air attacks, using their radars to find and bomb Japanese barges. Kenney also directed Whitehead to begin hitting supply areas and troop concentrations around Hollandia to reduce any possible opposition to the amphibious invasion.[53]

Elimination of the Japanese air threat at Hollandia did not reduce the hazards caused by a continuing foe of aircrews—the weather. Sunday, April 16, 1944, earned the nickname "Black Sunday" for the losses suffered that day. In preparation for the invasion of Hollandia, 5th Air Force sent a large strike against Tadji. The 130 bombers and 40 fighters had no problems enroute to the target areas, but ran into low clouds on their way home and could not make it back to their home bases in the Markham Valley. Some crews made it into alternate landing sites, others got disoriented flying in the clouds and crashed, and some crews ran out of gas and made forced landings in the jungle or at sea. In all, 32 crewmen and 31 aircraft were lost: almost 20 percent of the strike force.[54] The weather forecasts called for storms, but there was no indication the weather would cause as many problems as it did that day. Kenney was upset, calling it "the worst blow I took in the whole war."[55] He clearly meant it. The losses bothered him, and he was concerned about the impact on morale. He immediately flew to Nadzab to investigate the situation and find out what went wrong. Although he could stop operations for one day to search for the missing crews, he was unable to do much more; the upcoming invasions at Hollandia and Aitape had to take priority over searching for missing squadron mates.[56]

Less than a week later, on the morning of April 22, 1944, the Reckless operation began. One regiment of the 41st Division landed at Aitape to take control of the airfield at Tadji, while the remainder of the division landed at Humboldt Bay; the 24th Division went ashore at Tanahmerah Bay. The deception plan had completely fooled the Japanese, and there was no significant opposition at any of the landing sites.[57] Not surprisingly one group of participants found the amphibious landings "clicked probably better than any previous operation."[58]

The Persecution task force at Aitape landed at 6:45 in the morning, about a mile east of the intended landing site, a fortuitous error as it turned out—the new beach proved to be better than the one chosen by the planners. Soldiers quickly advanced inland to the airfields and discovered that the surprise attack had caught some of the Japanese still asleep![59] The air task force that accompanied the Persecution task force was headed by Air Commodore Scherger of the Australian Air Force, the first time an Australian officer had been appointed as the air task force commander.[60] Scherger, the commander of the RAAF Number 10 Operation Group, an organization roughly equivalent to Kenney's air task forces, had numerous operational and staff assignments, including a stint at the Allied Air Forces headquarters, and was well regarded for his ability to get along well with American officers.[61] His primary task was to get the airfield ready in two days so that fighters could move in when the escort carriers shifted westward to cover the main landings at Hollandia. Construction of the airfields rested with Wing Commander W. A. C. Dale, the task force engineer and the commander of RAAF Number 62 Works Wing. In addition to his own engineering unit, Dale would also have three American aviation engineer battalions. By early afternoon both of the airstrips had been captured, and engineers started making repairs.[62]

When the engineers began to survey the northernmost field (also called the fighter strip), they found a sod surface, not the paved coral they expected. In addition, the runway was shorter than predicted.[63] While these two factors would cause problems later, by the middle of the first afternoon engineers had started grading and extending the airstrip. The lack of Japanese opposition, both on the ground and in the air, allowed them to set up floodlights and continue working all night.[64] Dale declared the field open early in the morning of April 24, forty-one hours after the engineers had started working. The first fighters, American P-38s—one flown by Brigadier General Paul Wurtsmith, who commanded 5th Fighter Command—landed at 9:45; and by the end of the day a squadron of RAAF P-40s was on duty.[65] Heavy rains the next day rendered the runway unusable, forcing engineers to shut down the runway for three days while they laid steel mat; but by April 28 the field was open for good.[66]

The unopposed landings at Aitape were repeated further west as the 24th and 41st Divisions went ashore at Humboldt Bay and Tanahmerah Bay near Hollandia. The deception efforts had convinced the Japanese that the invasion would occur at Hansa Bay, and they had no indication that the Allies were landing anywhere else until the morning of April 22. There was no air opposition either; Kenney's attacks had forced the Japanese to abandon Hollandia. Large numbers of aircraft were later found on the ground at the three airfields, and those few that were flyable had fled for safer havens further west.[67]

The biggest snag in the initial assault came from the landing conditions the troops found at Tanahmerah Bay. Kenney and Whitehead were involved in all phases of planning for operations and had grown increasingly concerned about the conditions at the landing beaches at Tanahmerah Bay. Whitehead told Kenney that he had looked at reconnaissance photographs and thought that the ground behind the beach rose sharply, limiting the actual landing area and making it difficult for a division-sized force to unload its supplies and quickly move them away from the landing area.[68] After viewing the pictures himself, Kenney agreed with Whitehead's assessment and suggested landing a smaller force or ignoring the Tanahmerah Bay landing site altogether.[69]

Kenney reiterated his concerns about the landing beach, as well as his thoughts on the plan presented by the Navy for air support, at a meeting with all of the top-level commanders on April 9. Perhaps because his forces were not going to be a significant factor in the actual invasion, he voiced numerous complaints, albeit with little effect. Kenney objected to the lack of aircraft in the Navy's plan for the landing. Naval officers countered by pointing out that heavy doses of naval gunfire could support the landing, and not as many aircraft would be needed. Kenney thought this position was fundamentally wrong, and he continued to argue against it, though his remarks "did not seem to make any impression."[70] Kenney also brought up the conditions at Tanahmerah Bay and predicted the landing would prove "extremely difficult."[71] He suggested shifting the main effort to Humboldt Bay or holding back the forces completely and landing them further west, at Wakde and Sarmi, to speed up the advance even more. When told it was too late to change the plan, he blasted the ground commanders for their lack of flexibility, especially in light of the new information, but could not budge them.[72]

Although Kenney's concerns about the beach at Tanahmerah were ignored, in the end his forecast turned out to be correct. The main landing beach at Tanahmerah Bay was shallow and bordered on "a swamp armpit deep and extending inland from 100 to 200 yards."[73] Based on a variety of reports about the crowded conditions on the beach and the poor terrain, Eichelberger decided that follow-on landings would be made at Humboldt Bay and shifted the main effort to that area, the very action Kenney and Whitehead had suggested earlier.[74]

Fortunately, actual resistance to the invasion was slight, and the ground forces made their way inland rapidly. The main objectives for the landings, the three airfields on the Lake Sentani plain, were in American hands just four days after the invasion; and construction on the fields began almost immediately. The carrier task force on loan from Admiral Nimitz departed on April 24, and the escort carriers moved from Aitape down to Hollandia.[75]

Almost as soon as the engineers started working on the airfields, it became apparent that they would not be able to repair them as quickly as promised, a turn of events that surprised neither Kenney nor Whitehead.

Whitehead, who as the on-scene commander in New Guinea had had more experience overseeing the building of the airfields, had been concerned from the beginning about having the airfields operating in three weeks.[76] As the date drew closer he increased his protests, telling Kenney, "the more information we get on this general area, the less satisfactory it appears."[77]

Although engineers had plenty of aerial photographs to assist them in planning for the airfields at Hollandia, they did not have the benefit of ground reconnaissance to help verify their assumptions. Two weeks prior to the invasion several reconnaissance teams had been put ashore; but soon after the landing, local inhabitants tipped off the Japanese, who captured or killed many of the soldiers. Those who managed to stay alive hid in the jungle to avoid capture and could not make any reports.[78] Forced to rely on the aerial photographs, engineers focused on areas that the Japanese had already cleared and were using for their aircraft. The Japanese had built three airfields in the Hollandia area just north of Sentani Lake. Hollandia airfield had two runways: one 4,500 feet long, the other 6,000 feet long but capable of being lengthened to 8,000 feet.[79] According to the engineers, the soil at Hollandia was "moderately porous clayey silt," one of the worst foundations for building airfields because it would require about two feet of firmer fill material, such as gravel, to support the heavier Allied aircraft.[80] Two miles southeast of the Hollandia air strip was Sentani, built for Japanese bombers and 5,800 feet long, and Cyclops, a fighter airfield 3,700 feet long. In addition to these three main airfields there was a small strip near Humboldt Bay called Tami, which, even from the photographs, did not look like a good location.[81] Although there were no quarries or large amounts of gravel nearby, engineers concluded that the area contained good roads, plenty of water, and suitable materials for construction. They anticipated no problems making Hollandia into a large forward base, slated to hold ten bomber groups and eight fighter groups on six airfields. The plans also called for an enormous aircraft repair depot, 4 million square feet of covered storage, enough supplies to feed and arm 200,000 soldiers for six months, and six hospitals. Appropriately, 25,000 engineers, among them 7,500 aviation engineers, sailed to Hollandia—about 40 percent of the total force.[82]

Although Hollandia was the first operation with "detailed" engineering plans, it does not appear that this prior preparation was of much help in carrying out the operation.[83] All of the airfields turned out to be too short for the Allied requirements, none of them had adequate drainage, and the soil was not firm enough.[84] The fighter strip at Cyclops did open for transport aircraft on April 27, five days after the landing; a squadron of P-40s moved into the field on May 3 to relieve the escort carriers off the coast.[85] The runway at Hollandia had 5,000 feet available on May 3, but had to be surfaced with limestone before it was capable of allowing takeoffs and landings in any kind of weather. Heavy rainfall soon frustrated the construction efforts; despite the "complete cooperation" of the engineers, Hollandia airfield was not in steady operation until late May.[86] In short, building the airfields turned out to be much tougher than expected. Six weeks after the invasion White-head reported that the strip at Hollandia was only a "semi-all weather" land-ing surface and that there was still no runway capable of handling heavy bombers.[87] The construction problems and the speed of subsequent opera-tions made it clear that the area would never be made into the massive advance location that the planners had forecast.[88]

The problems in developing the airfields were caused by a variety of fac-tors. MacArthur's chief engineer, Major General Hugh Casey, was convinced that the engineers doing the work deserved much of the blame. The fields did consist of a sandy clay as the terrain intelligence had predicted, but they were also covered by six to eight inches of soft topsoil. This top layer of soil should have been removed prior to beginning work on the runways, but in the haste to get the airfields done, it was not.[89] In addition, the engineers in the invasion force did not pay enough attention to making preparations for drainage. As a result, when it rained in Hollandia, a frequent occurrence dur-ing this time of the year, water stayed on the runways rather than being car-ried away, making the subsoil very unstable and incapable of carrying heavy loads. The situation prompted Casey to write a memorandum to all engi-neers, stressing the importance of drainage and pointing out that it was im-possible to build runways "on a bed of muck."[90]

Construction efforts were also hampered by problems in getting heavy machinery to the airfields. The roads leading from the landing areas to the airfield complex turned out to be little more than small dirt tracks. Traffic over these paths during the first few days, especially on the road from Hum-boldt Bay, coupled with heavy rains, quickly made the tracks impassable. None of the heavy engineering equipment was able to move over the roads, and the work on the Cyclops field was done with light tools and captured Japanese equipment. Problems on the roads also left the troops inland short of supplies and required pulling engineers off of the airfields for road repairs.[91] The supply situation was so desperate that bombers had to be pressed into service dropping food and supplies, and an alternate airfield at Tami near Humboldt Bay was built solely to fly food and ammunition to the forces inland.[92] The muddy roads also created problems in establishing the early warning network, as no radars or their associated equipment could move. Fortunately, the Japanese did not take advantage of the Allies' rela-tive weakness in Hollandia: they attempted only six raids in twelve days, and many of those were done by single aircraft at night—annoying to be sure, and sometimes dangerous, but not enough to cause any severe problems.[93]

From almost every aspect, the invasion of Hollandia was a complete success. The planning between Kenney and the naval air commanders appeared detailed and well thought out. The procedures for geographical separation of the various air components, assisted by the exchange of liaison officers, worked well; there were no complaints afterwards about the lack of coordination or support. How well this system would have worked under the stress of heavy enemy air attacks was anyone's guess and not a subject of much discussion. The planning sessions, and the knowledge that future invasions might involve aircraft carriers, did prompt the development of standard operating procedures between carrier and land-based aircraft during an amphibious landing.[94] Despite Kenney's trepidation, relying on the carriers did not cause any adverse consequences. In short, the operation was a well-planned, well-executed example of air, sea, and land warfare supported by highly accurate intelligence estimates and blessed with little resistance from the enemy.[95]

When judged against the primary objective of the landing, which was to build a "major air base, minor naval facilities, and an intermediate supply base, for the purpose of supporting further operations,"[96] the operation was a bust. Problems in airfield and road construction made it impossible to fulfill the plans envisioned for the area. The problems in the Hollandia area can be partially explained by the poor decisions on drainage, made by the engineers on the spot. More important, incomplete information on the terrain led to very optimistic engineering estimates—a concern Kenney and Whitehead had both voiced, but their counsel was ignored. Even with only a vague idea of the terrain around Hollandia, the two years of fighting in New Guinea should have convinced any engineer that the estimates about the ability of the trails to handle the heavy equipment from the landing beaches to the airfields were ludicrous. Few, if any, of the "trails" in New Guinea had ever been speedily converted into roads capable of handling heavy equipment, and enough Japanese airfields had been captured previously to give the planners some idea of their construction techniques.[97] In short, the engineering plans were too optimistic about both the speed with which the construction could be done and the extent of the work required.

Sarmi-Wakde-Biak

Even before the problems with the airfields at Hollandia became clear, Kenney was lobbying MacArthur to speed up attacks further west. The move to

Hollandia effectively removed most of his aircraft from the war; he now faced the embarrassing problem of having plenty of aircraft, but no way of using them.[98] ULTRA intelligence revealed that the Japanese were rushing air reinforcements into the area, and without new airfields Kenney would be unable to stop any Japanese air attacks.[99] He was particularly interested in grabbing several small islands off the northern coast of New Guinea, where there would be fewer problems in building runways for bombers because the coral foundations could support the heavier aircraft with little additional work. Kenney estimated that in those areas the engineers could have a run-way ready in a "few days" rather than weeks or even months.[100] At one of the final planning conferences for the Hollandia attack, Kenney first pitched his idea of seizing the island of Wakde, 140 miles northwest of Hollandia, and the adjacent area of Sarmi in New Guinea.[101] Kenney brought up the idea again at a meeting in Port Moresby on April 25, and MacArthur approved the invasion for May 15.[102] A few days later, when the problems at Hollandia were becoming clear, Kenney went back to MacArthur and pressed him to bypass the landing on New Guinea for an attack on Biak, an island 325 miles west of Hollandia. Photographs showed that the terrain around Sarmi, like that at Hollandia, would not support heavy bombers, and this time the rec-ommendation was heeded.[103] With the problems in building airfields at Hol-landia, Kenney desperately needed Wakde and Biak not only to speed MacArthur's advance to the Philippines and beat down the burgeoning Japanese air strength in western New Guinea, but also to attack Japanese air bases in the Caroline Islands in support of Nimitz's Central Pacific advance.[104]

The landings at Wakde, Sarmi, and Biak reverted to the familiar pattern of earlier New Guinea operations without the support of aircraft carriers. Kenney gained control of the air, then isolated the landing zone, destroyed the shore defenses, and provided direct support during the invasion itself until the airfield was secure. At the same time his aircraft continued to fly reconnaissance missions, support ground operations in the bypassed areas, and transport troops and supplies.[105] With the additional forces on hand from the transfer of forces from the South Pacific, Kenney now had the luxury of assigning 5th Air Force the task of directly supporting the attack for the inva-sion of Wakde. The 13th Air Task Force would bomb airfields in the Caro-line Islands in support of Admiral Nimitz's operations as well as patrol the seas and attack targets in eastern New Guinea and New Britain. RAAF Com-mand meanwhile remained committed to the area in New Guinea west of Noemfoor Island and raided installations in the Timor and Arafua Sea areas to hold some of the Japanese air reinforcements away from MacArthur's ground operations.[106]

The attacks on Wakde and Sarmi went off as scheduled in late May. Although the Japanese had guessed the trajectory of MacArthur's advance, the speed with which he moved surprised them, making it difficult to assemble enough forces for a strong defense. In addition, they continued to be handicapped by their lack of heavy equipment and airfields.[107] The Japanese on Wakde fought hard, but had only a limited number of soldiers to defend the island. The airfield was initially captured on May 18, and repairs began the next day. By May 21 the field was ready for aircraft, although many of the dispersal areas were not completed for another week.[108]

The Biak landing early on the morning of May 27 likewise went smoothly; capturing the airfields, however, turned into a long and bloody affair. The position of Biak, only 900 miles south of Mindanao, made it a critical point in the crumbling Japanese defensive perimeter; and they were determined to protect it for as long as possible. The Japanese commander on the island correctly guessed that the primary objective of an invasion would be the only possible site for an airfield—a small strip of land along the southern coast of the island that currently contained several Japanese runways. Overlooking this area was a series of 500-foot-high limestone cliffs riddled with caves, a perfect location for a stout defensive stand.[109] Once again MacArthur's advance hit sooner than expected, and many of the Japanese defensive preparations were incomplete. Most important, the garrison had not been reinforced with troops earmarked for that purpose from the 35th Division.[110] Despite being short of troops, the Japanese put up a vicious fight. Although the airfield was in American hands by June 8, the almost impregnable positions in the cliffs overlooking the site made it impossible to do much more. The Japanese lobbed artillery shells and mortars onto the runways, stopping the engineers from repairing the airfields. Even after a portion of the runway was repaired, the Japanese shelling kept the field closed to aircraft.[111]

While the ground forces carried on their grim struggle to capture the airfields, radio intercept operators monitored Japanese activities far from the island and detected ominous signs. The invasion of Wakde and Biak threatened to topple the Japanese defensive perimeter and triggered a series of moves by military commanders to retain control over the area. About one hundred Japanese naval aircraft were flown from bases in the Philippines and Central Pacific to the western region of New Guinea. Beginning on June 1, the Japanese made several raids; but because none of the attacks was in great strength, Kenney's fighters managed to hold them off and Allied bombers destroyed Japanese aircraft on the ground at their fields.[112]

In an attempt to get better results, the Japanese shifted to night attacks against Wakde, with exceptionally good success. Because of problems in developing the airfields at Hollandia, Wakde was the only forward location available to Kenney for heavy bombers. Despite the efforts of the engineers, they were not able to build dispersal areas around the island; and, much like the Japanese situation, Wakde was packed with aircraft. The presence of a night fighter squadron, a ground radar station, and a wireless unit from the RAAF could not stop two night raids from hitting their mark and destroying at least thirteen aircraft while damaging many others.[113]

From Kenney's earliest days in command, an increase in Japanese air activity had been a tip-off that a convoy was in the offing. The situation during the battle for Biak was no different. On May 29 the Japanese army and navy staffs agreed to reinforce Biak, setting in motion plans for transporting the 2nd Amphibious Brigade from Mindanao to Biak. This convoy (code-named KON), consisting of a transport group with two cruisers and three destroyers screened by two cruisers, five destroyers, and a battleship, departed Davao in Mindanao on June 2.[114] Intercepted radio messages alerted Kenney and other allied commanders to the convoy's departure for Biak, and they quickly rushed forces to cut if off.[115] On the night of June 3 the Japanese withdrew much of the screening group, based on reports that an American carrier task force was moving towards Biak (which was not true) and that the convoy was being followed by American submarines and B-24 "Snoopers" (which was true). The transport group and three additional destroyers continued south towards Sorong in western New Guinea.[116]

After a refueling stop, the convoy departed Sorong for Biak at midnight on June 8 with six destroyers each loaded with 200 soldiers. Radio intercepts and reconnaissance reports helped track the convoy, but Japanese bombing of Wakde and a limited number of aircraft thwarted Kenney's efforts to hit the convoy.[117] The only long-range aircraft available were B-25s from the 17th Reconnaissance Squadron, which spotted the convoy and attacked it on June 8 at 12:45 p.m., just 200 miles from Biak. The ten B-25s radioed their report and then bore in at wave-top height to attack the warships. This attack would not be a repeat of the Bismarck Sea—there were too few of Kenney's attackers, and they faced destroyers more heavily armed than the Japanese merchant shipping. Three of the B-25s were hit and crashed almost immediately, killing all aboard, while the returning seven aircraft were so badly damaged that the squadron had to be removed from combat. In return they sank the destroyer *Harusame* and inflicted some minor damage on the other ships.[118] After rescuing the survivors of the *Harusame*, the convoy continued to Biak, arriving near the northern coast that night. One of the destroyers sighted an Allied naval task force, and the Japanese quickly retired after discharging about 100 troops.[119] A third KON convoy was canceled when the Japanese received word of shelling and air attacks against Tinian and Saipan, meaning that these islands would be the site of the next American attack. To contest the landing on Saipan the Japanese dispatched most of the naval surface units there, ending any further effort to reinforce Biak.[120] The Japanese attempt to strengthen Biak was a close-run affair; despite overwhelming American air and sea superiority, the Japanese put an additional 1000 troops on the island.[121]

Perhaps to compensate for a rather ineffectual showing in stopping the convoy, Kenney's version of the convoy attacks was substantially different from what actually occurred and greatly exaggerated the impact of air power during the operation. Kenney recorded that ten B-24s attacked the convoy on June 4, sinking two destroyers and damaging two cruisers. A Japanese officer in the convoy, however, told investigators after the war that although the ships were attacked, they did not suffer any losses.[122] Kenney also maintained that his forces made two attacks on June 6 in which several destroyers and cruisers received direct hits. The Japanese reported that one ship was "heavily attacked," but it was not damaged.[123] Notwithstanding the brave and courageous efforts of the B-25 aircrews who attacked the convoy on June 8, Kenney's version of events was untrue. In his account, probably based on the initial postflight reconstructions by the crews, the B-25s sank four destroyers and damaged one other (actual results were one sunk, three damaged). Following the air attack he claimed the remaining ships "made a 180 degree turn and went back home," an outcome that Kenney might have hoped for but one that did not happen, as Kenney surely knew.[124] As he so often did, however, Kenney stuck to the original version. His published account makes no reference to the surface naval actions, claiming instead that after the B-25 attack the ships that remained afloat "turned around and headed northwest at full speed."[125]

Although the Japanese attempts to send reinforcements to Biak had been stymied, fighting on the island continued unabated. American forces maneuvered to split the Japanese defenses and eventually burned and blasted them out of the caves overlooking the airfield. The last desperate attempt by the Japanese to recapture the runways came on June 9, but the Japanese positions in caves overlooking the airfield continued to slow repair work and made it impossible to use the runway.[126] It took another week of bloody fighting to eliminate the Japanese positions enough to allow the engineers to finish their repairs, and P-40s finally began flying operations on June 23.[127]

The delay in establishing the runways on Biak threatened to slow the pace of the war, and Kenney looked elsewhere for likely airfields. Owi island, just 3 miles south of Biak, had been overlooked in the advanced planning, but seemed a good bet; it was a coral island, could handle the weight of the heavy bombers, and was unoccupied.[128] Engineers scouted Owi, and on June 9 construction on the first runway began. A week later they had completed 4,500 feet of runway, enough to allow ten P-38s and one B-25 to make emergency landings. By June 21 the airfield was complete, and a P-38 fighter group began flying operations.[129]

As combat operations continued on Biak, Kenney was simultaneously planning for landings further westward and northward. The island of Noemfoor on the far western end of New Guinea was isolated by air action and quickly captured in early July. About a month later, Allied forces captured the Sansapor region of New Guinea.[130] To reduce any Japanese air interference with the landings near Sansapor, Nimitz's carriers hit the Japanese air bases on Palau, while Kenney's airmen went after airfields on the island group known as the Halmaheras. Once again, signals intelligence provided Kenney with a clear picture of the Japanese buildup. By Kenney's estimation there were about 200 aircraft in the Halmaheras at the end of July, along with almost 800 in the Philippines. He could not understand why the Japanese were not using the aircraft to attack his airfields that were now tightly packed with aircraft. Rather than assess whatever impediments they might have, Kenney concluded that the Japanese inaction was another example of their inability to understand air power.[131]

Kenney's airmen attacked airfields in the Halmaheras in late July and met little resistance while destroying about 100 aircraft, an experience that, according to Kenney, "left everyone contemptuous of the capabilities of the Nip air force."[132] In truth, the conclusion reveals more about Kenney's state of mind regarding the Japanese capabilities than the unanimity of opinion within his command. By the beginning of August it appeared that most of the Japanese aircraft had been destroyed or moved northward to the Philippines.[133]

Organizational Changes

During the series of westward invasions in New Guinea, Kenney's command underwent a significant organizational change. In absorbing the addition of air units from the 13th Air Force from the South Pacific theater, Kenney could no longer remain the commander of 5th Air Force. A new organizational headquarters was needed to encompass both organizations. Kenney, who now enjoyed MacArthur's greatest confidence, would remain in overall command of the two American air forces. MacArthur's initial suggestion for the name of Kenney's new headquarters was 1st Air Army, but his idea was rejected in

Washington in favor of Far East Air Forces.[134] Kenney assumed command of the provisional headquarters of the Far East Air Forces on June 15, 1944, and the headquarters was given permanent status on August 5, 1944.[135] White- head took over as commander of 5th Air Force, and Major General St. Clair Streett was named the head of 13th Air Force.[136] Kenney retained his title as the commander of the Allied Air Forces and on June 15 was placed in charge of air units remaining in the Solomon Islands, including the 1st Marine Air Wing and the Royal New Zealand Air Force, which were part of a command called Aircraft Northern Solomons under United States Marine Corps Major General Ralph J. Mitchell.[137] While these changes increased the number of air- craft available to Kenney, they also codified the existing organizational frame- work that had been worked out over the past two years in the Southwest Pacific. Kenney retained overall command of the air organizations and handed down the general priority of missions and the tasks for a given period of time. He then let the respective air force headquarters and air task forces do the detailed planning for missions.

The air task forces had proven themselves as important tools for con- ducting air operations in the Southwest Pacific, but for a long time Kenney could not get official recognition of them, forcing him to take officers from flying squadrons and move them into the headquarters to plan missions. While the organizational framework improved flying operations, the lack of manpower in both the flying units and the headquarters wore officers to a frazzle.[138] While neither the Army Air Forces headquarters nor the War Department was as enthusiastic as Kenney about the benefits of an air task force, in late 1943 the War Department decided, over Kenney's objections, that the headquarters of a bombardment wing would provide a suitable sub- stitute for an Air Task Force. In February 1944, 1st Air Task Force was re- named as the 308th Bombardment Wing, the 2nd became the 309th Bom- bardment Wing, and the 3rd the 310th Bombardment Wing.[139] Although the names of the organizations changed, they continued to function as the old air task forces and controlled many different types of aircraft for various periods of time, depending on the operation. In this regard these three bom- bardment wings were unlike similarly named wings in any other theater, which only contained bomber aircraft.[140] Every operation in the Southwest Pacific would have an air task force, only with a different name.

ALTHOUGH KENNEY had preached the same plan for air operations in Mac- Arthur's march westward through New Guinea, the leap to Hollandia brought with it carrier-based aircraft and introduced some new problems for

Kenney. For practical reasons he did not want to rely on aircraft carriers for support of an amphibious landing. In the event, the invasion of Hollandia went smoothly. Kenney had largely eliminated any potential Japanese air threat, and there was no attempt to reinforce the airfields during the attack. With the campaigning in the western end of New Guinea complete, Kenney looked forward to MacArthur's move to the Philippines.

NINE

RETURN TO THE PHILIPPINES

October 1944 to December 1944

"The main lesson . . . we should draw from this operation
is to stick to land-based support."

MacArthur's long-awaited return to the Philippines in the fall of 1944 would
not be the flawless operation that he might have hoped. The introduction of
aircraft carriers for the Hollandia operation marked a new stage in the
advance, a course of action MacArthur followed when afforded the opportunity to invade Leyte in the central Philippines. The invasion of Hollandia had
been marked by a notable lack of Japanese resistance, especially in the air.
During the fighting for Leyte, on the other hand, the Japanese would mount
stiff resistance, revealing that the war was far from over—an ominous warning of the fighting that would occur if the home islands of Japan were invaded.

To Leyte

MacArthur's scheduled plans for the Philippines underwent a drastic change
in late August, when Admiral Halsey began flying missions against targets
in the Philippine archipelago. Based on the lack of an effectual Japanese air
reaction to the raids and a report from a carrier pilot who had been rescued
by guerrilla forces, Halsey recommended canceling the planned invasion of
Yap and moving up the invasion of Leyte, a proposal that carried with it
enormous changes to the current plans.

Nimitz agreed with Halsey's proposal and offered to turn over to Mac-
Arthur the carriers and the army corps scheduled to invade the island of Yap
if the JCS approved the move. While the JCS agreed in principle to Nimitz's
suggestion, they asked MacArthur for his thoughts.[1] At the time, however,
MacArthur was aboard a destroyer observing radio silence as it accompanied

the task force to Morotai, leaving Lieutenant General Richard Sutherland, MacArthur's long-serving chief of staff, to answer the query. Initially he told the JCS and Nimitz that Halsey's report was wrong; but rather than reject Nimitz's proposal outright Sutherland temporized and told the JCS that he needed more details about the attacks.[2] After receiving the additional information Sutherland seized the opportunity, telling the JCS that MacArthur would be ready to invade Leyte on October 20, 1944. The JCS, in turn, gave the design their quick approval.[3] Although Sutherland's recommendation followed Halsey's new report, it seems unlikely that the new information played much of a role in this decision. Intercepted Japanese radio messages, as well as guerrilla operations within the Philippines, gave MacArthur's staff a very detailed accounting of the Japanese forces, a picture far more pessimistic than Halsey's report. Sutherland knew, for example, that many of the Japanese aircraft had been withdrawn northward to the island of Luzon, a move that partly accounted for the lack of opposition to the carrier pilots. In the end, Sutherland decided to disregard the more credible information and go ahead with the attack, probably basing his decision on MacArthur's likely reaction to the same situation more than a belief in the weakness of the defenses. If Sutherland failed to grab this chance, it might have meant bypassing the Philippines altogether.[4]

Kenney had been thinking about speeding up the advance to the Philippines too, although this time his plans were more modest, hoping only to omit the invasion of Talaud for an assault on Mindanao in the southern Philippines. Kenney later claimed credit for advocating an early invasion of Luzon, but it is unlikely that he would have come up with the idea of going there on his own, for the same reason he objected to the invasion of Hollandia—it would be beyond the range of his aircraft. As Sutherland was responding to the proposed changes, Kenney was, in fact, visiting the different bases in his command. He met with Whitehead at the new 5th Air Force headquarters on Owi to discuss the idea of omitting the Talaud operation.[5] Even Kenney's plan would entail some risk, and Whitehead worried about the impact Japanese aircraft might have if he could not move his forces forward. The feeble reaction to the air attacks on Halmaheras had convinced Kenney that the Japanese would have little effect on operations despite a lack of intermediate bases. He brushed off Whitehead's concerns, arguing, "Jap air is shot."[6] When Kenney returned to his headquarters at Hollandia on September 15 and learned about the decision to invade Leyte in October, he told Whitehead, "The program that you and I talked over on shortening up the move into the Philippines is child's play compared with what has happened in the last couple of days."[7] Kenney played no part in the actual decision, despite his later claims, but wholeheartedly supported Sutherland's decision and promised to be present when Sutherland broke the news to MacArthur.[8]

The leap to Leyte meant that MacArthur would once again rely on aircraft carriers rather than land-based air power for the invasion. Kenney had earlier warned against such a move for several reasons, most importantly the short loiter time Navy aircraft had over their targets, their limited range, and their small bomb loads.[9] After hearing about the decision to advance the attack on Leyte, Whitehead reminded Kenney of the shortcomings of carrier aircraft in an attempt to stop or modify the change in plans.[10] Whitehead's warnings went unheeded.

Although Kenney retained some uneasiness about relying on the carriers, his perception of the state of the Japanese forces in the Philippines and desire to meet MacArthur's goals overrode his fears. Based on reports about the performance of Japanese air units and what he had heard during the attacks in the Halmaheras, Kenney was convinced that the Japanese were "on the downhill grade,"[11] predicting that "the war will officially end when we take the Philippines—perhaps by the time we land on Luzon."[12] Kenney's decision was helped by his perception of the failure of the Japanese leaders to understand air power. "I didn't think that his air leadership and staff work could be so bad," he confided to Arnold. "He has handled his air force like an amateur, frittering it away in a manner that is really disgraceful from a professional viewpoint."[13] Furthermore, he detected a change in their strategy, forecasting that they had "seen the futility of trying to hold islands or isolated spots" and were likely to withdraw from the Philippines.[14] Kenney's racial attitudes helped distort his views as well: "I failed to appreciate [that] the percentage of Japanese males that can be made into combat aviators is much smaller than ours. Too much of their population is peasant class—rice planters, fishermen, richsa [*sic*] pullers—who are too dumb, too slow thinking and utterly lacking in mechanical knowledge or adaptability."[15] These racial liabilities were largely responsible for the problems the Japanese airmen faced:

> The newcomers to the game are incapable of even flying their equipment, much less become real flyers. In common with most of their race they become confused when faced with an unforeseen emergency. Japan hasn't the years of time required to teach this class of plodding, thick-headed, half fed, stupid recruits how to fight against the well drilled show we have out here. It takes intelligence to fight in the air. We have it. The Jap had quite a bit a year ago. He does not have it now.[16]

Kenney was so confident of Japanese weakness that he even began to believe that Halsey's carriers would not be needed for the invasion. The American fleet could be released the day after the amphibious landing "to seek out and destroy the Jap fleet or anything else worth hitting," he predicted.[17] While the invasion of Leyte was something of a "gamble," the weakness of the Japanese convinced him it was a gamble worth taking. "If my hunch is right, that the Japs are about through, we are all right," he told Whitehead. If they were able to cobble together some resistance on Leyte, especially in the air, "we are in for a lot of trouble"—prophetic words for the battle of Leyte Gulf.[18]

Balikpapan

During the month between the decision in mid-September to invade Leyte and the actual attack on October 20, 1944, commanders, staff officers, soldiers, sailors, and airmen frantically prepared for the largest amphibious invasion in the Pacific to date. While Kenney spent most of his time overseeing preparations for the invasion, he also ordered a series of air attacks on the oil refineries at Balikpapan in Borneo.

Kenney had regarded the sources of Japanese oil as potential war-winning targets since his arrival in Australia, but the closest refineries were over 1,000 miles away, at the limit of the range of his bombers in Australia. According to Kenney, the most important site for Japanese oil production was the area around Palembang in southern Sumatra, while Balikpapan in eastern Borneo contained critical oil refineries. Under Dutch control before the war, the refineries at Balikpapan were the second-largest refining center in southeast Asia.[19] Before leaving the area in January 1942, Dutch technicians destroyed some of the equipment, which hobbled Japanese efforts at extracting oil for a time. The Japanese were eventually able to refine about 2,500,000 barrels a year, the bulk of it as aviation fuel.[20] In a characteristic bit of Kenney overstatement, he asserted that these targets constituted "the finest and most decisive set of targets for bombing anywhere in the world."[21] There was no way that any bombers Kenney had available could reach Palembang—it was simply too far away. Balikpapan, however, was barely within range and continued to attract Kenney's attention.

The closest Allied base to Balikpapan was at Darwin in northwestern Australia, and B-24s from there made sporadic attacks on the oil targets. On the night of August 13, 1943, B-24s from the 380th Bombardment Group flew the 2,400-mile, seventeen-hour round trip mission to Balikpapan. Aircrews reported setting both refinery areas afire and seeing "at least 7 large oil tanks" explode.[22] Although two of the ten aircraft on the mission were lost and later photo reconnaissance showed that the refineries had not been destroyed, both Kenney and Whitehead considered the raid worthwhile because it critically reduced Japanese oil supplies over the next ninety days.[23] The B-24s occasionally returned to Balikpapan, but only sporadically and only at night. The lack of long-range fighters that could escort the bombers and the robust Japanese air defenses in the area led Kenney to believe that a daylight raid would result in prohibitively high losses.[24] The occasional raids and the possibility of future attacks did tie down a portion of the Japanese fighter force in defending the refineries, but did not stop oil production.[25]

The distance from Darwin to Balikpapan not only made it impossible to conduct bombing attacks in daylight, but also reduced the bomb loads that the B-24s could carry. Solving this problem required a bomber with longer range, which accounts for Kenney's continuing interest in the Boeing B-29 Superfortress. The decision in March 1944 by the JCS to approve MacArthur's bold move to Hollandia also sanctioned Admiral Nimitz's invasion of the Marianas, future air bases from which the B-29s could attack the Japanese home islands, effectively ending Kenney's hopes for the new bomber.

In the midst of planning for the Hollandia landing, Kenney received a visit from Major General Laurence Kuter, Arnold's assistant chief of staff in charge of planning, a fervent believer in the efficacy of strategic bombardment who was determined to pit the B-29s against Japan proper.[26] Kenney later referred to Kuter as one of "the Young Turks," the primary supporters behind the plan for the Marianas, a stance that pitted them against Kenney and MacArthur.[27] Kuter tried to explain the rationale behind the B-29 decision; but Kenney paid little attention and returned to his sales efforts, pointing out that missions from Darwin to Balikpapan would provide an opportunity to introduce the B-29 crews and airplanes into combat against a group of relatively benign targets.[28] Kenney also maintained that the most important oil target in the region was not Palembang but Balikpapan. Even if the B-29s could not be assigned permanently, he continued to press for their use against Balikpapan, even offering to service the aircraft in Darwin if needed.[29] Despite Kenny's blandishments, Kuter was unimpressed. He told Arnold that Kenney's evidence on Balikpapan was not convincing and that Palembang remained the primary oil target in southeast Asia. More important, those two targets were the only "strategic objectives" within reach of Kenney's bases, making it clear that Kuter saw no reason to hand over B-29s to Kenney and MacArthur.[30] Despite the setback in obtaining the long-range bombers, Kenney would not take no for an answer. In August 1944, he met with his old friend and Arnold's current chief of staff, Major General Barney Giles, and urged Giles to send four groups of B-29s to Darwin. Giles was apparently impressed by what he heard and pressed Kenney's demand on Arnold, but the request was denied.[31]

Not long after his meeting with Giles, Kenney began serious preparations to attack the refineries at Balikpapan. The original aim of the missions was to reduce the amount of aviation fuel in the Philippines and ground the Japanese aircraft, rendering them ineffective during the invasion. Since Kenney knew full well that the effects of such an attack would not be felt for at least a month or two, he planned to attack the oil targets in late September or early October, well ahead of the original invasion date for Leyte of late December. An October mission would provide airfields close enough to Balikpapan for the B-24 bombers to carry a large bomb load and allow enough time for the fuel shortages to reduce or stop air operations in the Philippines in time for the invasion of Leyte.[32] Once again he submitted a request for B-29s, but scaled his request back to two groups, claiming that the loss of Balikpapan "would throw a heavy burden on Japan."[33] In what by now must have been a familiar disappointment for Kenney, Arnold declined.[34] When the Leyte invasion was moved up to October 20, Whitehead wanted to cancel the Balikpapan operation, forecasting that given the timing of the missions, there would probably be little impact on the Japanese air forces in the Philippines.[35] Kenney pressed ahead; he had a "hunch" that the combination of the loss of Balikpapan and the invasion of the Philippines would convince the decision makers in Tokyo to end the war.[36]

Kenney usually regarded Whitehead's 5th Air Force, his old command, as the elite air unit in his command; for that reason they were given the primary role in any operation. Kenney must have been aware of his partiality and acceded to St. Clair Streett's request that 13th Air Force be allowed to plan and lead the raids on Balikpapan, believing that they would earn some "prestige" by doing so.[37]

Distance from the Allied air bases to Balikpapan still remained the planners' biggest problem. The closest airdrome capable of supporting the bombers was at Noemfoor, 1,080 nautical miles from the oil targets. To carry enough fuel for the mission and a 2,500-pound load of bombs, the amount considered necessary to inflict serious damage, the bombers had to reduce the normal ammunition load for their guns by 60 percent, another indication of Kenney's belief in the weakness of the Japanese air force.[38] It would have been difficult, but very possible, to send some fighters along on the mission as protection against the Japanese fighters; but when these difficulties were combined with the prevailing attitudes about the weakness of the air defenses around Balikpapan, it was easy for mission planners to decide that the bombers would not need a fighter escort to the target.[39] Unfortunately, the Japanese did not comply with these assumptions.

Just after midnight on September 30, 1944, the B-24s took off for Balikpapan, and nine and a half hours later 64 of the bombers arrived over Balikpapan. They met what one report termed a "violent air reaction" highlighted by "stiff opposition."[40] Japanese fighters intercepted the bomber formation fifteen minutes before the target and continued their attacks for half an hour afterwards. At least 5 bombers were lost in the running battle, and several more landed so badly shot up that they literally "crash-landed."[41] Thirty-nine B-24s returned to Balikpapan on October 3 and were again hammered by the Japanese fighters: 7 bombers, all from the 307th Bombardment Group, were lost in the target area; several more aircraft were so heavily damaged that they had to be scrapped.[42] The two-day tally was grim. Out of the 104 bombers sent out, 12 had not returned, some had been so badly damaged that they were written off, and others required extensive repairs. In total almost 40 percent of the bombers that flew the missions were either lost or out of commission.[43] Although some of the crews shot down were rescued by the submarines *Redfin* and *Mingo* posted near Balikpapan or by seaplanes located along the flight path to and from the target, the losses were still devastating.[44]

After the horrific second mission, Kenney flew to Noemfoor to investigate. Understandably, he found morale "not too good."[45] As the commander of 13th Air Force made changes to the mission profiles, Kenney spent his time with the crews and "got the kids to let their hair down."[46] Although Kenney sympathized with them, he did not back off from his plan for future attacks on Balikpapan. Instead he stressed the importance of the mission, likely emphasizing his belief that destroying Balikpapan and capturing the Philippines might bring an end to the war. He also tried to convince them that the changes in tactics, along with additional bombers from 5th Air Force and some long-range fighters, would cut their losses.[47] The need for fighter escort to the target was made even more apparent by reports Kenney received of Japanese air reinforcements being flown in to defend the oil refineries, a move that seemingly confirmed the value that the Japanese attached to these targets.[48]

How much Kenney improved morale is uncertain, but he did make good on his promises for the next mission to Balikpapan. Planning for the mission was extremely thorough and included raids the nights prior to the attack, as well as aircraft dedicated to confusing the Japanese air defense radars.[49] Kenney also provided additional bombers from 5th Air Force and long-range fighters to escort the bombers. Reportedly some fifty fighter pilots volunteered to go with the bombers even without enough gas to return home—they planned on being rescued by seaplanes after they bailed out—but Kenney did not have to resort to such desperate measures.[50] During a visit to the Southwest Pacific a few months earlier, Charles Lindbergh had experimented with the ever-present problem of increasing the range of the P-38s. After several flights he suggested a few changes to the operating procedures. By reducing the engine's revolutions per minute, leaning out the fuel mixture, and increasing the manifold pressure while cruising to the targets, P-38s were able to increase their range to almost 2,000 miles. The new procedure created its own problems. The changes fouled spark plugs and burned up engine cylinder heads, thereby increasing the work for the hard-pressed mechanics, but spare engines and parts were now relatively easy to obtain, making these problems a small price to pay.[51] The P-47s could also fly farther than ever before thanks to three external fuel tanks and the newly captured and repaired air strip at Morotai. They could make it all the way to Balikpapan and had enough fuel to spend at least twenty-five minutes orbiting in the area.[52]

The changes paid off during the next missions. Despite what some members of 13th Air Force described as "stiff" enemy air resistance, on October 10, 1944, the strike force of 106 bombers and 35 fighters overwhelmed the defenders and came away with only 4 bombers and 1 fighter missing.[53] A repeat performance four days later, including some 100 bombers and 60 fighters, brought similar results. Two bombers and 5 fighters were lost, although at least four of the fighter pilots were rescued. A final, almost anticlimactic, raid on Balikpapan was flown October 18. The bombers found the oil refineries obscured by clouds, which had also grounded the Japanese fighters, and simply dropped their bombs when the navigators guessed they were over the targets. Even with no enemy opposition, one B-24 and two P-38s were lost during the long mission.[54]

The mission on October 18 was the last one flown to Balikpapan. The invasion of Leyte would occur in only two more days and all of the aircraft in the command were needed to support MacArthur's return to the Philippines. From September 30 until October 18, Kenney's airmen had flown more than 300 bombing missions and dropped over 400 tons of bombs while losing twenty-two B-24s. Kenney typically put the missions, and his decision, in the best possible light, claiming that they had "finished Balikpapan off for the rest of the war."[55] Contemporary damage assessments were less sanguine, however, finding the damage inflicted "surprisingly small."[56] Some critical equipment at one plant was put out of action, but other areas of the complex escaped relatively free from damage.[57] To be sure, the aviators on the mission gained valuable experience in long-distance missions, but the loss of twenty-two bombers and nine fighters seemed a large price to pay for experience that could have been gained more cheaply in other ways.[58]

Based on Kenney's objectives, the missions can only be judged a failure. While he believed at one point that the attacks could affect air operations in the Philippines, moving the invasion of Leyte up from December to October obviated this rationale even before the missions were flown. He knew full well that the attacks occurred too late to influence the air battles in the Philippines, yet insisted on them, basing his reasoning largely on a "hunch" about the impact that the bombing raids would have on Tokyo. There is no evidence, however, that the attacks had any influence on Japanese political and military leaders. Not only was the damage done by the raids too small to have any impact, but submarines were causing far more havoc with the oil supply than Kenney, and most other Allied commanders at the time, realized.[59] Submarine attacks had virtually stopped oil shipments from Balikpapan to Manila by June 1944. Japanese tankers still sailed, but were now forced to travel south to Singapore and then north, hugging the coast of China. By the time of Kenney's attacks, fuel reserves in Japan were "critically low."[60] Submarines had already forced Japanese leaders to face a potential oil shortage. A postwar survey concluded that Kenney's raids had no "strategic effect because more oil was always available . . . than could be shipped out."[61]

Although the B-24s' missions to Balikpapan were largely ineffective, the question remains of whether it would have been better to send B-29s to Kenney rather than basing them in China. Leaving aside the political effect of the decision, from a military perspective the overall record of the aircraft from the Chinese bases was, according to the official history, "not a successful one."[62] Problems during production of the aircraft caused delays in training aircrews, and the first aircraft did not arrive in China until April 1944. They flew the first combat mission on June 5, and the first mission against Japan occurred two days later; but when the missions from China ended in January 1945, only nine missions had been flown against targets in Japan. A variety of logistical and technical problems burdened the effort and severely limited plans for employing the bombers.[63]

A postwar survey validated at least part of Kenney's claims for using the bombers rather than sending them to China. The United States Strategic Bombing Survey, a team of civilian analysts and military officers commissioned by President Roosevelt to investigate the effects of bombing on Germany and Japan, concluded that prior to capturing the Marianas Islands and flying missions against Japan itself, the B-29s would have been better used in attacking Japanese shipping and "in destroying oil and metal plants in the southern areas."[64] While using the B-29s in the Southwest Pacific may have been a more efficient use of the aircraft, which was the implicit criterion used by the Strategic Bombing Survey, there is little evidence to suggest that it would have been any more effective in ending the war. As the survey also noted, the submarine blockade and the capture of the Marianas Islands rendered Kenney's approach moot. Whatever the merits of Kenney's argument, it seems clear that Arnold had no intention of putting the B-29s under his and MacArthur's control.

If Kenney had been able to start bombing the oil refineries in May 1944, the disruption in petroleum might have adversely impacted air and naval operations in the Southwest Pacific; but it seems unlikely that this loss would have convinced, or even encouraged, Japanese leaders to surrender.[65] The best evidence against Kenney's supposition is the fact that the surrender of Japan followed a series of devastating events, including a complete naval blockade, firebombing of the largest cities, the dropping of two atomic bombs, and swift Russian victories against the Japanese forces in Manchuria. By almost any measure, any one of these other events alone exceeded the shock caused by the bombing of Balikpapan. Kenney's contention about the value of bombing Balikpapan, one that was probably shared by many other officers as well as politicians, was that the military conditions for defeat (the loss of oil refineries in this case) would automatically (and quickly) lead to the political decision to surrender. Such a belief bore little resemblance to the process that actually ended World War II.[66]

Return to the Philippines

As Kenney pursued his hope of inducing a Japanese surrender through the bombing of the oil refineries at Balikpapan, he was also involved with planning for the invasion of Leyte. As in the preparations for Hollandia, air operations for the invasion of Leyte, code-named King Two, involved both aircraft carriers and land-based aircraft. Just as in the Hollandia operation, there would be no single air commander for King Two. Instead, the invasion area was divided geographically and each commander was allocated responsibility for a given area, with no attempt to introduce arrangements for using the forces in concert.[67]

The Third Fleet fast carrier task forces under the command of Admiral Halsey were assigned the task of protecting the invasion force from the Japanese fleet and air reinforcements that might be sent from Formosa or the northern Philippines to Leyte. Ten days prior to the invasion date (termed A day by MacArthur to distinguish it from D day in Normandy), Halsey's carriers would work from the bases furthest away to those nearby, moving their attacks from the Japanese airfields on Okinawa to Formosa to northern Luzon. Four days before A day, the Third Fleet would shift southward and attack enemy positions on Leyte and Cebu, while bombers from Army Air Force units in China attacked Formosa.[68] During the invasion itself the fleet would be positioned about one hundred miles east of Luzon and guard against any Japanese naval attacks (Figure 4).

Direct support and protection, in the form of air cover and bombing during the amphibious landing, would be provided by the escort carriers and other ships assigned to Admiral Kinkaid, the Allied Naval Forces commander. Kinkaid would remain in charge of air operations until both he and Kenney agreed that land-based aviation was established ashore and could take the place of the escort carriers.[69]

While Kenney's aircraft would not participate directly in the invasion, they continued to carry out air strikes anywhere from Mindanao southward and patrolled the western flank of the Philippines for a Japanese attempt to send a naval force against the American armada.[70] Most important, the Allied Air Forces prepared to move into Leyte quickly and take over responsibility for supporting the invasion from the carriers. Kenney designated Whitehead's 5th Air Force as the assault air force, with Colonel David Hutchinson and the staff of the 308th Bombardment Wing as the air task force headquarters.[71] Hutchinson was told to have two fighter groups and one night fighter squadron operating on Leyte airfields in five days. Ten days later Kenney planned to have three additional groups, including a medium bomber unit, ready for action.[72]

It was critical for Kenney's aircraft to get onto Leyte quickly and take over from Kinkaid's escort carriers as soon as possible. As Kenney had pointed out to MacArthur earlier, the ships themselves could not stay in the area indefinitely; they needed to be rearmed and refueled.[73] If the carriers were forced to leave before the airfields became operational, the soldiers of 6th Army on the ground would be vulnerable to attacks from whatever Japanese aircraft remained. In addition, there would be no way to cut off reinforcements from other islands in the Philippines. As the engineers emphasized, "the rapid development of airdromes on Leyte . . . would be of critical importance."[74]

Capturing the airfields on Leyte was also uppermost in the mind of Lieutenant General Walter Krueger, the commander of 6th Army, as he planned the two corps landing on the eastern coast of Leyte. Two divisions of X Corps would land near Tacloban, capture the airfield, and then move inland to control the northern portion of the island. Further south, responsibility for the territory around the airfield at Dulag fell to XXIV Corps, recently

Figure 4. Philippine Islands (Wesley Frank Craven and James L. Cate, eds., *The Army Air Forces in World War II*, vol. 5, *The Pacific: Matterhorn to Nagasaki, June 1944 to August 1945* [Chicago: University of Chicago Press, 1953], p. 277).

diverted from their planned attack on Yap. XXIV Corps would advance westward to control the area around the remaining three airdromes and eliminate the Japanese presence in the southern part of the island.[75]

As Allied plans for the invasion of Leyte moved forward, so did Japanese plans for the island's defense. Japanese military leaders were committed to extracting a stiff price for the Philippines. Losing this territory would cut off Japan from its armies and the resources in the southern area, making the homeland extremely vulnerable to invasion. Since the Japanese did not know where the American forces would attack, they developed four different variations of the Sho-Go (victory) plan, all based on the fundamental assumption that every available reinforcement would be rushed to the threatened area and used in a "decisive battle" with the American forces. This battle, Japanese military leaders hoped, would inflict huge losses and convince the American people to end the war. The four options were Sho-Go 1 for an invasion of the Philippines, Sho-Go 2 for Formosa, Sho-Go 3 for southern Japan, and Sho-Go 4 for the northern Japanese islands.[76]

Since a basic premise of the Sho-Go 1 plan was that additional reinforcements, especially aircraft, would be sent to whatever area was threatened, an additional thirty airfields were built in the Philippines. To preserve their naval aircraft, which had been decimated in earlier forays against the American carriers and ineffective at stopping the amphibious landings, the Japanese elected to change tactics. Rather than attacking the carriers prior to the arrival of the amphibious force, they planned to concentrate on the troop transports during the landing phase—a decision that helps explain the lack of air opposition Halsey encountered, which was the impetus behind his proposal to speed up the invasion of the Philippines.[77] The Japanese Naval staff also developed plans for a decisive sea battle based on a similar premise—to lure the protecting naval craft away and concentrate on the transports. Because the Americans could invade the Philippines at a number of spots, ground commanders elected to make their defensive stand on Luzon rather than one of the smaller central or southern islands.[78]

On the eve of the American invasion of Leyte, the defense of the Philippines rested with the commander of the 14th Area Army, General Yamashita Tomoyuki. At his disposal, but not under his command, was the 4th Air Army under Lieutenant General Tominaga Kyoji, who reported to Field Marshal Count Terauchi Hisaishi, head of the Southern Army. Tominaga had between 400 and 500 hundred aircraft in and around the island of Luzon, but could only count on about half of those being operational.[79] Naval aircraft of the 1st Air Fleet in the Philippines had been badly mauled in their earlier attacks against the American carriers and were in the process of refitting their units.

Although it numbered about 400 aircraft, again only half that number could fly at any one time. These units would be reinforced by 300 aircraft from the 2nd Air Fleet in Formosa.[80] Kenney's Far East Air Forces, with over 2,600 combat aircraft, greatly outnumbered the Japanese; but without any airfields in range, he was essentially powerless in attacking the Philippines.[81]

The defense of the southern and central islands in the Philippines fell to Lieutenant General Suzuki Sasaki, the commander of 35th Army. Leyte itself was defended by the 16th Division, which was charged with keeping the air bases near Tacloban, Dulag, and Burauen in Japanese hands. In the case of an American attack on Leyte, Suzuki planned to send parts of two other divisions through the port of Ormoc, on the western coast of the island, as reinforcements.[82]

Radio intercepts provided a wealth of information about the strength of the Japanese air units in the Philippines, but American knowledge about the Japanese intentions was limited.[83] Although aware that losing the Philippines would cut off the home islands of Japan from oil and other natural resources in the southern area of the empire, American intelligence officers generally assumed that the logical course of action for the Japanese would be to preserve their limited numbers of working aircraft for a defense of Formosa, Luzon, or the home islands. The possibility of air strikes against the Leyte invasion force was not dismissed, but large numbers of attackers seemed unlikely.[84] Likewise, most of the high-ranking American naval commanders dismissed the possibility of a large-scale naval engagement for Leyte.[85]

Kenney's attitudes about the ability of Japanese airmen to impact operations adhered to this general outlook and had not changed since late July, despite the losses suffered during the recent Balikpapan raids. The Japanese were "on the downhill grade," he boasted.[86] As Kenney departed Hollandia with MacArthur onboard the *Nashville* he felt uncomfortable and out of his element, but downplayed the thought of a serious air battle. He was confident that only submarines and mines could cause trouble for the invasion force.[87]

As the *Nashville* sailed towards Leyte, reports began arriving about the attacks by Halsey's carriers on the Japanese air bases in Formosa and the Philippines. The Japanese abandoned their short-lived intent to withhold attacks against the aircraft carriers (largely because they found they were losing too many aircraft on the ground) and met Halsey's raiders in force. Japanese pilots damaged two cruisers, but failed to sink any of the American ships.[88] The attacks, however, did inflict heavy losses on the Japanese. Second Air Fleet was down to about 230 aircraft, and less than 200 of the army aircraft remained in the Philippines.[89]

On the morning of October 20, 1944, hundreds of amphibious landing craft in Operation King Two steamed toward the beaches of Leyte. Since the Japanese planned a fighting retreat that would decimate the American units as they advanced inland, the initial resistance on the beachheads was quickly dispatched. The landing by X Corps near Tacloban took place on two beaches, the northernmost one termed White Beach, the one to the south, Red. The amphibious engineers at White Beach encountered "almost no opposition"[90]—largely because the Japanese did not expect a landing that far north on the island—allowing the Americans to quickly unload troops and equipment. Thirteen miles south at Red Beach, the landing plan quickly began to unravel. A sandbar 100 yards from the shoreline grounded most of the larger amphibious craft, including the 300-foot-long LSTs (landing ship tank), which carried up to 2,000 tons of cargo and most of the heavy equipment. One LST made it to shore, but when another lowered its forward ramp on the sandbar to discharge its cargo, a bulldozer promptly sank into the eight feet of water, jamming the loading ramp and disabling the landing craft. Large numbers of enemy troops near Red Beach, the anticipated landing area, put up heavy resistance, lobbying mortar shells and pouring machine gun fire into the grounded ships.[91]

The existence of the sandbar did not come as a total surprise to the engineers in the landing force. The beaches in the Philippines had been extensively studied; according to the 6th Army engineer, "the survey definitely showed the LSTs would ground 250 to 300 feet off Red Beach."[92] Since there were valid tactical reasons for using this landing beach, the engineers proposed shifting two LSTs loaded with pontoon causeways from the southern convoy to X Corps. Once the enemy troops were removed from the landing site, the pontoons could be unloaded and used to move the matériel the 300 feet from the sandbar to the shore. Control over the LSTs, however, fell to officers in the Allied Naval Forces, who argued that the LSTs should not be transferred until they were needed. A small problem it seemed, but one that proved to have important consequences.[93]

Once the problems with the predicted sandbar became evident, LSTs with the pontoon causeways began making their way to Red Beach, but the other supply ships could not simply remain stationary; they had to be unloaded and sent back for more equipment. Some troops and equipment were hurriedly transferred to smaller craft and shuttled to shore, but this method was time consuming. Successive waves of equipment and troops were told to move north and discharge their cargoes on the best available spot, a flat spit of land just above White Beach: Tacloban airfield.[94] Amphibious engineers were able to rapidly unload vast amounts of cargo (the peak during the Leyte invasion was 100 tons an hour), and they quickly stacked an estimated 4,000 tons of equipment on the runway.[95]

From Kenney's position on the *Nashville,* he did not see the problems developing on his new airfield at Tacloban. On the afternoon of A day, October 20, he accompanied MacArthur for the latter's triumphant return to the Philippines. Over the next several days he and MacArthur stayed aboard ship, making several trips ashore to monitor the progress of the attack and to participate in a variety of official functions.[96] It was not until October 23, two days before his units were scheduled to take over the air duties over Leyte, that Kenney discovered that the LSTs were using the runway at Tacloban to unload troops, supplies, and ammunition. He quickly went to both Krueger and MacArthur in an effort to stop it. Kenney returned the next day and found twenty-eight more ships had tried to unload, but the air task force commander had stopped them by invoking the authority of Kenney and Krueger.[97] By now the damage was done. The decision not to move the causeways had clogged the airfield with troops, supplies, and equipment, making it impossible for the engineers to do any work. Kenney threatened to bulldoze any supplies into the ocean if they were not removed in a hurry, but with little immediate effect.[98] It was clear that Kenney would not be able to take over air support of the invasion from Admiral Kinkaid on October 25.[99]

In addition to clearing the airfield at Tacloban of equipment, engineers also battled with a host of other problems in developing the landing site. The runway was littered with land mines that had to be cleared away too. Next engineers discovered that the landing surface was only 4,300 feet long, not 6,000 feet as projected, requiring them to shift the runway ten degrees to get the desired length. They also found that the soil was too soft to support the American aircraft. Coral or gravel was needed before the steel landing mats could be laid; but the supplies piled on the runway and the resulting congestion slowed the delivery of coral, adding to the construction delays.[100]

As Kenney tried desperately to push the work on Tacloban along, his naval counterpart, Admiral Kinkaid, had his hands full with the Japanese reaction to the invasion. By this stage in the war the Japanese navy was no match for the massive carrier task forces the American Navy was able to put to sea. The naval plan for the Sho-Go plan for the Philippines depended on luring away carriers in order to overwhelm and destroy the amphibious landing force. The resulting clash was the largest, and according to most naval historians the greatest, sea battle ever fought: the Battle of Leyte Gulf.[101]

Upon initiation of the Sho-Go plan, the Japanese planned to send a carrier task force, albeit with almost empty decks, under Vice Admiral Ozawa Jisaburo to lure away Halsey's carriers, which they suspected would be stationed to the northeast of Luzon. If Halsey took the bait, Vice Admiral Kurita Takeo's force could easily blast its way through the escort carriers and other surface units screening the transports in Leyte Gulf and wreak havoc on the landings. Kurita's force actually split into two parts. Kurita himself would attack from the north, through the San Bernardino Strait, while Vice Admiral Nishimura Shoji sailed through the Sulu Sea and Surigao Strait to the south. It was hoped that the resulting pincer would crush the landing force. Simultaneously, Japanese air units were held back from attacking the American landing force until air reinforcements could be rushed into the Philippines to combine large-scale air raids with the naval action.

The first confirmed warnings about the American invasion of Leyte arrived in Tokyo on October 17; official orders activating the Sho-Go plan for the Philippines were issued the next day, with October 24 tentatively designated as the day of the attack (later changed to October 25).[102] The Japanese attack started out very nearly as planned when Halsey took the bait and steamed northward to engage Ozawa's carriers. Further south, however, the plan started to unravel. Kurita's force was spotted by submarines and then ripped apart by Kinkaid's 7th Fleet. Although he lost much of his original force, Kurita regrouped and headed back towards Leyte as Kinkaid turned against the remaining portion of the Japanese force, sailing through the Surigao Strait. The divided command at Leyte, however, was about to reveal a fatal flaw. Kinkaid's maneuvering and Halsey's dash north had left only the escort carriers guarding the landing force. At dawn on October 25 Kurita as spotted moving towards the vulnerable supply ships and troopships afloat in Leyte Gulf. Thanks to the gallant actions of innumerable naval officers and sailors, as well as poor communications and indecisive leadership on Kurita's part, the Japanese turned away just 45 miles from Leyte—a lucky break for American soldiers on the beach.

Japanese air opposition on the first few days after the landing at Leyte had been weak, as units awaited October 25 and the infusion of reinforcements. Halsey's previous raids on the Philippine airfields inflicted large losses; and on October 20, the 1st Air Fleet had fewer than 50 flyable aircraft, while the 4th Air Army was down to about 100.[103] Given the value they placed on the Philippines, the Japanese were willing to make up these losses. The 7th Air Division from the Celebes flew into Luzon, joining numerous aircraft from Japan. By October 23, there were roughly 250 Japanese naval aircraft in the islands, along with almost 200 army planes.[104] Mass attacks began the next day, with almost 200 naval aircraft hitting Halsey's carriers and about 100 army aircraft bombing the landing forces in Leyte Gulf. Over the next several days a new, terrifying tactic appeared—the kamikaze, or suicide, attacks.

Although there had been suicide attacks previously in the Pacific, the desperate situation the Japanese faced in October 1944 forced them to organize such extreme measures on a regular basis. Tokko, or special-attack units, were specifically organized to carry out such missions. Although the name Tokko applied to all such units and the term kamikaze originally was only used to refer to naval air units, the latter name was adopted by American forces as the general designation for a suicide mission. The first kamikaze attack was carried out on October 21, but massed efforts that brought home the power of this weapon did not start until the morning of October 25. Although using aircraft in this manner was expensive (an aircraft and its pilot on a conventional bombing mission could be used many times over), a suicide attack could produce impressive results. Alongside the kamikaze attacks, other army and navy aircraft carried out conventional bombing missions in large numbers; after October 24 the Japanese managed to fly over one hundred missions a day against the invasion force—a notable change from their previous methods.[105]

On October 25, as Kinkaid's forces were dealing with Kurita's attack, Kenney moved ashore with MacArthur and experienced the Japanese air attacks firsthand. While inspecting the progress on Tacloban he "hit the dirt three times in an hour."[106] Understandably anxious after this experience to bring his fighter units forward, he found that it would be some time before he could do so. Work on the airdromes had been slowed by the Japanese bombing raids as well as by Navy aircraft forced to land ashore because of damage to the escort carriers. With only 2,000 feet of the old Japanese landing strip available, twenty-five of the sixty-five Navy aircraft that landed on Tacloban were wrecked and had to be shoved into the water. Similar problems also affected the engineers at Dulag, where the combination of enemy attacks and emergency landings made work almost impossible.[107]

At the same time, engineering officers looked at some of the planned airfields further inland, and they discovered that those areas were ill suited for airfield development. At a conference on October 24, 6th Army engineers tried to talk Kenney into concentrating all of the engineering efforts on Tacloban and Dulag. Perhaps because he wanted an airfield capable of handling the heavy bombers (even when completed, neither Tacloban nor Dulag could fulfill that need), he insisted that the engineers continue working at the other locations.[108]

By the evening of October 26 engineers were putting the finishing touches on the runway and dispersal areas at Tacloban, and Kenney ordered the first P-38s in the next day.[109] The aircraft carriers had taken a beating during the sea battles and needed immediate relief. Kinkaid had lost over one hundred aircraft and two of his escort carriers, with at least half of the remaining number incapacitated in some way. Even the undamaged ships were running short of fuel. He needed relief badly.[110] Late on October 25, Kinkaid requested help from Kenney in covering Leyte Gulf:

> Can [fighters] be flown in tomorrow? Apparently the enemy has flown in a large number of aircraft into the Philippines in addition strong Japanese surface units got through San Bernadino Strait last nite [*sic*]. Our CVEs [escort carriers] have been crippled severely by repeated air and surface attacks today. Probably less than half the group can function at all. The maximum CVE air effort has been extended in self defense with subsequent inability to provide [fighter] cover for Leyte. . . . Task groups 38.1 and 38.2 will be here tomorrow morning and will be able to furnish [fighter] cover but those groups should be hitting enemy surface vessels in the area as well as attacking enemy aircraft in the air and on the ground. It is of utmost importance that land based [fighters] be established in Leyte immediately.[111]

Halsey, facing many of the same problems as Kinkaid, also pleaded for relief that night. "After 17 days of battle my fast carriers are unable to provide extended support for Leyte but 2 groups are available October 27. The pilots are exhausted, and the carriers are low in provisions, bombs, and torpedoes. When will land-based air take over at Leyte?"[112] In effect, Halsey's message confirmed the very problems Kenney had cited earlier about the carriers, but the confession was probably of little comfort at the time. For his part, Halsey was not aware of the myriad of difficulties involved at the airfield at Tacloban. All he cared about was the fact that Kenney was supposed to take over the air duties five days after the invasion.[113]

Powerless to accelerate the construction, embarrassed by the Navy's demands, and concerned about the strength of the Japanese attacks, Kenney grew increasingly frustrated and irritated over what he perceived to be irrational actions by the Navy. He clashed frequently with Captain Richard Whitehead, a member of Kinkaid's staff and the officer in charge of directing aircraft in the amphibious landing area. Kenney could not understand why the Navy failed to put some of their aircraft over land or why they remained on the ground after getting warning of an enemy air attack.[114] The last straw came on October 26, as Kenney was making plans to bring forward the first P-38s, when the Navy, according to Kenney, "immediately started giving instructions" about using the aircraft. He vowed to take over responsibility for the whole area "as soon as one squadron arrives."[115] Kenney convinced MacArthur of the need to get rid of the Navy as soon as the first P-38s landed; the subsequent directive not only put Kenney in control of air operations in Leyte Gulf, but also ordered the Navy away from any targets in the Philippines.[116]

Although Kenney did move one squadron into Tacloban on October 27, he was in no position to take over air operations. He had planes but little else. A temporary fighter command post, six air defense radars, and an RAAF wireless unit had landed on Leyte during the initial stages of the invasion to provide the essential command and control network for the fighters; but heavy rainfall delayed the installation of the equipment, and ground observers had to be pressed into service to provide early warning of Japanese air attacks.[117] A typhoon on the night of October 29 slowed the movement of any additional fighters into Leyte; and on October 30 Whitehead, who had arrived at Leyte to command operations, only had 20 P-38s to defend against Japanese attacks. Kenney brushed off Whitehead's concerns despite the fact that his deputy faced almost 300 Japanese aircraft in the Philippines.[118]

Kenney needed more airfields to get more aircraft into Leyte, but bad weather plagued the engineer's efforts. Two typhoons and several smaller storms pounded Leyte with 24 inches of rain during the first forty days of the operation, and the rainfall recorded in November was almost twice the usual amount. "Construction under these conditions," recalled the 6th Army engineer, "became a nightmare."[119] The rains not only hampered construction of the airfields, but also turned roads into muddy bogs, making it impossible to move fuel, ammunition, or equipment anywhere. Engineers were yanked off the airfields to help repair roads, a move that delayed airfield construction further and frustrated Kenney, since additional engineering battalions did not arrive until November 12.[120] Despite Kenney's instruction to continue building at all the planned sites, conditions at the proposed airfield near San Pablo got too bad and construction was quickly stopped. The airfields at Buri and Bayug were used for a time, but they also proved unusable and eventually were abandoned.[121] With only Tacloban and Dulag operating, and neither capable of handling any bombers, engineers cast about for additional sites. The best location in terms of terrain was near Tanauan, then the current site of the 6th Army headquarters. Fortunately, Krueger was aware of the desperate need for more airfields and agreed to move his headquarters. Work began on the site on November 28, and by the middle of December the airfield was operating.[122]

The lack of airfields and the inability to defend against Japanese attacks had an immediate impact on the course of the fighting on Leyte as the campaign progressed through November and December. While rainfall pounded the Allies, the Japanese forces' location offered favorable weather, allowing them to hit Kenney's airfields, supply areas, and the ships bringing additional troops and equipment to Leyte. Kenney began taking great risks and pushed as much of his air strength forward as possible. The airfields at Tacloban and Dulag overflowed with aircraft and supplies, making them inviting targets for the Japanese. In the first two weeks of operation at Tacloban, a quarter of the P-38s lost were destroyed on the ground by enemy air attacks. During November and December Kenney wrote off about 100 aircraft each month, a situation that prompted him to plead for more aircraft. Rather than promise relief, Arnold warned Kenney that the rate at which he was chewing up aircraft placed an excessive burden on aircraft production and resources.[123] Six weeks after the landings Kenney still had less than 200 available aircraft on Leyte, while the Japanese continued to pour aircraft into Luzon.[124]

Stopping the Japanese air attacks became particularly difficult because of the nature of the suicide attacks against American ships.[125] Defenses that would stop a regular aircraft were simply ineffective in preventing these new attacks. It was necessary to completely disable the aircraft or kill the pilot before it got close to the target. When the Japanese shifted to nighttime or dawn attacks, Kenney's daytime fighters like the P-38s were useless. A squadron of P-61 night fighters was sent to Leyte, but they proved too slow to catch the Japanese fighters. The night raids became so troublesome that Halsey prodded Kenney into replacing the P-61s with a Marine Corps night fighter squadron, a move that must have galled Kenney but one that proved more effective in stopping the night attacks.[126]

While aircraft on Leyte provided local air defense, Kenney searched for a way to prevent the Japanese aircraft from ever getting airborne. ULTRA intercepts tracked the aircraft as they moved up from Borneo and Malaya, permitting Kenney's bombers flying from the recently completed airfield on Morotai to attack the Japanese aircraft at these staging bases before they flew off for the Philippines.[127] Kenney also began investigating other possibilities for airfields. He flew to newly captured Palau in late November and managed to get some space for a B-24 bomb group there so that they could hit targets in the southern part of Luzon.[128] The bulk of the Japanese airfields on Luzon, however, remained inaccessible except to aircraft flying from the carriers.

Despite his desire to take complete control of air operations, Kenney could not make good on his promise. Almost immediately after getting his aircraft into Tacloban, he was forced to ask MacArthur for Halsey's help against the airfields on Luzon. The carriers were eventually forced to remain in the vicinity of the Philippines until late November, forcing Halsey to cancel a planned attack against Tokyo and the Japanese battle fleet.[129] This turn of events frustrated Halsey so much that after the war he complained of

"Kenney's inability to give Leyte effective air support. I had to stand by and attend to his knitting for him."[130] While the actual situation was more complicated, Halsey's comment underscores the hostility between Kenney and the naval air commanders.[131]

Along with their unrelenting air attacks, the Japanese also began to move large numbers of ground forces into the port of Ormoc in western Leyte. The enthusiastic, but misleading, reports by the Japanese navy about the destruction of the American fleet convinced Japanese army headquarters in Tokyo that it was possible to gain temporary air superiority and wage the decisive battle for the Philippines on Leyte rather than waiting for the Americans to attack Luzon.[132] The first reinforcements began arriving at Ormoc from other islands in the southern Philippines on October 23, and by the end of the month over 6,000 men from two Japanese divisions had been unloaded. Although still able to break the Japanese codes, Allied intercept operators and intelligence officers during this period were focused more on deciphering the actions of the Japanese battle fleet during the Battle of Leyte Gulf than monitoring small-ship movements. Any encounters with these convoys were normally accomplished with naval aircraft and were the result of good luck, not good intelligence.[133] As more and more reinforcements began arriving and the outline of Japanese intentions became clearer, ULTRA intercepts often, but not always, provided a picture of when and where the convoys were moving.[134]

For example, on the afternoon of November 1, 1944, a large convoy arrived at Ormoc carrying the veteran, well-trained 1st Division from Manchuria. There had been no ULTRA warnings, and Japanese deception efforts helped keep most of Halsey's carriers away from the area. The four merchant ships and their escorts were picked up by a B-24 and strafed by several P-38s, but none of the ships suffered any serious damage. The convoy was attacked again the next day by twenty-four B-24s and one vessel was sunk, but only after all of the 12,000 soldiers and 90 percent of their equipment had already been unloaded.[135]

Kenney found himself handicapped by a lack of information as well as the tactical situation. He had few aircraft on Leyte and was unable to base any bombers on the island. The P-38s could carry bombs and the pilots were trained to drop them, but there were usually too few aircraft and too many demands. To Kenney's mind, taking control of the air claimed first priority, and on November 2 only eight P-38s were available for strikes against this convoy.[136] On occasion he was even forced to ask Halsey for help in stopping the shipping. On November 10, an intercepted radio message revealed that a Japanese convoy was due at Ormoc at 8:00 A.M. the next day. Halsey's carriers had completed strikes on Japanese air bases on Luzon, and Kenney asked if Halsey could attack the ships before they unloaded. Although Kenney made the request grudgingly, he realized that it was necessary because his aircraft, flying from bases further away, simply could not make it to Ormoc before the convoy was unloaded. Kenney's comment also sheds some light on one of the reasons behind the service tensions—public recognition of the service contribution. "Let him [Halsey] have the headline if he will stop the reinforcement," Kenney remarked.[137] The decision turned out to be a fortunate one in many respects. Not only did Halsey's attack utterly destroy the convoy, but bad weather at Morotai prevented any of Kenney's aircraft from taking off.[138]

Although eventually the Allies were able to stop the Japanese from sending troops and supplies to Leyte, the damage had been done. In two weeks the Japanese sent 22,000 troops into Ormoc, doubling the strength of the Japanese force on Leyte. By the end of the fighting, about 35,000 soldiers fought on Leyte as reinforcements.[139] The transfer of the crack 1st Division was especially significant; the Japanese claimed this movement was the "most successful major reinforcement of the Leyte campaign," while Krueger believed "this unit, more than any other hostile unit on Leyte, was responsible for the extension of the Leyte Operation."[140]

Another factor in extending the Leyte fighting was problems in building airfields. This failure not only increased the number of casualties in the Leyte campaign, but also delayed the attack on Luzon and possibly lengthened the war. Explanations, by both participants and historians, of the failure to bring more aircraft into Leyte tend to focus on poor terrain intelligence about Leyte or the engineering problems involved in building the airfields, but these interpretations do not tell the whole story.[141] The long-time American presence in the Philippines provided some knowledge of the country, and MacArthur himself had spent two weeks on Leyte in 1903 surveying Tacloban. Additionally, American forces had used a small commercial airstrip in the area before the war.[142] The Japanese had reportedly lengthened the airstrip at Tacloban and made other improvements. Although the runway was not concrete or covered with any sort of paved surface, it was considered an all-weather surface because, according to several studies, "the rain packs the sandy soil and makes it even firmer than when dry."[143]

Other than this limited amount of information about the airfield at Tacloban, however, there was little for engineers to go on in deciding where to build the airfields. The decision to attack at Leyte without capturing any intervening bases put the area out of range for reconnaissance aircraft until the beginning of October.[144] Even when aircraft were in position to fly to

Leyte, bad weather limited opportunities for visual reconnaissance, as did a request from the Navy to limit the number of friendly aircraft flights over Leyte out of fear that the aircraft might be attacked by American forces.[145] While there was a definite lack of the appropriate kind of photographs needed to adequately plan for building airfields, ground reconnaissance reports had proven enormously helpful in making decisions about where an airfield could be built in other areas and might have been expected to be used for Leyte also. There were plenty of friendly agents on the island who could provide information, but most reports dealt with the number of Japanese troops on the island and where they were located. From the perspective of an engineer assigned the task of planning runways, these reports were disappointing. Agents did give some general information about the terrain, but they were neither trained nor equipped to provide the critical soil assessments.[146]

In the end though, the lack of aerial photographs and reports on the terrain (which aviation engineers found "faulty and considerably exaggerated"[147]) caused only minor problems during the planning for the invasion of Leyte. In fact, engineers had enough information to forecast the general kinds of problems they actually encountered on Leyte. Colonel William J. Ely, the second-highest-ranking engineer in the 6th Army and the liaison officer to MacArthur's headquarters, anticipated the problems with uncanny accuracy. Ely opposed both the scale of the engineering projects and the time available, arguing that there were too many construction requirements and too few engineers. He also pointed out that the attack would occur during the time of year when heavy rains and typhoons were most likely, factors that would only add to the problems. In addition, he claimed that the soil in the Leyte Valley, where three of the airfields were supposed to be built, was ill suited to runways and would require large amounts of additional work. To meet the demands of the attack, he recommended either adding more engineers to the operation, changing the proposed landing site to another island, or reducing the requirements. Despite support from 6th Army, Ely's recommendations were downplayed at MacArthur's headquarters.[148]

While engineers faced some daunting challenges, few historians or participants link the difficulties in building airfields to the more important problem in the fighting—the failure to gain air superiority. The problem was not just the inability to bring aircraft forward, but the consequences of that for the commanders and troops on the ground and at sea. General Krueger, for example, has been criticized for the slow pace of the campaign, but his position is easier to understand given his worries about a Japanese attack on his northern flank.[149] As historian Edward Drea points out, one of Krueger's problems was the ambiguous intelligence indications he received. As late as

November 8, Krueger's intelligence officer was worried about the possibility of a landing at Carigara Bay on their exposed northern flank.[150] By this stage of the war Krueger had grown accustomed to fighting with almost total air superiority, but he was now thrust into an environment in which the situation was, at best, neutral. This not only allowed the Japanese to ship additional reinforcements into Ormoc, but also presented the very real possibility of a landing at Carigara Bay. The threat of such a move gave Krueger pause; it helps explain his decision to consolidate his position, resulting in slow progress in finishing the Leyte campaign.[151]

In previous operations Krueger might have turned to Kenney for help using reconnaissance aircraft to spot ships heading for a landing, while other aircraft waited on alert to attack the landing force before it hit Krueger's flank. On Leyte in late 1944 such an option was unavailable. The lack of bases and the presence of hostile air forces meant that no reconnaissance aircraft could be brought forward. The first close air support mission, by Kenney's P-40s, was not flown until the end of November; and the total number eventually flown was small.[152] In short, the inability to gain control of the air was a key component in Krueger's decision-making process.

Based on the success of previous operations, Kenney believed that the Japanese were very weak in the air and postulated that his forces could handle any possible contingency. The whole plan was "unsound," he thought, unless the Japanese air and naval forces were "reduced so far that they could be of little more than nuisance value,"[153] the situation he thought existed. Kenney's support for the invasion makes it clear that he never expected such a stiff and prolonged reaction to the landing on Leyte. Similarly, Admiral Barbey wrote a fellow officer that Japanese efforts in defending Leyte were "more determined . . . than had been anticipated."[154] The confidence about the likely Japanese reaction probably made it easy to dismiss or downplay concerns about construction and also left Kenney and the other commanders unprepared to deal with the resistance they did encounter.

There was also little recognition among any of the commanders that the air battle for the Philippines would be fundamentally different from any other invasion. Although ground combat in the Central Pacific differed in many ways from fighting in the jungles of the Southwest Pacific, air warfare in both areas had been very similar up until Leyte.[155] On both the small islands that dotted the Central Pacific and the garrisoned areas in New Guinea, there were a limited number of airfields that the Japanese could use. In addition, the very long distances from Japan made it difficult to quickly rush in large numbers of aircraft. In an amphibious assault on an island in the Central Pacific, for example, it was relatively easy for aircraft from the carriers to eliminate the Japanese air threat, provide air support for their ground troops, and at the same time guard against the Japanese fleet. Likewise in Kenney's theater he had to keep track of only a few airfields that could threaten MacArthur's operations and had excellent intelligence on the influx of reinforcements. As Kenney explained to Arnold nearly two years before Leyte:

> In the Pacific theater we have a number of islands garrisoned by small forces. These islands are nothing more or less than aerodromes or aerodrome areas from which modern fire-power is launched. Sometimes they are true islands like Wake or Midway, sometimes they are localities on large land masses. Port Moresby, Lae and Buna are all on the island of New Guinea, but the only practicable way to go from one to the other is by air or by water: they are all islands as far as warfare is concerned.[156]

The air battle in the Philippines was dramatically different. To begin with there were many more airfields in the Philippines than the other locations. At Wewak in New Guinea the Japanese had built four airfields, at Hollandia three; even the largest Japanese base in the Southwest Pacific, Rabaul, had only five airfields. In contrast, there were around seventy airstrips on the island of Luzon and roughly fifty more in the central and southern Philippine islands, allowing the Japanese to disperse their aircraft very effectively, increasing the problems in destroying the planes on the ground.[157] In addition, the distance between Japan and the Philippines was relatively short, making it possible and practical to rapidly reinforce the air units in the fighting. The increased number of airfields and the ability to send in more aircraft combined to make the air battle in the Philippines very different from previous experiences; yet none of the air commanders, Kenney included, seemed to anticipate this difference or believe that it would have any impact. Confidence that the Japanese air arm was largely defeated and a lack of awareness about the differences in the conditions of air warfare they faced led commanders into a false sense of security and made them willing to overlook the problems in airfield construction identified by the engineers.

Once ashore engineers found their efforts stymied by a variety of factors, and estimates of the Japanese reactions proved inaccurate. The unloading of the LSTs on the Tacloban airfield, caused by using a beach with a sandbar and failing to have pontoon causeways in the proper position, resulted in at least a two-day delay in repairing the field. Further delays resulted from problems in getting steel landing mats to the airfields.[158] Rather than being readily available, the mats were stowed deep in the hold of the freighters because the convoy had originally been loaded for a landing on Yap, where coral provided plenty of support for the runways. The rapid change from Yap to Leyte made it impossible to unload and reload the ships, creating more problems for airfield construction.[159] As Ely predicted, heavy rainfall during October and November also played a role. Three typhoons and twice the normal amount of rain forced engineers to repeat the same jobs many times over, and as a result they had to be pulled off the airdromes and put on road construction in order to get equipment to where it was needed.[160]

The problems in building the airfields and the difficulties caused by the robust Japanese air response highlighted shortcomings in the planning for the invasion and the inability of the Army and Navy air commanders to meld their forces. Despite the comments by some officers, including MacArthur's intelligence chief, Major General Willoughby, and the amphibious commander in the Southwest Pacific, Admiral Barbey, that Kenney took over control of air operations too soon, there was, in fact, no other option.[161] The escort carriers had to be withdrawn. Halsey wanted to move his carrier task forces away from an area where they were being pounded by suicide bombers.[162] There had not been a firm date set for Kenney to take over air operations during the planning for the invasion, although five days was the assumed target date for completion of the first airfield. The invasion plan only called for Kenney to assume air support duties "at the earliest practicable date after the establishment of fighters and light bombers in the Leyte area," when both he and Kinkaid agreed. The directive also gave air control over the invasion area to either Kenney or Kinkaid and did not allow them to control the other's air units even for brief periods of time.[163] In short, there had been no planning for the contingency that the commanders actually faced: some of the airfields open, but not as many as anticipated; a strong enemy air reaction; and difficulty in keeping the carriers close by.

One possible alternative would have been for Kenney and Kinkaid to combine their forces, forming a more potent combination. Unfortunately, there was no procedure at the time for integrating air units, and the lack of coordination between the land-based aircraft and the carriers was clearly evident during the invasion of Leyte. Some of the problems were small and easily resolved. The Marine night fighter pilots on Leyte, for instance, were initially confused by procedures used by the Army ground controllers, but the difficulties were alleviated through practice.[164] Other problems were not so easily resolved. Kenney's aircraft were charged with patrolling and defending the westward approaches to Leyte, through which the Japanese fleet passed before the battle of Leyte Gulf. While the airmen spotted some of the fleet, they were not used to attack the ships.[165] Whitehead suspected that this was a deliberate move by the Navy to gain all of the publicity in sinking the Japanese fleet.[166] In reality, some of Kenney's bombers on Morotai attempted to go after the ships as they left the Leyte area, but a combination of poor bombing and bad intelligence rendered their efforts ineffective—only one light cruiser, already heavily damaged in the sea battle, was sunk.[167]

Solutions to the problems of combining air operations were not abundant in 1944. Admiral Kinkaid suggested placing all of the air reconnaissance and land-based aircraft that would be used in any way during the operation under the control of the naval commander. While this arrangement would allow the naval commander to determine search areas and coordinate attacks with surface units, it was unlikely to gain support from officers like Kenney.[168] Some naval officers, in fact, saw Kenney as the problem. The commander of one carrier task force, Vice Admiral John S. McCain, told Kinkaid that the aircraft from the escort carriers should have been put on land along with some Marine squadrons. The problem, McCain argued, was that "the Army don't understand the sea. They don't understand search and strike. They don't know how to defend ships. They are cocky, courageous and will try anything once, but their higher-ups [Kenney] do not have the know how."[169] McCain urged Kinkaid to go around Kenney and talk directly to MacArthur. Kenney, McCain believed, "has a closed mind on the subject."[170]

As he had throughout the war, Kenney had little use for the complaints or suggestions of naval officers and made few attempts to get along or work together with them. On occasion Kenney would request Halsey's help in attacking the airfields on Luzon or sinking the convoys off of Ormoc, but those cases were the exception rather than the rule. If Halsey's comments after the fact were any indication, he probably made his dissatisfaction with Kenney's requests quite clear. In any case, there were few, if any, attempts to define what targets had the highest priority or to combine the efforts of the two services.

The most divisive fights between Kinkaid and Kenney came in late November over protection of the ships in Leyte Gulf. During refueling operations on November 27, suicide bombers hit a battleship and destroyer, prompting Kinkaid to complain that the aircraft assigned to protect the ships were nowhere in sight. Kenney retorted that there were aircraft in the air, but that they could not get close enough to the ships to attack the Japanese bombers because of the antiaircraft fire.[171] Two days later another battleship and destroyer were hit. On board the *Maryland,* thirty-one men were killed and another thirty injured.[172] Understandably upset with the growing list of casualties, Kinkaid accused Kenney of not fulfilling his obligations.[173] At the same time Kenney was also under intense pressure. Air operations during the Leyte operation had not gone at all the way he had planned. Japanese air reinforcements continued to arrive in large numbers, and he still only had a little over one hundred aircraft (the complement of one of the large aircraft carriers) to deal with a variety of tasks.[174] Kenney became enraged by Kinkaid's comments and told the naval commander to put the comments "in writing" so that he could "prefer charges against him for false official statements,"[175] harsh words for two men who were supposed to be working together.

Although Kenney and Kinkaid blamed each other for the problems, both bore some of the responsibility for these incidents. An investigation afterwards revealed that the attack on November 27 came from a spot with no radar coverage, which hid the enemy aircraft until very late, and that delays in relaying the information from the ships to the P-38s prevented the aircraft from arriving before the Japanese attacked the ships. In addition, the report pointed out a variety of problems and blamed the failure on a variety of factors, including a lack of awareness on the part of the ground controllers, an inability of sea and land radar sites to work together, and poor radio discipline.[176]

Tension between all the commanders was undoubtedly growing high at the end of November, exacerbated by the unexpectedly intense fighting they had encountered. Not only did the ground combat on Leyte continue to drag on, but towards the end of the month the Japanese staged an attack of their own against the American airfields. No less than the Americans, the Japanese realized that control of the air was a deciding factor in the fighting. General Yamashita was growing increasingly concerned about the buildup of Kenney's forces and directed Suzuki to put more effort into recapturing the fields. The Japanese were not finished yet. The 4th Army Air Force commander, Tominaga, planned a major assault using air transports against the airfields on Leyte. On November 22 an airborne raiding detachment landed at Buri and Bayug airfields and staged a quick hit-and-run raid. A larger assault was planned for December 5; but weather problems grounded many of the planes, and only about half of the regiment made the assault. In the end the Japanese effort was plagued by multiple errors. In the judgment of historian Stanley Falk, the assaults were hampered by communications problems and poor coordination. In addition, the Japanese had very poor intelligence, landing at airfields that had been abandoned because of construction problems. They also could not transport a large enough force to give the American defenders serious problems. For very high costs, the Japanese inflicted little serious damage.[177]

The remaining phase of the complicated Japanese air assault was ended by the American amphibious landing near Ormoc that effectively sealed off the island from reinforcements. Meanwhile, Kenney's air strength on Leyte continued to grow, and by the end of December he had almost 350 aircraft on the island.[178] The landing on Mindoro on December 15 cut off Leyte even further, and by the end of December most of the heavy fighting was over. Eighth Army and 13th Air Force took over control of operations on December 26, while 6th Army and 5th Air Force prepared for the invasion of Luzon.

In assessing the results of the invasion of Leyte, Kenney downplayed the problems caused by the Japanese, putting the best face he could on events, stressing what might have happened. His attitude was that "the Jap missed an opportunity to give us a bloody nose."[179] Things would have been much worse, he claimed, if not for "his naval dumbness, his wretched gunnery, his stupid handling of his air forces and his incredibly inaccurate bombing."[180] Kenney was convinced that even though the Japanese could not have won the war, they could have caused serious trouble and perhaps prevailed on Leyte if they had pressed their attack harder.

Not surprisingly perhaps, the overwhelming lesson for Kenney was the importance of land-based aircraft. "Carrier-based aircraft, even in the overwhelming numbers we are using, do not supply the answer for air cover and support," he concluded.[181] "The main lesson I believe we should draw from this operation is to stick to land-based support whenever we attempt an amphibious expedition against a hostile shore."[182]

THE RETURN to the Philippines had not been a smooth journey. The pattern of operations Kenney had grown used to during the first two years of war had changed. The introduction of aircraft carriers, beginning with the invasion of Hollandia, meant that MacArthur could now advance without seizing nearby air bases. While Kenney still carried out many of the familiar roles with his aircraft, he now had to integrate operations with aircraft carriers. For the most part the air commanders cooperated by separating their forces in space and time. Although there were no complications when this was tried in Hollandia, differences in the conditions at Leyte produced problems. The fighting on Leyte made it clear that the war was far from over. Not only was the invasion of Luzon ahead, but it appeared that the worst was still to come.

LUZON AND BEYOND

January 1945 to August 1945

"We cannot take another chance like Leyte."

Even before the fighting ended on Leyte, Kenney had started looking forward to the next invasions and returned to his headquarters at Hollandia to review the plans for the attacks against Mindoro and Luzon. Although he was convinced that the Japanese could not win the war, the initiation of the large-scale suicide attacks, the persistence of the air raids, and the reinforcements flowing into Leyte scared Kenney into a more cautious approach. "We cannot take another chance like Leyte," he told his staff, vowing that "land-based air must support the next operation"[1]—a pledge he was determined to keep throughout the fighting in the Philippines and on to Japan.

Mindoro

The campaign on Leyte convinced Kenney that he and his planners had badly underestimated the number of aircraft needed for the next invasions.[2] He told Sutherland and Chamberlin that he needed a minimum of two heavy-bomb groups, three groups of medium bombers, and three fighter groups in Leyte for the Mindoro assault, plus the use of Halsey's carriers against Japanese airfields on Formosa and Luzon. For the attack on Luzon, Kenney wanted an additional two fighter groups, four or five bomber groups, and more help from Halsey against Formosa, which was within range of the Luzon landing beaches. Assembling this fleet of aircraft, not to mention the required people and equipment, would take time. Given the delays already incurred in building the Leyte airfields, Kenney recommended moving the date of the Mindoro invasion from December 5 to December 15 or 20 and delaying the attack on Luzon until early January.[3] Although Sutherland agreed with Kenney in principle, neither was anxious to tell MacArthur about the need to postpone the invasions; both knew that their commander wanted to proceed as quickly as possible.[4]

Eventually, of course, MacArthur would have to be informed about the problems in attacking Mindoro. Kenney returned to Leyte on November 10 and found that the fighting on the island was still not progressing as quickly as planned. Sutherland and Kenney met with MacArthur to discuss the plans for Mindoro and Luzon, a session Kenney termed "a real brawl."[5] MacArthur refused to listen to any suggestions about delays.

Despite the rejection, Kenney and others continued to work on MacArthur to convince him that the original dates for Mindoro and Luzon were just not feasible. Not only would the airfields on Leyte not be ready in time, but the shipping needed for the invasion force would be tied up by Krueger's proposal for a landing at Ormoc. In addition, the aircraft carriers had been in operations almost continuously and badly needed a break from combat.[6] Whitehead, overseeing operations on Leyte, updated Kenney on the pace of construction and predicted that by the scheduled date for Mindoro he would have only four fighter groups and one medium bomber group on Leyte, a number far less than Kenney considered necessary. Whitehead also met with MacArthur and updated him on the construction and its effect on bringing forward more aircraft. Although very "disappointed" with Whitehead's estimates, MacArthur stood by his original timetable.[7]

Shortly before Whitehead's meeting, Admirals Kinkaid and Nimitz had informed MacArthur that the fast carrier task groups would not be able to stay around indefinitely and provide air cover. Nimitz told MacArthur that Halsey's carriers and men needed two weeks of rest before they would be ready for the Mindoro invasion. Kinkaid had some of the small escort carriers on hand, but was reluctant to put them close to the Japanese air bases, given the strength of the air attacks.[8] Even with the steady calls for a delay, MacArthur would not budge. Kenney continued to work out plans for the Mindoro and Luzon attacks and returned to Leyte for another planning conference on November 26. Before the formal meeting, Kenney met with MacArthur privately and lobbied for a delay of ten days. If MacArthur did not agree, Kenney could not promise that he would have enough fighters available, forcing MacArthur to rely on the escort carriers for protection. MacArthur remained obstinate, and Kenney threatened to bring up his recommendation for a delay at the planning conference, a comment that made MacArthur "sore as hell." The airman held his ground, however, and asked MacArthur "if he wanted me to yes him or give him my best professional advice on air matters." Probably because of their long association through the war and MacArthur's trust in Kenney's judgments about air operations, MacArthur did not throw Kenney out, but told him to "tell . . . the truth as

I saw it and not to mind if he did get excited once in awhile,"[9] a remark that indicates how close the two had grown over the course of the war.

As the top commanders met to discuss air operations for the invasion of Mindoro, the kamikaze attacks loomed as large as ever. The day before the meeting, suicide raiders slammed into Halsey's big carriers attacking the airfields on Luzon, sinking one carrier and several other vessels and forcing the Americans to withdraw.

Despite his earlier promise to bring up the ten-day delay during the meeting, Kenney evidently decided against a public confrontation with MacArthur over a postponement, perhaps fearing the retribution if he did so or rationalizing that the action would have not done any good. Instead, he turned his anger on the Navy. He blasted their refusal to risk the escort carriers with the convoy or send them forward to relieve Kenney's aircraft in defending Leyte so that he could cover the convoy. Not surprisingly, his intemperate remarks about the Navy's fear of losing the escort carriers did little to help solve the problem; instead they turned the discussions into another "brawl."[10] After much debate, Kinkaid, under intense pressure and against his better judgment, agreed to use six escort carriers, along with his small fleet of old battleships, destroyers, and cruisers, to accompany the convoy on December 5.[11]

The naval commander almost immediately began having doubts about the risks involved in sending ships into such an environment. Over the next couple of days he heard from the commanders of the various task forces, urging a reconsideration of the situation in light of the ferocious Japanese air attacks.[12] During refueling operations on November 27, twenty-five to thirty Japanese aircraft attacked one of Kinkaid's task groups, damaging a battleship and two cruisers. Near sunset two days later, the same group was hit, severely damaging the battleship *Maryland*.[13] Kinkaid was growing more and more exasperated with the persistent attacks and grumbled about Kenney's air protection. Although at one point Kenney privately admitted that he did not understand why his aircraft could not stop the suicide attacks, he was decidedly unsympathetic, an attitude that led him to make his comments about Kinkaid putting his complaints in writing so that Kenney could file charges for a false official statement.[14] Perhaps if the two had worked together they could have convinced MacArthur about the danger from the Japanese attacks on the shipping for the Mindoro invasion, but the frayed nerves of the commanders since the invasion of Leyte, Kenney's tactless comments, and the tensions between the services made this level of cooperation almost impossible.

With no help from Kenney and with the evidence of the Japanese attacks fresh in his mind, Kinkaid set out alone to change MacArthur's mind about delaying the invasion of Mindoro and Luzon. On the evening of November 30, Kinkaid resumed his argument about the risks involved in sending the escort carriers to Mindoro, bolstering his case by producing a message from Nimitz, urging a delay of ten days. Kinkaid also hinted that he was obliged to go over MacArthur's head and tell Admiral King in Washington about his reservations, a statement that made "MacArthur hit the roof."[15] That same evening Halsey also sent word that he would like to postpone the attack on Mindoro. The combined efforts finally had the desired effect, MacArthur gave in and moved the date for Mindoro to December 15 and scheduled the attack on Luzon for January 9, 1945.[16]

The delay not only freed up amphibious vessels for Krueger's attack on Ormoc, but also allowed time for the construction of an additional airfield on Leyte, which Kenney desperately needed if he was going to support the invasion of Mindoro.[17] The air plan for the upcoming invasion focused almost entirely on stopping the suicide attacks. Aircraft in 13th Air Force and the RAAF Command went after airfields in Borneo and the Celebes to prevent any reinforcements from the southern area. Carriers would have responsibility for striking the airfields on Luzon north of Manila Bay, while Kenney's aircraft could hit any target in the Philippines south of Manila. Whitehead's 5th Air Force planned on covering the convoy at dusk as well as the Allied shipping in the Mindanao Sea, while aircraft from the escort carriers would remain over the convoy at all other times and provide any bombing on the beach the day of the invasion.[18]

Despite frequent attacks on the Japanese airfields, their air strength in the Philippines remained high. While the exact numbers varied from day to day, on December 9 the 4th Air Army had about 133 operational planes and the Japanese navy an additional 100 or so flyable aircraft. On the day prior to the invasion of Mindoro, 150 more aircraft were sent from Formosa to the Philippines.[19] Although Kenney had more aircraft at his disposal in the entire region, airfield construction problems continued to restrict the number he could push into combat: only about 286 aircraft a day were available on Leyte.[20] Fortunately, it did not look like the American soldiers would face much tough fighting once ashore. The Japanese did not consider Mindoro a likely landing spot and left fewer than 1,000 troops on the island.[21]

Early on the morning of December 13, the invasion convoy for Mindoro assembled off the coast of Leyte and threaded its way westward under heavy air protection. Japanese reconnaissance aircraft spotted the convoy's departure, and that afternoon ten attackers from an airfield on Cebu met the convoy as it approached the southern tip of the island of Negro. Despite the massive effort put forth to defend the American ships, a Japanese bomber made it through, slamming into the cruiser *Nashville* and killing 175, including the commander of the air task force, Colonel Jack Murtha, and wounding 100 more.[22]

Halsey's continued assaults on the Japanese airfields on Luzon reduced the number of aircraft taking off to attack the convoy, and Kenney's forces stymied the Japanese air forces on the southern islands; yet it appeared that nothing could totally stop the kamikazes. The next day Japanese aircraft flew almost seventy missions, more than half of them suicide attacks, against the convoy bound for Mindoro, and an additional thirteen sorties the day after. Although the Japanese failed to stop the landing, they did sink two LSTs and a small tanker and damaged several more ships.[23] From December 16 until January 5, the Japanese flew over three hundred missions, about half of them kamikaze attacks, against cargo ships near Mindoro or the airfields being built on the island.[24]

The actions of the Japanese ground forces on Mindoro did not match the ferocity of the air attacks. After the landing, American troops quickly routed the outnumbered Japanese, and by the middle of the first afternoon engineers had already started construction of the first runway.[25] In contrast to the problems encountered on Leyte, Mindoro was a "gold mine" for building airfields.[26] The position of the island in the Philippines archipelago, combined with a high central mountain range, sheltered the southwestern corner of the island from the rainfall experienced on Leyte, greatly speeding the construction efforts.[27] Kenney planned on moving as many units as he could from 5th Air Force into Mindoro, where they would be in position for the invasion of Luzon. At the same time, 13th Air Force units would move to Leyte and work with 8th Army, while the RAAF Command shifted northward to Morotai.[28] Five days after the Mindoro landing, Kenney moved in the first fighter group; and by the end of December engineers had completed a second all-weather runway.[29]

The Japanese were not content to leave Mindoro alone. Hoping to slow down MacArthur's advance to Luzon, a surface task force of two cruisers and six destroyers steamed toward Mindoro to attack the supply ships offshore and shell the island. Although signals intelligence provided some indication of the impending attack, the Japanese were poised to inflict severe damage if they had not been spotted by a Navy reconnaissance pilot about 180 miles west of the landing area at Mindoro late in the afternoon of December 26. Although Kinkaid formed a surface group to attack the Japanese force, it would not arrive from Leyte Gulf until the next day, plenty of time for the Japanese to cause trouble. The defense of Mindoro rested with the 105 aircraft already on the island. The American aircrews had little or no training in night attacks and no equipment to find or hit the ships accurately, yet they heroically made repeated attacks throughout the night. Although the Japanese lost only one destroyer in the running battle, they received enough damage on the other ships that they turned back after some ineffective shelling of the island. The cost of this success was heavy: of the 105 aircraft on Mindoro, 26 were lost. Some were downed by gunfire from the ships, but many others were put out of commission by damage caused by night landings under enemy shelling on unimproved airfields. Still others were unable to land on Mindoro at all and ran out of gas enroute to Leyte.[30]

Mindoro had been captured at remarkably low cost, with most of the damage coming from the Japanese air attacks. A total of three large Liberty ships, two carrying ammunition and fuel for aircraft, were sunk off the island and two LSTs, a destroyer, and several other landing craft were damaged. The airfields did not escape unscathed. On the night of January 2, 1945, a kamikaze attack destroyed fifteen P-38s and seven A-20s.[31] The island proved an ideal location for Kenney's aircraft. By the time of the invasion of Luzon on January 9, five fighter groups, two bomber groups, and an assortment of other squadrons were flying from several airfields.[32] Despite Kenney's earlier prediction, it was apparent that the Japanese air threat had not disappeared. As the forces moved northward to Luzon, the air attacks would remain one of Kenney's biggest headaches during the amphibious attack in Lingayen Gulf.

Luzon

Much of the planning for Luzon occurred at the same time as the fighting on Leyte and the planning for the attack on Mindoro. Generally, Kenney immersed himself in the details of future attacks, leaving responsibility for ongoing operations to his respective subordinate commanders: Whitehead at 5th Air Force, Major General St. Clair Streett with 13th, and Air Vice-Marshal William Bostock with RAAF Command.[33] Kenney gave them wide latitude to develop appropriate tactics and techniques based on their individual situations. He commanded by assigning them a specific area of operations and general missions, but did not interfere as long as they continued to produce results, as indicated by the number of airplanes shot down and ships sunk.[34] For the invasion of Luzon, Kenney again tapped 5th Air Force as the air arm that would accompany Krueger's 6th Army during its landing at the Lingayen Gulf and the drive south to Manila (Figure 5).[35]

General Yamashita Tomoyuki, Krueger's adversary, had limited options for defending Luzon. He could not depend on air support for a great deal of

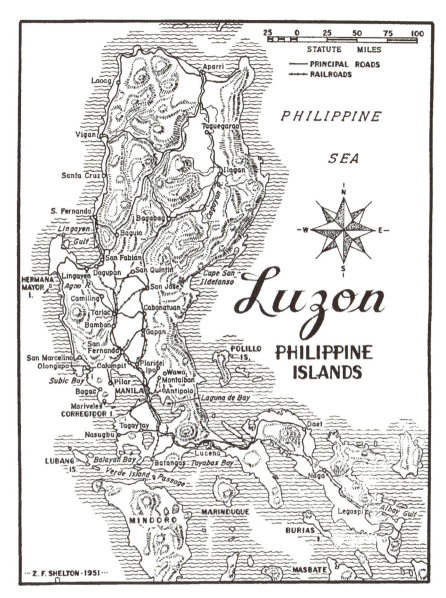

Figure 5. Luzon (Wesley Frank Craven and James L. Cate, eds., *The Army Air Forces in World War II*, vol. 5, *The Pacific: Matterhorn to Nagasaki, June 1944 to August 1945* [Chicago: University of Chicago Press, 1953], p. 417).

assistance, and a large portion of his ground units had been chewed up on Leyte. Rather than defend against the Americans on the beaches and then retreat to the peninsula of Battan, as MacArthur had done, Yamashita divided his forces into three groups to carry out a protracted defense of Luzon and inflict as many American casualties as possible.[36] The Shobu group occupied the mountains northeast and east of the anticipated landing zone in the Lingayen Gulf, threatening Krueger's left flank as he advanced south toward Manila. In the mountains west of the airfield complex at Clark Field, 50 miles north of Manila, was the Kembu Group. Its primary purpose was to keep the airfields out of the Americans' hands for as long as possible and threaten Krueger's right flank. The Shimbu group, deployed in the high terrain of southern Luzon, east of Manila, controlled the reservoirs and water supply of Manila and threatened any American advance from the south. Although Yamashita could not count on air support for his ground operations, at the beginning of January about 150 aircraft remained, scattered among some fifty airfields, plenty of firepower for the Japanese to contest the American landing.[37] In contrast with his optimism before Leyte, Kenney was anxious about the impending battle, convinced that the Japanese were "going to throw everything . . . into the defense of Luzon."[38]

As in the previous landing operations that combined carrier- and land-based aircraft at Hollandia and Leyte, there was no centralized air command for Luzon; instead, roles and tasks were divided among a whole host of participants. Halsey's carrier task forces would cut off reinforcements coming from Formosa and the Ryukyus Islands to the Philippines and then sail south to strike airfields in northern Luzon; B-29s based in the Marianas would then take over and suppress the reinforcements. Escort carriers under Kinkaid planned on covering the invasion force and providing air support for the ground troops on landing. The airfields at Mindoro brought Kenney's aircraft within 160 miles of Manila and allowed him finally to begin heavy attacks against the Japanese airfields on Luzon. To prevent any interference with the Navy's operations, Kenney's planes would remain south of the Lingayen Gulf and attack the airfields around Clark Field and Manila, isolate the landing area, and be ready to take over air operations from the escort carriers a week after the amphibious assault. Aircraft could cross the boundaries erected between the services, but only with the permission of the commander responsible for the area. The only procedure put in place to allow aircraft from the different services to work together was restricted to missions over the invasion beaches. In that event, the planes would come under the control of Kinkaid's air officer.[39]

Once again, rapid construction of the airfields was critical. Kenney needed to take over responsibility for the air missions from the escort carriers a week after the landing.[40] Chastened by the fiasco with the LSTs at Tacloban and other problems on Leyte, Kenney paid close attention to all aspects of the planning, extracting a promise from the landing force commander that the supplies would be unloaded to the east of the landing beach and the planned airfield. In addition, he wanted the engineers who would stake out the runways, and the steel runway matting they would need, landed in the first wave of ships.[41]

The convoy for the invasion of Luzon departed from Leyte on January 2, 1945, and soon came under heavy air attacks. The Japanese had anticipated this move and intensified their efforts as the ships sailed northward up the western side of Luzon. As the convoy neared Panay on January 4, an escort carrier was hit and sunk. Despite far-ranging air attacks and the protection afforded by fifty to sixty American aircraft flying over the convoy, the next day the Japanese struck hard, damaging nine Allied ships, including two cruisers, two escort carriers, and three destroyers.[42] As horrifying as the kamikaze attacks had been so far, every soldier and sailor afloat braced for the worst as the naval task force entered the Lingayen Gulf on January 6, 1945. At the end of that terrifying day one mine sweeper had been sunk and sixteen more vessels were damaged, including the battleships *New Mexico* and *California*, which were severely damaged. The attacks, inflicted by a surprisingly small number of aircraft, killed 170 men and wounded another 500.[43] According to the Japanese, there were only fifty-eight kamikaze aircraft and seventeen escorts sent out that day; meaning that they exchanged roughly three and a half kamikaze aircraft for every ship hit.[44] A variety of factors had combined to help the Japanese. The bravery of their pilots; the mountainous terrain surrounding the gulf, which hid the aircraft from radar detection and delayed early warning of the attacks; and the tight quarters in the gulf, which restricted the ability of the ships to maneuver against the attacks, all added to the Japanese success.

American commanders reacted to the events that day by filling the skies over Luzon to find anything that moved. MacArthur asked Halsey to move his carriers south to assist Kenney in hitting the airfields around Clark and Manila. For his part, Kenney sent 120 aircraft over the Clark airfields at low altitude to shoot up and bomb everything that looked like it could fly.[45] Unsure of the location of the bases the Japanese were using, MacArthur also asked for an increase in the B-29 raids against Formosa and Okinawa to prevent any attacks from that area.[46] Although this huge effort could not completely shut down the kamikaze attacks, it may have convinced the Japanese that they were approaching the point of diminishing returns. In retrospect, January 6 proved to be the apex of the kamikaze effort during the Philippine campaign. The next day only twelve missions were flown; on January 8, the Japanese began evacuating their aircraft from Luzon. Planes that could not be repaired enough to fly away were kept on the island to carry out the last kamikaze attacks on January 13, 1945.[47] On that same day Kenney's headquarters declared that the Japanese air units in the Philippines were no longer an "integral offensive force."[48]

Although the Japanese initiated kamikaze attacks out of desperation, they proved a very effective method of air attack, especially against ships. The first concentrated kamikaze attack during the invasion of Leyte cost the Japanese 16 aircraft, but in return they sank an escort carrier and damaged 6 other ships. By comparison, conventional air attacks against Halsey's fleet prior to the Leyte invasion damaged just 2 American cruisers while the Japanese lost 126 aircraft.[49] Over the course of the Philippines campaign the Japanese army launched 338 "special attack," or kamikaze, flights, and the Japanese navy about 300 more. The results were impressive. Suicide attacks sank at least 19 ships, including 2 escort carriers. Additionally, the 121 hits and 53 near misses caused heavy damage to 30 ships, with 37 more slightly damaged.[50] At a time when the chances of hitting a maneuvering ship with regular bombing methods was slight, the Japanese had a precision guided weapon: one out of every three kamikaze aircraft was causing some kind of damage.[51]

Based largely on estimates that the attacks were even more effective and sank 116 American ships, Japanese officers concluded that their impressive results more than made up for the loss of aircraft. Unwilling or unable to end the war, and taking huge losses in conventional air attacks, they believed the effectiveness of the kamikaze attacks compensated for the high attrition rate. For American sailors, soldiers, airmen, and marines, the kamikaze were a recurring, and horrifying, phenomenon in the closing months of the war in the Pacific.

Kenney, along with most other Americans, had trouble understanding the attacks. He realized that the quality of the Japanese pilots had decreased from 1942, but did not foresee the reaction being the planned suicide attacks.[52] Based on reports that some Japanese pilots had been found manacled by their ankles to the rudder pedals and that other aircraft were found with the canopy locked from the outside, he concluded that the Japanese pilots were being forced to fly such missions against their will. Although he spent little time analyzing why they would resort to such measures, he found it "comforting to find that the Japs themselves didn't trust their 'volunteers' too far."[53] Although it is unclear where Kenney obtained these reports, the most recent historical research does not corroborate his belief. Only in the last desperate months of the war were the pilots not volunteers.[54]

With most of the Japanese aircraft gone from Luzon and Yamashita deployed in the mountains to delay the American advance, the Japanese offered little opposition on the beaches of Lingayen Gulf in the early morning hours of January 9. Sixth Army quickly moved ashore and rapidly began expanding the beachhead.[55] Despite Kenney's efforts during the planning phase, construction of the airfield near the beach got off to a slow start. Heavy surf delayed the landing of the engineers and the steel landing mats for several days. With no enemy air attacks and good weather, however, the delays had little impact, and construction proceeded quickly. The Lingayen airfield opened on schedule, and by January 17 Kenney had enough aircraft on the ground to release the escort carriers.[56] Engineers planned a second airfield at Dagupan, but found the site unsuitable and substituted an area near Mangaldan. The airfield at Mangaldan, commanded by United States Marine Corps Colonel Clayton C. Jerome, was completed by January 22; and in early February a fighter group from 5th Air Force and two Marine air groups began flying daily missions under the direction of the 308th Bombardment Wing.[57]

Previously, the demand for air missions usually exceeded the number of aircraft available, but the situation on Luzon was markedly different. As Krueger advanced south toward Manila, all of Kenney's aircraft were at his disposal. The departure of Japanese aircraft allowed American forces to dominate the air over the battlefield, releasing planes previously dedicated to defending against Japanese air attacks. With the Japanese air threat vanquished, there was also no need to bomb airfields or send up fighter patrols.

Other air missions, much called for in earlier days, had faded too. Krueger originally planned to isolate the Japanese in the mountains by using aircraft to bomb the bridges and highways leading into the Cagayan Valley.[58] The Japanese decision to stay in the mountains obviated the need for these missions, and Krueger asked Kenney to stop bombing bridges and railroad cars because the repairs were slowing the American advance more than enemy action was.[59] Restricted from bombing roads and railroads, with little ground movement by the Japanese, no large supply areas to attack, and an abundance of aircraft, Whitehead had the luxury of assigning an air task force to each corps. The 308th Bombardment Wing was attached to I Corps, the 309th to XI Corps, and the 310th to XIV. These pairings allowed closer planning between the ground and air commanders; naturally, ground commanders were enthusiastic about having unlimited access to a previously scarce asset. Over 90 percent of the air effort expended during the fighting on Luzon was in direct support of the ground forces.[60]

Ground operations were greatly enhanced by the abundance of aircraft. Near the end of January, Krueger's troops had captured the area around

Clark Field and were approaching Manila. MacArthur pressed the 6th Army commander to drive faster; but Yamashita's Shimbu group, perched in the mountains east of Manila, worried Krueger because of the danger it posed to his left flank.[61] The situation was similar to Leyte, when Krueger fretted about the possibility of a Japanese landing and subsequently slowed his progress. One of the biggest differences now was in the air. On Luzon the threat to Krueger's flank was partially solved by assigning aircraft to guard Krueger's left—an option unavailable during the earlier fighting on Leyte.[62]

Ground commanders generally praised the effects of the air support missions on Leyte, but attacks on friendly forces during the first few weeks of the invasion marred the endeavor. At the end of January Krueger voiced strong complaints that 5th Air Force aircraft had bombed and strafed friendly forces and ships. Kenney pressed Whitehead on the issue and urged that "every precaution" be taken to avoid such incidents.[63] A few days later Krueger protested when P-51s strafed his troops, killing one soldier and wounding six others. When the initial investigation revealed no P-51 missions in the area at the time of the attack, Kenney immediately suspected that Japanese aircraft might have been used.[64] In reality, no airworthy Japanese planes remained on Luzon, and the problems between the air and ground forces were generally self-inflicted. The incidents stemmed from a variety of factors, including some similar to those that had plagued the air support efforts almost two years earlier in the Papuan campaign: pilots bombing the wrong target, poor communication between the soldiers and pilots, and ground troops operating in areas where aircraft did not need permission prior to dropping their bombs.[65] Operations in close support of the ground forces had not significantly improved, in part because of the low priority Kenney placed on such missions.

Krueger's 6th Army captured Manila on March 3, 1945, but Yamashita's forces did not surrender until the war ended. By early March, however, Kenney had already started preparing for the next step in the Allied advance to Tokyo: the invasion of Okinawa. Kenney's role in this operation was more restricted, limited to attacking the airfields on Formosa, the likely launching sites for kamikaze attacks on the fleet, and cutting off ships sailing to Japan. Before moving northward, however, MacArthur planned on liberating the southern Philippines with the 8th Army and using the Australians to take control of Borneo. Whatever MacArthur's reasons for undertaking these operations, Kenney, along with the JCS and the Australians, did not believe they were needed.[66] He tried to convince MacArthur that dedicating air units to an unnecessary southern offensive meant a six-month delay in moving them into the northern Philippines, where they could be used to strike Formosa and Japan.[67]

Despite Kenney's objections, MacArthur pressed ahead. Thirteenth Air Force teamed with 8th Army for operations in the central and southern Philippines, beginning with the invasion of Palawan at the end of February. Fighting continued in the southern Philippines until the end of June, when Eichelberger declared the fighting on Mindanao over. Like 5th Air Force on Luzon, 13th Air Force, which included four Marine air groups, flew most of its missions in direct support of the ground troops. No Japanese aircraft remained in the area to worry about, and 8th Army engineers asked that aircraft not bomb docks, harbors, and bridges unless the ground commander specifically requested the mission. The majority of the aircraft were deployed in close support of the ground advance, for airdrops and aerial resupply, and as air cover for the convoys moving between the various landing sites.[68] Although Kenney monitored the activities during the operations, he focused his attention more on building air bases and supply depots as far forward as possible to bomb Formosa, blockade Japan, and, if necessary, provide air support for an invasion.[69]

Trip to Washington

As Eichelberger began operations in the southern Philippines near the end of February 1945, Kenney grew concerned about reports he was receiving from Washington. Kenney had asked that one of his trusted staff officers, Brigadier General Freddie Smith, be sent back to the Philippines to replace Major General St. Clair Streett, for whom Arnold had requested a stateside reassignment. Before leaving Army Air Forces headquarters in Washington, Smith overheard several derogatory remarks about Kenney from both Arnold and other members of the staff. The situation seemed so bad that when he arrived in the Philippines Smith urged Kenney to make a trip to Washington and "make peace with Arnold."[70]

Although Arnold supplied Kenney with people, planes, and parts throughout the war, and the two corresponded frequently, by late 1944 their relationship had soured. Of their several disagreements, perhaps the most damaging one occurred over the basing of the B-29s. Kenney's crusade for the big bombers in the Southwest Pacific clearly aligned him with MacArthur and ran counter to Arnold's desire to attack the Japanese homeland from the Marianas. Kenney's comments at various meetings with naval officers, calling such bombing "stunts" or "nuisance raids," no doubt raised Arnold's ire.[71] Even after it was clear that he was not going to get any of the bombers, Kenney continued his badgering, reportedly predicting "that the Japs would shoot [the B-29s] out of the air," drastically lowering morale.[72] These remarks prompted Arnold to relay a warning through Smith that Kenney had better stop his "agitation" about the B-29 or risk being relieved of his command.[73] Given the strength of Kenney's relationship with MacArthur, it seems unlikely that Arnold could have made good on the threat, but it does reveal the depth of the discord between the two airmen.

Interference from Arnold's headquarters in Kenney's conduct of the air war also irritated the theater air commander. Kenney, likely echoing MacArthur's attitude, routinely rejected requests or suggestions from Washington and often voiced his displeasure at any meddling in local matters.[74] Kenney knew that Arnold himself did not write the messages and suspected officers he described as "Young Turks" of causing the problems. These high-ranking officers, men like Haywood Hansell and Laurence Kuter, were younger than Kenney, but had been rapidly promoted when the service expanded during the war. Their lack of experience, he argued, was evidenced by the number of impractical ideas they suggested.[75]

The duties of Kenney and Arnold also gave them different perspectives on the war that contributed to their misunderstandings. As a member of the JCS and as commanding general of the Army Air Forces, Arnold focused on the entire global struggle as well as the future of an independent United States Air Force. His position forced him to make difficult choices in a number of areas. He had to balance the number of airplanes and people parceled out to the various theaters, as well as weigh the benefits of continued production of current aircraft and equipment against researching and developing new models.[76] In contrast, Kenney, as a theater air commander, devoted his attention to more immediate decisions about what he had to fight with each day and in the near future. Arnold had to produce equipment for a variety of climates and areas, whereas Kenney emphasized what worked in the Southwest Pacific, maintaining that the tactics and equipment developed in his area could easily be transferred to any other combat area.

Their different perspectives also led to disagreements about assignments for officers. Arnold hoped to rotate men from his staff to the combat areas for some experience, but could never get Kenney to agree.[77] After clearing out the "dead wood" in the command, Kenney promoted officers who had proven themselves in combat and guarded against bringing in senior officers with no combat experience and credibility. Like all commanders, Kenney relied on officers he trusted, and proof of that trust came after serving in combat in his theater. He returned one general officer with the curt comment, "His mind is not flexible enough and he does not think clearly or fast enough [for this combat area]."[78] At one point Arnold asked that Whitehead be sent home, a request that brought a howl of protest from Kenney in reply; he told Arnold that he would rather lose his right arm than Whitehead.[79] Although Arnold eventually managed to force Kenney to take some officers, the experiment failed shortly afterwards. Kenney felt that he was getting Arnold's "cast-offs" and ended the endeavor, no doubt with MacArthur's backing.[80]

Arnold also believed that Kenney kept pilots who had shot down large numbers of enemy aircraft in action too long. After shooting down five aircraft a pilot was called an ace, a status that marked him as one of the best pilots as well as a valuable publicity asset.[81] When the Japanese shot down two of the top aces in Kenney's command, Colonel Richard Kearby and Captain Thomas Lynch, just days apart in March 1944, Arnold grew concerned about the impact this would have on public opinion and the morale of the pilots. He cautioned Kenney to "weigh very carefully the potential value of [his] heroes."[82] Despite Arnold's concern, Kenney kept his leading ace, Major Richard Bong, in combat. Bong was sent home to the United States for a publicity tour in April 1944, after breaking the American World War I record for the number of enemy aircraft shot down, but returned to the Southwest Pacific in September. Kenney made a half-hearted effort to comply with Arnold's request that Bong be kept out of combat, but claimed that the ace continued to shoot down Japanese aircraft in self-defense. Arnold warned Kenney, "I don't think it is necessary for me to remind you of Kearby. Do you think we should stop this business before there is a duplication of that situation or are the results worthwhile in spite of possible losses of experienced pilots?"[83] Kenney obviously thought the results worthwhile—Bong continued to fly until December 1944, when he was sent home with forty victories and the Medal of Honor.[84]

While the differing perspectives and conflicting pressures on the two officers are important to understanding their disagreements, the root of the tension between the two men was Kenney's loyalty. Although Kenney identified more closely with Arnold as an airman, he felt that he owed his primary loyalty to his immediate commander, Douglas MacArthur.[85] As Kenney put it, "Every once in awhile Arnold would get sore at me about something or other. He thought I was still working for him, but I wasn't. I was working for MacArthur."[86] Kenney believed that Arnold exerted a great deal of influence over air operations in Europe and hoped to do the same in the Pacific. MacArthur, on the other hand, "resented" interference from Washington and would never have agreed to the level of control over theater air operations that Arnold wanted to implement. While for the most part Kenney aligned himself with MacArthur, in his own mind he thought he acted more as a buffer between the two than as an active participant in the tensions.[87]

While the main purpose of Kenney's trip to Washington in March 1945, was to patch up his differences with Arnold, he also attended a number of meetings on a topic that occupied everyone in Washington—ending the war in the Pacific. Kenney met with officers in the Pentagon, who asked his views on how long the Japanese would hold out and what American command structure he envisioned for the invasion of Japan. Not surprisingly, Kenney favored MacArthur as the overall commander and felt that the sooner the invasion could take place the sooner the war would end.[88] The ferocity of the resistance on Leyte and Luzon had not altered Kenney's belief that Japan was ready to surrender. He told General Marshall that a landing could be made in Japan "anytime we could get ships to take troops there."[89] Although Kenney's contention was motivated in part by a desire to move scarce shipping to the Pacific as soon as possible, he truly believed that the Japanese air units were "through."[90] While that was true enough in the conventional sense of measuring the capabilities of an air force, the Japanese still retained thousands of aircraft for kamikaze attacks against an invasion of the homeland.[91]

Kenney met Arnold, who was recuperating from a heart attack, in Florida on March 17; according to Kenney, they "buried the hatchet."[92] During the meeting Kenney also persuaded Arnold to send him some long-range bombers to bomb the southern Japanese island of Kyushu directly from the Philippines. Although cut off from the B-29s, Kenney was promised the Consolidated B-32 Dominator, an aircraft originally built as a counterpart to the B-29, but never mass-produced. Arnold was considering canceling the contract, but Kenney asked that the first thirty aircraft be sent to the Philippines for a combat test. Kenney flew the aircraft during his visit in Washington and came away impressed with its flying characteristics.[93]

During his time in Washington Kenney made his third visit to the White House to meet with President Roosevelt. Kenney gave the president his impressions of the fighting in the Philippines and repeated his estimate that the invasion of Japan could take place "as soon as we could get the shipping."[94] Kenney found Roosevelt sickly: "He does not look well: his hand shakes when he picks anything up; told me he had lost about 25 [pounds] and had no appetite."[95] It was Kenney's last visit with Roosevelt; the president died just a few weeks later.

Kenney returned to the Philippines at the end of March, pleased about the long-range bombers and relieved to have patched up his relationship with Arnold. Just before his return Kenney received some more good news: promotion to general. In his promotion recommendation, MacArthur summed up his thoughts on Kenney's contribution: "I believe that no, repeat, no officer suggested for promotion to General has rendered more outstanding and brilliant service than Kenney. . . . Nothing that Spaatz [the American air commander in Europe] or any other air officer has accomplished in the war compares to what Kenney has contributed and none in my opinion is his equal in ability."[96]

Okinawa

While Kenney was in Washington the invasion of Okinawa began. Although none of Kenney's aircraft were directly involved in the landing, airmen continued to fly large numbers of missions in support of the operation through attacks on airfields and other targets on Formosa. Fifth Air Force actually began striking Formosa in late January and continued intermittent attacks, depending on the pace and needs of the fighting on Luzon, from that time on.[97] A shortage of suitable landing fields for heavy bombers that had the range to reach Formosa plagued Kenney's efforts to support the invasion. He hoped to build airfields in the northern part of Luzon, but could not convince MacArthur of the need for more construction; he based most of the long-range aircraft on airfields in the Clark Field area.[98]

Kenney's air efforts in support of the Okinawa invasion continued from the start of the landing on April 1, 1945, until organized resistance on the island ended on June 21.[99] While the fighting on the ground was horrific and bloody, the distance of Kenney's air units on the Philippines from the battle area on Okinawa limited the contribution they could make. The continued Japanese kamikaze attacks on the ships off Okinawa, however, did require Kenney's assistance, primarily in bombing the airfields on Formosa (Figure 6).

The Okinawa invasion saw the largest and deadliest kamikaze attacks of the war, a source of fear for every sailor in the fleet. To carry out an offensive of this magnitude the Japanese army air force and naval air force combined their efforts. They launched the first major offensive over a thirty-six-hour period on April 6 and 7, sending 355 kamikazes against the Allied fleet. Although the Japanese lost 222 aircraft, they hit 30 ships, sank 6, and seriously damaged 10 others.[100] Throughout the Okinawa campaign the Japanese staged nine more major attacks and dozens of smaller missions, flying close to 1,900 kamikaze missions, sinking 25 ships and damaging over 250 others. Although the percentage of ships hit per kamikaze aircraft was less than it had been during the Philippine campaign, the sheer number of attacks and the staggering loss of life were terrifying.[101] One reporter provided vivid testimony of the psychological effect of the battle. "The strain of waiting, the anticipated terror, made vivid by past experience, sent some men into hysteria, insanity, breakdown."[102]

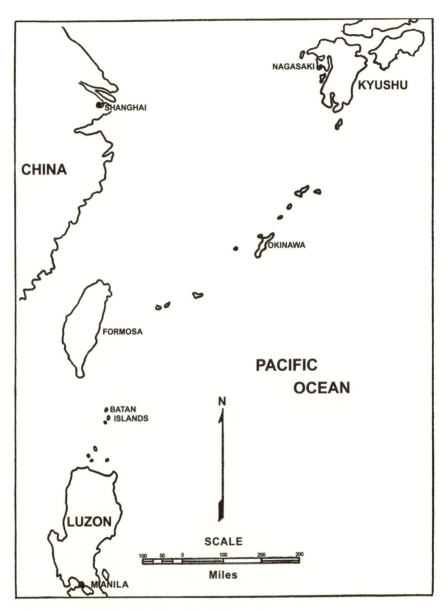

Figure 6. Formosa, Okinawa, and Kyushu (George C. Kenney, *General Kenney Reports* [New York: Duell, Sloan and Pearce, 1949; reprint, Washington Office of Air Force History, 1987], p. 548).

Kenney did his part in suppressing the kamikaze missions by bombing the fifty-three airfields on Formosa to destroy any aircraft capable of attacking the fleet off Okinawa. After several days of bombing, Kenney's intelligence officers speculated that only about ninety planes remained on Formosa. Believing that most of the Japanese aircraft had been destroyed, Kenney turned his bombers loose on other targets, including electrical plants, factories, and sugar mills being used to produce synthetic gasoline.[103] This last target caused a contemptuous comment from Navy admirals suffering through the kamikaze attacks, who assumed that most of the attacks originated from Formosa. No doubt assuming the worst, they blamed Kenney for going after trivial targets instead of stopping the kamikazes. When Halsey was told, incorrectly, that all Kenney's flyers had done was attack sugar mills and other equipment, he "blew up."[104] No doubt the misunderstanding was never cleared up, adding to the mistrust that each service felt toward the other.

Although the intelligence estimates about the number of aircraft on Formosa were wildly inaccurate (a postwar investigation found that there were about 700 aircraft on the island), the attacks by Kenney's flyers and the earlier carrier missions forced the Japanese to hide many of the aircraft on small airfields that were far away from the main bases, disperse others far from any kind of runway, and even park some planes in towns. Still other aircraft were dismantled and hidden in sections, to be reassembled at a later date.[105] All of these actions kept the aircraft safe from destruction, but made it difficult to fly missions. Only 250 of the almost 2,000 kamikaze attacks originated from Formosa. The majority of such flights originated from bases in Kyushu; but to sow uncertainty in the minds of the American commanders about the locations of the kamikaze bases, pilots were told to fly in such a manner that the Americans would suspect Formosa was the actual launching point,[106] a tactic that obviously worked well.

Planning for OLYMPIC

Even before the end of the fighting on Okinawa, Kenney became deeply involved in discussions over the transfer of Army forces and planning for the invasion of the Japanese home islands. The JCS directive for the invasion of Japan was formally issued on May 25, 1945. Although both MacArthur and Nimitz wanted to be named the overall commander, the JCS compromised, putting Nimitz in charge of the naval portion and MacArthur in command of the ground assault. The actual plan of the invasion would be worked out by cooperation between the two commanders. The invasion of Kyushu, code-named OLYMPIC, was scheduled for November 1, 1945. The attack on the main island of Honshu, code-named CORONET, would follow on March 1, 1946.[107]

A major sticking point in planning sessions before the invasion was the question of control over the various ground, naval, and air forces. Throughout the war in the Pacific both MacArthur and Nimitz had commanded units belonging to the other service. Army ground and air units had been assigned to Nimitz's Central Pacific command, and many of them were still under his direction as they battled the Japanese on Okinawa. Similarly, MacArthur commanded naval units (the 7th Fleet) in the Southwest Pacific. Because of the decision to divide command for the invasion of Japan along service lines, those Army units currently under Nimitz had to be transferred to MacArthur and the Navy units under MacArthur to Nimitz.[108]

Negotiations between the two staffs began in mid-April. While many of the discussions focused on shifting operational control of the units and transferring supplies, Kenney focused on the allocation of airfields under construction on Okinawa. He realized that without airfields he would be unable to support the invasion of Japan. Although the participants hammered out only a tentative agreement at this session, Kenney won two important concessions from Nimitz's staff. He convinced them of the need to build more airfields on Formosa and the importance of turning 7th Air Force over to his control as soon as possible.[109]

Kenney hoped to take control of 7th Air Force and "pack" Okinawa with as many units as he could to begin bombing southern Japan in July.[110] Unfortunately, the tenacious Japanese defense of the island, the slow delivery of supplies, and construction problems all hindered the development of airfields and frustrated Kenney's plans. Since everyone else wanted to "pack" Okinawa with their aircraft too, he was limited in the number of groups he called forward, despite the earlier promises extracted from Nimitz's staff. During May and June Kenney participated in numerous meetings on airfield construction and the priority for moving different units onto Okinawa. By the middle of May the Navy had agreed to build airfields for fifty-one groups, and Kenney gained control over the Army aircraft on Okinawa. A month later engineers had finished five airfields and had six more under construction, allowing Kenney to move his air task force headquarters forward.[111]

Kenney's air plan for the invasion of Kyushu followed the well-established pattern of previous operations. Although some of his fellow Army Air Force officers hoped that the fire-bombing raids by the B-29s against Japanese cities would produce a surrender, neither Kenney nor Whitehead had much confidence in this approach. Kenney told General Arnold, "I am as great a believer in the efficacy of air power to win wars as anyone in the Air Force, but I do not subscribe to any thesis that a few thousand tons of bombs can knock out a nation as highly organized militarily as Japan."[112] Kenney warned that the leaders of Japan would not "become panic stricken simply because a few thousand or even a few hundred thousand civilians are killed by air bombardment."[113] While his arguments about using the B-29s against the Japanese home islands were partially motivated by his desire to have the bomber for use elsewhere, even after the heavy bombing began he felt that the only way to end the war was to invade, or at least threaten to invade, Japan.[114]

The air plan followed the general scheme that Kenney and Whitehead had used throughout the war. Fifth Air Force would again serve as the air assault force and focus its early efforts on eliminating the ability of the Japanese to launch air attacks from western Japan, while simultaneously isolating southern Japan from reinforcements or supplies from China—only then would airmen turn their attention to isolating Kyushu from the rest of Japan by attacking roads and railroads as well as small boats and barges along the cost. Finally, 5th Air Force would cover the actual landing on Kyushu.[115]

Integrating the huge number of airplanes flying over Japan promised to be a headache for all parties. Once again there would be no single air commander for OLYMPIC. Instead, air planners separated aircraft by geographical boundaries. An added complication to the air operations for OLYMPIC was the addition of the B-29 bombers. Although General Arnold technically commanded those bombers from Washington, he sent General Carl Spaatz over from Europe to head the strategic air forces in the Pacific, an independent command that made him equal in rank to both MacArthur and Nimitz. MacArthur objected to Spaatz's presence in the theater and could not understand why Arnold would not turn the aircraft over to Kenney. According to Kenney, MacArthur considered the plan an example of "unwarranted interference" and "accused the Air Forces of trying to show they could win the war by themselves."[116] Kenney, in anticipation of the war ending and wary of his future in an independent Air Force, did not protest Spaatz's arrival or the organizational changes. Although he privately complained that the addition of a new air command in the Pacific was "another needless complication,"[117] his talk with Arnold seemed to have convinced him that open disagreements between Army air officers would hurt the drive for service independence. Publicly, Kenney wholeheartedly supported Arnold's plan and persuaded MacArthur that it was workable.[118] When Spaatz arrived in the Pacific in early July, Kenney quickly made arrangements to discuss any disputes privately and "present a unified front to all comers."[119]

Kenney's agreement with Spaatz, however, did little to solve the problem of bringing together the various American aircraft over Japan. With so many planes trying to hit targets in one area, Kenney argued that it would have been better to "put all of the participating air forces under one control and issue one set of orders assigning times, routes, and targets and let the kids do their stuff."[120] Such an approach had not been done earlier, and with the end of the war in sight, interservice tensions that might have been submerged were becoming more pronounced. As usual, Kenney assumed the worst from the Navy. At one point naval officers proposed dividing the enemy airspace at the coastline: the Navy would take care of targets on the sea, restricting the Army Air Forces to land targets. Kenney thought the idea was driven by the Navy's constant desire "to get the credit for all operations over the sea."[121] No stranger at attempts to gain publicity, Kenney promised to just ignore the restrictions and "hit targets whenever their importance justified it."[122] He felt that a Navy protest over the sinking of a Japanese ship would just bring on bad publicity because of the difficulty they faced in "proving we were wrong in sinking Japanese vessels."[123]

At a conference in early August, air commanders finally agreed to divide the Japanese airspace at 135 degrees east longitude (just west of Osaka). Kenney's air units had free rein and could attack any targets west of the line, but their primary objective was to destroy the Japanese air units and isolate southern Kyushu. Likewise, the carrier aircraft flying east of the line would concentrate on destroying every Japanese aircraft they could find. The B-29s in Spaatz's strategic air force continued to pound Japanese cities, but had to provide prior notice of their attacks to both Kenney and the Navy so that they could keep away from the areas at the time of the B-29 raids. In general, aircraft were expected to stay in their respective areas, but could cross the boundary line with twenty-four hours' advance warning or in an emergency.[124] The only change to these boundaries for the actual landing was the addition of a new area around southern Kyushu the week prior to the amphibious assault. In this area 5th Fleet would supply most of the aircraft and be in charge of the various missions. Kenney's air units would be on call to support the landing and retained responsibility for attacking targets on Kyushu outside of the immediate landing beaches.[125]

At the same time that commanders and planners were finalizing arrangements for air operations, Kenney grappled with the continuing problem of moving his aircraft forward to attack Kyushu. Although over half of the airfields on Okinawa had been allocated to him, by early August only four fighter groups and two night fighter squadrons were on the island; the rest were delayed by a lack of shipping. Kenney had taken over control of 7th

Air Force in the middle of July and used those aircraft to bomb Kyushu; but problems in getting supplies to Okinawa limited operations.[126] Although one attack by Kenney's units destroyed 57 potential kamikaze aircraft at one Japanese air base, the missions barely made a dent in the roughly 10,000 aircraft available for defending the home islands.[127] With problems getting aircraft and supplies to Okinawa and a focus on first eliminating the Japanese air threat, Kenney did not have enough additional aircraft to isolate Kyushu. As a result, during June and July the Japanese doubled the number of soldiers near the invasion beaches.[128] Near the end of July, MacArthur's headquarters finally realized the significance of the Japanese moves and pushed Kenney for more transportation bombing. The ability to build up defenses on the beaches resulted, in part, from Kenney's decision to go after aircraft and supplies rather than the roads and railroads. While different priorities might have reduced the ground defenses, it seems likely that suicide planes would have also made a huge impact on the invasion.[129]

The dropping of the atomic bombs on Japan in early August made the planning and speculating regarding the invasion irrelevant. Kenney knew very little about the atomic bombs before the first attack on Hiroshima on August 6, 1945. Marshall sent MacArthur a message in early July restricting certain cities in Japan for air attack, and Kenney was later told that he would receive twelve hours warning of a special mission.[130] On receipt of this warning he was to keep aircraft 50 miles away from the designated target four hours before and six hours after the target time.[131] Although restricted from the areas where the atomic bombs exploded, Kenney's aircraft continued flying after the two nuclear detonations on August 6 and 9. Kenney halted operations on August 12, but after a two-day respite, during which frantic peace negotiations between Japan and the United States took place, President Harry S. Truman ordered more attacks for August 15. The president's announcement of the Japanese agreement to surrender came as aircraft were already enroute to their targets, and they had to be recalled. Kenney's airmen continued to fly reconnaissance missions over Japan to provide an American presence and to serve as a warning to Japanese leaders against renewing hostilities. During reconnaissance missions on August 17 and 18, Japanese fighters attacked some of the new B-32s that Kenney had lobbied for during his trip to Washington in March. The bombers shot down at least three Japanese planes, the last losses in a long war. The march to Tokyo was over.[132]

KENNEY LEARNED HIS LESSONS from the experiences at Leyte. He took no chances with the landings on Mindoro and Luzon, expending great effort to ensure that his land-based aircraft would be in position to support the operations. The kamikaze threat posed the biggest challenge to Kenney over this period. Although large numbers of Japanese aircraft were destroyed, determined attackers still menaced the American fleet. For the invasion of Japan Kenney planned to stick to his template of previous operations, gaining control of the air, isolating the battle area, and then supporting the ground advance. As the end of war neared, Kenney also reestablished his ties with General Arnold and the Army Air Forces. Although he retained his primary loyalty to MacArthur, as victory grew closer concerns about the interservice rivalries after the war gradually assumed more prominence.

ELEVEN

CONCLUSION

"It may be truthfully said that no air commander
ever did so much with so little."

On the morning of September 2, 1945, George Kenney stood on the deck of
the battleship *Missouri* and witnessed the official surrender ceremony ending the war in the Pacific. As he watched the official proceedings he might
have been tempted to contrast his position as victor with the situation he
faced three years earlier. After the attack on Pearl Harbor on December 7,
1941, Japanese forces had advanced virtually unimpeded through the Pacific.
By the time of Kenney's arrival in Australia in late July 1942, it was unclear
where, or when, the Japanese would stop. They had swiftly taken control of
the East Indies (present-day Malaysia and Indonesia), a location they termed
the "southern resources area," and along the way eliminated the American
Air Force prior to capturing the Philippine Islands.

Kenney's arrival coincided with the start of two major offensives in the
Southwest Pacific. During the early days of the war the Japanese had captured Rabaul, located on the northeastern tip of New Britain, a base from
which they could defend the southern part of their defensive perimeter. In a
bid to wrest control of the eastern part of New Guinea and isolate Australia
in late July 1942, Japanese forces landed on the northern coast of New
Guinea and marched overland to capture Port Moresby. General Douglas
MacArthur, the top American and Allied commander in the Southwest Pacific
theater, was determined to stop the Japanese advance and remove this threat
to Australia. About the same time as the Japanese attack on New Guinea,
American forces landed in the Solomon Islands at Guadalcanal to maintain
control of the sea and air lanes between the United States and Australia.
Although this offensive did not fall under MacArthur's direction, the American landing at Guadalcanal required his support, especially in the use of air
power (see Figure 1, p. 50).

Prior to Kenney's arrival, the Allied air forces had been largely ineffectual in air combat against the Japanese. The surprise attack by the Japanese
on December 8, 1941, decimated the American air units at Clark Field, and

air power contributed little to the defensive stand in the Philippines. In other early battles of the war in the Pacific a variety of factors, including a lack of spare parts, too few aircraft, inappropriate tactics, and poor training handicapped Allied airmen in their efforts to stem the Japanese advance. Although the incumbent Allied Air Forces commander, Major General George Brett, struggled to overcome the multitude of problems he faced, by June 1942 MacArthur had lost confidence in Brett's ability to effectively lead the air operation.

Gaining the trust and confidence of Douglas MacArthur became Kenney's first priority and was perhaps his greatest challenge when he assumed command. Kenney had been apprised of the troubles between Brett and MacArthur before leaving the United States and was well aware of the need to get along with the theater commander. Kenney faced two formidable obstacles in accomplishing this objective. MacArthur was known for having an extremely tight-knit and loyal staff that controlled both access and information to the commander. These officers left the Philippines with MacArthur and on their arrival in Australia earned the nickname "the Bataan Gang." Kenney also had to contend with the animosity, which had been building up over the past two decades, between air and ground officers about the role of air power. Soldiers believed that air power would be useful in combat, but should be closely harnessed to the ground fighting. Airmen, on the other hand, argued that air power could best be employed as a consolidated force in pursuit of theater objectives under the control of a single air commander.

Early on, Kenney made a concerted effort to tackle these roadblocks. His most important move came when he outmaneuvered MacArthur's chief of staff, Major General Richard Sutherland, an imperious officer who had kept the previous air commanders away from MacArthur, and established direct access to the theater commander. Kenney's showdown with Sutherland dovetailed with efforts aimed at gaining Douglas MacArthur's trust and confidence, a campaign that included everything from speaking with MacArthur regularly during the day to social visits in the evening. Kenney's outgoing, aggressive personality, coupled with his professional knowledge and enterprising attitude, appealed to MacArthur. The two men established a close personal and professional relationship, allowing Kenney to overcome the potential hazards posed by MacArthur's staff and the institutional differences between airmen and ground officers.

No matter how good the personal chemistry between MacArthur and Kenney, Kenney's success was not preordained. The airman had to demonstrate his ability as commander. In making decisions Kenney drew on a long career spent learning about air warfare. His combat duty as an observation pilot in World War I provided a wealth of experience, including a sense of the chaos and uncertainty of warfare and the reaction of warriors under fire. In addition, he had taken away some specific lessons on air combat. The horrific losses his squadron experienced seared into him the importance of training before sending young men to war, while his personal trials in flying missions and nearly getting shot down by enemy aircraft imparted a real sense of the importance of gaining control of the air.

After World War I, Kenney served in a variety of areas in the Army Air Corps. He learned about the new science of aeronautics and researched the problems and possibilities involved in modifying and building aircraft, duty that gave him some insight into both the technical advantages and the limitations of air power. Kenney also spent many years in military schools and on staffs, time he used to expand his understanding from a narrow focus on flying to a broader view of the problems involved in organizing and employing an air force in combat. At the premier military school for airmen, the Air Corps Tactical School, Kenney investigated and codified doctrine on attack aviation and explored low-altitude bombing methods. As the operations officer in the first separate combat air headquarters in the United States Army, called General Headquarters Air Force, Kenney saw the problems air units encountered during the exercises and simulated combat maneuvers. Even before the United States entered the war, indeed even before the war in Europe started, Kenney's exposure to the myriad of situations that an air commander might face allowed him to think and write about what components were needed to build a combat air force and how air power should be used in warfare.[1] Of course, Kenney's experiences could not, and did not, prepare him for every possibility he would face in the war. He knew little of the improving ability of American intelligence organizations to intercept and decode radio communications and the benefits such information provided to a commander. In addition, Kenney, like most Army officers, was given little training or education in naval warfare and had little appreciation for how the Navy planned to wage war. He had also spent little time as a commander and was never in charge of a flying unit larger than a squadron prior to assuming command of a numbered air force. On balance, though, he had been an avid student of air power and led large procurement organizations during the buildup of the Army Air Forces.

In carrying out an air campaign, Kenney's priority was to "get control of the air situation before you try anything else."[2] He had personally witnessed the difficulty of carrying out missions without air superiority in the skies over western Europe in World War I and continued to believe that this was an absolutely vital first step in modern warfare. Gaining air superiority was necessary before commanders could seriously consider other air, ground, or sea operations. Since the Japanese aircraft factories and other industrial targets were beyond the range of Allied aircraft in the Southwest Pacific, Kenney sought to achieve air superiority by destroying Japanese aircraft on the ground and shooting them down in the sky. He argued that the plan sounded "simple but actually it is a long and difficult job."[3]

Kenney maintained his commitment to gaining air superiority through every campaign in the war. During the fighting for Port Moresby and Guadalcanal that began in July and August 1942, Kenney dispatched bombers to eliminate Japanese aircraft on the ground at Rabaul. He reasoned that these attacks would reduce Japanese air strength in the region, supporting both MacArthur's fighting in New Guinea and the offensive on Guadalcanal. In addition, he pushed for improvements in the air defense network around New Guinea, an effort aided by the Allies' ability to intercept Japanese radio transmissions and provide early warning of enemy bombing raids. The advanced warning allowed Allied pilots to exploit hit-and-run tactics, which highlighted the advantages of their aircraft, allowing them to down Japanese aircraft without suffering excessive losses.

Alongside Kenney's effort at gaining control of the air, he also used aircraft to isolate the Japanese garrisons in eastern New Guinea by bombing the ships bringing supplies to the island or attacking the reinforcements being transported over land. Kenney believed that these types of missions, known as interdiction, offered the best use of air power in support of ground warfare. He instituted low-altitude tactics, introduced new munitions, and took advantage of the Allied information on Japanese movements to cut off the battle areas of New Guinea during the last half of 1942.

While Kenney realized the importance of using air power to support ground combat, he argued strongly for flying interdiction missions and against dedicating aircraft to bombing the enemy positions at the front lines, called close air support. Nevertheless, at times during the fighting in the Papuan Campaign on New Guinea, Kenney dispatched aircraft on close air support missions, though with less than ideal results. Pilots had difficulty locating and attacking targets on the ground through the thick jungle canopy and often could not locate their own forces, mistakenly bombing American troops on several occasions.

Despite the problems with the close air support missions, Kenney's attitude and ability to produce success increased his stock with MacArthur, allowing Kenney to become a close advisor to the theater commander, offering advice on a wide range of issues. Rather than oppose the Japanese headlong in the steamy jungle of New Guinea, Kenney offered to airlift ground forces and outflank the Japanese advance. Although some members of MacArthur's staff thought Kenney's suggestion unreasonable, MacArthur quickly grasped the benefits of the plan and enthusiastically accepted Kenney's offer. Soon transports were flying soldiers, food, ammunition, and even artillery pieces to the front lines in Papua and flying out the sick and wounded.

Kenney viewed the Papuan campaign, which ended in January 1943, as a template for future operations in the Southwest Pacific. Although a map of the Southwest Pacific in early 1943 showed huge chunks of territory under Japanese control, in reality this defensive perimeter rested on relatively small forces deployed in a series of points along the coast of New Guinea and on island outposts. The terrain and geography of the region restricted the Japanese to these areas that could be isolated and then defeated or simply bypassed. To carry out this operational scheme, Kenney planned to take control of the air in advance of the next objective, while simultaneously isolating the Japanese ground forces from reinforcements and supplies. The garrisons thus weakened and unprotected, Kenney concentrated his air units on bombing the enemy positions near the amphibious landing area both prior to and during an invasion. In some cases, Allied ground forces could even be air transported into an area and resupplied by aircraft—eliminating the need for the amphibious landings altogether. Once the ground soldiers rid the area of enemy forces, engineers moved in to build the airfield from which the next advance could be mounted, and the whole process was repeated.[4] Although the details of each specific operation varied, this general outline of MacArthur's operations in the Southwest Pacific remained the same: bypassing the most strongly held Japanese positions and defeating the remaining outposts.

Although Kenney's contribution to this scheme of maneuver was important, MacArthur had some idea about the potential of air power even before Kenney's arrival. As the Army chief of staff, he advanced the idea of forming a General Headquarters Air Force. Moreover, he was primed for exploiting the advantages of air power after suffering through the devastating Japanese surprise air attack that wiped out virtually all of the aircraft in the Philippines, forcing American troops to fight without the benefit of friendly air cover. MacArthur proved a willing student of air power and he and Kenney spent a great deal of time discussing future operations and, specifically, the potential of air power to hasten MacArthur's return to the Philippines and the eventual defeat of Japan. The highly successful "leapfrog" strategy used by MacArthur to avoid the strongly held, but widely separated, Japanese garrisons required air superiority and depended on the aggressive, flexible, and focused use of aviation to interdict men and supplies, harass enemy communications, transport Allied soldiers and matériel to battle, provide protection for shipping and amphibious assaults, and fly in direct support of the ground fighting. Kenney helped convince MacArthur of the particular advantages offered by aircraft, but MacArthur's support of his air commander provided Kenney the opportunity to implement his ideas. General Arnold summed up the importance of the relationship between the two when he told Kenney, "I don't believe the units could possibly perform the missions in the manner that they are doing without the most sympathetic support from General MacArthur. It requires complete understanding between General MacArthur and you."[5]

Although the general outline of MacArthur's operations became clear with the end of the fighting in Papua, several months would pass until ground forces could carry out this scheme. The temporary hiatus in ground fighting offered no respite for airmen. During the first half of 1943, Kenney's aviators fought to gain and maintain air superiority and isolate the Japanese forces in New Guinea.

Although dogmatic in his beliefs about the proper sequence of air operations, Kenney demonstrated great flexibility in carrying out the missions. Indeed, Kenney's mental agility and willingness to sponsor innovations are the hallmarks of his command. In carrying out his aim of gaining air superiority, Kenney needed to be able to engage and defeat Japanese fighters. Very early in the war he realized that the failure to develop long-range fighters was a serious shortcoming, and he eagerly sought ways to increase the distance his fighters could fly and accompany the bombers to their targets. Perhaps the most dramatic and far-reaching change Kenney made from the prewar thinking involved the shift from high-altitude bombing of enemy ships to low-altitude attacks. Despite his later claims to the contrary, Kenney did not invent this tactic. He did, however, eagerly adopt it; and the low-level bombing of enemy ships became routine in the Southwest Pacific. Although inspired by his previous work on low-altitude attacks while an instructor at the Air Corps Tactical School, Kenney made the change to low-level bombing for more pragmatic reasons. The weather in the Southwest Pacific and the number of operational aircraft available at any one time made it impossible to put as many aircraft in the air as the doctrine manuals recommended. Further, the inaccuracy of high-altitude bombing made it extremely difficult to sink maneuvering ships, no matter how many aircraft were available. The move to low-altitude bombing, along with regular and more realistic training, improved munitions suitable for low-level bombing, and superb intelligence about Japanese shipping movements, made it possible for Kenney's airmen to begin sinking many more Japanese vessels. The most dramatic and public success occurred in early March 1943, when the

Japanese attempted to send reinforcements from Rabaul to their garrison at Lae. Kenney's aircraft located and tracked the sixteen-ship convoy for two days prior to devastating the formation off the coast of New Guinea on the morning of March 3, 1943, in the Battle of the Bismarck Sea. The results sent a clear signal to the Japanese high command that they could no longer dispatch large-scale reinforcements to eastern New Guinea, effectively sealing the fate of the garrisons.

Though Kenney did not personally produce every new or innovative idea, his focus on improving methods and a willingness to jettison established routines encouraged innovation in his command. He created an atmosphere within his organization that allowed creative thinking to flourish, producing ideas that ranged from sawing trucks in half so that they could fit into air transport planes to grafting a tailgun turret onto the nose of the B-24 to increase its forward firepower.

While many of the changes Kenney introduced involved technical and tactical adaptations, he also instituted a number of organizational changes. When he first arrived in Australia he found command arrangements ill suited to the demands of the theater. Kenney's predecessor, Major General George Brett, had combined American and Australian air units into one command, even to the point of mixing nationalities in the same aircraft. Although Brett adopted these measures largely out of necessity, the policy irritated MacArthur, who objected to the idea of American forces being under the command of officers from another nation. Kenney moved quickly to separate Australian and American air units into discrete organizations, a separation he found useful for improving both combat effectiveness and his relationship with MacArthur.

The long distances and poor communications between MacArthur's headquarters in Brisbane (where most of the high-level planning took place) and the forward airfields in New Guinea forced Kenney to delegate much of the responsibility for daily operations to a commander near the airfields. For this crucial position Kenney tapped Major General Ennis Whitehead, who commanded 5th Air Force Advanced Echelon, dubbed "Advon" for short, at Port Moresby and was responsible for overseeing daily missions. Perhaps because they entered the military at the same time and were part of the same service "generation," Kenney and Whitehead shared the same outlook on warfare and rarely disagreed on a course of action. Often, Kenney's tasks for the upcoming air operations, which he outlined in frequent letters to Whitehead, had already been foreseen and planned at Advon headquarters. Kenney had great respect for Whitehead's ability and confidence in his judgment, leading to total trust in his deputy. The two made an outstanding team. There is no doubt that much of Kenney's success rested on the talent and ability of his subordinates, especially Whitehead. Kenney admitted as much when he called Whitehead "my strong right arm all through the war."[6] With White-head in charge of offensive operations from Port Moresby, Kenney named Air Vice Marshal William Bostock to head the separate Royal Australian Air Force (RAAF) Command based in Australia. Although RAAF Command contained some American units, it was primarily an Australian outfit, dedicated to the air and sea defense of the country.

In June 1943, MacArthur's amphibious assaults along the northern coast of New Guinea began in earnest. Through the rest of the year, in a series of well-integrated air, land, and sea operations, MacArthur's forces moved westward to outflank the Japanese position at Rabaul. Kenney stuck to his basic template of operations, but continued to add innovative methods. Despite attempts to increase the range of his fighters, they still lacked the ability to fly from the Allied bases in eastern New Guinea near Buna and Port Moresby to the Japanese airfields at Wewak. To overcome this handicap he built a forward airfield close to Wewak. This forward site, combined with an intricate plan to deceive the Japanese as to the location of the actual airfield, made it possible to spring a devastating raid on the Japanese airfields and gain air superiority over the Huon Peninsula—the essential precursor to the amphibious assaults. During the inland advance through the Markham Valley that followed, American air units worked closely with Australian ground forces, providing transportation, food, and fire power to quickly capture territory before the Japanese could move in and build strong defensive positions.

Although MacArthur had originally planned to invade Rabaul after gaining control of the Huon Peninsula, the American advance through New Guinea, coupled with Admiral Halsey's control over the Solomons and Admiral Nimitz's advance in the Central Pacific, made it possible to bypass Rabaul. MacArthur could now turn his full attention to controlling the rest of New Guinea and moving on to the Philippines. In early 1944, as MacArthur's staff planned the impending operations in New Guinea, the JCS in Washington searched for ways to speed up the war in the Pacific. MacArthur suggested combining all of the naval, air, and ground forces under his command, a proposal the Navy rejected, arguing that the forces allocated to MacArthur's thrust should be sent to the Central Pacific. In the midst of these negotiations, Kenney came forward with a bold proposition. The next step in MacArthur's conquest of New Guinea was an invasion of the Admiralty Islands, scheduled for April 1944. When Kenney received reports from aircrews that the Japanese had deserted the islands, he suggested an early invasion. This was a risky move, but if successful would isolate Rabaul completely, accelerate MacArthur's return to the Philippines, and ensure that the Navy did not steal the show in the Pacific. Despite other intelligence reports that contradicted Kenney's information, MacArthur pressed ahead with the attack. Although Kenney's contention that the Japanese had deserted turned out to be wrong, the attack surprised the Japanese on the islands and resulted in an impressive victory for MacArthur. He could now move westward and on to the Philippines.

Kenney became a close advisor to MacArthur during the war, but it is possible to overstate his influence. On occasion MacArthur ignored Kenney's advice, as in the planning for the attack on Hollandia in April 1944. Prior to this operation in western New Guinea, MacArthur's advances had always enjoyed the protection of Kenney's aircraft. An invasion at Hollandia would avoid the strong Japanese position at Hansa Bay but was too far from friendly air bases for air cover during the landing, forcing MacArthur to rely on aircraft carriers for protection. Kenney argued forcefully against this plan, maintaining that the planes on the carriers had limited range and could carry only small bomb loads, making them ill equipped to support the amphibious attack. He also pointed out the serious limitations of the aircraft carriers themselves, such as the need to routinely stop flying operations in order to take on fuel, food, and ammunition. The result, he feared, was that carriers could continue operations for only a limited time and might have to leave an area at a crucial moment.

Despite Kenney's complaints, the attack on Hollandia went forward without the protection of land-based aircraft. The ability to outflank the largest concentration of Japanese forces in New Guinea and prevent a long and bloody ground fight, the need for a supply base that could support the invasion of the Philippines, and the chance to speed up the rate of MacArthur's advance all outweighed the air commander's advice.

Kenney's aircraft did not cover the actual landing at Hollandia, but they still managed to eliminate the Japanese aircraft in the area prior to the invasion. The air attacks on Hollandia at the end of March 1944 blended many aspects of Kenney's success in the Southwest Pacific, beginning with exquisite timing keyed by excellent intelligence. Kenney's airmen struck after the Japanese had packed the airfield with planes and equipment, but prior to their move westward to a location that would have allowed the Japanese to oppose the landing at Hollandia from a safe distance. Tactically, the conduct of the mission was characteristic of Kenney's approach—long-range fighters escorting a low-level bombing force. The attack surprised the Japanese and brought spectacular results with few American losses. Lacking any air presence in western New Guinea and deceived into thinking that the attack would occur elsewhere, the Japanese could offer little resistance to the invasion at Hollandia.

Although engineers found that they had overstated the usefulness of Hollandia to support air bases and supply depots, few could deny the importance of gaining this site for containing the Japanese presence in New Guinea and supporting future operations. The aircraft carriers returned to the Central Pacific fleet after the invasion of Hollandia, allowing a return to earlier methods. For the remainder of the fighting in New Guinea, ground forces moved forward under air protection to capture an airfield, which could then be used to support the next leap forward.

During the following months Kenney and other Allied commanders grew increasingly convinced that the Japanese military had been seriously weakened and no longer presented a viable fighting force. After meeting little resistance on several bombing raids in the Philippines, Admiral Halsey suggested eliminating the scheduled invasion of Mindanao in the southern Philippines for an assault on Leyte. Invading Leyte earlier than planned would accelerate the American invasion of Luzon, a move that would completely sever the sea lanes between Japan and the southern resources area and place American forces in a prime position for invading Japan. Bypassing Mindanao, however, also meant no land-based air support for the invasion of Leyte, forcing MacArthur once again to rely on the aircraft carriers. This time Kenney chose not to voice any criticism about using the carriers without the benefit of land-based aircraft.

Although the landing on Leyte on October 20, 1944, encountered no major problems, the entire campaign took much longer and was far costlier than anticipated, in part because of the decision to rely solely on aircraft carriers. They ably covered the initial landing, but after being battered by Japanese surface and air attacks, and needing refurbishment, they were forced to depart soon after the invasion—as Kenney had earlier feared. At the same time, building the airfields on Leyte to support land-based planes turned out to be very difficult and took much longer than originally planned, further eroding the Allied air advantage. Although engineers had accurately predicted many of the problems encountered, their concerns were ignored because of MacArthur's desire to return to the Philippines as quickly as possible and a willingness among the top commanders to disregard the possibility of a strong Japanese reaction to the invasion.

Kenney and the other air commanders erred badly in their planning for Leyte. In addition to discounting the engineers' concerns, they failed to recognize the important differences between earlier campaigns and the battle for air superiority in the Philippines. In previous operations in the Central and Southwest Pacific against isolated Japanese outposts with a limited number of airfields, it was possible to destroy every aircraft at a base and cut off the flow of replacement planes. Neither was possible in the Philippines. The number of airfields scattered throughout the islands allowed the Japanese to disperse their aircraft, making it exceedingly difficult to find and destroy all of them, while the relatively short distance between Japanese-held Formosa and Luzon allowed the Japanese to pour large numbers of reinforcements into the fighting.

Changes in Japanese tactics exacerbated these miscalculations. In contrast to previous operations, in which the Japanese sent out small numbers of aircraft and were largely ineffective in disrupting American operations, during the battle for Leyte the steady flow of reinforcements allowed the Japanese to use large formations. Additionally, they unleashed the deadly kamikaze attacks, which proved almost impossible to stop. Problems in building the airfields coupled with miscalculations about the enemy and the changes in Japanese tactics forfeited the American advantage of air superiority. The combined effect of fighting without control of the air and dealing with the Japanese ground reinforcements sent to Leyte slowed the American advance and the conquest of the island.

Kenney proved a quick study and learned from his experiences on Leyte. In the upcoming invasions on Mindoro and Luzon in the Philippines and the planning for the invasion of the Japanese home islands, he went to great lengths to ensure that his aircraft were always in position to support the landing, regardless of the planned support from the carriers.

Although the threat posed by Japanese air attacks remained Kenney's first priority, aircraft under his command flew other missions, aimed at cutting off reinforcements and directly supporting the movement of the ground forces. When the Japanese withdrew their aircraft from the Philippines in early January 1945, shortly after the Allied landing on Luzon, the fear of Japanese air attacks disappeared. Japanese ground forces, dug into mountain redoubts, had no supply lines that could be cut off. With two of the usual tasks obviated by the situation and with a multitude of aircraft on hand, Kenney turned most of his planes loose on missions in direct support of the ground forces.

After American soldiers captured Manila in March 1945, Kenney turned his attention northward: first, in support of the landings at Okinawa with attacks on the airfields on Formosa, and later in preparation for an American invasion of the Japanese homeland. In both cases, Kenney made few changes from the methods he had developed during the course of the war: first gain air superiority, then cut off the battle area, and finally, on the day of the assault, put every available aircraft over the landing area. In the end, the atomic bombs and the Soviet Union's entry into the war made the planned invasion unnecessary.

Throughout the war, MacArthur and Kenney maintained a close professional and personal relationship, and Kenney played an important role in shaping the general conduct of MacArthur's operations in the Southwest Pacific. In spite of their relationship, the two men did not always see eye-to-eye, and it is clear that MacArthur accepted Kenney's advice only when it was in line with his goals. For instance, MacArthur gladly followed Kenney's suggestions for speeding the advance, such as the airlifting of troops to New Guinea in 1942 to outflank the Japanese advance on Port Moresby, even though the plan drew dire warnings from the rest of MacArthur's staff. By contrast, when Kenney attempted to dissuade MacArthur and suggested a course of action that threatened to slow the pace of warfare, as he tried to do in warning about the risks involved in relying on carriers during the invasion of Hollandia, his cautions fell on deaf ears. In short, Kenney's influence on the actual conduct of the war varied to the extent that it was in agreement with MacArthur's overarching goals.[7]

Kenney's position as the theater air commander brought him into close contact with the other Army and Navy commanders. Although Kenney was an aviator, he was also a career Army officer and had met many of the other commanders and staff officers prior to the war. Soon after taking command Kenney effectively bypassed MacArthur's difficult chief of staff, Major General Richard Sutherland. Although Kenney's personality was important in this confrontation, his prior dealings with Sutherland at the Army War College assisted the airman by giving him insight into Sutherland's personality and character. Kenney had also known Generals Walter Krueger and Robert Eichelberger, the principal ground commanders, and worked closely with them in planning operations. Although both men criticized Kenney for problems encountered with bombing missions in close proximity to friendly ground forces, they registered few complaints about the priority Kenney placed on missions or his selection of targets.

In contrast with the generally good relations he had with Army officers, Kenney's relationship with the Navy was very adversarial. In the years prior to World War II he had little personal contact with Naval officers and received only a limited education in naval warfare. The interservice rivalries of those years, particularly the tension between the Air Corps and the Navy over the mission of coastal defense, certainly influenced his attitude. During the war he clashed frequently with a number of Navy officers. He had his most long-running disagreements with Admiral Daniel Barbey, an amphibious expert, over the way to carry out air operations during an amphibious landing. Barbey, who arrived in Australia in early 1943, argued for the procedures used by the Navy: standing air patrols over the convoys and landings at dawn to hide the ships under the cover of darkness and surprise the defending forces. Kenney, on the other hand, maintained that standing air patrols were wasteful and inefficient. He urged later landing times so that his aircraft could bomb the beaches just before the troops landed. In the end, various combinations of the methods were used in operations, but the constant bickering between the services kept the disputes simmering. Throughout the war Kenney distrusted the Navy's intentions and remained extremely suspicious of naval officers' attempts to interfere in air operations. During the campaign on Leyte, Kenney's quarrels with Admiral Thomas Kinkaid, MacArthur's naval commander, prevented the two from combining forces at a time when cooperation was badly needed. While the weight of American material superiority masked many of the problems caused by conflicts between the services, Kenney's combativeness did little to improve interservice cooperation.

Although Kenney's direct superior was Douglas MacArthur, he continued to depend on General "Hap" Arnold, commanding general of the Army Air Forces, for the supplies and people needed to fight the war. The problem of divided loyalty between officers with very different perspectives and agendas created a source of tension and conflict for Kenney throughout the war. Arnold did his best, within the constraints of the strategic framework of the war, to accommodate Kenney's numerous requests and was generally impressed by Kenney's leadership and the ability of the air units in the Southwest Pacific to produce impressive results with a minimum of aircraft. By the middle of 1944, a variety of factors caused their relationship to deteriorate. While Kenney and Arnold clashed over such things as rotating officers from the headquarters in Washington to the theater for combat duty and the low priority given to the Southwest Pacific for spare parts and people, their biggest disagreement was over Kenney's continued efforts to obtain the long-range B-29 bomber for MacArthur's theater. Arnold maintained that the aircraft could best be used for the strategic bombing of the Japanese homeland, leading him to support efforts to base B-29s in China and the Marianas Islands. Kenney contended that the B-29s could be used more profitably to bomb oil facilities in the East Indies and cut off the oil and other natural resources from that area to Japan, a plan that would have based the bombers in Australia.

Although Arnold grew tired of Kenney's insistent lobbying for the B-29s, Kenney's penchant for taking his grievances outside the bounds of the service was an even greater irritant. The most egregious example occurred in early 1944, with Kenney's assertion, along with that of other officers from MacArthur's command, that Japan could be defeated more quickly by using the forces in the Central Pacific under Admiral Nimitz to advance Mac-Arthur's Southwest Pacific drive to the Philippines. Arnold's reason for supporting a separate Central Pacific advance was to capture the Marianas Islands for B-29 attacks on Japan. Kenney blasted this logic, telling naval planners that basing the B-29 in the Marianas was a "stunt" and would only accomplish "nuisance raids."[8] Arnold found these disparaging comments about strategic bombing, made to officers outside of the service, particularly jarring. To Arnold and many other officers in the Army Air Forces, strategic bombing was the key mission for assuring an independent United States Air Force. While Kenney's loyalty to MacArthur was lauded by Arnold during combat operations, in arguing for the new bombers Kenney's actions made him appear disloyal. Toward the end of the war Kenney managed to patch up his differences with Arnold. In March 1945, with Germany close to defeat and the end of the war with Japan only a matter of time, both men turned their attention to future battles in Washington over an independent Air Force. Although Kenney remained loyal to MacArthur, he stopped his divisive comments and closed ranks with his fellow airmen over the coming interservice disputes. The problem of dual loyalty Kenney faced was never entirely resolved; rather its importance ebbed and flowed over the course of the war. During the more critical times of the war Kenney put aside his service loyalty and sided with the theater commander. With the end of fighting in sight, however, loyalty to service assumed a larger role, given the enduring tensions between the armed services of the United States.

KENNEY'S SUCCESS as an air commander was the result of both his personal background and the setting he found himself in during the war. He did have the advantage of serving with a theater commander who learned to appreciate the benefits offered by air power, as well as outstanding subordinates who carried out the plans he formed. Kenney also benefited from highly accurate intelligence about the enemy. Arguably, of all the commanders in the Southwest Pacific Kenney benefited the most from ULTRA, or signals, intelligence. Because radio communications were integral to all aspects of air operations, the ability to intercept and decode Japanese radio transmissions, even those of a routine nature, gave Kenney an extremely accurate picture of Japanese air strength, an important advantage when making decisions. ULTRA allowed Kenney to concentrate on a single area without undue concern about air attacks or the size of the Japanese forces in other areas. It let him choose lucrative targets for concentrated raids, such as the bombing of the airfields at Wewak and Hollandia, after the Japanese flew in large numbers of reinforcements. Without this covert information Kenney would have been forced to carry out many missions against airfields that might, or might not, contain enemy aircraft. More frequent raids would have reduced the impact on Japanese air operations at greater cost to Kenney's forces. Intercepted radio messages also provided a critical advantage in defending against enemy air attacks. ULTRA provided early warning of an impending air raid and gave Allied fighters enough time to gain altitude and be in a position to attack the Japanese formations before they reached their targets. In short, this intelligence advantage allowed Kenney to concentrate his air forces, both offensively and defensively, when and where they would have the greatest effect on Japanese operations.

Kenney also used ULTRA to great advantage in sealing off the Japanese garrisons. Searching for and finding ships in the vast expanses of the ocean was not an easy task. Without foreknowledge of the Japanese sailing schedules, Kenney would have had to assign more aircraft to scouting enemy ship movements, leaving fewer available for other missions. Dramatic successes such as the Battle of the Bismarck Sea in March 1943, when Kenney's aircraft destroyed a convoy bringing troops and supplies from Rabaul to New Guinea, would not have been possible. Although Kenney exercised little influence over establishing the intelligence network or shaping its operating arrangements, he was an enthusiastic supporter and consumer of their efforts.[9]

Knowledge about the enemy's capabilities and intentions explains only part of Kenney's success; equally important was having the means to carry out the missions. When Kenney first arrived in Australia, he faced a numerically superior foe; while the insightful use of intelligence to concentrate the air missions made up part of this deficit, building an effective supply and maintenance organization was vital to having a larger proportion of planes airborne. Kenney moved supply depots closer to the combat air bases and focused the people working in the rear echelon on the goal of increasing the number of combat-ready aircraft. While pilots and other aviators received much of the publicity, Kenney realized the importance of the hardworking mechanics and armorers to winning the war and searched for ways to raise their morale by awarding military decorations and improving living conditions. Although the number of aircraft under his command increased slowly, the total number of sorties flown grew rapidly through strenuous efforts aimed at flying the same few aircraft more often. Kenney also benefited from the enormous productive capacity of the United States during the war. While he never had as many aircraft as he thought he needed, the overall strength of the command did increase. By the time the war ended, Kenney had 1,800 aircraft, a large supply of spare parts, and trained mechanics capable of keeping close to 80 percent of the aircraft flying at any given time.[10]

War, of course, is not a one-sided enterprise. The actions of one party cannot be judged against some absolute standard, but must be measured against a particular adversary at a particular moment in time. In this regard, Kenney's strengths and methods exacerbated the weaknesses of the Japanese. They never seriously considered the possibility that their radio codes had been broken; and relative to the Allied successes, they were usually not able to exploit the information they did gain through signals intelligence. The disparity between the two sides in this area gave Kenney a sizable advantage in planning air operations.[11]

Likewise, Kenney benefited from an increasing material advantage during the war. Although Japanese aircraft production did expand, it never kept pace with American production; and the supply and maintenance organizations of the Japanese air arms were woefully incompetent. Similarly, the Japanese did not increase their pilot training programs until late; as a result, Japanese pilots became less experienced and less capable as the war progressed. Although the lack of surviving sources makes it difficult to reconstruct an exact comparison, it appears that at the same time that Kenney's maintenance crews could keep 70 to 80 percent of the aircraft ready for combat, Japanese mechanics kept something less than 50 percent of their aircraft in flying shape. The combination of small numbers of aircraft piloted by ill-trained aviators was a death spiral, resulting in greater and greater losses.[12] Though he didn't hold an advantage in terms of actual numbers of aircraft, Kenney nevertheless had an edge in the number of missions flown and the quality of the aviators he sent into combat.

Kenney's tactics also met with great success against the Japanese. The low-level attacks against merchant shipping were extremely effective and resulted in relatively few losses, largely because the Japanese ships were only lightly armed and ill equipped to defend against air attacks. The relatively few antiaircraft guns and the weaknesses in the air raid warning networks around Japanese airfields also made low-altitude attacks against these bases effective and generally resulted in few American casualties.

A lack of heavy equipment and trained engineers hampered the ability of the Japanese to build airfields, further contributing to Kenney's success. American aviation engineers played a vital role throughout the fighting in the Pacific, and their construction feats made it possible to fight the war. Conversely, the Japanese found themselves handicapped by a lack of heavy equipment and labor in this very important area. Unable to disperse their aircraft around the perimeter of an airfield or build more bases, the Japanese clustered their aircraft together, making them easy to destroy in large numbers at a time. The lack of heavy equipment also made it difficult to repair runways, quickly rendering the fields unusable.[13] Although the exact tactics Kenney advocated might not have been as successful in other combat areas, his mental flexibility and willingness to innovate suggest that he would have adapted to any situation.

Kenney's actions in the war were partly the result of his prewar thinking about air warfare and partly the result of adapting to the particular environment. He proved to be both well prepared for his role and capable of accommodating a wide range of problems, an important combination in any commander. None of the success he enjoyed was inevitable; rather it was the result of decisions and choices he made about fighting the war. He built and maintained a strong and effective working relationship with MacArthur while at the same time balancing the conflicting pressures on a theater air commander. Kenney loved flying and was a fervent believer in air power, but he was not enamored of one type of aircraft or one particular use of air power. The challenge for the theater air commander, he believed, was building an air organization that made the most out of the capabilities of air power in modern warfare.

Throughout the war Kenney remained focused on using the advantages that air power offered, especially the ability to avoid large concentrations of enemy forces and outflank the enemy through the air. This task, however, required first gaining control of the air by defeating the opposing air force. This mission became Kenney's first priority, and he continually preached the importance of air superiority to MacArthur. After neutralizing or defeating the enemy threat, aircraft could then be used to isolate the enemy positions, support the ground advance, or transport troops and equipment to the battle area. Although the basic strategy of outflanking the enemy is as old as war itself, MacArthur's campaign in the Southwest Pacific would not have been possible without air power. General George C. Kenney, MacArthur's airman, proved instrumental to the Allied victory.

NOTES

Introduction

1. USS *Missouri* Deck Log, August 31, September 2, 1945, Quintin S. Lander Papers, MHI; General Headquarters, U.S. Army Pacific, "Instructions for Personnel Attending Surrender Ceremony," September 2, 1945, KP; George C. Kenney, *General Kenney Reports* (New York: Duell, Sloan, and Pearce, 1949; reprinted, Washington, D.C.: Office of Air Force History, 1987) pp. 576–578.

2. Ronald H. Spector, *Eagle against the Sun* (New York: Free Press, 1984; reprinted, Vintage Books, 1985), p. 226.

3. D. Clayton James, *A Time for Giants* (New York: Franklin Watts, 1987), p. 202.

4. Geoffrey Perret, *Winged Victory: The Army Air Forces in World War II* (New York: Random House, 1993) p. 465.

5. Donald M. Goldstein, "Ennis C. Whitehead, Aerospace Commander and Pioneer" (Ph.D. diss., University of Denver, 1970), pp. 2, 436; idem, "Ennis C. Whitehead: Aerial Tactician," in *We Shall Return!* ed. William M. Leary (Lexington: The University Press of Kentucky, 1988), p. 207.

6. David Horner, "Strategy and Higher Command," in *RAAF in the Southwest Pacific 1942–1945* (Canberra: RAAF Air Power Studies Centre, 1993), p. 54.

7. Spector, *Eagle*, p. 228.

8. Herman Wolk has done the most to illuminate Kenney's contributions: Herman S. Wolk, "George C. Kenney: The Great Innovator," in *Makers of the United States Air Force*, ed. John L. Frisbee (Washington, D.C.: Office of Air Force History, 1987), pp. 127–150, covers Kenney's entire career, while "George C. Kenney: MacArthur's Premier Airman," in Leary, 88–114, concentrates on Kenney's role in World War II. Alexus Gregory Grynkewich's thesis on Kenney, "'Advisable in the National Interest?' The Relief of General George C. Kenney," (M.A. thesis, University of Georgia, 1994), concentrates on Kenney's relationship with other Air Force leaders and his dismissal as the commander of Strategic Air Command in 1948. By comparison, one of Kenney's ground counterparts, Lieutenant General Robert L. Eichelberger, has been the subject of two biographical studies and one edited volume, John F. Shortal, *Forged by Fire: General Robert L. Eichelberger and the Pacific War* (Columbia: University of South Carolina Press, 1987); Paul Chwialkowski, *In Caesar's Shadow: The Life of General Robert Eichelberger* (Westport, Conn.: Greenwood Press, 1993); Jay Luvaas, ed., *Dear Miss Em: General Eichelberger's War in the Pacific, 1942–1945* (Westport, Conn.: Greenwood Press, 1972).

9. Stanley L. Falk, "Gaps in the Published History of the Air Force: Challenge for Historians," *The Historian* 44 (Aug. 1982): 457–458; Noel F. Parrish, "The Influence of Air Power upon Historians," pp. 36–37, and David MacIssac, "Leadership in the Old Air Force: A Postgraduate Assignment," pp. 91–92, in *The Harmon Memorial Lectures in Military History, 1959–1987,* ed. Harry R. Borowski (Washington, D.C.: Office of Air Force History, 1988).

10. Philip S. Meilinger, *American Airpower Biography: A Survey of the Field* (Maxwell Air Force Base, Ala.: Air University Press, 1995), pp. 60–62.

1. *The Early Years*

Epigraph: George C. Kenney, interview with James C. Hasdorff, August 10–21, 1974, Bay Harbor Island, Florida, p. 9, file K239.0512-806, HRA.

1. Roland W. Kenney, "The Kenney Family Tree," unpublished manuscript, Farmington, Connecticut, 1973, Allen County Public Library, Fort Wayne, Indiana, pp. 3–4, 15, 44–45, copy in author's possession. Information on the early Kenney family can also be found in Florance L. K. Robertson, "Keeney, Keny Family of Milton, Mass., and Nova Scotia, Canada," in *Genealogies of Mayflower Families,* selected and introduced by Gary Boyd Roberts (Baltimore: Genealogical Publishing Co., 1985), pp. 413–434.

2. Roland W. Kenney, "Kenney Family Tree," pp. 3–5. There were numerous variations of the family name in the colonial records such as Keayne, Keny, Kene, Keyne, Kenny, Keney, Kanney, Keene, and Keen, p. 2.

3. "Yarmouth Genealogies, No. 70, The Churchill Family," *Yarmouth Herald*, December 6, 1898, p.1, December 27, 1898, p. 1, General George C. Kenney papers, file 168.7103-25, HRA.

4. George Rawlyk, *Nova Scotia's Massachusetts: A Study of Massachusetts–Nova Scotia Relations, 1630–1784* (Montreal: McGill-Queen's University Press, 1973), pp. 217–219; Edwin Crowell, *History of Barrington Township* (Yarmouth, Nova Scotia: n.p., 1923; reprint ed. Belleville, Ontario: Mika Publishing, 1973), pp. 66–73; Marcus Lee Hansen and John Bartlet Brebner, *The Mingling of the Canadian and American Peoples* (New Haven, Conn.: Yale University Press for the Carnegie Endowment for International Peace, 1940), p. 30.

5. Rawlyk, pp. 217–228; Crowell, pp. 82–85; John Bartlet Brebner, *The Neutral Yankees of Nova Scotia* (New York: Columbia University Press, 1937), pp. 26–29, 55–56; Roland W. Kenney, "Kenney Family Tree," pp. 5–21.

6. Roland W. Kenney, "Kenney Family Tree," pp. 19, 21; Crowell, pp. 153, 147, 504.

7. Quoted from Rawlyk, p. 221–222. Also see Brebner, Chapter 7; Crowell, p. 61. Rawlyk uses a figure of 5,000 immigrants, Crowell 7,000.

8. Brebner, pp. 309–310; Rawlyk, pp. 222–223.

9. Roland W. Kenney, "Kenney Family Tree," pp. 32–33.

10. Edith Porter, interview with James Kenney, p. 6, Yarmouth, Nova Scotia, 1982; Roland Kenney, letter to James Kenney, February 27, 1994, both in author's possession.

11. Roland W. Kenney, "Kenney Family Tree," p. 33; James Kenney, letter to author, February 26, 1994.

12. Roland W. Kenney, "Kenney Family Tree," p. 32. There is no record of the move, but Joseph Kenney is first listed in the poll tax records in 1900, the year after George was born. Brookline Massachusetts Poll Tax list, Public Library of Brookline, Massachusetts. I am grateful to Cindy Battis, Collection Development Librarian, Public Library of Brookline, for providing this information.

13. Roland W. Kenney, "Kenney Family Tree," p. 36.

14. Hansen, pp. 208–210, 242; David D. Harvey, *Americans in Canada: Migration and Settlement Since 1840* (Lewiston, NY: Edwin Mellen Press, 1991), p. 45; Crowell, pp. 422–423.

15. Hansen, p. 209. While Hansen is referring to an earlier time period, the same phenomenon held true during the time that Joe Kenney emigrated, see p. 242.

16. Harvey, pp. iv–v; Kenneth Lines, *British and Canadian Immigration to the United States Since 1920* (San Francisco, Calif.: R & E Research Associates, 1978), pp. 2, 57–58. For more on the problems in tracing these cross-border movements see Hansen, pp. vi, 246–247.

17. See, for example, "Battle of the Pacific," *Time*, January 18, 1943, p. 28, for the circumstances of Kenney's birth. In all of his biographical sketches and oral history interviews Kenney repeats the same story.

18. James Kenney, letter to author, February 26, 1994.

19. Dorothy Dodson (George Kenney's niece), interview with author, Arlington, Virginia, May 22, 1995. Later in life Arthur Kenney, George's younger brother, had difficulty proving his citizenship because he did not have a birth certificate. Arthur claimed that George encountered similar problems. Arthur Kenney, interview with

James Kenney, Los Angeles, California, 1980, p. 4. There was no record of George's naturalization, but, as far as the records show, his assertion about his citizenship was never questioned.

20. Brookline Poll Tax list; Brookline Directory, Public Library of Brookline, Massachusetts.

21. Edith Porter, interview with James Kenney, pp. 9, 11.

22. Roland W. Kenney, "Kenney Family Tree," p. 33; Edith Porter, interview with James Kenney, pp. 7, 9.

23. William R. Callahan, "Brookline Boy Takes Command of Our Air Force in Pacific," *Boston Globe,* September 16, 1942, p. 1.

24. Lawrence Dame, "A Flying General," *Boston Herald,* September 8, 1945, p. 1.

25. Certificate from MIT, from James Kenney, copy in author's possession.

26. Callahan, pp. 1, 4; Robert Cromie, "Kenney of the Fifth," *Chicago Sunday Tribune,* November 14, 1943, p. 1; Margarite Kenney, letter to author, April 3, 1994.

27. Brookline Poll Tax list, Brookline Directory, Public Library of Brookline, Massachusetts.

28. Edith Porter, interview with James Kenney, p. 6; James Kenney, letter to author, February 26, 1994.

29. Roland Kenney, letter to James Kenney, February 27, 1994, copy in author's possession.

30. Kenney does not mention his father in any oral histories or interviews, and his grandfather was the only family member Kenney mentioned in the essay. George C. Kenney, "Personalities," handwritten manuscript, n.d., file 168.7103-26, HRA. William Knudsen was a member of the National Defense Advisory Commission during World War II in charge of coordinating aircraft production, I. B. Holley Jr., *Buying Aircraft: Matériel Procurement for the Army Air Forces* (Washington, D.C.: Center of Military History, 1989), pp. 254–257.

31. Roland W. Kenney, "Kenney Family Tree," p. 33; idem, "General George C. Kenney, USAF," unpublished manuscript, p. 1; Edith Porter, interview with James Kenney, pp. 4–6. Captain Churchill was also given a certificate of appreciation by the insurance company. I am grateful to Dorothy Dodson for showing the certificate to me.

32. *New York Times,* September 2, 1910, p. 1. Graham Wallace, *Claude Grahame-White A Biography* (London: Putnam, 1960), pp. 96–97.

33. Michael Paris, "The Rise of the Airmen: The Origins of Air Force Elitism: c. 1890–1918," *Journal of Contemporary History* 28 (Jan. 1993):130; Wallace, pp. 51–76.

34. *New York Times,* September 8, 1910, p. 4; September 14, 1910, p. 4; Wallace, pp. 104–105.

35. *New York Times,* September 16, 1910, p. 4.

36. *New York Times,* September 14, 1910, p. 4. His winnings included the $5,000 first prize in bombing accuracy. According to the *Times* this bombing competition was the first ever held in the United States.

37. Kenney, interview with Hasdorff, p. 8, Kenney mistakenly believed that the prize was $5,000. Cromie, p. 1.

38. Kenney, interview with Hasdorff, pp. 8–9; Wolk, "Innovator," p. 128. In the interview with Hasdorff, Kenney recalled that Grahame-White usually charged $10 for a fifteen-minute flight, a sum that Kenney did not have. In reality the aviator was so swamped by people wanting to fly that his manager charged $500 for a five-minute

flight, and Grahame-White earned over $2,000 flying passengers during the meet. Wallace, p. 102; *New York Times,* September 14, 1910.

39. Kenney, interview with Hasdorff, p. 9.

40. For insight into the public's fascination with aviation in this era, see Joseph J. Corn, *The Winged Gospel: America's Romance with Aviation, 1900–1950* (New York: Oxford University Press, 1983), passim, but in particular pp. 8–10, 135; Robert Wohl, *A Passion for Wings: Aviation and the Western Imagination, 1908–1918* (New Haven, Conn.: Yale University Press, 1994).

41. Kenney, interview with Hasdorff, pp. 10, 11; *New York Times,* September 9, 1910, p. 4. For Blériot see Mike Spick, *Milestones of Manned Flight* (New York: Smithmark Publishers, 1994), pp. 20–23.

42. Kenney, interview with Hasdorff, pp. 10, 11; James Kenney, letter to author, February 26, 1994; Cromie, p. 1; Wolk, "Innovator," p. 128.

43. Kenney, interview with Hasdorff, p. 2; Wolk, "Innovator," p. 127.

44. James Kenney, letter to author, February 26, 1994; Margarite Kenney, letter to author, April 3, 1994.

45. Kenney, interview with Hasdorff, p. 2; George C. Kenney, "Biographical Sketch," n.d. (1953?), file 168.7103-34, HRA. Louise Kenney died during an operation for a fibroid uterus. Louise C. Kenney Death Certificate, copy in author's possession; interview with Dorothy Dodson.

46. Kenney, interview with Hasdorff, p. 3; Kenney, "Biographical Sketch;" Samuel C. Prescott, *When M.I.T. Was "Boston Tech" 1861–1916* (Cambridge, Mass.: Technology Press, 1954), pp. 264–267.

47. Kenney, interview with Hasdorff, pp. 5–7; Dodson, interview with author; Roland W. Kenney, "Kenney Family Tree," p. 33; Dame, p. 1; Callahan, p. 1.

48. Kenney, interview with Hasdorff, pp. 5–6.

49. Ibid.

2. *Army Aviator*

Epigraph: Kenney, interview with Hasdorff, p. 19.

1. Ibid., p. 12; Cromie, p. 1.

2. I. B. Holley Jr., *Ideas and Weapons* (New Haven, Conn.: Yale University Press, 1952; reprinted, Washington, D.C.: Office of Air Force History, 1983), pp. 27, 37; John H. Morrow Jr., *The Great War in the Air: Military Aviation from 1909 to 1921* (Washington, D.C.: Smithsonian Institution Press, 1993), p. 265.

3. The course was later lengthened to twelve weeks. James J. Hudson, *Hostile Skies: A Combat History of the American Air Service in World War I* (Syracuse, N.Y.: Syracuse University Press, 1968), pp. 27–28; Maurer Maurer, *The U.S. Air Service in World War I,* 4 vols. (Washington, D.C.: Office of Air Force History, 1979), 4:xvii.

4. Hudson, p. 28; Hiram Bingham, *An Explorer in the Air Service* (New Haven, Conn.: Yale University Press, 1920), pp. 21, 47–48; Millie Glasebrook, ed., *American Aviators in the Great War 1914–1918* (Carson City, Nev.: Glasebrook Foundation, 1984), p. 141. For the universality of this training, see Lee Kennett, *The First Air War, 1914–1918* (New York: Free Press, 1981), p. 123.

5. Quote from George H. Beverley, *Pioneer in the U.S. Air Corps: The Memoirs of*

Brigadier General George H. Beverley (Manhattan, Kans.: Sunflower University Press, 1982), p. 14; Hudson, p. 28. The emphasis on military training and the account of the Lewis machine gun are common refrains in the personal narratives of World War I aviators. For other examples see Howard R. Craig, *Sunward I've Climbed: A Personal Narrative of Peace and War* (El Paso, Tex.: Texas Western Press, 1975), pp. 10–16; Norman Archibald, *Heaven High, Hell Deep, 1917–1918* (New York: Albert & Charles Boni, Inc., 1935; reprinted, New York: Arno Press, 1980), pp. 8–11; Dean C. Smith, *By the Seat of My Pants* (Boston: Little, Brown and Company, 1961), pp. 40–42.

6. Hudson, p. 28; Craig, pp. 10–16; Archibald, pp. 8–11; Smith, pp. 40–42.

7. Archibald, p. 10.

8. Smith, p. 41.

9. Certificate of Enlistment, courtesy of James Kenney, copy in author's possession; Caroline Ticknor, ed., *New England Aviators, 1914–1918,* 2 vols. (Boston: Houghton Mifflin, 1919), 1:202–203; Wolk, "Innovator," p. 128; Wolk, "Airman," p. 89.

10. Bingham, pp. 46, 53; Jack H. Nunn, "MIT: A University's Contributions to National Defense," *Military Affairs* 43, no. 3 (Oct. 1979): 121; Prescott, pp. 283–284. The other universities that established ground schools were the University of California, the University of Texas, the University of Illinois, Ohio State University, Cornell, Princeton, and Georgia Tech. Hudson, pp. 27–28.

11. Of the 797 who entered MIT throughout the war, 622, 77 percent, graduated. Glasebrook, p. 141.

12. Smith, pp. 54–62.

13. Hudson, pp. 29–30; Maurer, *Air Service in World War I,* 4:xviii. While officers usually enter active duty as a second lieutenant, for a time during World War I pilots were commissioned as first lieutenants. In January 1918 this policy changed, and pilots entered active duty as second lieutenants. Craig, p. 16.

14. Kenney, interview with Hasdorff, pp. 12–13; George C. Kenney, "Summary of Activities," n.d.(1953?), Kenney papers, file 168-7103-2, HRA; Ticknor, 1:202–203. For Bert Acosta see Wesley Phillips Newton, "Acosta, Bertram Blanchard," in *Dictionary of American Biography, Supplement Five,* ed., John A. Garraty (New York: Charles Scribner's Sons, 1977), pp. 2–3; Paul O'Neil, *Barnstormers and Speed Kings* (Alexandria, Va.: Time-Life Books, 1981), p. 84; Sterling Seagrave, *Soldiers of Fortune* (Alexandria, Va.: Time-Life Books, 1981), p. 45; John Edward Carver, *Airmen Without Portfolio: U.S. Mercenaries in Civil War Spain* (Westport, Conn.: Praeger, 1997), pp. 28–31, 108–109.

15. Kennett, pp. 105–107.

16. Kenney, interview with Hasdorff, pp. 12–15, quote on p. 13; Wolk, "Innovator," p. 128; Wolk, "Airman," p. 89.

17. "Summary of Activities" and "Biographical Sketch," George C. Kenney Military Personnel Record (201 file kept by the Adjutant General), National Personnel Records Center, National Archives and Records Administration, St. Louis, Missouri; Ticknor, 1:202–293. Kenney listed November 5 as his commissioning date, but his 201 file has November 8.

18. Kennett, pp. 1–21; Morrow, pp. 1–21.

19. Kennett, pp. 23–36; Morrow, pp. xv, 52–55, 63–64, 85–87, 338, 365.

20. Kennett, pp. 39, 41–68, 211–214.

21. Bingham, pp. 117–119, 126–129; Hudson, pp. 35–37.

22. Patrick report, found in Maurer, *Air Service in World War I,* 1:93, 97, quote on 1:97.

23. Ibid.

24. Hudson, p. 82; *History of the 91st Aero Squadron, 1917–1918* (Koblenz, Germany: Gebruder Breuer, 1919), pp. 1–3, file Sq-Photo-91-HI, HRA.

25. Kenney, interview with Hasdorff, pp. 16, 18–19.

26. Kennett, ch. 9; Wohl, *Passion,* ch. 7; idem, "The Bards of Aviation: Flight and French Culture 1909–1939," *Michigan Quarterly Review* 29 (Summer 1990): 303–327; Paris, pp. 123–141.

27. Colonel Walter C. Kilner, chief of training section, Air Service, American Expeditionary Force, quoted in Maurer, *Air Service in World War I,* 4: 330.

28. Hudson, pp. 131–133; Kennett, pp. 86–87; Lucien H. Thayer, *America's First Eagles: The Official History of the U.S. Air Service, A.E.F. (1917–1918),* ed. Donald Joseph McGee and Roger James Bender (San Jose, Calif.: R. James Bender Publishing, and Mesa, Ariz.: Champlin Fighter Museum Press, 1983), pp. 180, 201–202. Thayer was a second lieutenant assigned in September 1917 to the Air Service Headquarters as a historian, Maurer, *Air Service in World War I,* 1:2.

29. Morrow, pp. 147–148, 205, 338; Kenney, interview with Hasdorff, p. 25.

30. George C. Kenney Flying Log Books, Kenney papers, file 168.7013-2, HRA. Although Kenney claims this as a combat mission, it was actually classified as a familiarization flight for the squadron. The squadron was declared ready for duty on June 6 and flew its first combat mission the next day, June 7, Hudson, p. 83; Maurer, *Air Service in World War I,* 1:30, 260, 262.

31. *History of the 91st,* p. 6.

32. "Summary of Activities," p. 1; Ticknor, 1:202–203; Hudson, pp. 83.

33. Hudson, pp. 131–133; Thayer, pp. 180, 201–202; Maurer, *Air Service in World War I,* 1:262–265, 269.

34. Kenney Log Books, August 22, 1917. In his log books Kenney claims to have shot down a total of six aircraft, although he was only officially credited with two.

35. Quoted in Patrick report, Maurer, *Air Service in World War I,* 1:30.

36. Maurer, *Air Service in World War I,* 1:37.

37. Maurer, *Air Service in World War I,* 1:37, 3:1–2; Morrow, p. 337; Edward M. Coffman, *The War to End All Wars: The American Military Experience in World War I* (New York: Oxford University Press, 1968; reprinted, Madison: University of Wisconsin Press, 1986), pp. 207, 273–278; Alfred F. Hurley, *Billy Mitchell: Crusader for Air Power* (Bloomington: Indiana University Press, 1975), pp. 32–36.

38. Thayer, p. 180, 201–202; Maurer, *Air Service in World War I,* 2:38.

39. Maurer, *Air Service in World War I,* 1:269.

40. Kenney, interview with Hasdorff, p. 23; Kenney Log Books, September 15, 1917; Headquarters Air Service, First Army, American Expeditionary Forces, General Order number 13, October 2, 1918, courtesy of James Kenney, copy in author's possession; *91st Aero Squadron,* p. 11; Maurer, *Air Service in World War I,* 1:38, 3:675–676. Kenney used some artistic license in his memoir, stating that he shot down his first

aircraft on "the thirteenth." Kenney, *Reports,* p. 26. That is incorrect; neither his first claim nor his first credited victory came on that date.

41. Coffman, pp. 300–301, 328–329.

42. "Summary of Activities," p. 1.

43. Quoted in Maurer, *Air Service in World War I,* 1:275.

44. Ibid.

45. Maurer, *Air Service in World War I,* 1:275–276.

46. Kenney, interview with Hasdorff, pp. 23–25; "Fifth Air Force Biographies," file 720.293, HRA; Headquarters Air Service, First Army, American Expeditionary Force, General Order number 20, October 23, 1918, courtesy of James Kenney, copy in author's possession.

47. Thayer, p. 218.

48. William Badham, interview with George W. Goddard, n.p., May 20, 1966, p. 7, file K239.0512-989, HRA.

49. Lawrence Dame, "A Flying General," *Boston Herald,* September 8, 1945, p. 1.

50. "Summary of Activities," p. 1; Cromie, p. 1. For flight organization see table of organization, Observation Squadron, Air Service, Maurer, *Air Service in World War I,* 4:514, also 4:54. General Headquarters, AEF, Special Order number 77-A, March 18, 1919, Kenney papers, HRA. Wolk, "Innovator," p. 128, Wolk, "Airmen," p. 89, and DeWitt S. Copp, *A Few Great Captains* (Garden City, NY: Doubleday & Company, Inc., 1980), p. 280, incorrectly identify Kenney as the commander of the 91st Squadron.

51. "Biographical Sketch," p. 3; *History of the 91st,* pp. 18–20; Hurley, p. 33.

52. Hudson, p. 270; Thayer, pp. 218–219.

53. In every interview Kenney repeated this same complaint, but often cited different numbers for the losses his squadron suffered. The exact numbers are probably less important than Kenney's perception of the causes for the losses. In one session he stated that only nine of the original twenty-four pilots in the squadron survived the war. Kenney, interview with Goddard, p. 6. In another he claimed that only seven of the fifty-two pilots in the squadron were alive after the war. Kenney, interview with Hasdorff, p. 19. Also George C. Kenney, interview with Marvin Stanley, Washington, D.C., n.d., pp. 5–6, file K239.0512-747, HRA.

54. Kenney, interview with Goddard, p. 6.

55. For weather problems see Morrow, p. 272; for criticisms about training see Maurer, *Air Service in World War I,* 4: 57–58, 67–68, 132–133, 329–330.

56. Kenney, interview with Hasdorff, p. 20.

57. Letter, George Kenney to H. H. Arnold, December 10, 1942, p.4; Letter, George Kenney to H. H. Arnold, June 19, 1943, p. 2, KP.

58. Robert Frank Futrell, *Ideas, Concepts and Doctrine* (Maxwell Air Force Base, Alabama: Air University Press, 1971), p. 64.

59. Letter, Kenney to Arnold, October 21, 1943, KP.

60. Letter Donald Wilson to Edna Wilson, September 25, 1942, Donald Wilson Papers, Library of Congress.

61. Kenney, *Reports,* p. 43; Perret, p. 417.

62. Letter, Kenney to Arnold, February 19, 1944, p. 4, Murray Green Collection, United States Air Force Academy Library, Special Collections Division, United States Air Force Academy, Colorado.

3. Preparation for Command

Epigraph: Letter, Major General Frank M. Andrews to General Malin Craig, quoted in Copp, *Few Great Captains,* p. 354.

1. *91st Aero Squadron,* pp. 18–23.

2. "Biographical Sketch," p. 1; "Summary of Activities," p. 1; 201 File; Headquarters Mitchell Field, Special Order Number 96, June 24, 1919; War Department, Special Order Number 177-0, July 30, 1919, Kenney papers, file 168.7103-2, HRA.

3. Clarence C. Clendenen, *Blood on the Border: The United States Army and the Mexican Irregulars* (New York: Macmillan Company, 1969), pp. 341–359; Maurer Maurer, *Aviation in the U.S. Army, 1919–1939* (Washington, D.C.: Office of Air Force History, 1987), pp. 100–101.

4. Headquarters Southern Department, Fort Sam Houston, Texas, Special Order Number 208, August 11, 1919; Headquarters Southern Department, Fort Sam Houston, Texas, Special Order Number 260, October 10, 1919, Kenney papers, HRA; 201 file; Clendenen, p. 356; Maurer, *Aviation in U.S. Army,* pp. 100–107; Stacey C. Hinkle, *Wings over the Border: The Army Air Service Armed Patrol of the United States–Mexico Border 1919–1921,* Southwestern Studies Number 26 (El Paso, Tex.: Texas Western Press, 1970), pp. 3–39.

5. Hinkle, p. 8.

6. Kenney, interview with Hasdorff, p. 30.

7. Kenney, interview with Hasdorff, pp. 28–30; Maurer, *Aviation in U.S. Army,* p. 23; idem, *Air Service in World War I,* p. 507.

8. 14th Cavalry Headquarters, Fort Ringgold, Texas, Special Order Number 146, July 2, 1920; Headquarters Southern Department, Fort Sam Houston, Texas, Special Order Number 167, July 17, 1920, Kenney papers, HRA; Hinkle, pp. 52–53; Maurer, *Aviation in U.S. Army,* p. 47.

9. Futrell, pp. 34–35; Hurley, pp. 39–50.

10. Hurley, pp. 56–70.

11. Headquarters Southern Department, Fort Sam Houston, Texas, Special Order Number 167, July 17, 1920; War Department, Special Order Number 237, October 8, 1920, Kenney papers, file 168.7103-2, HRA; Kenney, "Biographical Sketch"; James Kenney, phone interview with author, January 10, 1996.

12. Kenney, interview with Hasdorff, pp. 30–31.

13. John F. Powers, "Founding of the Air Force Institute of Technology," *Air University Review* 15 (Sept.–Oct. 1964): 36–49; Maurer, *Aviation in U.S. Army,* pp. 65–66. The school was originally known as the Air School of Application; the name was changed in 1920 to the Air Service Engineering School.

14. Kenney, interview with Hasdorff, p. 31; Maurer, *Aviation in U.S. Army,* p. 65.

15. Kenney, interview with Hasdorff, p. 31; "Summary of Activities," p.1; "Biographical Sketch," p. 1.

16. Maurer, *Aviation in U.S. Army,* pp. 81–82. To preserve the nascent aircraft industrial base developed during the war, the Air Service divided orders for the bombers among different manufacturers; as a result Curtiss built an aircraft designed by Martin.

17. Letter, James Kenney to author, February 26, 1994; James Kenney, phone interview with author, January 10, 1996.

18. Ibid. E. C. Hoagland, phone interview with author, February 2, 1996.

19. War Department Special Order Number 115, May 16, 1923, Kenney papers, HRA; "Biographical Sketch," p. 2; "Summary of Activities," p. 2. My thanks to Dave Mets for his insights on aircraft armament.

20. War Department Special Order Number 115, May 15, 1925; War Department Special Order Number 158, July 7, 1925, Kenney papers, HRA.

21. John W. Masland and Laurence I. Radway, *Soldiers and Scholars: Military Education and National Policy* (Princeton, N.J.: Princeton University Press, 1957), p. 95.

22. Robert T. Finney, *History of the Air Corps Tactical School*, USAF Historical Study 100 (Maxwell AFB, Ala.: Air University, 1955; reprinted, Washington, D.C.: Center for Air Force History, 1992), pp. 8–9, 11–4, 16; Robert T. Finney, "Early Air Corps Training and Tactics," *Military Affairs* 20 (Fall 1956): 154–161; Maurer, *Aviation in U.S. Army*, pp. 64–65. My thanks to Peter Faber for his insight into the Tactical School.

23. War Department Special Order Number 83, April 8, 1926, Kenney papers, HRA.

24. Boyd L. Dastrup, *The U.S. Army Command and General Staff College: A Centennial History* (Manhattan, Kans.: Sunflower University Press, 1982), pp. 63–65; Timothy K. Nenninger, "Leavenworth and Its Critics: The U.S. Army Command and General Staff School, 1920–1940," *The Journal of Military History* 58 (April 1994): 201–203.

25. The Command and General Staff School, "Schedule for 1926–1927," p. 3, Archives, Combined Arms Research Library, U.S. Army Command and General Staff College, Fort Leavenworth, Kansas; Dastrup, pp. 75–76; Nenninger, "Leavenworth and Its Critics," pp. 201–203.

26. Dastrup, pp. 70–74; Nenninger, "Leavenworth and Its Critics," pp. 222–224.

27. D. K. R. Croswell, *The Chief of Staff: The Military Career of General Walter Bedell Smith* (Westport, Conn.: Greenwood Press, 1991), p. 57; Dastrup, p. 128.

28. Command and General Staff School, "Schedule for 1926–1927," passim. The classroom periods were called conferences.

29. Ibid., pp. 7–10.

30. Command and General Staff School, Class Roster, 1926–1927. Even as a percentage this was less than their strength in the army. In 1927 aviation personnel made up 7.5 percent of the army, whereas the airmen were slightly over 4 percent of the students in the Command and General Staff School that same year, Office of Statistical Control, Headquarters Army Air Forces, "Army Air Forces Statistical Digest," December 1945, p. 15.

31. Letter, Elaine McConnell, Archives, U.S. Army Command and General Staff College, to author, August 30, 1995, in author's possession.

32. Historian Timothy Nenninger maintains that "generally, Leavenworth had a most favorable reputation among U.S. Army officers who served during the interwar era," "Leavenworth and Its Critics," p. 203. While that may have been true for the ground officers, airmen were uniformly more negative about their educational experiences.

33. Thomas M. Coffey, *Hap: The Story of the U. S. Air Force and the Man Who Built It, General Henry H. "Hap" Arnold* (New York: Viking Press, 1982), p. 133.

34. Ibid., p. 134.

35. David R. Mets, *Master of Airpower* (Novato, Calif.: Presidio Press, 1988), pp. 98–99, quote on p. 99.

36. Richard G. Davis, *Carl A. Spaatz and the Air War in Europe* (Washington, D.C.: Center for Air Force History, 1993), p. 24.

37. Donald Wilson, *Wooing Peponi* (Monterey, Calif.: Angel Press, 1974), pp. 147–149, quote on p. 234.

38. Quoted in Copp, *Few Great Captains*, p. 152.

39. Laurence S. Kuter, "Growth of Air Power," unpublished manuscript, p. 121, USAF Academy Special Collections, USAF Academy Library, Colorado.

40. Wilson, p. 144.

41. Hurley, p. 101.

42. Quoted in Hurley, p. 101.

43. Hurley, pp. 101–109.

44. Greer, p. 29; Futrell, pp. 44–51.

45. E. C. Hoagland, phone interview with author, February 2, 1996.

46. Robert L. Eichelberger with Milton MacKaye, *Our Jungle Road to Tokyo* (New York: Viking Press, 1950), p. xv; Coffey, p. 132.

47. Eichelberger, p. xv; James, *Time for Giants*, p. 194.

48. War Department Special Order Number 75, March 31, 1927, Kenney Papers, HRA.

49. Finney, *History*, pp. 62–68.

50. Richard P. Hallion, *Strike From the Sky: The History of Battlefield Air Attack, 1911–1945* (Washington, D.C.: Smithsonian Institution Press, 1989), pp. 19–28.

51. United States Army Training Regulation 440-15, *Air Tactics*, October 15, 1935, pp. 11–13; Thomas H. Greer, *The Development of Air Doctrine in the Army Air Arm, 1917–1941*, USAF Historical Study Number 89 (Maxwell AFB, Ala.: Air University Press, 1955), p. 12; Lee Kennett, "Developments to 1939," in *Case Studies in the Development of Close Air Support*, ed. Benjamin Franklin Cooling (Washington, D.C.: Office of Air Force History, 1990), p. 43.

52. Hallion, p. 20. The British also used the terms "trench flights" and "battlefield bombing" for these missions. Kennett, *First Air War*, pp. 211, 221–222.

53. "Attack Aviation, 1925–1926," pp. 1, 9–13; George C. Kenney, "Conference on Attack Aviation," March 1930, file 248.2201B-1, HRA.

54. From at least 1925 the attack aviation teaching at the Tactical School focused on targets behind the front lines. "Attack Aviation, 1925–1926"; Kenney, "Conference"; Frank M. Andrews, "Is Attack Aviation Necessary or Justified?" May 15, 1928, ACTS thesis, Langley Field, Virginia, file 248.222-55D, HRA. For earlier thinking see Hallion, pp. 51–54; Kennett, "Developments," pp. 45–47.

55. Letter, Kenney to Lt. Col. H. A. Wells, Fort Benning, Georgia, Subject: Comments on test of infantry weapons against aircraft, April 18, 1930, file 248.2201, HRA.

56. Ibid.

57. Kenney, "Conference;" ACTS, "Attack Aviation," March 1930, file 248.2201B, HRA; Major Frank D. Lackland, memorandum to Assistant Commandant Air Corps Tactical School, May 8, 1929, pp. 5, 8, 13, file 248.222-10F, HRA. This paper was written in response to Kenney's question, "What is the best method of operation for attack aviation against ground targets in a [*sic*] warfare against a well organized enemy?"

58. Comparison of "Attack Aviation, 1925–1926" and "Attack Aviation" 1930, pp. 1–21; also see Kenney, "Conference" for historical examples.

59. Letter, Commandant Air Corps Tactical School to Chief of the Air Corps, Subject: Appointment of Instructors of the Tactical School as members of Boards to recommend types of aircraft, October 25, 1929; "Proceedings of a Board of Officers for the Purpose of Determining the General Requirements for an Attack Airplane," Langley Field, Virginia, April 8, 1929, file 248.122, HRA.

60. Kenney, interview with Hasdorff, p. 35; Kenney, interview with Stanley, pp. 6–7. In the school roster Kenney is the only instructor listed for attack aviation and observation. "Roster, Air Corps Tactical School, 1928–1929," file 248.12610, HRA. Prior to the 1934–1935 annual report there was no breakdown of instructors by section or subject area. ACTS, "Staff and Faculty Air Corps Tactical School, 1920–1934," file 248.1751, HRA; Finney, *History,* p. 99.

61. Kennett, in Cooling, pp. 45–49.

62. "Attack Aviation," 1930, pp. 22–24; Lackland memorandum, pp. 6–7.

63. Morrow, p. 237.

64. Stephen L. McFarland, *America's Pursuit of Precision Bombing, 1910–1945* (Washington, D.C.: Smithsonian Institution Press, 1995), pp. 84–85.

65. Gary C. Cox, *Beyond the Battle Line: US Air Attack Theory and Doctrine, 1919–1941* (Maxwell AFB, Ala.: Air University Press, 1996), pp. 30–32; Hallion, pp. 48–49; Kennett, in Cooling, 51–52.

66. Antiaircraft fire accounted for almost half of the losses on combat missions in the European theater (5,380 out of 11,687), but only 22 percent (546 out of 2,494) in Kenney's area. *Army Air Forces Statistical Digest,* pp. 255, 258; Kenneth P. Werrell, *Archie, Flak, AAA, and SAM: A Short Operational History of Ground-Based Air Defense* (Maxwell AFB, Ala.: Air University Press, 1988), pp. 53–57.

67. "Attack Aviation, 1925–1926," pp. 12–13; "Attack Aviation," 1930, pp. 34–35.

68. Lackland memorandum, p. 3; "Attack Aviation, 1925–1926," p. 13; McFarland, pp. 84–85.

69. Major L. S. Fraser, Captain George C. Kenney, Captain George H. Weems, "Report on bombing and machine gun firing conducted by the Air Corps Tactical School, April 13, 17, and 23, 1931, against targets representing a small infantry column," [May 1931], file 248.2201B, HRA.

70. Kenney, interview with Stanley, p. 9; "Summary of Activities," p. 2. In another interview Kenney said he developed the bomb several years after leaving the Tactical School. Kenney, interview with Hasdorff, pp. 72–75. In his memoirs he states that he came up with the idea in 1928, but the bombs were not tested until 1936, Kenney, *Reports,* p. 12.

71. Letters, Frank Andrews to Davenport Johnson, November 11, 1930 (reply to first request); Johnson to Andrews, November 17, 1930; Andrews to Johnson, November 22, 1930, Frank M. Andrews Papers, Library of Congress; Finney, *History,* p. 101.

72. Wilson, p. 144.

73. Andrews to Johnson, November 22, 1930; Harry P. Ball, *Of Responsible Command: A History of the U.S. Army War College* (Carlisle Barracks, Penn.: Alumni Association of the United States Army War College, 1983), pp. 211–212, 250–253; Croswell, p. 63; Oswald H. Saunders, "The Army War College," *The Military Engineer* 26 (March–April 1934), p. 102.

74. Colonel Leon B. Dromer, assistant commandant, Army War College, "General Orientation, the Army War College Course, 1932–1933," pp. 2–3, file 390-1, miscellaneous no. 1, 1932–1933, Curricular Archives of the Army War College, MHI; Ball, pp. 212–214, 227–230.

75. Dromer, pp. 4–6; Saunders, p. 103.

76. Ball, p. 248.

77. Army War College, "Class of 1933, Resident," Curricular Archives of the Army War College, MHI; Copp, p. 494, n. 2. The other Air Corps officers were Charles T. Phillips and David S. Seaton. In 1932, aviation personnel were 11 percent of the army. *Army Air Forces Statistical Digest,* p. 15.

78. Report of Committee Number 3, Army War College, "Tactical Doctrines," September 26, 1932, Curricular Archives of the Army War College, MHI.

79. George C. Kenney Record Card, Army War College; Report of Committee Number 8, "Promotion, Separation, and Assignment of Regular Army Officers in Time of Peace: Modifications to Develop Efficient and Well-Balanced Officer Personnel," October 26, 1932; Report of Committee Number 2, "War Reserves," November 16, 1932; Report of Committee Number 6, "Separate Strategic Surveys of the A.B.C. (Argentina, Brazil, and Chile) Countries of South America," December 21, 1932, Curricular Archives of the Army War College, MHI.

80. Report of Committee Number 3-B, "A Critical Study of the First German Army from August 12 to 24, 1914 and contrast it with a march under like conditions of an American force organized under the present tables of organization and having approximately equal infantry strength to that of the First Germany Army," January 23, 1933; Report of Committee Number 3-B, "Envelopment (The Winter Battle in Masuria, 8th and 10th German Armies, February 7 to 18, 1915)," February 18, 1933, Curricular Archives of the Army War College, MHI.

81. Ball, p. 246.

82. Finney, *History,* pp. 22–23, 33–34; Captain George C. Kenney, "The Proper Composition of the Air Force," Memorandum for the Assistant Commandant, The Army War College, April 29, 1933, p. 11, file 248.211-62K, HRA.

83. Allan R. Millett and Peter Maslowski, *For the Common Defense: A Military History of the United States of America,* rev. and expanded ed. (New York: Free Press, 1994), pp. 380–382, 402–404.

84. Kenney, "The Proper Composition of the Air Force," p. 1; Peter R. Faber, "Interwar U.S. Army Aviation and the Air Corps Tactical School: Incubators of American Airpower," in Philip Meilinger, ed., *The Paths of Heaven: The Evolution of Airpower Theory* (Maxwell AFB, Ala.: Air University Press, 1997), pp. 215–216.

85. Kenney, "Proper," pp. 2, 3.

86. Ibid., p. 2.

87. B. Q. Jones, "The Army War College," *Air Corps News Letter* 20, no. 23, December 1, 1937, p. 6, file 168.69, HRA.

88. Croswell, pp. 65–66.

89. Report of Committee Number 3, "Tactical Doctrines;" Report of Committee Number 8, "Promotion, Separation, and Assignment," Curricular Archives of the Army War College, MHI.

90. Quoted in Timothy Nenninger, "Creating Officers: The Leavenworth Experience, 1920–1940," *Military Review* 69 (Nov. 1989): 62.

91. For an example of the importance of a common language in an academic discipline, see Donald N. McCloskey, "Storytelling in Economics," in Cristopher Nash, ed., *Narrative in Culture: The Uses of Storytelling in the Sciences, Philosophy, and Literature* (London: Routledge, 1990). McCloskey writes, "Persuasion of the most rigorous kind has blanks to be filled at every other step, if it is about a difficult murder case, for example, or a difficult mathematical theorem," p. 19. Or, I would add, a military operation.

92. Army War College, "Class of 1933 Resident."

93. War Department Special Order Number 57, March 11, 1933, Kenney papers, HRA.

94. War Department, Office of the Chief of the Air Corps, Personnel Order Number 147, June 27, 1933; Letter, Oscar Westover, assistant chief of the Air Corps, to Kenney, June 27, 1933, Kenney papers, HRA; 201 file.

95. Headquarters Army Air Forces Plans Division, Record Group 18, entry 223, Box 4, National Archives and Records Administration, Washington, D.C; Jerold E. Brown, *Where Eagles Land: Planning and Development of U.S. Army Airfields, 1910–1941* (Westport, Conn.: Greenwood Press, 1990), p. 111.

96. Gulio [*sic*] Douhet, "Air Warfare," 1933, National Defense University Library, Fort McNair, D.C. Wolk, "Innovator," p. 130, dates this project to Kenney's term at the Tactical School, but the timing of the article makes that unlikely.

97. John F. Shiner, *Foulois and the US Army Air Corps* (Washington, D.C.: Office of Air Force History, 1983), p. 78–79, 97–98.

98. Copp, *Few Great Captains*, pp. 151, 282.

99. Shiner, *Foulois*, pp. 97–100.

100. Ibid., pp. 84–89; idem, "Birth of GHQ Air Force, *Military Affairs* 42 (Oct. 1978): 114–117; Maurer, *Aviation in U.S. Army*, pp. 284–298; Futrell, *Ideas*, pp. 67–68.

101. Shiner, *Foulois*, ch. 5; Maurer, *Aviation in U.S. Army*, pp. 299–317; Eldon W. Downs, "Army and the Airmail—1934," *The Airpower Historian* 9 (Jan. 1962): 35–51.

102. Shiner, *Foulois*, pp. 193–198, 207.

103. Training Regulation 440-15, "Employment of the Air Forces of the Army," October 15, 1935, Andrews papers, LOC; Maurer, *Aviation in U.S. Army*, pp. 319–325, 332–339; Futrell, pp. 40–41, 73–75; Shiner, *Foulois*, pp. 206–207.

104. Maurer, *Aviation in U.S. Army*, pp. 325–327.

105. "Memo on Conference on GHQ organization," n.d., Andrews papers, LOC; Headquarters GHQ AF, Special Order Number 1, July 25, 1934, Kenney papers, HRA.

106. Adjutant General Orders, AG 210.482, January 21, 1935, Kenney papers, HRA; War Department Special Order Number 35, February 11, 1935; Headquarters GHQ AF, General Order Number 2, March 2, 1935; Andrews papers, LOC.

107. Finney, *History*, pp. 101–103, 118; Army War College, "Roster, Class of 1933," Curricular Archives of the Army War College, MHI.

108. "Preliminary Report of Service Test of GHQ Air Force," Headquarters GHQ AF Bulletin Number 5, November 2, 1935, pp. 10–14, file 415.171, HRA.

109. Ibid., p. 14–15; Kenney, interview with Hasdorff, pp. 35–36; Copp, *Few Great Captains*, pp. 303, 342–343.

110. Kenney, interview with Hasdorff, p. 36.

111. "Preliminary Report of Service Test of GHQ Air Force," p. 13; Commanding General GHQ AF, "Report of 1935 Service Test of GHQ AF," February 1, 1936, pp. 11–15, 47–49, Andrews papers, LOC.

112. Maurer, *Aviation in U.S. Army,* pp. 339–343; Shiner, *Foulois,* pp. 114, 210; Copp, *Few Great Captains,* pp. 333–339.

113. War Department, Special Order Number 115, May 14, 1936, Kenney papers, HRA; Kenney, interview with Hasdorff, p. 37.

114. Jeffrey S. Underwood, *The Wings of Democracy: The Influence of Air Power on the Roosevelt Administration, 1933–1941* (College Station: Texas A&M University Press, 1991), p. 84; Copp, *Few Great Captains,* pp. 353–354; Shiner, *Foulois,* p. 210; Maurer, *Aviation in U.S. Army,* pp. 360–361; Robert W. Krauskopf, "The Army and the Strategic Bomber, 1930–1939, Part II," *Military Affairs* 22 (Summer 1958): 209, 215.

115. Kenney, interview with Hasdorff, p. 37.

116. Ibid.

117. Copp, *Few Great Captains,* pp. 350–353.

118. Kenney, interview with Hasdorff, p. 37.

119. Kenney's frequent contact with Andrews is spelled out in Copp, *Few Great Captains,* pp. 314, 331, 350–351, 353.

120. Underwood, p. 60; Copp, *Few Great Captains,* p. 302–303.

121. Underwood, pp. 68–70.

122. Memorandum from Craig to Westover, November 6, 1935, quoted in Underwood, p. 69.

123. Letter, Andrews to Craig, quoted in Copp, *Few Great Captains,* p. 354.

124. War Department, Special Order Number 162, June 26, 1936, Kenney papers, HRA; Kenney, interview with Hasdorff, pp. 37–38.

125. Letter, Kenney to Andrews, April 13, 1937; Letter, Kenney to Andrews, April 27, 1937; Andrews papers, LOC.

126. Letter, Andrews to Kenney, February 18, 1937; Letter, Andrews to Kenney, January 13, 1937, Andrews papers, LOC.

127. Letter, Andrews to Kenney, June 8, 1937, Andrews papers, LOC.

128. Copp, *Few Great Captains,* pp. 366–369.

129. Letter, Kenney to Andrews, January 3, 1937 [1938], Andrews papers, LOC.

130. Letters, Andrews to Kenney, January 6, 1938, January 18, 1938, Andrews papers, LOC.

131. Letter, Andrews to Hugh Knerr, June 13, 1938, Andrews papers, LOC; Kenney, interview with Hasdorff, pp. 38–39; War Department Special Order Number 114, May 16 1938, Kenney papers, HRA.

132. Copp, *Few Great Captains,* pp. 418–423; Maurer, *Aviation in U.S. Army,* pp. 406–408; Wolk, "Innovator," p. 132.

133. Copp, *Few Great Captains,* pp. 423–427; Maurer, *Aviation in U.S. Army,* pp. 408–411; Underwood, pp. 114–117.

134. George C. Kenney, interview with Murray Green, July 18, 1969, New York, New York, p. 29, United States Air Force Academy Library, Special Collections Branch, United States Air Force Academy, Colorado. My thanks to Duane Reed for a copy of this interview. Wolk, "Innovator," p. 132. Although the number of officers

in the Air Corps fluctuated from year to year, the officer corps was always quite small. In 1921 there were 975 Air Corps officers, in 1923, 867, and in 1926, 919. Although authorized by Congress in 1926 to have 1,650 officers, this goal was not reached until 1939. Maurer, *Aviation in U.S. Army,* pp. 48, 202, 350. By comparison, in 1996 there were over 76,000 officers in the U.S. Air Force. Tamar A. Mehuron, "USAF Almanac, 1997," *Air Force Magazine* 80 (May 1997), p. 31.

135. "Summary of Activities," p. 2; Kuter, p. 137; Futrell, *Ideas,* pp. 90–91.

136. Holley, *Buying Aircraft,* pp. 169–186; Futrell, *Ideas,* pp. 92–94.

137. Summary of Activities," p. 2; 201 file; Holley, *Buying Aircraft,* pp. 462–463, 468–469; Wesley Frank Craven and James L. Cate, eds., *The Army Air Forces in World War II,* vol. 6, *Men and Planes* (Chicago: University of Chicago Press, 1955), p. 187; Perret, pp. 37–38.

138. George C. Kenney, interview with Murray Green, New York, July 18, 1969, p. 1.

139. 201 file; "Biographical Sketch," p. 2. In his memoirs Hap Arnold claimed that after Germany invaded Poland, "I at once sent two of the best officers in the Air Corps, Lieutenant Colonel 'Tooey' Spaatz and Major George C. Kenney, to Europe as combat observers." H. H. Arnold, *Global Mission* (New York: Harper and Brothers, 1949), p. 192. In fact, since July 1938 the Air Corps had been trying to send observers to Europe. In January 1940 Great Britain and France acceded to the request, and a number of Air Corps officers were sent to observe aerial operations, Martin P. Claussen, "Material Research and Development in the Army Air Arm, 1914–1945," Army Air Forces Historical Study Number 50, pp. 156–160; Wesley Frank Craven and James Lea Cate, eds., *The Army Air Forces in World War II,* vol. 1, *Plans and Early Operations, January 1939 to August 1942* (Chicago: University of Chicago Press, 1948), p. 109.

140. Kenney, interview with Hasdorff, pp. 43–45; Kenney, interview with Stanley, pp. 13–16; "Summary of Activities," p. 3; Colonel J. M. Churchill, Assistant Chief of Staff, G-2, Memorandum, Subject: Air Corps Procurement, F. Y. 1941, April 18, 1940, file 248.501, HRA. This memorandum was prepared by Kenney.

141. Clare Boothe, *Europe in the Spring* (New York: Alfred A. Knopf, 1941), p. 174.

142. Ibid., pp. 171–174.

143. Kenney, interview with Hasdorff, p. 45; Claussen, pp. 98–100; Holley, *Buying Aircraft,* pp. 512–515.

144. 201 file; War Department Biography, "George C. Kenney," March 9, 1942, Knerr papers, LOC.

145. Claussen, pp. 54–55; Wesley Frank Craven and James L. Cate, eds., *The Army Air Forces in World War II,* vol. 4, *The Pacific: Guadalcanal to Saipan, August 1942 to July 1944* (Chicago: University of Chicago Press, 1950), pp. 294–296.

146. Craven and Cate, 4:296–298.

147. 201 file; War Department Biography; Holley, *Buying Aircraft,* pp. 97, 468–469.

148. 201 file.

149. Kenney, interview with Hasdorff, pp. 46–47; Kenney, *Reports,* pp. 8–9, 15. In one version of this story Kenney stated that Arnold promised to assign Kenney to an operational command when aircraft production reached 4,000 planes a month. While this may be true, there were also other factors that went into the timing of Kenney's move.

150. In commenting on General Hap Arnold, one author noted: "Unlike [Lieutenant General Ira C.] Eaker, [General Carl A.] Spaatz, or [Lieutenant General Frank M.]

Andrews, or for that matter any of his senior commanders *with the possible exception of George Kenney,* Hap Arnold had always been genuinely interested in scientific development." DeWitt S. Copp, *Forged in Fire* (Garden City, NY: Doubleday & Company, 1982), p. 412, emphasis added.

151. Nenninger, "Leavenworth and Its Critics," p. 212; Berlin, p. 158. Berlin notes that all of the U.S. Army corps commanders in World War II had served as instructors in one of the service schools.

152. George C. Kenney, "The Airplane in Modern Warfare," *U.S. Air Services,* July 1938, pp. 17–21.

153. Ibid., p. 22; Letter, Kenney to Arnold, May 18, 1942, Arnold papers, LOC, Washington, D.C.

154. Major General Donald Wilson, interview with Hugh N. Ahmann, Carmel, California, December 10–11, 1975, p. 149, file K239.0512-878, HRA.

155. Kenney, "The Airplane in Modern Warfare," p. 17.

156. Ibid., p. 18.

157. Ibid.

4. *Taking Command*

Epigraph: Kenney, *Reports,* p. 39.

1. Ibid., pp. 25, 26; Douglas Gillison, *Royal Australian Air Force, 1939–1942* (Canberra: Australian War Memorial, 1962), pp. 527–530; 543–562. During June, July, and August 1942, the Japanese used midget submarines to attack shipping in Sydney harbor, and there were frequent Japanese bombing attacks on northwestern Australia.

2. Wolk, "Innovator," p. 127; James Gould Cozzens, *A Time of War: Air Force Diaries and Pentagon Memos, 1943–1945,* ed. by Matthew J. Bruccoli (Columbia, S.C.: Bruccoli Clark, 1984) p. 257.

3. Boothe, p. 171.

4. K. S. Bartlett, "Brookline's Gen. Kenney Raining Armies on Japs in Southern Pacific," *Boston Globe,* January 31, 1943, p. 1; Daniel E. Barbey, *MacArthur's Amphibious Navy: Seventh Amphibious Force Operations 1943–1945* (Annapolis, Md.: United States Naval Institute, 1969), p. 27; Wilson, p. 258.

5. J. E. Hewitt, *Adversity in Success* (Victoria, Australia: Langate Publishing, 1980), pp. 83, 87, 174, 202, 224–225; N. M. Parnell, "Reminiscences of a Radio Operator," *American Aviation Historical Society Journal* 32 (Winter 1987): 265; Wilson, p. 144; Wilson, interview with Ahmann, p. 202; Letter, Margarite Kenney to author, April 3, 1994.

6. Kenney diary, July 7, 11, 1942, KP. Message, Maxwell to Marshall, June 29, 1942, Arnold papers, LOC; Marshall to MacArthur, July 6, 1942, RG 4, MMMA; Kenney, interview with Hasdorff, p. 108. Either out of professional courtesy or for personal reasons, Kenney does not say in his book that he had been tapped to relieve Brereton, who was not replaced. Instead, Kenney simply stated that his destination was a secret. Kenney, *Reports,* p. 7.

7. Kenney diary, July 13, 1942, KP.

8. Maurice Matloff and Edwin M. Snell, *Strategic Planning for Coalition Warfare, 1941–1942* (Washington, D.C.: Office of the Chief of Military History, 1953), pp. 9–31, 95–119; Grace P. Hayes, *The History of the Joint Chiefs of Staff in World*

War II: The War Against Japan (Washington: Naval Institute Press, 1982), p. 38; Spector, *Eagle*, pp. 123–124; Gerhard Weinberg, *A World At Arms* (Cambridge: Cambridge University Press, 1994), pp. 305–306.

9. Hayes, pp. 108–114.

10. Kenney diary, July 13, 1942, KP.

11. Kenney, *Reports,* p. 11; Hayes, pp. 118–120; Spector, pp. 206–207; Craven and Cate, 4:x, xi–xii.

12. Kenney, *Reports,* p. 11.

13. Craven and Cate, 1:175–188, 192; Louis Morton, *The Fall of the Philippines* (Washington, D.C.: Office of the Chief of Military History, 1953), pp. 23, 37–42. Walter Edmonds claims that only fifty-four pursuit planes and thirty-four B-17s were actually in combat flying condition on December 8, 1941. Part of the difference in the number of combat aircraft available resulted from varying judgments about the airworthiness or combat condition of aircraft under repair. Walter D. Edmonds, *They Fought with What They Had: The Story of the Army Air Forces in the Southwest Pacific, 1941–1942* (Boston: Little, Brown, 1951; reprinted, Washington, D.C.: Center for Air Force History, 1992), p. 71.

14. Lewis H. Brereton, *The Brereton Diaries* (New York: William Morrow and Co., 1946), pp. 5–44; Morton, pp. 43–45.

15. Craven and Cate, 4:209; Brereton, 44–52; Morton, pp. 84–90, 92–97; D. Clayton James, *The Years of MacArthur*, 3 vols. (Boston: Houghton Mifflin, 1970–1985), 2:3–6. William H. Bartsch, *Doomed at the Start: American Pursuit Pilots in the Philippines, 1941–1942* (College Station: Texas A&M University Press, 1992), passim.

16. Craven and Cate, 4:209; Brereton, 57–63; James, *Years*, 2:16–17.

17. In his memoirs MacArthur refrained from criticizing Brereton directly; he nevertheless made it clear that he thought Brereton deserved most of the blame. Douglas MacArthur, *Reminiscences* (New York: McGraw-Hill Book Company, 1964), p. 120. Brereton blamed the loss of the aircraft on the lack of preparation and infrastructure, along with Sutherland's meddling in air affairs and MacArthur's indecisiveness on December 8. Brereton wanted to carry out an air attack of Formosa, but Sutherland would not let him talk to MacArthur. The Japanese struck after permission for the attack had been received and the bombers were on the ground being readied for the mission. Sutherland stressed the fact that Brereton disobeyed previous orders to move the B-17s south and believed this move would have preserved the bomber force. Brereton, pp. 38–43, 64–66; Craven and Cate, 4:209. When MacArthur was writing his memoirs Sutherland urged him to address the issue and called Brereton's remarks about Sutherland's interference "egregious lies." Letter, Sutherland to MacArthur, August 1, 1951, RG 10, MMMA. Discussions about blame for the event have not abated with time. D. Clayton James, MacArthur's biographer, believes that "the question of where to put the blame for the Clark Field disaster continues in a tangle of personalities and contradictory data." D. Clayton James, "The Other Pearl Harbor," *MHQ: The Quarterly Journal of Military History* 7 (Winter 1995): 25–26. For other examinations of the attack, see Spector, *Eagle*, pp. 106–108; James, *Years*, 2:6–14; Edmonds, pp. 86–93; Morton, *Fall*, pp. 88–90; Robert F. Futrell, "Air Hostilities in the Philippines, 8 December 1941," *Air University Review* 16 (Jan.–Feb. 1965): 33–45; William H. Bartsch, "Was MacArthur Ill-Served by His Air Force Commanders in the Philippines?" *Air Power History* 44 (Summer 1997), pp. 44–63.

18. Matloff and Snell, *1941–1942*, pp. 165–166.

19. Hayes, pp. 88–103.

20. For a similar conclusion see Weinberg, p. 341. For a different perspective see Spector, who argues that the two advances "might well have led to disaster," Spector, *Eagle*, pp. xiii, 144–147.

21. Craven and Cate, 4:7.

22. Letter, R.C. Moore, deputy chief of staff, U.S. Army, to Brett, December 19, 1941, Whitlock papers, MHI; Message, Marshall to Brett, December 24, 1941, *The Papers of George Catlett Marshall*, ed. Larry I. Bland (Baltimore: Johns Hopkins University Press, 1991–), 3:38.

23. Craven and Cate, 1:231–233.

24. MacArthur, p. 145; George Brett with Jack Kofoed, "The MacArthur I Knew," *True*, October 1947, pp. 139–140.

25. Brett, "MacArthur," pp. 140, 142; David M. Horner, *High Command: Australia and Allied Strategy, 1939–1945* (Sydney: George Allen & Unwin, 1982), p. 180.

26. MacArthur's ego and his fear of rivals is recounted in James's biography, especially 2:717–720, and James, *Time for Giants*, pp. 240–241. Robert Eichelberger, who believed he suffered because of MacArthur's ego, recorded his views about MacArthur's fears in letters to his wife, Luvaas, passim; Paul Chiwalkowsi, *In Caesar's Shadow: The Life of General Robert Eichelberger* (Westport, Conn.: Greenwood Press, 1993), pp. 86–87.

27. George C. Kenney, interview with D. Clayton James, July 16, 1971, New York, New York, pp. 13–15, file 168.7103-24, HRA; Kenney, interview with Hasdorff, pp. 100–103; Kenney, interview with Green, p. 8. For Brett's thoughts see "MacArthur I Knew," pp. 141–142.

28. Paul P. Rogers, *The Good Years: MacArthur and Sutherland* (New York: Praeger, 1990), pp. 275, 278, quote on p. 278. Rogers worked as a clerk, stenographer, and typist in MacArthur's office during the war.

29. Douglas Gillison, pp. 473–477; Craven and Cate, 1:420. Colonels Eugene L. Eubank and Ross G. Hoyt headed the plans and operations directorates, Air Commodore Joseph G. Hewitt, RAAF, was the director of intelligence, while Group Captains F. R. W. Scherger and Carn S. Wiggins, were respectively directors of defense and communications.

30. Gillison, p. 478.

31. George Brett, "Comments of Gen. Brett Re: Personnel, Etc.," a compilation of statements given to Kenney on August 3, 1942, KP.

32. *Papers of Marshall*, 3:76–77.

33. Message, Brett to War Department, February 18, 1942, file 704.162A, HRA; Message, Brett to Arnold, April 10, 1942, RG 4, MMMA; Lieutenant General George H. Brett, "Report to Army Air Forces Headquarters," May 1942, section S, p. 4, file 730.101-1, HRA; Letter, Commanding General Allied Air Forces Southwest Pacific Area (Brett) to Commanding General Army Air Forces, May 13, 1942, section F; Kathleen Williams, "The AAF in Australia to the Summer of 1942," Army Air Forces Historical Studies no. 9, Assistant Chief of Air Staff, Intelligence, Historical Division, July 1944, pp. 77–80.

34. The prevailing interpretation of Brett's motives seems to be drawn largely from Kenney's observations. In Kenney's memoirs he notes, "In order to make it a truly

Allied organization, the Americans and Australians were thoroughly mixed every-where . . . even in the airplane crews." Kenney, *Reports,* p. 32. D. Clayton James echoes this view: "Brett held the Australian airmen in high esteem, carrying the Allied partnership so far as to require every American bomber pilot to have an Australian copilot and vice versa." James, *Years,* 2:197. For comments on Australians flying in American units, see Parnell, p. 260; E. Daniel Potts and Annette Potts, *Yanks Down Under, 1941–1945* (Melbourne: Oxford University Press, 1985), p. 277; Lex MacAuly, *Battle of the Bismarck Sea* (New York: St. Martins Press, 1991), pp. 26–27. Even as late as March 1943, Australian copilots were being used in some American squadrons, see Fifth Bomber Command, "Tactical Reports of Attacks on Bismarck Sea Convoy," March 1943, Richard K. Sutherland papers, RG 200, National Archives, Washington, D.C.

35. Gillison, p. 478; Craven and Cate, 1:420–431.

36. Williams, pp. 70–74, quote on p. 74.

37. "Report on Operations Carried Out May 21 to May 27, 1942," From: Air Officer Commanding, Northwestern Area, To: Headquarters Allied Air Forces, 4 June 1942, p. 2, file 706.01A, HRA; Hewitt, p. 35; Williams, p. 145.

38. MacArthur, p. 141; James, *Years,* 2:98–100; 117–124; Matloff and Snell, *1941–1942,* pp. 168–173. In describing MacArthur's staff, Ronald Spector notes, "MacArthur brought with him from the Philippines a group of loyal and deferen-tial—critics said sycophantic—subordinates who served as his key staff officers and assistants throughout the war," p. 146.

39. "Comments of General Brett"; Brett, "MacArthur," p. 146.

40. Hewitt, p. 30.

41. Luvaas, p. 30.

42. Walter Krueger, *From Down Under to Nippon* (Washington, D.C.: Combat Forces Press, 1953), p. 10; Senior Officers Debriefing Program, General George H. Decker with Lieutenant Colonel Dan H. Ralls, November 9, 1972, Washington, D.C., pp. 18–19, MHI; Senior Officers Debriefing Program, General Clyde D. Eddleman with Lieutenant Colonels Lowell G. Smith and Murray G. Swindler, January 28, 1975, p. 27, MHI.

43. Potts, p. 35.

44. Wilson, p. 270.

45. Potts, pp. 274–275; Paul P. Rogers, *The Bitter Years: MacArthur and Suther-land* (New York: Praeger Publishers, 1990), pp. 13–21.

46. Major General Robert C. Richardson, "Memorandum for General MacArthur," 4 July 1942, p. 2, RG 4, MMMA. General Marshall sent Richardson on the trip to inspect American forces and inform MacArthur on strategic plans. *Papers of Marshall,* 3:200.

47. Brett, "MacArthur," p. 143. A thorough reconstruction of the fighter group in the Philippines confirms MacArthur's assessment about the performance of the air units, Bartsch, pp. 427–431.

48. Message, MacArthur to Marshall, May 1, 1942, RG 4, MMMA; also MacArthur to Marshall, March 21, 1942, Arnold papers, LOC.

49. John Hammond Moore, *Over-Sexed, Over-Paid, and Over-Here: Americans in Australia 1941–1945* (St. Lucia: University of Queensland Press, 1981), pp. 21–38; Gillison, pp. 527–530, 554–564.

50. *The Reports of MacArthur,* 2 vols. (Washington, D.C.: Government Printing Office, 1966), 2:124–131; Weinberg, pp. 333–334.

51. Craven and Cate, 1:448–451; Gillison, pp. 513–524; James, *Years,* 2:157–163; Spector, pp. 159–161. Even after fifty years there is some confusion over this "friendly fire" incident. Most historians agree that the bombers came from the Australian base at Townsville, but they offer dramatically different numbers. Gillison claims that nineteen heavy bombers attacked; James, three B-26s; and Spector, using Samuel Eliot Morison's account, three B-17s. Gillison, p. 522; James, *Years,* 2:160; Spector, p. 161. Craven and Cate mention that the 19th Group admitted to attacking friendly naval units; Craven and Cate, 1:450. If the 19th was involved, then the aircraft were B-17s, although the number is still unclear. Based on the availability of aircraft, it is unlikely that there were nineteen bombers. Hence the Spector/Morison account seems most accurate.

52. Letter, MacArthur to Brett, June 1, 1942, Sutherland papers, NA; Message, MacArthur to War Department, June 18, 1942, Arnold papers, LOC.

53. Letter, Sutherland to Commander Allied Air Forces, June 3, 1942, Subject: Operation of B-17E Aircraft; Letter, Sutherland to Commander Allied Air Forces, June 4, 1942, Subject: Attacks Against Hostile Bomber Concentration in New Britain; Letter, MacArthur to Commander Allied Air Forces, June 10, 1942, Subject: Attacks Against Hostile Bomber Concentration in New Britain, Sutherland papers, NA.

54. Memo, Chief of Staff, Allied Air Forces to Chief of Staff, GHQ, June 5, 1942, Subject: Attacks Against Hostile Bomber Concentration in New Britain; Memo, Commander Allied Air Forces to Commander-in-Chief SWPA, June 11, 1942, Subject: Attacks Against Hostile Bomber Concentrations in New Britain, Sutherland papers, NA.

55. Richard K. Sutherland, typewritten note on page 1 of Memo, Commander Allied Air Forces to Commander-in-Chief SWPA, June 11, 1942, Subject: Attacks Against Hostile Bomber Concentrations in New Britain, Sutherland papers, NA.

56. Message, War Department to USAFIA, June 23, 1942, Sutherland papers, NA.

57. Message, MacArthur to Army Chief of Staff, June 26, 1942, Sutherland papers, NA.

58. Memorandum, Arnold to Assistant Chief of Staff, OPD, Subject: Operations in Australia, July 22, 1942, Arnold papers, LOC.

59. Kenney, *Reports,* p. 53; Craven and Cate, 4:98; Horner, *High Command,* pp. 207–208.

60. Kenney, *Reports,* p. 63.

61. Memorandum, Arnold to Assistant Chief of Staff, OPD, Subject: Operations in Australia, July 22, 1942, Arnold papers, LOC.

62. Interview, Samuel E. Anderson with Hugh N. Ahmann, June 28 to July 1, 1976, Santa Monica, California, p. 186, file 239.0512-905, HRA; Coffey, p. 271. The other members of the three-man team were Lieutenant Colonel Francis R. Stevens and Lieutenant Commander Lyndon B. Johnson. Stevens was killed on a bombing mission on June 9, and Johnson and Anderson left for Washington on June 18. Robert A. Caro, *The Years of Lyndon Johnson,* vol. 2, *Means of Ascent* (New York: Alfred A. Knopf, 1990), pp. 33–45.

63. Message, Marshall to MacArthur, June 29, 1942, RG 4, MMMA.

64. Message, MacArthur to Marshall, June 30, 1942, RG 4, MMMA.

65. Interview, Major General Thomas Darcy with Murray Green, Jupiter, Florida,

May 31, 1970, Box 62, Murray Green Collection, Special Collections, United States Air Force Academy Library, United States Air Force Academy, Colorado; DeWitt S. Copp, *Forged in Fire* (Garden City, N.Y.: Doubleday and Company, 1980), pp. 270–271; idem, *Few Great Captains,* pp. 305–307.

66. Lawrence S. Kuter, "Growth of Air Power," unpublished manuscript, USAF Academy Library Special Collections Branch, p. 196.

67. Message, Marshall to MacArthur, July 6, 1942, RG 4, MMMA.

68. Message, MacArthur to Marshall, July 7, 1942, RG 4 MMMA; July 11, 1942, KP. James, *Years,* 2:197, argues that the impetus for the relief came from MacArthur rather than Marshall, but the action seems to have been a mutual decision.

69. Kenney diary, July 15, 18, 1942, KP.

70. Kenney diary, July 29, 1942, KP; Kenney, *Reports,* pp. 28–29.

71. Kenney, *Reports,* p. 29.

72. MacArthur, pp. 85–86; James, *Years,* 1:306–311; George C. Kenney, *The MacArthur I Know* (New York: Duell, Sloan and Pearce, 1951), pp. 21–22.

73. James, *Years,* 1:354–363, 369–371, 378–381, 458–461; Shiner, *Foulois,* p. 260.

74. Brett, "MacArthur," p. 144. "Comments of Gen. Brett," KP.

75. James, *Years,* 2:274–275; Shiner, *Foulois,* pp. 193–211, 256–265.

76. Arnold, p. 331.

77. Brett, "MacArthur," p. 149.

78. Kenney, *Reports,* p. 29.

79. Kenney, interview with Hasdorff, p. 88.

80. Kenney diary, July 12, 13, 14, 1942, KP.

81. Kenney diary, July 12, 1942, KP.

82. Ibid. Kenney gives the impression in his book that these changes were made after his arrival, but according to his diary he knew that Major Generals Lincoln and Royce, and Brigadier Generals Perrin, Sneed, and Scanlon were not the type of officers needed in the command, and their leaving the Southwest Pacific was agreed to before Kenney left the United States. Kenney, *Reports,* pp. 11, 40, 44, 99, 115, 125.

83. "Comments of General Brett," KP

84. "Comments of General Brett," KP.

85. Kenney diary, July 12, 1942, KP; Message, MacArthur to Chief of Staff, War Department, May 24, 1942, Sutherland Papers, NA.

86. Kenney, *Reports,* pp. 11–12.

87. Goldstein, in Leary, pp. 178–181; Goldstein, "Pioneer," pp. 15–23, 30–48, 57, 69–71; Finney, *History,* pp. 102–103; 120–121.

88. Kenney, *Reports,* p. 153.

89. Martha Byrd, *Kenneth N. Walker: Airpower's Untempered Crusader* (Maxwell Air Force Base, Ala.: Air University Press, 1997), pp. 3–5, 23–24; Finney, *History,* pp. 102–103, 118–119.

90. Byrd, pp. 25–38; Steven L. McFarland, *America's Pursuit of Precision Bombing, 1910–1945* (Washington, D.C.: Smithsonian Institution Press, 1995), pp. 84–88.

91. Quoted in Futrell, *Ideas,* p. 64.

92. Kenney, *Reports,* p. 143.

93. September 15, 18, 1942, KP; Wilson, pp. 254–255.

94. Wilson, pp. 120–180, 236–241. For more details on Wilson's contribution to strategic bombing theory, at least from his perspective, see, Donald Wilson, "Origin

of a Theory for Air Strategy," *Aerospace Historian* 18 (March 1971): 19–25.

95. Kenney, *Reports,* p. 90.

96. Letter, Kenney to Arnold, May 1, 1943, KP.

97. Ibid. Although Arnold specifically asked for recommendations about older offi-
cers, one of the men Kenney recommended for retirement was Brigadier General
Elwood "Pete" Quesada, one of the youngest general officers in the Army Air Forces.
Why Kenney would make this assessment of Quesada is unclear. For more details on
Quesada's career, see Thomas Alexander Hughes, *Over Lord: General Pete Quesada
and the Triumph of Tactical Air Power in World War II* (New York: Free Press, 1995).

98. Kenney diary, September 4, 1942, July 30, 1942, KP.

99. Kenney, *Reports,* p. 56.

100. Quoted in Wolk, "Innovator," p. 138.

101. Message, Commanding General 5th Air Force to Commanding General Army
Air Forces, October 25, 1942, KP.

102. Kenney, *Reports,* p. 39.

103. Kenney diary, July 29, 1942, KP; Kenney, *Reports,* pp. 32–33, 47.

104. Kenney, *Reports,* p. 47.

105. Kenney diary, August 9, 1942, September 6, 1942, KP; Headquarters Allied
Air Forces, SWPA, General Order Number 62, November 8, 1942, file 706.193,
HRA. The Australian component was initially called Coastal Defense Command, but
this appellation lasted only two weeks. Gillison, pp. 585–598; George Odgers, *Air
War Against Japan, 1943–1945* (Canberra: Australian War Memorial, 1957; re-
printed, 1968), p. 8.

106. Kenney, *Reports,* p. 53; Craven and Cate, 4:98.

107. Brett Report, Summary Q, p. 1; "Comments of General Brett."

108. Gillison, pp. 473–477; Horner, *High Command,* pp. 350–353.

109. Kenney diary, August 23, 1942, KP; Gillison, pp. 587–596.

110. Letter, Jones to Bostock, November 20, 1942, RG4, MMMA.

111. Letter, Bostock to Secretary, Air Board, December 12, 1942; Air Vice Marshal
William Bostock, "RAAF Command-Organization," January 3, 1943, p. 1, RG 4,
MMMA.

112. Minutes, Australian Defence Committee, January 7, 1943, RG4, MMMA.

113. Kenney diary, August 23, September 21, 1942, KP; Kenney, *Reports,* p. 80.

114. "Comments of General Brett"; Alan Stephens, *Power Plus Attitude: Ideas, Strategy and Doctrine in the Royal Australian Air Force, 1921–1991* (Canberra: Australian
Government Printing Service, 1992), p. 64; Hewitt, p. 31.

115. Kenney, *Reports,* p. 80.

116. Kenney diary, July 30, 1942, KP; Kenney, *Reports,* pp. 35–38.

117. Kenney diary, July 30, 1942, KP; Kenney, *Reports,* pp. 35–36, 38, 41.

118. Kenney diary, August 5, 1942, KP; Kenney, *Reports,* pp. 78–79; Headquarters
Allied Air Force, General Order Number 63, November 11, 1942, file 706.193, HRA.

119. Kenney diary, August 1, 1942, KP.

120. Kenney diary, August 1, 1942; Kenney, *Reports,* pp. 42–43; Gillison, pp. 574–575;
Craven and Cate, 4:8–10.

121. Williams, pp. 40–43; Craven and Cate, 4:101.

122. Letter, Stephen J. Chamberlin to Brigadier General Brehon Somervell, Assistant Chief of Staff, G-4, War Department, February 26, 1942, Stephen J. Chamberlin papers, MHI.

123. Williams, pp. 33–37.

124. Wayne P. Rothgeb, *New Guinea Skies: A Fighter Pilot's View of World War II* (Ames: Iowa State University Press, 1992), pp. 103–104.

125. Williams, pp. 97–100; Craven and Cate, 4:8–10.

126. Kenney diary, August 15, 1942, KP; Kenney, *Reports*, pp. 44, 78–79; Office of the Chief Engineer, General Headquarters Army Forces, Pacific, *Engineers of the Southwest Pacific,* vol. 6, *Airfield and Air Base Development* (Washington, D.C.: Government Printing Office, 1951), pp. 63–64.

127. Kenney diary, August 28, 1942, KP; Kenney, *Reports*, p. 86.

128. Kenney, *Reports*, pp. 45, 61.

129. Kenney diary, August 21, 1942, KP.

130. Kenney, *Reports*, pp. 43, 52.

131. Kenney, interview with Hasdorff, p. 52; Kenney, interview with James, p. 44; Kenney, *Reports,* p. 215. Kenney presented some of the watches on September 30, 1943. George C. Kenney Scrapbook, file 168.7103-69, HRA.

132. General Richard H. Ellis, interview with Maurice Maryanow, August 17-21, 1987, Washington, D.C., pp. 53–54, 116–117, file K239.0512-740, HRA. Ellis flew in the Southwest Pacific and served as a group commander. He later went on to be the commander of Strategic Air Command.

133. Kenney, *Reports*, pp. 74–75.

134. Ibid., p. 194.

135. Lieutenant Walter A. Krell, quoted in Martin Caidin, *The Ragged, Rugged Warriors* (New York: E. P. Dutton, 1966), p. 343.

136. Letter, Arnold to Kenney, December 6, 1942, KP.

137. Kenney, *Reports*, p. 73.

138. Ibid., pp. 90, 120.

139. Message, Kenney to Arnold, November 27, 1942, KP; October 22, December 10, 1942, KP; Kenney, *Reports*, pp. 126, 129 , 141.

140. Kenney diary, July 12, 1942, KP; Kenney, *Reports*, 11.

141. Kenney, interview with James, p. 5; James, *Years*, 2: 77–78; Chwilakowski, pp. 67–68.

142. James, *Years,* 1:565–567; 2:77–78; Rogers, *Good Years,* pp. 36–40, 231–232.

143. Brereton, pp. 17–67.

144. Kenney, *Reports*, p. 33.

145. "Comments of Brett."

146. Report of Committee Number 3, "Tactical Doctrines," September 26, 1932, p. 1, Curricular Archives of the Army War College, MHI.

147. Kenney, *Reports,* p. 27; James, *Years,* 2:13.

148. Letter, Richard K. Sutherland to Commanding General Army Air Forces, Subject: Rating, March 28, 1943, KP.

149. Ibid.; Memorandum for the Commanding General, Army Air Forces, Subj: Rating of Service Pilot for Major General Sutherland, p. 2, n.d. [April 1943]. Letter, General Arnold to Major General Sutherland, April 17, 1943, KP; The *Official World War II Guide to the Army Air Forces* (New York: Bonanza Books, 1988; reprint of *The Official Guide to the Army Air Forces,* New York: Simon and Schuster, 1944), p. 49. Sutherland was awarded his official rating as a pilot under Philippine Army regulations when American forces recaptured the Philippines in 1945. Office Chief

of Air Corps, Army Headquarters, Commonwealth of the Philippines, Special Order Number 7, June 23, 1945, Sutherland papers, NA.

150. The struggle between ground and air officers over the control of air units occurred at the beginning of World War II in other theaters as well. The early experiences of the British in the Middle East affirmed the need for a separation of the responsibilities between air and ground commanders. See Shelford Bidwell and Graham Dominick, *Fire-Power: British Army Weapons and Theories of War, 1904–1945* (London: George Allen & Unwin, 1985), pp. 260–275, and Vincent Orange, *Coningham: A Biography of Air Marshal Sir Arthur Coningham* (London: Methuen, 1990; reprint, Washington: Center for Air Force History, 1992), pp. 77–126. The U.S. experiences during the invasion of North Africa resulted in a significant reorganization of forces. These changes were formalized in War Department Field Manual 100-20, *Command and Employment of Air Power,* July 21, 1943, described by some ground officers as the Army Air Force's "Declaration of Independence." Quoted in Futrell, *Ideas,* p. 138. On air doctrine and the struggle over the control of air units in North Africa, see Thomas H. Greer, *The Development of Air Doctrine in the Army Air Arm, 1917–1941,* USAF Historical Studies no. 89 (Maxwell Air Force Base, Ala.: Air University Press, 1955); I. B. Holley Jr., "RAF/USAAF Land/Air Operations: Mediterranean & Northwest Europe," *Air Power History* 38 (Winter 1991): 30–34; Richard H. Kohn and Joseph P. Harahan, eds., *Air Superiority in World War II and Korea* (Washington, D.C.: Office of Air Force History, 1983); Orange, pp. 127–156. The best single source is Daniel R. Mortensen, *Close Air Support Operations: North Africa* (Washington, D.C.: Research and Analysis Division Special Studies Series, U.S. Army Center of Military History, 1987).

151. James, *Years,* 2:200.

152. Kenney, *Reports,* pp. 52–53.

153. Kenney diary, August 4, 1942, KP.

154. Kenney, interview with Hasdorff, p. 62; Kenney, interview with James, pp. 5–6, 18.

155. Wilson, pp. 254–260; Clare Stevenson and Honor Darling, eds., *The WAAAF Book* (Sydney: Hale & Iremonger, 1984), pp. 135–136, 157–158.

156. Kenney, interview with Green, p. 12.

157. Horner, p. 58, in *RAAF in Southwest Pacific.*

158. Kenney, *MacArthur I Know,* p. 57; Kenney, *Reports,* p. 91.

159. Kenney diary, July 28, 1942, August 3, 1943, KP.

160. James, *Time for Giants,* p. 199.

161. James, *Years,* 2:246; Rogers, *Good Years,* p. 329.

162. Kenney, interview with James, p. 17; General Clyde D. Eddleman, interview with D. Clayton James, Washington, D.C., June 29, 1971, p. 8, RG 49, MMMA; Lieutenant General Clovis E. Byers, interview with D. Clayton James, Washington, D.C., June 24, 1971, p. 6, RG 4, MMMA.

5. *The Papuan Campaign*

Epigraph: Letter, Kenney to Arnold, January 1, 1943, p. 3, KP.

1. Message, MacArthur and Ghormley to COS and COMINCH, July 8, 1942, RG 4, MMMA; Matloff and Snell, *1941–1942,* p. 262; Spector, pp. 185–187.

2. "Joint Basic Plan for the Occupation and Defense of the Area New Britain, New Ireland, Admiralty Islands," Chamberlin papers, MHI; Samuel Milner, *Victory in Papua* (Washington, D.C.: Office of the Chief of Military History, 1957), pp. 50, 78–88; Craven and Cate, 4:22–24; James, *Years,* 2:191–192.

3. Milner, p. 56.

4. Milner, pp. 56–58.

5. Air Evaluation Board, Southwest Pacific Area, "The Battle of the Bismarck Sea and Development of Masthead Attacks," July 1, 1945, p. 23, file 168.7103-37, HRA.

6. Charles King, quoted in ibid., p. 14.

7. John Stanifer, quoted in Lex McAulay, *Into the Dragon's Jaws: The Fifth Air Force Over Rabaul* (Mesa, Ariz.: Champlin Fighter Museum Press, 1986), p. 14.

8. Craven and Cate, 4:113.

9. Kenney diary, August 3, 1942, KP.

10. Ibid; Kenney, *Reports,* pp. 44–45.

11. Kenney, *Reports,* p. 45.

12. Training Regulation 440-15, "Employment of the Air Forces of the Army," October 15, 1935; Frank M. Andrews, "Our Use of Air Power: The GHQ AF as an Instrument of Defense," *Army Ordnance* 18 (Nov.–Dec. 1937): 138–140, both in Andrews papers, LOC; Futrell, *Ideas,* pp. 33, 54–55, 65, 171.

13. George C. Kenney, "The Proper Composition of the Air Force," paper, Army War College, April 29, 1933, file 248.211-62K, HRA.

14. Kenney, "Airplane in Modern Warfare," p. 22.

15. Kenney, "Airplane in Modern Warfare," p. 19.

16. Kenney, *MacArthur I Know,* p. 52.

17. Kenney, *Reports,* p. 45.

18. Kenney diary, August 1, 1942, KP. Kenney exaggerated the number of enemy aircraft in his book and stated that the Japanese "had at least five times" the number of aircraft he had. Kenney, *Reports,* p. 62. The figures used in the official history vary: Craven and Cate, 4:101–102, cite 450 American and 401 Japanese aircraft; another report uses a figure of 575 American aircraft, United States Strategic Bombing Survey (USSBS), *Fifth Air Force in the War Against Japan* (Washington, D.C.: Government Printing Office, 1947), p. 14.

19. Kenney, *Reports,* pp. 51–52.

20. Kenney diary, July 13, 1942; September 2, 7, 1942, KP.

21. Kenney, *Reports,* p. 59.

22. Ibid., pp. 59–61.

23. United States Strategic Bombing Survey (USSBS), *Japanese Air Power* (Washington, D.C.: Government Printing Office, 1946), p. 11; Craven and Cate, 4:35.

24. John B. Lundstrom, *The First Team and the Guadalcanal Campaign* (Annapolis, Md.: Naval Institute Press, 1994), p. 72, for a different view.

25. Richard L. Watson, "Air Action in the Papuan Campaign July 21, 1942 to January 23, 1943," Army Air Forces Historical Studies no. 17, Assistant Chief of Air Staff, Intelligence, Historical Division, August 1944, p. 10.

26. Craven and Cate, 4:111.

27. Message, Marshall to MacArthur, September 15, 1942, RG, MMMA.

28. Message MacArthur to Marshall, September 16, 1942, RG 4, MMMA.

29. Ibid.; Kenney, *Reports,* p. 115.

30. Kenney, *Reports*, pp. 63, 89

31. Craven and Cate, 4:212–214.

32. Caidin, pp. 227, 286–288; John F. Kreis, *Air Warfare and Air Base Air Defense, 1914–1973*, (Washington, D.C.: Office of Air Force History, 1988), pp. 239–242; Kenney, *Reports*, pp. 38, 69; Craven and Cate, 1:476–477; 4:24.

33. Kenney diary, July 30, 1942, KP.

34. Kenney, *Reports*, pp. 89, 98.

35. George Raynor Thompson, Dixie R. Harris, Pauline M. Oakes, and Dulany Terrett, *United States Army in World War II: The Signal Corps: The Test* (Washington, D.C.: Office of the Chief of Military History, 1957), pp. 94, 98; Craven and Cate, 4:83.

36. Craven and Cate, 4:96

37. Thompson et al., *Signal Corps: The Test*, pp. 111–112. The SCR-268s were augmented by SCR-516s, an updated version of the SCR-268 with better low-altitude coverage, but about the same range. Ibid., p. 99.

38. Letter, Whitehead to Kenney, October 24, 1942, KP; Thompson et al., *Signal Corps: The Test*, pp. 211–217, 326–327.

39. USSBS, *Fifth Air Force*, p. 87.

40. Eric A. Feldt, *The Coastwatchers* (New York: Oxford University Press, 1946), pp. 4–7, 12; Allison Ind, *Allied Intelligence Bureau* (New York: David McKay Company, 1958), pp. 17–20; Charles A. Willoughby and John Chamberlain, *MacArthur, 1941–1951* (New York: McGraw-Hill, 1954), pp. 145–150; Kreis, *Air Warfare*, pp. 222–223.

41. Feldt, p. 168.

42. Feldt, pp. 168–171, 176–177, 186; Ind, pp. 67–78.

43. Feldt, pp. 17, 178–179, 186; Ind, pp. 80–83. For a more positive assessment of the coastwatchers, see *Piercing the Fog: Intelligence and Army Air Forces Operations in World War II*, ed. John F. Kreis (Washington, D.C.: Air Force History, 1996), pp. 259–261, 276.

44. Edward J. Drea, *MacArthur's ULTRA: Codebreaking and the War Against Japan, 1942–1945* (Lawrence: University Press of Kansas, 1992), p. xi.

45. Ibid., pp. 20–22; Kreis, *Piercing the Fog*, pp. 252–253.

46. Jack Bleakley, *The Eavesdroppers* (Canberra: Australian Government Publishing Service, 1991), pp. 6–10. For American efforts, see Drea, *MacArthur's ULTRA*, pp. 8–12; Spector, p. 447–448.

47. Bleakley, pp. 51, 70.

48. "Central Bureau Technical Records, Part J-Field Sections," CRS B5436/1, Australian Archives. My thanks to Edward Drea for a copy of this report. Kreis, *Piercing the Fog*, pp. 258, 261.

49. Bleakley sketches out this mission, pp. 52–53. For other examples see "Operational History of the 126th Radio Intelligence Company" February 1944, SRH-227, reprinted in James L. Gilbert and John P. Finnegan, eds., *U.S. Army Signals Intelligence in World War II: A Documentary History* (Washington, D.C.: Center of Military History, 1993), p. 209.

50. "Central Bureau Technical Records"; Bleakley, pp. 55, 72, 75; Geoffrey Ballard, *On ULTRA Active Service* (Richmond, Australia: Spectrum Publications, 1991), p. 164.

51. "Central Bureau Technical Records"; Bleakley, p. 75.

52. "Central Bureau Technical Records"; "Achievements of the Signal Security Agency in World War II," 1945, SRH-349, reprinted in Gilbert and Finnegan, pp. 96–97; Ballard, p. 203.

53. "Central Bureau Technical Records"; Kreis, *Piercing the Fog*, pp. 258–259, 275–277.

54. Ballard, p. 197.

55. Ballard, p. 182; Bleakley, pp. 75–76.

56. Howard W. Brown, "Reminiscences of Lieutenant Colonel Howard W. Brown," SRH-045, reprinted in *Listening to the Enemy*, ed. Ronald H. Spector (Wilmington, Del.: Scholarly Resources, 1988), pp. 55–57, quote on p. 69; Spector, *Eagle*, p. 447.

57. "Central Bureau Technical Records."

58. Hewitt, pp. 83, 174, 202, 224.

59. Bleakley, pp. 75–76; Kreis, *Piercing the Fog*, pp. 361–362.

60. Milner, pp. 61–71.

61. Craven and Cate, 4:22–24, 96; Milner, pp. 50, 78; *Reports of MacArthur*, 2:143.

62. Kenney diary, August 13, 1942, KP; Message, MacArthur to Marshall, September 16, 1942, RG 4, MMMA.

63. Message, Arnold to Kenney, November 18, 1942, KP; Memorandum to Chief of the Air Corps, From Commanding General GHQ Air Force, Reference: Methods and results to be expected from an attack of naval targets at sea by army aircraft, April 18, 1936, Andrews papers, LOC. At one time instructors at the Air Corps Tactical School recommended at least twelve bombers to hit a battleship. John G. Williams, "A Bomb Sight View of the Red Navy," Air Corps Tactical School, Maxwell Field, Alabama, 1937–1938, file 248.222-86, HRA.

64. Carl von Clausewitz, *On War*, ed. and trans. Michael Howard and Peter Paret (Princeton: Princeton University Press, 1976), pp. 119–121. For an analysis of the failure of airmen to consider this problem in general, see Barry D. Watts, *The Foundations of U.S. Air Doctrine: The Problem of Friction in War* (Maxwell, Air Force Base, Ala.: Air University Press, 1984).

65. Message, Kenney to Arnold, November 27, 1942, KP.

66. Kenney, *Reports*, p. 66.

67. Message, Kenney to Arnold, November 27, 1942, KP.

68. Letter, Kenney to Major General Muir S. Fairchild, director of military requirements, December 8, 1942, KP.

69. Kenney diary, August 13, 1942, KP.

70. Major Frank O. Brown, "Report on Skip Bombing," March 14, 1943, Appendix 9 in Watson, pp. 170–173.

71. In his memoir Kenney intimated that he and his aide thought up the idea by themselves. Kenney, *Reports*, pp. 21–22. This was not the case, as Kenney himself noted on several occasions. George C. Kenney, "Air Power in the Southwest Pacific," *Air Force* 27 (June 1944): 10; Kenney, interview with Hasdorff, p. 77. For the British and German use, see Timothy D. Gann, *Fifth Air Force Light and Medium Bomber Operations during 1942 and 1943* (Maxwell Air Force Base, Ala.: Air University Press, 1993), pp. 8–10; H. H. Arnold Journal, "Trip to England," April 1941, Arnold

papers, LOC; Arnold, *Global Mission,* pp. 230–231. For Australian missions, see Lex MacAuly, *Battle of Bismarck Sea,* p. 21. For American testing, see Proof Department, Bombing Section, Army Air Forces Proving Ground, Eglin Field, Florida, "Final Report on Minimum Altitude Attack on Water-Borne Surface Vessels with Aircraft Bombs," December 7, 1942; War Department Training Circular Number 46, July 25, 1942, Box 12, Folder 3, Emmett O'Donnel papers, Special Collections, United States Air Force Academy Library.

72. Headquarters Advon 5AF Report, "Skip Bombing," Sutherland papers, NA.

73. Gann, p. 10; Craven and Cate, 4:141.

74. Letter, Harmon to Marshall, September 9, 1942, p. 3, Harmon papers, MHI.

75. Letter, Nathan F. Twining, Commanding General 13th Air Force to Commander Aircraft, South Pacific Area, Subject: Tentative Tactical Doctrine, April 28, 1943, file 750.549-1, HRA.

76. Letter, Arnold to Each Air Force Commander Throughout the World, Subject: Employment of Air Forces, October 30, 1942, Arnold papers, LOC. For an overview of the extent of the problem in both Europe and the Pacific, see McFarland, *Precision Bombing,* pp. 168–193.

77. Ibid.

78. Headquarters Army Air Forces, Routing and Record Sheet, Subject: Bombing Presentation data, November 19, 1942; Routing and Record Sheet, "Kenney's bombing methods," November 28, 1942; Letter, Arnold to Commanding General Second Air Force, December 12, 1942, Arnold papers, LOC.

79. Kenney diary, August 13, 1942, KP; Kenney, *Reports,* p. 66.

80. Message, Kenney to Arnold, November 3, 1942, KP.

81. Kenney diary, September 3, 1942, KP.

82. Feldt, pp. 178–179; Ind, pp. 80–83.

83. Milner, pp. 81–89.

84. Ibid., pp. 91–95.

85. Ibid., pp. 76–78.

86. Drea, pp. 44–46; Kenney, *Reports,* p. 76.

87. Kenney diary, August 25, 1942, KP; *Reports of MacArthur,* 2:153–154; Watson, pp. 29–30; Milner, pp. 78–81. Most of the "hunches" Kenney mentioned in his memoir about this operation were actually analysis based on good intelligence about the Japanese actions. Compare Kenney, *Reports,* pp. 82–83, and Drea, pp. 44–45.

88. John Mordike, "Turning the Japanese Tide: Air Power at Milne Bay August–September 1942," in *RAAF in Southwest Pacific,* pp. 78–79.

89. Kenney diary, August 26, 1942, KP.

90. Kenney, *Reports,* pp. 84–88; *Reports of MacArthur,* 2:155–157; Milner, pp. 81–88; Craven and Cate, 4:96–97.

91. Mordike, in *RAAF in Southwest Pacific,* p. 88; *Reports of MacArthur,* 2:153–157; Craven and Cate, 4:97; quote from Eric Bergerud, *Touched With Fire: The Land War in the South Pacific* (New York: Viking, 1996), p. 256.

92. Milner, pp. 81–88.

93. Gregory M. Franzwa and William J. Ely, *Lief Sverdrup* (Gerald, Mo.: Patrice Press, 1980), pp. 115–129. Sverdrup was one of the engineers who was sent to look for land routes.

94. James, *Years,* 2:239, 241–242; Milner, pp. 105, 168; Samuel Eliot Morison,

History of the United States Naval Operations in World War II, vol. 6, *Breaking the Bismarcks Barrier* (Boston: Little, Brown and Company, 1950), p. 32.

95. William H. Carleton, "History of the Directorate of Air Transport, Allied Air Forces–Southwest Pacific Area and the 322d Troop Carrier Wing," pp. 1–7, file 706.306, HRA; Erickson S. Nichols, "Historical Record of the Air Transport Command for the six months ending June 30th, 1942," file 733.01, HRA.

96. Kenney diary, May 22, 1942, KP; Milner, pp. 42–43, 64–65, 76.

97. Kenney diary, September 11, 12, 15, 1942, KP; Message, Ritchie to Marshall, September 21, 1942, Arnold papers, LOC; Kenney, *Reports,* p. 99; Milner, pp. 92–95; David M. Horner, *Crisis of Command* (Canberra: Australian National University, 1978), pp. 164, 169.

98. Kenney, "Airplane in Modern Warfare," pp. 21–22.

99. Wilson, interview with Ahmann, p. 149.

100. Futrell, *Ideas,* p. 178.

101. Kenney diary, September 29, 1942, KP.

102. Goldstein, "Pioneer," pp. 112–113.

103. Kenney diary, August 2, 1942, KP; Milner, pp. 105–107, 115–118; Franzwa, pp. 130–136.

104. Kenney diary, September 29, 1942, KP. Other comments about using the Wanigela in Kenney diary, September 18, 24, 1942, KP.

105. Craven and Cate, 4:115–116.

106. Kenney diary, August 2, 18, September 4, 18, 24, 1942, KP.

107. Milner, pp. 101–107.

108. Kenney diary, October 5, 1942; December 9, 10, 1942, KP.

109. "Lessons from New Guinea Operations, Jul 42–Apr 43," Allied Translator and Interpreter Section (ATIS) Enemy Publications Number 285, January 18, 1945, pp. 13–14, quoted in *Reports of MacArthur,* 2:160, n. 118.

110. Milner, pp. 98–100.

111. Ernest Gerber, quoted in Bergerud, p. 217.

112. Milner, pp. 140–143.

113. Watson, p. 99.

114. Craven and Cate, 4:118.

115. Letter, MacArthur to Kenney, September 6, 1942, KP.

116. Message, MacArthur to Marshall, September 16, 1942, RG 4, MMMA.

117. Ibid.

118. Draft message, Chief of Staff, SWPA, to War Department, September 30, 1942, KP.

119. Kenney, *Reports,* pp. 112–114.

120. Henry H. Arnold Journal, "Trip to Southwest Pacific," p. 15, Arnold papers, LOC.

121. Message, Ritchie to Marshall, September 21, 1942, Arnold papers, LOC.

122. Brown, p. 2.

123. Major R. E. Smyser Jr., "Airdromes for War," *The Military Engineer* 33 (Dec. 1941):562.

124. Lenore Fine and Jesse A. Remington, *United States Army in World War II: The Corps of Engineers: Construction in the United States* (Washington, D.C.: Office of the Chief of Military History, 1972), pp. 614–615.

125. Colonel Stuart C. Godfrey, "Engineers with the Army Air Forces," *The Military*

Engineer, 33 (Nov. 1941): 487–488; Blance D. Coll, Jean E. Keith, and Herbert H. Rosenthal, *United States Army in World War II: The Corps of Engineers: Troops and Equipment* (Washington, D.C.: Office of the Chief of Military History, 1958), p. 18.

126. Godfrey, pp. 487–488; Smyser, pp. 562–566; Major General Henry H. Arnold, "The Air Forces and Military Engineers," *The Military Engineer* 33 (Dec. 1941): 548; Coll et al., pp. 25–26, 53–63.

127. Douglas MacArthur, quoted in William C. Baldwin, "Engineers in the Southwest Pacific, 1941–1944," *The Military Engineer* 83 (March–April 1993):76; Spector, *Eagle,* p. 299.

128. Wesley Frank Craven and James L. Cate, eds., *The Army Air Forces in World War II,* vol. 7, *Services Around the World* (Chicago, University of Chicago Press, 1958), pp. 277–278.

129. Hugh J. Casey, *Engineer Memoirs Major General Hugh J. Casey, U. S. Army* (Washington, D.C.: Office of History, U.S. Army Corps of Engineers, 1993), pp. 191–192, 196–197.

130. Kenney diary, October 18, 31, 1942; Karl C. Dod, *United States Army in World War II: The Corps of Engineers: The War against Japan* (Washington, D.C.: Office of the Chief of Military History, 1966), pp. 184–188, 220.

131. Milner, pp. 169–170, 198–199; Morison, 6:47.

132. Kenney diary, December 11, 1942, KP; Letters, Robert L. Eichelberger to Richard Sutherland, December 4, 7, 8, 1942, Robert L. Eichelberger papers, Special Collections Library, Duke University, Durham, North Carolina.

133. *Reports of MacArthur,* 2:174–175.

134. Ibid., 2:179.

135. Ibid., 2:179, 198, n. 92.

136. USSBS, *Fifth Air Force,* pp. 14, 43. The number of missions reaching a target varied by month, but it went from 1,000 in September to at least 2,000 every month beginning in October.

137. Extracted from Historical Division, Office of the Assistant Chief of Air Staff, Intelligence, Headquarters Army Air Forces, "The Bismarck Sea Action March 1–4, 1943," September 1, 1943, p. 24, file 105.1-8, HRA.

138. Kenney, "Airplane in Modern Warfare," pp. 18, 22.

139. Ibid., p. 18.

140. It was not clear to the participants that the Allies had gained control of the air at this time. Spector, *Eagle,* p. 215, argues that the air battle was over by this time.

141. Craven and Cate, 4:126–127; Milner, pp. 375–376; Eichelberger, p. 40; Nicola Baker, *More Than Little Heroes: Australian Army Air Liaison Officers in the Second World War,* Canberra Studies on Strategy and Defence no. 106 (Canberra: Strategic and Defence Studies Centre, 1994), pp. 47–66; Joe Gray Taylor, "American Experience in the Southwest Pacific," in Cooling, p. 305.

142. Office of the Chief Engineer, General Headquarters Army Forces, Pacific, *Engineers of the Southwest Pacific, 1941–1945,* vol. 3, *Engineer Intelligence* (Washington, D.C.: Government Printing Office, 1950, p. 29.

143. Milner, pp. 177–178, 182, 185, 285; Craven and Cate, 4:125–127; Shortal, p. 45.

144. Eichelberger, p. 40. One notable friendly fire incident involved the death of Byron Darnton, a reporter from the *New York Times,* Eichelberger, pp. 66–67; Milner, p. 108.

145. Kenney diary, November 11, 1942; Letter, Kenney to Arnold, December 14, 1942, KP.

146. Kenney diary, November 20, 1942, KP; Letter, Kenney to Fairchild, p. 2; Shortal, p. 50.

147. Message, Kenney to Chief of Air Staff, RAAF; Message, Kenney to Secretary, Air Board, December 9, 1942, KP.

148. Milner, p. 375; Shortal, p. 50.

149. Eichelberger, p. 34.

150. Kenney diary, December 10, 1942, KP; Milner, p. 255.

151. Watson, p. 80.

152. *Reports of MacArthur*, 2:183; Milner, pp. 346, 374.

153. Quoted in Milner, p. 374, also pp. 144–146.

154. Kenney, "Modern Warfare," p. 22.

155. Letter, Kenney to Arnold, January 1, 1943, p. 2, KP.

156. Arnold, *Global Mission*, p. 382.

157. USSBS, *Japanese Air Power*, pp. 34–36, 40. For a personal account of the training and experience a Japanese pilot brought to war in 1942 against American aircrews in the Southwest Pacific, see Saburo Sakai with Martin Caidin and Fred Saito, *Samurai!* (Garden City, N.Y.: Doubleday, 1978).

158. Kenney, *Reports*, p. 69.

159. Ibid.

160. Letter, Kenney to Arnold, January 1, 1943, p. 1, KP; Letter, Kenney to Dorothy Glazier, February 10, 1943, I am grateful to Dorothy Dodson for sharing this letter with me. His impressions on first going to New Guinea are recorded in Kenney, *Reports*, p. 92.

161. Letter, Kenney to Arnold, January 1, 1943, p. 2, KP.

162. Letter, Kenney to Arnold, December 10, 1942, KP.

163. Letter, Kenney to Arnold, October 24, 1942, quoted in Craven and Cate, 4:119.

164. "Notes to discuss with General Arnold," September 24, 1942, KP.

165. Kenney diary, December 16, 1942, KP.

166. Edward V. Rickenbacker, *Rickenbacker*, (Englewood Cliffs, N.J.: Prentice-Hall, 1967), pp. 332–333; James, *Years*, 2:281.

6. *Moving Westward*

Epigraph: Letter, Kenney to Fairchild, December 8, 1942, KP.

1. Maurice Matloff, *Strategic Planning for Coalition Warfare, 1943–1944* (Washington, D.C.: Office of the Chief of Miltary History, 1959), pp. 18–33.

2. USSBS, *The Allied Campaign against Rabaul* (Washington, D.C.: Government Printing Office, 1946), pp. 12–13; Odgers, p. 91.

3. John Miller Jr., *United States Army in World War II: Cartwheel: The Reduction of Rabaul* (Washington, D.C.: Office of the Chief of Military History, 1959), pp. 1–2.

4. Miller, pp. 32–35.

5. Kenney diary, December 16, 1942, KP; Miller, pp. 30–36; Craven and Cate, 4:135.

6. Kenney, *Reports*, pp. 56–57, 71–73.

7. Air Evaluation Board, SWPA, "Air Transport Operations, Battle of Wau," June 10, 1945, p. 12–13, file 706.310, HRA.

8. Extracted from USSBS, *Fifth Air Force,* p. 14, 43; "Aircraft Attrition—Southwest Pacific Area," July 15, 1943, file 706.215, HRA.

9. Craven and Cate, 4:141, 154; Kenney, *Reports,* p. 182; Gann, p. 8.

10. Craven and Cate, 4:106; Kenney, *Reports,* p. 76; Gann, p. 7; John Alcorn, "The Grim Reapers: 3rd Bomb Group," *American Aviation Historical Society Journal* 20 (Spring 1975): 12.

11. Kenney, *Reports,* pp. 105–106.

12. Letter, Kenney to Fairchild, December 8, 1942, KP.

13. Letter, Kenney to Colonel Alvin Crawford, December 9, 1942, KP.

14. Kenney, "Air Power in Southwest Pacific," p. 59.

15. Letter, Kenney to Group Captain Wackett, President Commonwealth Aircraft Corporation, December 8, 1942; Letter, Kenney to Secretary, Air Board, December 30, 1942, Subject: Flying-Officer Snooker, December 30, 1942, KP.

16. "History of the Fifth Air Service Command," p. 42, file 733.01, HRA.

17. Letter, Kenney to Fairchild, December 8, 1942, KP; also Kenney diary, August 5, 1942, KP.

18. Caidin, pp. 316–317, for some examples of innovation in the South Pacific.

19. Jane M. Howell and Christopher A. Higgins, "Champions of Change: Identifying, Understanding, and Supporting Champions of Technological Innovations," *Organizational Dynamics* (Summer 1990): 52–54; Richard L. Daft, *Organization Theory and Design,* 4th ed. (St. Paul, Minn.: West Publishing Company, 1992), pp. 271–272, 486.

20. Letter, Kenney to Arnold, Subject: Report on Modifications Recommended for B-24 Airplanes, January 14, 1943; Kenney diary, January 16, 1943, KP; John S. Alcorn, *The Jolly Rogers: History of the 90th Bomb Group during World War II* (Temple City, Calif.: Historical Aviation Album, 1981), pp. 70–74.

21. Alcorn, *Jolly Rogers,* pp. 73–74, 139.

22. Gillison, pp. 638–639.

23. Letter, Whitehead to Kenney, May 19, 1943, p. 1, Ennis C. Whitehead papers, HRA; Letter, Whitehead to Kenney, April 9, 1944, file 730.161-3, HRA.

24. Kenney, "Air Power in Southwest Pacific," pp. 59–60.

25. Kenney diary, August 11, 1942, KP; Kenney, *Reports,* p. 162.

26. For Kenney's intelligence organization see Kreis, *Piercing the Fog,* pp. 257–263.

27. Kenney diary, January 1, 3, 1943, KP.

28. Kenney diary, January 4, 1943, KP; Kenney, *Reports,* p. 176.

29. Kenney diary, August 21, 1942; October 5, 1942, KP; Kenney, *Reports,* p. 167.

30. Byrd, pp. 107–117.

31. Kenney diary, January 5, 1943, KP.

32. Quoted in Byrd, p. 121.

33. Headquarters United States Army, Japan, "18th Army Operations," Japanese Monograph no. 37, 1950, pp. 182–184, reprinted in *The War in Asia and the Pacific 1937–1949: Japanese and Chinese Studies and Documents,* ed. Donald S. Detwiler and Charles B. Burdick, 15 vols. (New York: Garland Publishing, 1980), vol. 7; AEB, SWPA, "The Battle of the Bismark [*sic*] Sea and Development of Masthead Attacks,"

1 July 1945, pp. 1–7, 27, file 168.7103-37, HRA; Kenney, *Reports,* pp. 176–177; Drea, *MacArthur's ULTRA,* pp. 63–66.

34. "18th Army Operations," p. 184.

35. "The Bismarck Sea Action," pp. 24–25.

36. "Air Transport Operations, Battle of Wau," p. 17.

37. Ibid., pp. 17–19. Kenney used a figure of 194 flights, Kenney, *Reports,* pp. 186–187.

38. Vice Admiral Mikawa Gunichi, Captain Ohmae Toshikazu, and Rear Admiral Kimura Masafuku, in Special Projects Section, Assistant Chief of Staff, Intelligence, Advanced Echelon, Headquarters Far East Air Forces, "A Japanese Version of the Battle of the Bismarck Sea, 1–4 March 1943," September 1945, pp. 23, 30, 49, reprinted in Detwiler, vol. 5; "18th Army Operations," pp. 105–106; Drea, *MacArthur's ULTRA,* pp. 67–68.

39. Kenney, *Reports,* p. 198.

40. Headquarters Allied Air Forces, SWPA, "Intelligence Summary number 76," p. 1, February 10, 1943, Sutherland papers, NA.

41. Headquarters Allied Air Forces, SWPA, "Intelligence Summary number 80," February 23, 1943, p. 1, Sutherland papers, NA.

42. Drea, *MacArthur's ULTRA,* p. 69.

43. Letter, Kenney to Whitehead, February 25, 1943, KP.

44. Kenney diary, February 25, 26, 1943, KP.

45. Letter Kenney to Whitehead, February 25, 1943, KP; Kenney, *Reports,* pp. 199–200. Drea suggests that intercepted messages made it clear that Lae was the destination. Kenney viewed the landing site more ambiguously, either because he was worried about the accuracy of the data or because he was concerned that if he was more precise he would divulge the source of the information. Drea, *MacArthur's ULTRA,* pp. 69–70. Even on the day of the actual attack an intelligence summary from Kenney's headquarters stated that the exact destination of the convoy was "uncertain." Allied Air Forces, SWPA, Intelligence Summary Number 82, March 3, 1943, p. 1, Sutherland papers, NA.

46. Kenney diary, February 25, 26, 1943, KP; Craven and Cate, 4:141–142.

47. Kenney diary, February 27, 1943, KP; Headquarters Advanced Echelon 5AF, "Report on Destruction of Japanese Convoy in Bismark [*sic*] Sea March 1 to 5, 1943," 6 April 1943, p. 2, Sutherland papers, NA; McAulay, *Battle of Bismarck Sea,* pp. 21–22.

48. Lieutenant General Francis C. Gideon, interview with Mark C. Cleary, July 7, 1982, Larkspur, Colorado, p. 33, file K239.0512-1338, HRA.

49. "Central Bureau Technical Records."

50. Kenney diary, March 1, 2, 1943, KP; Kenney, *Reports,* pp. 202–203.

51. Robert W. Reed, 19th Bombardment Squadron, "Tactical Study of Attack on Convoy near Lae, New Guinea," March 1943, in Sutherland papers, NA.

52. AEB, p. 15.

53. Fifth Bomber Command Orders for Major Assault on Convoy, 0955, 3 March 1943, found in AEB, "Development of Masthead Attacks," p. 61; Kenney diary, March 3, 1943, KP.

54. Masuda Reiji, quoted in Haruko Taya Cook and Theodore F. Cook, *Japan at War: An Oral History* (New York: New Press, 1992), p. 301.

55. AEB, "Development of Masthead Attacks," pp. 20–22; McAulay, *Battle of Bismarck Sea,* p. 101.

56. Kenney diary, March 4, 5, 1943, KP.

57. Letter, Intelligence Officer, 63rd Bombardment Squadron, to Commanding Officer, 43rd Bombardment Group, Subject: Narrative Report of Attacks on "Lae Convoy" March 2–3, 1943, March 12, 1943, Sutherland papers, box 64, NA. Kenney dates this attack on March 3, Kenney, *Reports,* p. 204, a claim that is often repeated, see McAulay, *Battle of Bismarck Sea,* pp. 102–103, 115; James T. Murphy with A. B. Feuer, *Skip Bombing* (Westport, Conn.: Praeger, 1993), p. 119.

58. Wilson, p. 269.

59. Murphy, p. 119.

60. Ibid., p. 120.

61. Morison, 4:62. Historian John Dower disagrees with this assessment and views the actions as part of a cycle of atrocities, John Dower, *War without Mercy: Race and Power in the Pacific War* (New York: Pantheon Books, 1986), p. 67.

62. Major Edward F. Hoover, 5th Bomber Command, quoted in Vern Haugland, *The AAF against Japan* (New York: Harper and Brothers Publishers, 1948), p. 163.

63. Number 30 Squadron RAAF, "Attack on Convoy off Lae, 5/3/43," in Sutherland papers, box 64, NA, and Wilson, p. 269. The statement about flyers becoming sick is from Hoover, quoted in Haugland, p. 163, also cited in Dower, p. 67.

64. Letter, Kenney to Arnold, January 1, 1943, KP.

65. Kenney diary, December 12, 1942, also entries for December 29, 31, 1942, KP.

66. Kenney diary, March 5, 1943, KP; Kenney, *Reports,* p. 205; Letter, Wilson to Whitehead, March 5, 1943, KP; James, *Years,* 2:295–296.

67. United States Strategic Bombing Survey, *Interrogations of Japanese Officials,* 2 vols. (Washington, D.C.: Government Printing Office, n.d.), 1:498; Drea, *MacArthur's ULTRA,* p. 71.

68. USSBS, *Japanese Air Power,* pp. 12, 14.

69. Headquarters Advanced Echelon 5AF, p. 2; AEB, "Development of Masthead Attacks," pp. 1, 18; Alan Stephens, "Australia's Forgotten Victory: The Battle of the Bismarck Sea," in *RAAF in Southwest Pacific,* pp. 110–111.

70. AEB, "Development of Masthead Attacks," p. 49; Letter, Wilson to Whitehead, March 5, 1943, KP.

71. AEB, "Development of Masthead Attacks," p. 9.

72. Kenney, "Air Power in Southwest Pacific," p. 60.

73. Morison, 6:63, attributes Kenney's success in the battle to a "fair measure of good luck."

74. *New York Times,* March 4, 1943, p.1.

75. Ibid.

76. *New York Times,* March 5, 6, 7, 1943; "Right Guess and Great Tactics Won Us Bismarck Sea Victory," *Newsweek,* March 15, 1943, pp. 17–18; "Battle of the Pacific," *Time,* March 15, 1945, p. 20.

77. Allied Translation and Interpreter Service, SWPA, "Bismarck Sea Operation February–March 1943 Part Two," April 8, 1943, file 710.625-12, HRA, part one of the report was published on March 29, 1943; Drea, *MacArthur's ULTRA,* pp. 71–72.

78. Memorandum, Brigadier General Edgar P. Sorenson, Assistant Chief of Air Staff, Intelligence, to Lieutenant General George C. Kenney, Subject: Proposed Release

of Revised Information re Bismarck Sea Action, August 12, 1943, file 142.16-15, HRA; Messages, Marshall to MacArthur September 7, 8, 1943, RG 4, MMMA.

79. Memorandum, Sorenson to Kenney.

80. Message, MacArthur to Marshall, September 7, 1943, RG 4, MMMA.

81. Letter, Kenney to Arnold, Subject: Proposed Release of Revised Information re: Bismarck Sea Action, September 14, 1943, RG 4, MMMA.

82. Ibid.

83. Ibid.

84. Kenney, interview with James, pp. 22–23.

85. "A Japanese Version of the Battle of the Bismarck Sea." The evidence produced by this investigation was thought to have been so damaging and so contrary to Kenney's and MacArthur's findings that the report was destroyed. See "Report on the Battle of the Bismarck Sea," file 142.15-16, HRA; Craven and Cate, 4:717, n. 49; and James, *Years,* 2:300, for comments asserting this claim. The authors listed in the "Japanese Version of the Battle of the Bismarck Sea" and the chronology of this investigation reflect the information previously thought to have been destroyed.

86. Kenney, *Reports,* pp. 205–206.

87. Gavin Long, *MacArthur as Military Commander* (New York: Van Norstrand Reinhold Company, 1969), pp. 118, 136.

88. James, *Years,* 2:303.

89. Message, Kenney to Arnold, December 26, 1942, RG 4, MMMA.

90. Kenney's press coverage was extensive. He was on the cover of *Life,* March 22, 1943; the caption read "Victor of Bismarck Sea."

91. John Stanaway, *Possum, Clover & Hades: The 475th Fighter Group in World War II* (Atglen, Penn.: Schiffer Military/Aviation History, 1993), p. 14.

92. *Reports of MacArthur,* 2:204.

93. "18th Army Operations," p. 184.

94. "Reply to written questions by Vice Admiral Gunicki Mikawa," in "A Japanese Version of the Battle of the Bismarck Sea," p. 25. Also *Reports of MacArthur,* 2:205; "18th Army Operations," pp. 189–191.

95. Commander Doi Yasumi, staff officer, Southeast Area Fleet, November 20, 1945, in *Interrogations of Japanese Officials,* 2:398.

96. "A Japanese Version of the Battle of the Bismarck Sea," pp. 4, 23–25; "18th Army Operations," pp. 179–182; Kenney, interview with Stanley, p. 35; James, *Years,* 2:296; Craven and Cate, 4:146–147; Miller, p. 41; Drea, *MacArthur's ULTRA,* p. 71.

97. Letter, Kenney to Arnold, September 14, 1943.

98. Morton, p. 385; Miller, pp. 6–8, 11–12; Matloff, pp. 91–92.

99. Kenney, *Reports,* p. 198; Miller, p. 12, n. 12.

100. Kenney diary, February 28, 1943, KP; Kenney, *Reports,* p. 201.

101. Miller, pp. 11–12.

102. Morton, pp. 390–391, Miller, pp. 12–14.

103. Hayes, pp. 312–315.

104. Morton, p. 398–399; Miller, pp. 16–19.

105. Kenney diary March 17, 25, 1943, KP; Kenney, *Reports,* pp. 215–217. Kenney's meeting with Roosevelt took place on March 17, and Kenney returned to the White House on March 25 for the presentation of the Medal of Honor to Kenneth Walker's family. In a memo written to the president between the two meetings, Gen-

eral Marshall praised Kenney's exploits, Memorandum, Marshall to Roosevelt, March 22, 1943, cited in Perret, p. 530, n. 14. In addition, Kenney noted that Arnold was called to the White House for a meeting on March 21, 1943. Kenney diary, March 21, 22, 1943, KP.

106. Kenney diary, March 14, 1943, KP; Arthur H. Vandenberg Jr., with the collaboration of Joe Alex Morris, *The Private Papers of Senator Vandenberg* (Boston: Houghton Mifflin, 1952), pp. 77–78.

107. Philip J. Briggs, "General MacArthur and the Presidential Election of 1944," *Presidential Studies Quarterly* 22 (Winter 1992): 33–40; Vandenberg, pp. 75–89; James, *Years*, 2:403–440.

108. Kenney diary, March 14, 1943, KP.

109. Letter, Kenney to Arnold, December 10, 1942, p. 3; Letter, Kenney to William Ritchie, G-3, War Department, April 14, 1943, KP.

110. Morton, 411–415; Miller, 42–44; Morison, 6:117–127; Gillison, p. 700.

111. Morison, 6:127. In reality, U.S. forces had lost a destroyer, a tanker, and about twenty-five planes.

112. Morison, 6:128–129; Craven and Cate, 4:231–214.

113. Allied Air Forces, SWPA, Intelligence Summary, Number 89, March 27, 1943; Number 90, March 30, 1943; Number 92, April 7, 1943, in Sutherland papers, NA.

114. Kenney, *Reports*, pp. 228–229.

115. Bleakley, pp. 81–82.

116. Kenney, *Reports*, pp. 234, 241.

117. Ibid. Kenney reiterates this point in Kenney diary, June 30, 1943, KP.

118. Kenney diary, March 4, 1943, KP; Letter, Whitehead to Kenney, March 5, 1943, KP. The organization was initially named the Buna Air Task Force.

119. Kenney diary, March 5, 1943; Letter, Whitehead to Kenney, March 5, 1943, KP; Wilson interview with Moore, p. 3; St. Clair Street interview with Beverly Moore, September 19, 1945, pp. 2–3, file 706.201, HRA.

120. Colonel H. P. Dexter, "Report on Air Support in Southwest Pacific Area During the Period November 1, 1943 to February 1, 1943," April 10, 1944, p. 7–10, file 706.4501, HRA; Advanced Headquarters, Allied Land Forces, SWPA, "Army-Air Cooperation in New Guinea," August 1944, KP; USSBS, *Fifth Air Force*, pp. 8–11, 89–90.

121. "Notes to discuss with General Arnold," September 24, 1942; Letter, Kenney to Colonel William L. Ritchie, Operations Division, War Department, April 14, 1943, pp. 3–4, KP.

122. Jarred V. Crabb, interview with Lieutenant Colonel Julian and Major Goldstein, April 17, 28, 1970, USAF Academy, Colorado, pp. 120–122, file K239.0512-622, HRA; Ronald Yoshino, *Lightning Strikes: The 475th Fighter Group in the Pacific War, 1943–1945* (Manhattan, Kans.: Sunflower University Press, 1988), pp. 32–34; Robert R. Herrring, ed., *History of the 308th Bombardment Wing* (San Angelo, Tex.: Newsfoto Publishing Co., 1945); Herbert O. Johansen, "Our Air Task Force," *Air Force* 27 (Dec. 1944): 7, 40.

123. Hewitt, p. 96.

124. War Department Field Manual 31-35, *Aviation in Support of Ground Forces*, April 9, 1942, file 170-121031-35, HRA; Futrell, pp. 133–134, 136.

125. Kenney diary, January 11, 1943, KP.

126. Letter, Kenney to Whitehead, February 14, 1943, Whitehead papers, HRA; Baker, pp. 70–71.

127. Letter, Kenney to Whitehead, February 14, 1943.

128. Kenney diary, January 11, 1943, KP.

129. Letter, Whitehead to Kenney, February 16, 1943, Whitehead papers.

130. Headquarters Allied Air Forces, "Standard Operating Procedure for Attack Aviation in Close Support, SWPA," July 1943, p. 9, file 710.4501, HRA.

131. Alfred D. Chandler Jr., *The Papers of Dwight David Eisenhower: The War Years II* (Baltimore, Md.: Johns Hopkins Press, 1970), pp. 873–874; Futrell, pp. 136–138.

132. War Department Field Manual 100-20, *Command and Employment of Air Power*, July 21, 1943, p. 2. All capital letters in the original.

133. Ibid., p. 4, 8–13.

134. St. Clair Street, interview with Moore, pp. 2–3; Crabb, p. 7.

135. Quoted in Wolk, "Innovator," p. 148. For similar views of other officers, see Futrell, p. 138.

136. Kenney diary, August 30, 1942, KP.

137. Miller, pp. 52–53.

138. GHQ, SWPA, "G-2 Estimate of the enemy situation 'Chronicle,'" Landers papers, MHI.

139. Barbey, p. 57, also p. 42; Letter, Barbey to Brigadier General H. W. Buse Jr., Subject: Draft of New Britain Campaign, July 10, 1962, Barbey papers, NHC.

140. Letter, Whitehead to Kenney, February 10, 1943, KP.

141. Interview, Rear Admiral Charles Adair with John T. Mason Jr., U.S. Naval Institute Oral History Program, February 26, 1975, Washington, D.C., pp. 178–185, NHC.

142. Letter, Kenney to Arnold, October 21, 1943, p. 3, KP.

143. Barbey, p. 3.

144. Letter, Captain Ray D. Tarbuck to Barbey, May 19, 1961, quoted in Gerald E. Wheeler, *Kinkaid of the Seventh Fleet* (Washington, D.C.: Naval Historical Center, 1995), p. 362.

145. Kenney diary, June 18, 1943, KP. Suggestively, in Kenney's book he consistently misspelled both Barbey's and Carpender's name. He spelled Barbey as Barby and Carpender as Carpenter. Kenney, *Reports,* passim.

146. Miller, pp. 50–58; Krueger, p. 223; Barbey, pp. 65–68; Kenney, *Reports,* pp. 265–266.

7. *Isolating Rabaul*

Epigraph: Letter, Kenney to Arnold, October 21, 1943, p. 1, KP.

1. Letter, Kenney to Arnold, June 19, 1943, KP.

2. Miller, pp. 194–195.

3. Ballard, p. 206; Letter, Whitehead to Kenney, February 10, 1943, p. 1, KP.

4. Headquarters Allied Air Forces, SWPA, Intelligence Summary Number 103, May 15, 1943; Number 123, July 24, 1943; Number 124, July 28, 1943; Number 129, August 14, 1943, Sutherland papers, NA.

5. Drea, *MacArthur's ULTRA,* pp. 79–81, Miller, pp. 45–48; *Reports of MacArthur,* 2:215.

6. Letter, Kenney to Whitehead, May 11, 1943, KP.

7. USSBS, *Fifth Air Force,* pp. 11, 13–14.

8. Letter, Kenney to Bostock, May 20, 1943, cited in Odgers, pp. 56–57.

9. Kenney diary, February 19, 1943, KP.

10. Memorandum, Kenney to Wilson, June 10, 1943; Letter, Kenney to Arnold, August 25, 1943, KP.

11. Letter, Kenney to Arnold, May 18, 1942, Arnold papers, LOC.

12. Feldt, pp. 181, 187, 194, 199–200, 203.

13. Office of the Chief Engineer, *Engineers,* 3:46–47, 80–84. The research required makes it clear that the process did not just rely, as the official Air Force history contends, on "common sense and the luck or skill of the surveying parties." Craven and Cate, 7:278.

14. Lieutenant Colonel William J. Ellison, "Airdrome Construction in the Southwest Pacific," *Aviation Engineer Notes,* June 1944, p. 2, COE V, 25, 17; Captain Everette E. Frazier, "Experiences on the location of airdromes in New Guinea," p. 5, file 733.01, HRA; Casey, p. 148.

15. Frazier, "Experiences," pp. 5–6; Casey, pp. 148–149; Office of the Chief Engineer, "Technical Memorandum Number 8," February 23, 1944, COE X, 117, 1.

16. Ellison, p. 3; Brigadier General Samuel D. Sturgis, "Air Power as Affected by Airdrome Construction," *The Military Engineer* 40 (Sept. 1948): 417; Fine and Remington, pp. 620–621, 625–630; Dod, pp. 218–219.

17. Franzwa, pp. 137–143, 153; Dod, p. 230.

18. Captain Everette E. Frazier, "Experiences on the Location of Airdromes in New Guinea," file 733.01, HRA; idem, "Airfield Reconnaissance in New Guinea," *Aviation Engineer Notes,* March 1945, p. 4, COE V, 25, 17; Kenney diary, June 6, 8, 1943, KP; Colonel Harry F. Cunningham, Assistant Chief of Staff, Intelligence, Headquarters Advance Echelon Fifth Air Force, "Brief Narrative of Tsili-Tsili (Marilinan)-Lae-Wewak Operations by Advon 5," December 26, 1943, p. 2, KP; Kenney, *Reports,* pp. 251–254.

19. Kenney, *Reports,* p. 253, 271.

20. Frazier, "Airfield Reconnaissance," pp. 4–5.

21. Kenney diary, June 8, 1943, KP; Kenney, *Reports,* p. 254.

22. Kenney diary, June 6, 1943, KP; Kenney, *Reports,* p. 253.

23. Letter, Kenney to Arnold, June 19, 1943, p. 3, KP.

24. Ibid., p. 4; Kenney diary, June 30, 1943, KP. Kenney also recounts the episode in Kenney, *Reports,* p. 268.

25. Letter, Arnold to Kenney, July 1, 1943; Message, Marshall to MacArthur, July 4, 1943, KP.

26. Kenney, *Reports,* p. 268.

27. Kenney diary, July 4, 1943, KP.

28. Ibid.; Letter, Kenney to Arnold, July 26, 1943, p. 4, KP; Kenney, *Reports,* p. 281.

29. Kenney diary, August 28, 1943, KP; Kenney, *Reports,* pp. 281–282.

30. Hayes, p. 316.

31. Kenney diary, July 6, 1943, KP, Kenney, *Reports,* pp. 262–263, 267, 269.

32. Message, Kenney to 1 Wireless Unit, June 12, 1943, quoted in Bleakley, p. 100.

33. Letter, Whitehead to Kenney, July 9, 1943; Letter, Whitehead to Kenney, July 18, 1943, KP.

34. Letter, Whitehead to Kenney, July 9, 1943, KP.

35. Kenney diary, June, 16, 17, 1943, KP.

36. Frazier, "Airfield Reconnaissance," p. 5; Casey, 6:166–167; Dod, pp. 247–249.

37. Kenney diary, July 10, July 26, August 5, 1943; Cunningham, p. 3, KP. Colonel David W. "Photo" Hutchinson replaced Moore on August 27, Craven and Cate, 4:176.

38. Kenney diary, July 7, 1943, KP; Kenney, *Reports*, pp. 269–270.

39. Kenney, *Reports*, p. 270.

40. "Airborne 2 1/2 ton trucks," *Aviation Engineer Notes*, June 1944, p. 16, COE V, 25, 17.

41. Headquarters Allied Air Forces, SWPA, Intelligence Summary Number 129, August 14, 1943, Sutherland papers, NA; Drea, *MacArthur's ULTRA*, p. 83; August 14, 15, 1943, KP. Kenney, *Reports*, p. 275, places the reconnaissance flight on August 14.

42. Drea, *MacArthur's ULTRA*, p. 83. Kenney, *Reports*, p. 276, claims eleven Japanese bombers were shot down.

43. Letter, Kenney to Arnold, August 25, 1943, p. 1, KP.

44. Drea, *MacArthur's ULTRA*, p. 85; Craven and Cate, 4:178–180. Kenney claimed that there were 225 Japanese aircraft at the four airfields around Wewak and that the first day's attack destroyed over 150. Kenney, *Reports*, pp. 276, 278.

45. Headquarters Allied Air Forces, SWPA, Intelligence Summary Number 131, August 21, 1943, Sutherland papers, NA; Bleakley, p. 104.

46. Colonel Kaneko Rinsuke, Imperial Japanese Army, staff officer, 8th Area Army, July 1943 to August 1943, supply officer, 4th Air Force staff, August 1943 to September 1944, in USSBS, *Interrogations*, 2:405; Drea, *MacArthur's ULTRA*, pp. 79–81.

47. Weinberg, p. 551; Kreis, *Piercing the Fog*, pp. 292–296.

48. Kreis, *Air Warfare*, p. 252.

49. Major William J. Ellison Jr. "Advice from the 808th Engineers," September 25, 1943, p. 1, COE X, 116, 4; Office of the Chief Engineer, GHQ SWPA, "Engineer Construction in the Southwest Pacific Area," March 1, 1944, p. 35, COE X, 101, 2.

50. Ellison, p. 2. For other estimates on the problems faced by the lack of heavy equipment, see Casey, p. 119–120. The size and equipment of an aviation engineer battalion is found in Colonel Stuart C. Godfrey, "Engineers with the Army Air Forces," *Military Engineer* 33 (Nov. 1941): 488–489.

51. Drea, *MacArthur's ULTRA*, pp. 82–83; Godfrey, p. 489; S. D. Sturgis Jr., "Air Power as Affected by Airdrome Construction," *Military Engineer* 40 (Aug. 1948):355.

52. Drea, *MacArthur's ULTRA*, pp. 84–85.

53. Kenney, *Reports*, pp. 283–284; Bleakley, p. 104.

54. Kenney, *Reports*, pp. 258–259, 266–267.

55. Letter, Kenney to Arnold, July 28, 1943, KP.

56. Ibid.

57. Letters, Kenney to Arnold, June 19, 1943, pp. 2–3; September 7, 1943, p. 2, KP.

58. Letter, Kenney to Arnold, September 7, 1943, p. 7, KP.

59. Ibid., p. 3.

60. Letters, Arnold to Kenney, July 16, 1943, p. 2; October 8, 1943, p. 2, KP.

61. Letter, Arnold to Kenney, October 8, 1943, pp. 2–3, KP.

62. Letter, Kenney to Arnold, 19 June 1943, p. 3, KP.

63. Letter, Arnold to Kenney, July 5, 1943, p. 2, KP, emphasis in original.

64. Letter, Arnold to Kenney, July 5, 1943, KP.

65. Letter, Kenney to Arnold, July 28, 1943, KP.

66. Kenney diary, June 20, 1943, KP.

67. Kenney diary, June 20, 1943; Letter, Kenney to Whitehead, July 31, 1943, p. 1; Letter, Kenney to Arnold, August 25, 1943, KP.

68. Kenney diary, June 20, 1943; Letter, Kenney to Arnold, July 28, 1943, pp. 4–5; Kenney, *Reports*, p. 264. Kenney later put a 75-gallon tank into the radio compartment, a move engineers in the United States would make the aircraft "very unstable." Letter, Kenney to Arnold, November 6, 1943, file 710.3271, HRA; Major General O. P. Echols, Assistant Chief of Air Staff, Materiel, Maintenance, and Distribution, to Secretary of the Air Staff, Subject: Letter to General Arnold, November 6, 1943, from General Kenney, December 11, 1943, Arnold papers, LOC.

69. Kenney diary, June 19, 1943, KP; Letter, Kenney to Arnold, June 19, 1943, pp. 6–7, KP.

70. Letter, Arnold to Kenney, July 16, 1943, KP.

71. Letter, Kenney to Arnold, August 25, 1943, KP.

72. Letter, Kenney to Arnold, September 7, 1943, KP.

73. Letter, Kenney to Whitehead, July 20, 1943, KP.

74. Kenney diary, May 24, 31, June 2, 1943, KP.

75. Letter, Kenney to Whitehead, July 20, 1943, p. 3, KP.

76. Letter, Whitehead to Kenney, July 20, 1943, pp. 3–4; Transcript, telephone conversation between Kenney and Whitehead, October 27, 1942, KP.

77. Barbey, p. 70–71, 88; Baker, pp. 92–93; Craven and Cate, 4:181.

78. From: Commander Task Force 76 (Commander Seventh Amphibious Force), To: The Commander in Chief U.S. Fleet, October 23, 1943, Subject Lae Operation, Report Upon, p. 1, Barbey papers, NHC.

79. Krueger, p. 9; Barbey, p. 59.

80. Barbey, p. 59.

81. Barbey, pp. 70–71 for his complaint; "Lae Operation, Report Upon," p. 2, for the air cover provided.

82. Kenney, "Report on bombing and machine gun firing."

83. Letter, Whitehead to Kenney, May 19, 1943, May 20, 1943; Letters, Kenney to Arnold, July 28, 1943, p. 4; August 25, 1943, p. 4; September 7, 1943, p. 4.

84. Letter, Major General Barney M. Giles, Chief of the Air Staff, to Kenney, August 12, 1943, KP.

85. Letter, Arnold to Kenney, October 8, 1943, KP.

86. Lae Operation, Report Upon," p. 7; Barbey, pp. 70–71; Craven and Cate, 4:183, Miller, p. 193; Odgers, p. 75. Kenney does not mention the disagreements over the air cover or the use of the Navy destroyer for radar coverage, Kenney, *Reports*, pp. 291–292.

87. Kenney, *Reports*, p. 291, mentions about one hundred attacking aircraft. Barbey, pp. 80–84, says seventy attackers, while Craven and Cate, 4:183, give no specific number.

88. Kenney diary, March 12, 1943, KP.

89. Letter, Whitehead to Kenney, July 31, 1943, KP; Kenney, *Reports,* p. 288; Colonel H. P. Dexter "Report on Air Support in Southwest Pacific Area during the Period 1 Novermer 1943 to 1 February 1944," p. 35, April 10, 1944, file 706.4501, HRA; Miller, p. 191.

90. Letter, Kenney to Arnold, September 7, 1943, pp. 5–6, KP; Dexter Report, p. 35; Memorandum To Commanding General, Fifth Air Force, From Headquarters Advanced Echelon Fifth Air Force, Subject: Plan of Operations for Attack on Lae, July 31, 1943, KP; Kenney, *Reports,* pp. 291–294.

91. Kenney, *Reports,* pp. 294–296; Miller, pp. 211–212.

92. Kenney, Memorandum to Sutherland, Subject: "Dayton" Plan, September 1, 1943, file 730.322-4, HRA.

93. Horner, *High Command,* pp. 272–273; Miller, pp. 215–216; Kenney, *Reports,* p. 300.

94. Barbey, p. 89.

95. Craven and Cate, 4:187.

96. From: Commander Task Force 76 (Commander Seventh Amphibious Force), To: The Commander in Chief U.S. Fleet, Subject: Finschhafen Operation, Report Upon, pp. 8–9, enclosures A, B, Barbey papers, NHC; Barbey, pp. 88–96. An example of the problems with using Kenney's memoir as a history of the war can be seen in this episode. His only comments on the amphibious attack at Finschhafen are on this raid. He ignores the planning problems with Barbey, the use of the *Reid* for early warning of the attack, and the rest of the operation, concentrating instead on the operations in the Markham Valley. See Kenney, *Reports,* ch. 12.

97. Barbey, p. 95.

98. Kenney, *Reports,* p. 307; Craven and Cate, 4:189.

99. September 22, 1943, KP; Jarred V. Crabb, "Fifth Air Force Against Japan, September 1942–August 1945," unpublished manuscript, February 4, 1946, Air University Library, Maxwell Air Force Base, Alabama.

100. *Reports of MacArthur,* 2:224–225.

101. Letter, Whitehead to Kenney, September 18, 1943, p. 4, Whitehead papers.

102. Kenney diary, September 24, 1943; Letter, Kenney to Arnold, October 10, 1943, pp. 2–3, KP; Kenney, *Reports,* pp. 300–302.

103. Australian Military Forces, "Report by 7 Australian Division on Operation Outlook, September 1, 1943 to September 16, 1943," p. 18, COE, X, 73, 3.

104. Letter, Kenney to Arnold, October 10, 1943, p. 3, KP; Craven and Cate, 4:190–192.

105. "Notes for Memorandum, Conference between Southwest Pacific Area and South Pacific Area," September 10, 1943, KP; Letter, Kenney to Whitehead, October 19, 1943, p. 1, KP.

106. Letter, Whitehead to Kenney, February 16, 1943, Whitehead papers.

107. Letter, Whitehead to Kenney, July 20, 1943, p.1, KP. By comparison, the loss rate during the day for the same aircraft was 0.3 percent.

108. Letter, Whitehead to Kenney, July 18, 1943, pp. 1–2; Letter, Whitehead to Commanding General 5th Air Force, Subject: Night operations by heavy bombers, July 18, 1943, KP.

109. Letter, Whitehead to Kenney, July 18, 1943, pp. 1–2, KP; Letter, Whitehead to Kenney, October 21, 1943, pp. 1–2, Whitehead papers.

110. Letter, Kenney to Whitehead, July 20, 1943, p. 2, KP.

111. Bleakley, p. 116.

112. Drea, *MacArthur's ULTRA,* p. 89; Bleakley, p. 116.

113. Message, Ritchie to Marshall, October 14, 1943, RG4, MMMA.

114. Kenney diary, October 12, 1943, KP; Francis C. Gideon, interview with Mark C. Clear, July 7, 1982, Larkspur, Colorado, pp. 37–44, file K239.0512-1338, HRA; Kenney, *Reports,* pp. 313–315; Hewitt, pp. 169–175, 182–183. In his book Kenney gives a higher number of allied aircraft.

115. McAulay, *Dragon's Jaws,* p. 31; Craven and Cate, 4:321. Naval historian Samuel Eliot Morison provides even lower figures, Morison, 6:275, n. 4.

116. Admirals Jinichi Kusaka and Naosaburo Irifune, Commander Tomoyoshi Hori, and Lieutenant Commander Masamichi Watanabe, quoted in USSBS, *Rabaul,* p. 58.

117. Letter, Whitehead to Kenney, May 7, 1943, p. 2, KP; Letter, Whitehead to Kenney, October 18, 1942, pp. 2, 3, Whitehead papers.

118. Letters, Whitehead to Kenney, October 18, 1943, p. 2; October 21, 1943, Whitehead papers.

119. *Army Air Force Statistical Digest,* p. 258. Of the losses on combat missions in Kenney's command roughly 60 percent were caused by enemy action (1,488 out of 2,494, 59.6 percent). By comparison, even with the notoriously bad weather over in Europe, the majority of the losses on combat missions in that theater were due to enemy action (9,654 out of 11,687, 82.6 percent), *Army Air Force Statistical Digest,* p. 255.

120. Kenney diary, October 13, 18, 1943, KP; Letter, Whitehead to Kenney, October 21, 1943, Whitehead papers; Kenney, *Reports,* pp. 314–318.

121. Miller, pp. 248–250; Craven, 4:259–260. Kenney erroneously remarked, "No opposition to the landing was encountered," Kenney, *Reports,* p. 318.

122. Kenney diary, November 2, 1943, KP; Kenney, *Reports,* pp. 319–321.

123. Kenney, *Reports,* p. 319; Letter, Whitehead to Kenney, November 4, 1943, p. 1, file 730.322-5, HRA.

124. Letter, Whitehead to Kenney, November 4, 1943; Drea, *MacArthur's ULTRA,* pp. 89–90.

125. Kenney, *Reports,* pp. 319–321, quote on p. 321; Letter, Kenney to Arnold, November 6, 1943, file 710.3271, HRA.

126. James, *Years,* 2:337.

127. Miller, pp. 232–234, 248–252.

128. Craven and Cate, 4:259–260.

129. Kenney diary, November 5, 1943, KP; Letter, Whitehead to Kenney, November 7, 1943, p. 1, Whitehead papers.

130. William F. Halsey and J. Bryan III, *Admiral Halsey's Story* (New York: McGraw-Hill Book Company, 1947), p. 183.

131. Letter, Whitehead to Kenney, November 7, 1943; Letter, Kenney to Whitehead, November 7, 1943, Whitehead papers.

132. Morton, pp. 575–577; Morison, 6:392–409.

133. Letter, Arnold to Kenney, July 5, 1943; Letter, Arnold to Kenney, August 31, 1943, KP.

134. Letter, Arnold to Kenney, October 8, 1943, KP.

135. Letter, Arnold to Kenney, October 11, 1943, p. 1, KP.

136. Ibid.

137. Stephen L. McFarland and Wesley Phillips Newton, *To Command the Sky: The Battle for Air Superiority Over Germany, 1942–1944* (Washington, D.C.: Smithsonian Institution Press, 1991), pp. 127–129.

138. Letter, Kenney to Arnold, October 21, 1943, p. 1, KP.

139. Ibid., p. 2.

140. Ibid., pp. 2–4.

141. Ibid., p. 4.

142. Letter, Arnold to Kenney, October 26, 1943, p. 1, KP.

143. Letter, Arnold to Brereton, January 19, 1944, Arnold papers, LOC.

144. January 5, 1944; Transcript, Teleconference between Kenney and Sutherland, January 6, 1944, KP; Kenney, *Reports,* pp. 342–343.

145. McFarland and Newton, p. 245.

146. Letter, Whitehead to Kenney, October 21, 1943, p. 1, file 730.322-5, HRA.

147. Letter, Whitehead to Kenney, October 18, 1943, Whitehead papers.

148. Kenney diary, November 7, 1943, KP.

149. Letter, Kenney to Whitehead, September 17, 1943, pp. 1–2, KP; Letter, Whitehead to Kenney, November 7, 1943, Whitehead papers.

150. Letter, Whitehead to Kenney, November 7, 1943, Whitehead papers.

151. Morton, pp. 514–520; Matloff, pp. 206–207; Miller, pp. 222–225.

152. Miller, pp. 272–282; Kenney, *Reports,* pp. 326–327; Morison, 6:369–370; James, *Years,* 2:341.

153. Miller, pp. 273–274; Morison, 6:383.

154. Wheeler, pp. 351–352.

155. Ibid., pp. 181–227, 295–344.

156. December 24, 25, 26, 1943, KP; Wheeler, p. 352.

157. Kenney diary, December 25, 1943, KP; Barbey, p. 119.

158. Willoughby, pp. 152–153.

159. From: Commander Task Force 76 (Commander Seventh Amphibious Force), To: The Commander in Chief U.S. Fleet, February 3, 1944, Subject: Cape Gloucester Operation, Report Upon, pp. 7–12, Barbey papers, NHC; December 26, 1943, KP.

160. Ibid., pp. 10–12.

161. Kenney diary, December 26, 1943, KP; Kenney, *Reports,* pp. 334–335.

162. Miller, pp. 293–294.

163. Kenney diary, December 26, 1943, KP.

164. Kenney diary, December 29, 1943; January 3, 1944, KP; Hayes, pp. 544–545.

165. January 15, 16, 1944, KP; Kenney, *Reports,* pp. 339–346.

166. Wesley Frank Craven and James L. Cate, eds., *The Army Air Forces in World War II,* vol. 5, *The Pacific: Matterhorn to Nagasaki, June 1944 to August 1945* (Chicago: University of Chicago Press, 1953), pp. 6–7; Kenneth P. Werrell, *Blankets of Fire: U.S. Bombers over Japan during World War II* (Washington, D.C.: Smithsonian Institution Press, 1996), pp. 56–61, 72.

167. Craven and Cate, 5:8–9.

168. Stanley L. Falk, "General Kenney, The Indirect Approach, and the B-29s," *Aerospace Historian* 27 (Fall 1981): 151. B-24 data based on figures in Craven and Cate, 4:169. Historian R. J. Overy's comparison of bomber aircraft lists the maximum bomb load of the B-24 as 8,000 pounds and the B-29 as 20,000, and their

respective ranges as 2,100 miles and 4,200 miles. R. J. Overy, *The Air War, 1939–1945* (New York: Stein and Day, 1980), p. 113. During World War II aircraft could not carry the maximum bomb load and reach the maximum range at the same time. There was a tradeoff between bombs and fuel, and a heavier bomb load restricted the distance an aircraft could fly. Conversely, the farther the target, the fewer bombs could be carried.

169. For example, letter, Kenney to Colonel Alvin Crawford, December 9, 1942, p.2, KP. Also Craven and Cate, 5:12.

170. Falk, "Indirect Approach," pp. 147–149.

171. Letter, Kenney to Arnold, December 10, 1942, p. 4, KP.

172. Letter, Kenney to Arnold, July 28, 1943, KP.

173. Letter, Arnold to Kenney, August 31, 1943, KP.

174. Craven and Cate, 5:17; Hayes, pp. 492–494.

175. Hayes, pp. 470–471.

176. Hayes, pp. 490, 498–500; Craven and Cate, 5:18–30; Matloff, pp. 377–378.

177. Letter, Kenney to Arnold, October 10, 1943, p. 6, KP.

178. Letter, Kenney to Arnold, October 29, 1943, quoted in Falk, "Indirect Approach," pp. 150–151.

179. Ibid.

180. Office of the Chief Engineer, GHQ SWPA, "Technical Memorandum 3," October 11, 1943, COE X, 101, 3.

181. Letter, Kenney to Colonel V. E. Bertrandias, October 30, 1945[sic][1943], KP; Office of the Chief Engineer, *Engineers,* 6:18.

182. Letter, Giles to Kenney, November 18, 1943, Arnold papers, LOC.

183. Ibid.

184. Colonel William L. Ritchie, Memorandum for General Kenney, "Notes on Conference in General Arnold's Office, January 14, 1944," January 15, 1944, KP.

185. Falk, "Indirect Approach," p. 153.

186. Office of the Chief Engineer, *Engineers,* 6:18–19. Although the runway was lengthened and strengthened to handle the B-29s, the isolation of Darwin caused other problems in bringing supplies to the area. The terminal where the oil was delivered, for example, was 4 miles from the field, and the pipeline used to carry fuel to the airfield was already at maximum capacity. The engineers estimated that to have enough fuel for the B-29s they would need to install another pipeline and build two large storage tanks. Kenney's version of events overstates his authority over construction matters in Australia and overlooks the construction problems. Kenney, *Reports,* pp. 341–342.

187. Letter, Kenney to Arnold, February 19, 1944, box 46, Murray Green Collection, USAF Academy Library, Special Collections Branch, USAF Academy, Colorado; Kenney diary, January 27, 1944, KP. Hayes, p. 547, provides a slightly different quote.

188. Matloff, pp. 455–457.

189. Kenney diary, January 27, 1944, KP; Letter, Kenney to Arnold, February 19, 1944, Green Collection; Kenney, *Reports,* p. 348.

190. Matloff, pp. 457–459; Craven and Cate, 4:551–552.

191. Craven and Cate, 4:552–554.

192. Hayes, p. 592; Craven and Cate, 5:28–31.

193. Miller, pp. 317–319.

194. Letter, Kenney to Whitehead. February 24, 1944; February 24, 1944, KP; Craven 4:558–559; Miller, pp. 319–321.

195. Matloff, pp. 326–333.

196. Kenney diary, February 24, 1944, KP.

197. Letter, Kenney to Whitehead, February 24, 1944, p. 2, KP.

198. Ibid.

199. Kenney diary, February 28, 1944, KP.

200. Ibid.

201. Letter, Kenney to Whitehead, February 24, 1944, KP.

202. Bleakley, pp. 115, 125.

203. Kenney diary, February 28, 1944, KP.

204. *Reports of MacArthur,* 2:244-245.

205. Spector, *Eagle,* pp. 283–284; Miller, pp. 347–350; Morison, 6:432-448.

8. *Westward to Hollandia*

Epigraph: Letter, Kenney to CinC SWPA, July 11, 1944, Subject: Application of the Reno V Plan, Phases I and II, file 730.161-3, HRA.

1. Letter, Kenney to Whitehead, March 6, 1944, p.1, Whitehead papers.

2. Robert Ross Smith, *United States Army in World War II: The Pacific: The Approach to the Philippines* (Washington, D.C.: Office of the Chief of Military History, 1953), pp. 16–18.

3. Kenney, *Reports,* p. 371.

4. Kenney diary, February 19, 1944, KP; Message, MacArthur to Sutherland, February 16, 1944, Sutherland papers, NA.

5. Kenney diary, March 11, 1944, KP; Hayes, p. 595.

6. Kenney, *Reports,* 2:263.

7. *Reports of MacArthur,* 2:248–251, 257–258.

8. Edward J. Drea, "ULTRA Intelligence and General Douglas MacArthur's Leap to Hollandia, January–April 1944," in *Intelligence and Military Operations,* ed. Michael I. Handel (London: Frank Cass, 1990), pp. 324–328; Drea, *MacArthur's ULTRA,* pp. 97–98.

9. Letter, Kenney to Whitehead, February 24, 1944, p. 2, KP.

10. Letter, Kenney to CinC SWPA, July 11, 1944, Subject: Application of the Reno V Plan, Phases I and II, file 730.161-3, HRA. Kenney voiced another complaint on August 16, 1944, KP.

11. Letter, Kenney to Arnold, November 14, 1944, p. 6, KP.

12. Letter, Kenney to Whitehead, March 6, 1944, p. 2, Whitehead papers. Kenney claimed that it was his idea to bypass Hansa Bay and invade at Hollandia; but given his trepidation about the plan, especially the reliance on the aircraft carriers, it seems unlikely that he would have proposed such a move. Kenney, *Reports,* p. 369.

13. Letter, Kenney to Whitehead, March 6, 1944, p. 3.

14. Letter, Whitehead to Kenney, "By-Passing Hansa Bay-Wewak-Tadji Areas," March 7, 1944, p. 2, file 730.161-3, HRA.

15. Ibid.; Ennis C. Whitehead, "GHQ Modified Plan 'D'," March 7, 1944, Whitehead papers; Letter, Whitehead to Kenney, March 9, 1944, pp. 1–2, KP.

16. Craven and Cate, 4:769, n. 17; Smith, *Approach*, pp. 29–32.

17. Kenney, *Reports*, p. 373.

18. Smith, *Approach*, pp. 29–32, 43; Office of the Chief Engineer, *Engineers*, 6:237.

19. Craven and Cate, 4:583–584.

20. Headquarters Advance Echelon Fifth Air Force, "Plan of operations in support of the Aitape-Hollandia Operation," April 1, 1944, in AEB SWPA, "Report Number 24, Hollandia-Aitape Campaign" May 10, 1946, file 138.8-24, HRA; Report on Tanaherah [*sic*] Bay–Humboldt Bay–Aitape Operation, May 6, 1944, pp. 1–6, Barbey papers, NHC.

21. "General Headquarters Operations Instructions Number 46," March 28, 1944, in AEB, Report 24. The actual dividing line was 141 degrees, 30 minutes east longitude.

22. Ibid.; "Headquarters Allied Air Forces Operations Instruction Number 49," March 30, 1944, in AEB, Report 24; Barbey, pp. 161–162.

23. Letter, Kenney to Whitehead, March 6, 1944, Whitehead papers.

24. "G-2 estimate with respect to an operation against Hollandia," February 14, 1944, pp. 4–5, Lander papers, MHI.

25. Kenney diary, March 23, 26, 1944, KP; Kenney, *Reports*, p. 377; James, *Years*, 2:399–402.

26. "Headquarters Allied Air Forces Operations Instructions Number 49," in AEB, Report 24.

27. Hayes, pp. 566–567.

28. Kenney diary, March 29, 1944, April 9, 10, 1944, KP; "Headquarters Allied Air Forces Operations Instructions Number 49"; Craven and Cate, 4:586.

29. Wilson, interview with Moore, p. 5; Kenney, interview with James, p. 2; "Headquarters Allied Air Forces Operations Instruction Number 49"; Headquarters Advance Echelon Fifth Air Force, "Plan of Air Operations in Support of the Aitape-Hollandia Operation," April 1, 1944, in AEB, Report 24; Smith, *Approach*, p. 26; Samuel Eliot Morison, *History of United States Naval Operations in World War II*, vol. 8, *New Guinea and the Marianas* (Boston: Little, Brown, and Company, 1953), pp. 49–51.

30. "Allied Air Force Operations Instruction Number 49."

31. Bleakley, pp. 126–128.

32. Office of the Assistant Chief of Staff, A-2, Headquarters Advanced Echelon Fifth Air Force, Memorandum to: Commanding General, March 29, 1944, KP; Air Evaluation Board, Southwest Pacific Area, "Report Number 23 Neutralization of Wewak, 11–27 March 1944," May 10, 1946, pp. 33–34, 143–144, file 138.8-23, HRA.

33. Drea, "Leap to Hollandia," pp. 333–335.

34. Letter, Kenney to Whitehead, March 10, 1944, file 730.161-3, HRA; Drea, *MacArthur's ULTRA*, p. 109.

35. Letter, Whitehead to Kenney, March 12, 1944, file 730.161-3, HRA.

36. Craven and Cate, 4:579–580; USSBS, *Fifth Air Force*, p. 14.

37. Letter, Kenney to Arnold, November 3, 1942, KP.

38. Yoshino, pp. 64–65. The older H models had a range of 430 miles.

39. Kenney, *Reports*, pp. 373–374.

40. Kenney diary, March 21, 1944, KP.

41. Bleakley, pp. 133–134.

42. Bleakley, pp. 133–135; Raynor, pp. 242; Drea, *MacArthur's ULTRA*, pp. 23, 109–112; Drea, "Leap to Hollandia," pp. 330–336.

43. Captain Komoto H., Imperial Japanese Navy, November 12, 1945, in USSBS, *Interrogations*, 1:288–290; Lieutenant Colonel Kitamori Nobuo, staff officer (Communications), Second Area Army, quoted in *Reports of MacArthur*, 2:263, n. 44.

44. AEB, Report 24, p. 31.

45. Komoto, in USSBS, *Interrogations*, 1:288–290; Craven and Cate, 4:594–595; Drea, "Leap to Hollandia," p. 336. Kenney, *Reports*, pp. 380–381. Kenney makes no mention of the signals intelligence.

46. Drea, *MacArthur's ULTRA*, p. 110; idem, "Leap to Hollandia," pp. 332, 336.

47. Bleakley, p. 134; Colonel Kaneko Rinsuka, 4th Air Army headquarters, Imperial Japanese Army, in USSBS, *Interrogations*, 2:407; Drea, "Leap to Hollandia," p. 336.

48. USSBS, *Japanese Air Power*, pp. 34–36, 42; Overy, pp. 95, 138–145.

49. AEB, Report 24, p. v; Kaneko, in USSBS, *Interrogations*, 2:406.

50. AEB, Report 24, p. v; Kaneko, in USSBS *Interrogations*, 2:406–407.

51. *Reports of MacArthur*, 2:263.

52. Willoughby, pp. 180–182; Drea, *MacArthur's ULTRA*, p. 116–118; Kenney diary, March 30, 1944, KP; Kenney, *Reports*, p. 384.

53. Kenney diary, May 8, 1943, KP; Crabb, pp. 32–33; Drea, "Leap to Hollandia," p. 331–332; Kenney, *Reports*, pp. 375, 386–387.

54. Kenney, *Reports*, p. 388. The losses vary depending on the source. AEB, Report 24, pp. 84–85, lists twenty-nine aircraft lost and fifty-five aircrew members missing or dead; Craven and Cate, 4:597, fifty-three aircrew missing or dead; Hewitt, p. 237, has the same figures as Kenney; Alcorn, *Jolly Rogers*, pp. 128–129, lists twenty-six aircraft and thirty-two crewmen lost; Yoshino, p. 69, twenty-nine aircraft and fifty-three aircrew missing or dead. All agree it was a grim episode.

55. Kenney, *Reports*, p. 388.

56. AEB, Report 24, p. 84.

57. Smith, *Approach*, p. 105.

58. *Put 'em Across: A History of the Second Engineer Special Brigade* (Harrisburg, Penn.: Telegraph Press, 1946; reprint, Washington, D.C.: Office of History, Corps of Engineers, 1988), p. 76.

59. Smith, *Approach*, p. 105.

60. RAAF War History Section, "Precis of Activities of RAAF Airfield Construction Squadrons in New Guinea and Borneo Campaigns," 1947, COE X, 75, 16.

61. Harry Rayner, *Scherger* (Canberra: Australian War Memorial, 1984), pp. 60–63, 69–76; Alan Stephens, "RAAF Operational Commanders," in *RAAF in Southwest Pacific*, pp. 36–29; Odgers, p. 206.

62. RAAF, "Precis"; Office of the Chief Engineer, *Engineers*, 6:237–238; Smith, *Approach*, p. 108.

63. RAAF, "Precis."

64. Smith, *Approach*, pp. 108–109.

65. RAAF, "Precis;" Kenney, *Reports*, pp. 391–392.

66. Office of the Chief Engineer, *Engineers*, 6:238.

67. Smith, *Approach,* pp. 53–55, 68–69.

68. Letter, Whitehead to Kenney, Subject: Hollandia Operation, April 6, 1944, file 730.161-3, HRA.

69. Kenney, *Reports,* p. 385. Kenney largely ignored Whitehead's role in this recommendation. Craven and Cate, 4:610. Admiral Barbey had similar concerns, Palo E. Coletta, "Daniel E. Barbey: Amphibious Warfare Expert," in Leary, p. 226.

70. Kenney diary, April 9, 1944, KP.

71. Ibid.

72. Kenney diary, April 9, 1944, KP; Letter, Kenney to Whitehead, April 9, 1944, file 730.161-3, HRA; Kenney, *Reports,* p. 385; Morison, 8:75.

73. *Put 'em Across,* p. 76.

74. Smith, *Approach,* p. 47; *Put 'em Across,* p. 79. Smith, *Approach,* p. 55, stated that the bad situation on the beach was "contrary to estimates." That is incorrect; there was good evidence that the beaches were bad, but Krueger decided not to change the plan. Morison, 8:75; Coletta, p. 226.

75. Smith, *Approach,* pp. 67, 76; Office of the Chief Engineer, *Engineers,* 6:225; Craven and Cate, 4:599.

76. Letter, Whitehead to Kenney, Subject: By-Passing Hansa Bay–Wewak-Tadji Areas, March 7, 1944, p. 2, file 730.161-3, HRA; Ennis C. Whitehead, "GHQ Modified Plan 'D'," March 7, 1944, Whitehead papers; Letter, Whitehead to Kenney, March 9, 1944, pp. 1–2, KP; Letter, Whitehead to Kenney, March 12, 1944, file 730.161-3, HRA; Letter, Whitehead to Kenney, April 6, 1944, Subject: Hollandia Operation, file 730.161-3, HRA.

77. Letter, Whitehead to Kenney, April 9, 1944, file 730.161-3, HRA.

78. Smith, *Approach,* p. 49.

79. Engineer Intelligence Section, Office of the Chief Engineer, GHQ SWPA, "Humboldt Bay–Hollandia–Tanahmerah Bay Areas," p. 6, March 5, 1944, file 706.6101-61A, HRA; Allied Geographical Section, SWPA, "Locality Study of Hollandia," Terrain Study Number 78, p. 23, March 6, 1944, in Eichelberger papers, Duke University, Special Collections Library, Durham, North Carolina.

80. Engineer Intelligence Section, Office of the Chief Engineer, GHQ SWPA, "Engineer Annex 78A to Allied Geographical Section Terrain Study Number 78," p. 6, April 6, 1944, RG 4, MMMA; Sturgis, "Air Power," p. 417.

81. Allied Geographical Section, "Locality Study of Hollandia," p. 23.

82. Ibid., pp. 43–44; Engineer Intelligence Section, "Humboldt Bay–Hollandia–Tanahmerah Bay Areas," pp. 7–8; Headquarters Allied Air Forces, SWPA, Operations Instructions Number 49, in AEB, Report 24; Dod, p. 527; Baldwin, p. 76.

83. Office of the Chief Engineer, *Engineers,* 6:226.

84. Dod, pp. 532, 549–550.

85. Craven and Cate, 4:607; Office of the Chief Engineer, *Engineers,* 6:230.

86. Message, Commander 310th Bomb Wing to Commander Advon 5, May 16, 1944, in Eichelberger papers; Office of the Chief Engineer, *Engineers,* 6:230.

87. Letter, Whitehead to Kenney, June 8, 1944, file 730.161-3, HRA.

88. Dod, p. 534.

89. Office of the Chief Engineer, *Engineers,* 6:232.

90. Office of the Chief Engineer, GHQ SWPA, Special Technical Memorandum Number 1, "Drainage," June 7, 1944, COE S,112, 10.

91. Reckless Task Force, "History of the Hollandia Operation," p. 19, July 1944, Eichelberger papers; Office of the Chief Engineer, *Engineers,* p. 230.

92. Smith, *Approach,* p. 67; Craven and Cate, 4:607, 609; Lowell W. Newton, "Jungle Airfields," *Air Power History* 42 (Fall 1995): 20.

93. Craven and Cate, 4:608.

94. Headquarters Allied Air Forces, SWPA, Standing Operating Procedures Instructions Number 12, "Cooperative Action of Land-Based and Carrier-Based Aircraft in Support of Landing Operations," May 9, 1944, file 706.204, HRA.

95. Drea, *MacArthur's ULTRA,* pp. 121–122.

96. "Operations Instructions Number 46."

97. None of the reports written after this operation give any indication that this contingency should have been foreseen. See, for example, "History of the Hollandia Operation"; Reckless Task Force (I Corps), "Report of the Engineer Hollandia Operation April 22–August 25, 1944," COE X, 95, 3.

98. Kenney, *Reports,* pp. 394, 404.

99. Captain Komoto H., Staff 23rd Air Flotilla, Imperial Japanese Navy, in USSBS, *Interrogation,* 2:287–288; Drea, *MacArthur's ULTRA,* p. 126.

100. Kenney, *Reports,* p. 395.

101. Kenney diary, April 9, 1944, KP; Letter, Allied Air Forces SWPA to GHQ SWPA, April 12, 1944, cited in Smith, *Approach,* p. 208.

102. Kenney, *Reports,* p. 395.

103. Craven and Cate, 4:620.

104. Kenney, *Reports,* p. 395; Drea, *MacArthur's ULTRA,* p. 128; Smith, *Approach,* pp. 206–208; James, *Years,* 2:459.

105. Kenney, *Reports,* p. 397; "The Sarmi-Wakde-Biak Operation," May–June 1944, KP.

106. "The Sarmi-Wakde-Biak Operation"; Smith, *Approach,* pp. 214–215; Craven and Cate, 4:623–624.

107. *Reports of MacArthur,* 2:276–277.

108. "The Sarmi-Wakde-Biak Operation"; *Reports of MacArthur,* 2:279-280; Craven and Cate, 4:628–629; Smith, *Approach,* p. 231.

109. *Reports of MacArthur,* 2:283; Smith, *Approach,* pp. 300–302.

110. *Reports of MacArthur,* 2:283, 285.

111. Smith, *Approach,* pp. 325, 336, 340.

112. Kenney, *Reports,* p. 402; *Reports of MacArthur,* 2:287; Smith, *Approach,* pp. 349–350; Morison, 8:118–119, 122.

113. Kenney, *Reports,* p. 404; Craven and Cate, 4:629–630, 638; Bleakley, pp. 152–154; Morison, 8:125.

114. Captain Shimanouchi Momochio, Imperial Japanese Navy, November 26, 1945, in USSBS, *Interrogations,* 2:450, 452; *Reports of MacArthur,* 2:288–289.

115. Drea, *MacArthur's ULTRA,* pp. 138–139; John Prados, *Combined Fleet Decoded: The Secret History of American Intelligence and the Japanese Navy in World War II* (New York: Random House, 1995), pp. 556–558.

116. Shimanouchi, in USSBS, *Interrogations,* 2:452; *Reports of MacArthur,* 2:289; Drea, *MacArthur's ULTRA,* pp. 139–140.

117. Craven and Cate, 4:638; James, *Years,* 2:461–462; Drea, *MacArthur's ULTRA,* p. 140.

118. Shimanouchi, in USSBS, *Interrogations,* 2:452; Commander Chihaya Masa-taka, Staff 4th Advanced Southern Fleet, Imperial Japanese Navy, October 29, 1945, in ibid., 1:201; Komoto, in ibid., 2:289; Craven and Cate, 4:638.

119. *Reports of MacArthur,* 2:291; Craven and Cate, 4:639; Morison, 8:123–124. Smith, *Approach,* pp. 354–358, states that the destroyers were towing barges and that those accounted for the one hundred troops landed. The Japanese sources do not mention the barges.

120. *Reports of MacArthur,* 2: 291–292; Smith, *Approach,* pp. 358–359.

121. Morison, 8:132.

122. Kenney, *Reports,* p. 402; Shimanouchi, in USSBS, *Interrogations,* 2:452.

123. Kenney, *Reports,* p. 402; Shimanouchi, in USSBS, *Interrogations,* 2:452; *Reports of MacArthur,* 2:289.

124. Message, Kenney to Army Air Forces headquarters, July 21, 1944, cited in "The Sarmi-Wakde-Biak Operation," May–June 1944, in KP.

125. Kenney, *Reports,* p. 403.

126. *Reports of MacArthur,* 2:296; Smith, *Approach,* p. 340.

127. Dod, p. 541; Smith, *Approach,* pp. 375, 393.

128. Office of the Chief Engineer, *Engineers,* 6:250.

129. Office of the Chief Engineer, *Engineers,* 6:250; Dod, pp. 539, 541; Smith, *Approach,* pp. 340–341.

130. Smith, *Approach,* pp. 397–448.

131. Kenney, *Reports,* p. 417; Ballard, p. 287.

132. Kenney, *Reports,* p. 417; *Reports of MacArthur,* 2:303. In this instance, Kenney's estimates of the number of aircraft destroyed are very close to the losses reported by the Japanese.

133. Kenney, *Reports,* p. 420.

134. Kenney diary, May 16, 1944, KP.

135. Kenney diary, June 11, 1944, KP; Headquarters FEAF, General Order Number 1 and Number 4, June 15, 1944, KP; Craven and Cate, 4:648.

136. Letters, Kenney to Whitehead, April 9, 1944, file 730.161-3, HRA; May 5, 1944, KP.

137. Craven and Cate, 4:647; Charles W. Boggs Jr., *Marine Aviation in the Philippines* (Washington, D.C.: Historical Division, Headquarters United States Marine Corps, 1951), pp. 1–4.

138. "Notes to discuss with General Arnold," September 24, 1942, KP; Letters, Kenney to Whitehead, October 29, 1943, p. 1; Kenney to Ritchie, April 14, 1943, p.4, KP.

139. Letter, Kenney to Commanding General, United States Army Forces Far East, October 23, 1943; Letters, Kenney to Whitehead, October 29, 1943; November 2, 1943, p.2; February 1, 1944, KP.

140. St. Clair Street, interview with Moore, p. 2; Crabb, p. 7; Herring, n.p.

9. *Return to the Philippines*

Epigraph: Letter, Kenney to Arnold, November 14, 1944, p. 7, KP.

1. Messages, JCS to MacArthur, September 13, 1944; MacArthur to JCS, Sep-

tember 14, 1944, RG4, MMMA; Letter, Kenney to Whitehead, September 16, 1944, Whitehead papers; Hayes, p. 620; Craven and Cate, 5:306–307.

2. Message, MacArthur to JCS, September 14, 1944, RG 4, MMMA.

3. Messages, MacArthur to JCS, September 15, 1944; JCS to MacArthur, September 15, 1944; RG 4, MMMA; Hayes, pp. 620–621; Matloff, pp. 512–513.

4. Drea, *MacArthur's ULTRA,* p. 158.

5. Kenney diary, September 13, 14, 15, 16, 1944, KP; Kenney, *Reports,* pp. 426–428, 431.

6. Kenney diary, September 12, 1944, KP.

7. Letter, Kenney to Whitehead, September 16, 1944, p.1, Whitehead papers.

8. Kenney, *Reports,* p. 432, for how he reconstructed his role in the decision. Kenney diary, September 14, 15, 16, 1944, KP; Letter, Kenney to Whitehead, September 16, 1944, p. 1, Whitehead papers; Headquarters Far East Air Forces, "Leyte," [1945?], p. 5, file 720.3069, HRA.

9. Letter, Kenney to CinC SWPA, July 11, 1944, Subject: Application of the Reno V Plan, Phases I and II, file 730.161-3, HRA. Kenney voiced another complaint on August 16, 1944, KP.

10. Goldstein, "Pioneer," pp. 205–208.

11. Kenney diary, September 13, 1944, KP.

12. Letter, Kenney to Arnold, September 17, 1944, p. 4, file 706.311, HRA.

13. Ibid., p. 5.

14. Letter, Kenney to Whitehead, August 1, 1944, file 730.161-3, HRA.

15. Letter, Kenney to Arnold, September 17, 1944, p. 5, file 706.311, HRA.

16. Ibid.

17. Kenney diary, September 22, 1944, KP.

18. Letter, Kenney to Whitehead, September 16, 1944, p. 2, Whitehead papers.

19. Odgers, p. 480.

20. Ibid; Netherlands Military Oil Intelligence Service, "General Description of All Installations at Balikpapan," p. 4, September 20, 1944, file 730-306.5, HRA; Letter, Kenney to Arnold, April 1, 1944, KP; United States Strategic Bombing Survey, *Oil in Japan's War* (Washington, D.C.: Government Printing Office, 1946), pp. 45–47, 49–50.

21. Letter, Kenney to Arnold, October 29, 1943, quoted in Falk, "Indirect Approach," p. 151.

22. Kenney diary, August 13, 1943, KP; Crabb, section 2, p. 8.

23. Crabb, section 2, p. 8; Craven and Cate, 4:169–170, 722, n. 26. Goldstein, "Pioneer," pp. 286, n. 47, states that 37 percent of the bombers were lost, a figure that does not match other sources.

24. Odgers, p. 120.

25. Komoto, in USSBS, *Interrogations,* 2:287.

26. I. B. Holley Jr., "An Air Force General: Laurence Sherman Kuter," *Aerospace Historian* 27 (June 1980):88-90; Haywood S. Hansell Jr., "General Laurence S. Kuter 1905–1979," *Aerospace Historian* 27 (June 1980): 91–94.

27. Kenney diary, March 28, 1944; February 19, 1945, KP. Another of the "Young Turks" Kenney mentioned was Major General Haywood Hansell, a close contemporary of Kuter. For insight into Hansell's background and beliefs, see Haywood S. Hansell Jr., *The Air Plan that Defeated Hitler* (Atlanta: Higgins-McArthur/Longino &

Porter, 1972), and idem, *The Strategic Air War against Germany and Japan: A Memoir* (Washington, D.C.: Office of Air Force History, 1986).

28. Message, Kuter to Arnold, April 2, 1944, KP.

29. Letter, Kenney to Arnold, April 1, 1944, KP.

30. Message, Kuter to Arnold, April 2, 1944.

31. Kenney diary, August 7, 13, 1944, KP; Falk, "Indirect Approach," p. 154; Craven and Cate, 7:284.

32. Kenney diary, September 12, 1944; Kenney, *Reports,* p. 426.

33. Message, Kenney to Arnold, September 8, 1944, KP.

34. Kenney diary, September 12, 1944, KP.

35. Kenney diary, September 17, 1944, KP; Kenney, *Reports,* p. 433.

36. Kenney diary, September 14, 1944, KP.

37. Kenney diary, September 12, 1944, KP; Kenney, *Reports,* p. 427; Craven and Cate, 5:316–317.

38. Thirteenth Air Force, "Attacks Against Strategic Enemy Oil Centers," [1945], file 750.424-1, HRA.

39. Craven and Cate, 5:317.

40. Thirteenth Air Force, "Attacks"; Craven and Cate, 5:318–319.

41. Thirteenth Air Force, "Attacks."

42. "Balikpapan Strikes"; Thirteenth Air Force, "Attacks"; Craven and Cate, 5:319.

43. Crabb, section 2, p. 13.

44. Letter, Commander Submarines 7th Fleet to Commander 7th Fleet, "Narrative accounts of Lifeguard duties performed by submarines of Task Force 71 off Balikpapan, Borneo, September 24 to October 24," November 23, 1944, file 706.301, HRA; Craven and Cate, 5:317.

45. Kenney diary, October 6, 1944, KP.

46. Ibid.

47. Ibid.; Kenney, *Reports,* p. 438.

48. Kenney, *Reports,* p. 437.

49. Craven and Cate, 5:320.

50. Kenney diary, October 6, 1944, KP.

51. Yoshino, pp. 81–83. For Kenney's version see Kenney *Reports,* pp. 411–415.

52. Message, Kenney to Arnold, October 15, 1944, KP. Craven and Cate, 5:320, state that the P-47s carried two fuel tanks, one of 310 gallons under one wing and a 165-gallon tank on the other wing, a configuration that would have been very unstable, especially right after takeoff. Kenney reported using two 165-gallon tanks on each wing and using a 75-gallon tank on the belly of the aircraft, a more plausible arrangement.

53. Thirteenth Air Force, "Attacks"; "Balikpapan Strikes"; Kenney, *Reports,* p. 439.

54. Thirteenth Air Force, "Attacks."

55. Kenney, *Reports,* p. 440.

56. Allied Air Force Intelligence Summary No. 247, October 29, 1944, file 706.307A, HRA.

57. Ibid.; Craven and Cate, 5:322.

58. Craven and Cate, 5:322, posited that long-distance flying experience was the "greatest gain" from these missions.

59. Stephen Peter Rosen, *Winning the Next War: Innovation and the Modern Military* (Ithaca, N.Y.: Cornell University Press, 1991), p. 145.

60. USSBS, *The War against Japanese Transportation 1941–1945* (Washington, D.C.: Government Printing Office, 1947), pp. 50, 103–104; quote from *MacArthur Reports,* 2:305; Spector, *Eagle,* p. 486.

61. USSBS, *Oil in Japan's War* (Washington, D.C.: Government Printing Office, 1946), p. 65.

62. Craven and Cate, 5:175.

63. Ibid, 5:55–57, 78, 99–100; Hansell, *Strategic Air War,* pp. 142–166.

64. USSBS, *Summary Report (Pacific War)* (Washington, D.C.: Government Printing Office, 1946), p. 29. The authoritative study of the Strategic Bombing Survey is David MacIssac, *Strategic Bombing in World War Two* (New York: Garland Publishing, 1976).

65. Falk, "Indirect Approach," p. 154, for a similar conclusion.

66. See Barton J. Bernstein, "Understanding the Bomb and the Japanese Surrender: Missed Opportunities, Little-Known Near Disasters, and Modern Memory," *Diplomatic History* 19 (Spring 1995): 251–255; Thomas B. Allen and Norman Polmar, *Code-Name Downfall* (New York: Simon & Schuster, 1995); Roy Skates, *The Invasion of Japan: Alternative to the Bomb* (Columbia: University of South Carolina Press, 1994).

On the problem of war termination in general, Fred C. Ikle, *Every War Must End* (New York: Columbia University Press, 1971); Stephen J. Cimbala, *Conflict Termination and Military Strategy: Coercion, Persuasion, and War* (Boulder: Westview Press, 1987); William T. R. Fox, ed., *Annals of the American Academy of Political and Social Science* 392 (Nov. 1970); Michael Handel, "The Study of War Termination," *The Journal of Strategic Studies* 1 (May 1978): 51–75.

67. Major General Stephen Chamberlin and Vice Admiral Forest P. Sherman, Memorandum to CinC SWPA, CinC POA, "Coordination of Operations," September 21, 1944, file 720.322, HRA; Message, Advanced Headquarters GHQ SWPA, to Commander 3rd Fleet, Allied Naval Forces, Allied Air Forces, September 30, 1944, in "Appendix 6 to Annex G Operation Plan 13-44," file 720.311, HRA (hereafter Operation Plan 13-44).

68. Commander Task Force 78 to Commander in Chief U.S. Fleet, "Leyte Operation," November 10, 1944, p. 5; Operation Plan 13-44; Allied Naval Forces, SWPA, Task Force 73 Naval Air Force and Commander Aircraft, Seventh Fleet, "Operation Plan 8-44," October 15, 1944, pp. 2–3, Archives United States Marine Corps Library, Quantico, Virginia; Boggs, pp. 12–13.

69. Commander Task Force 78, "Leyte Operation," pp. 2–3; Operation Plan 13-44; Commander Allied Air Forces, "Operations Instruction 71," September 24, 1944, p. 4, Archives, United States Marine Corps Library; Headquarters FEAF, "Leyte," p. 15, n.d. [1945], file 720.3069, HRA.

70. FEAF, p. 13–14.

71. Letter, Whitehead to Kenney, September 18, 1944, file 730.161-3, HRA; Herring, n.p.

72. Allied Air Forces, Operations Instruction 71.

73. Kenney, "Application of the Reno V Plan."

74. Office of the Chief Engineer, *Engineers,* 6:284.

75. M. Hamlin Cannon, *United States Army in World War II: The Pacific: Leyte: The Return to the Philippines* (Washington, D.C.: Office of the Chief of Military History, 1954), pp. 31–34.

76. Prados, pp. 586–590; *MacArthur Reports*, 2:307–309.

77. *MacArthur Reports*, 2:319–320, 322–325, 343, 345.

78. *MacArthur Reports*, 2:326–327.

79. Estimates of Japanese aircraft strength vary depending on the source. Major Takahashi Kohei, Air Liaison Officer, 35th Army in 10th Information and Historical Service, Headquarters Eighth Army, "Staff Study of Operations of the Japanese 35th Army on Leyte," pp. 1, 3, Eichelberger papers; Commander Yamaguchi Meriyoshi, Operations Officer Second Air Fleet, Commander First Combined Base Force, Imperial Japanese Navy, October 26, 1945, in USSBS, *Interrogations*, 1:178; *MacArthur Reports*, 2:331; Drea, *MacArthur's ULTRA*, pp. 162–163.

80. Yamaguchi, in USSBS, *Interrogations*, 1:178; *Reports of MacArthur*, 2:331–333.

81. Craven and Cate, 5:337. Aircraft strength for August 31, 1944.

82. *MacArthur Reports*, 2:326-327, 340-342, 357.

83. Drea, *MacArthur's ULTRA*, p. 155.

84. Allied Air Forces, "Operations Instruction 71," Annex 3 (Intelligence), pp. 1–4; "G-2 Estimate of the enemy situation with respect to an operation against the Leyte Gulf Area," September 30, 1944, pp. 8–10, 14, Landers papers, MHI.

85. Spector, *Eagle*, p. 426; Barbey, p. 279; Prados, pp. 603–604.

86. Kenney diary, September 13, 1944, KP.

87. Kenney diary, October 16, 1944, KP.

88. Craven and Cate, 5:353; Wheeler, p. 389.

89. Drea, *MacArthur's ULTRA*, pp. 162–163, gives slightly higher numbers than previous sources. See Takahashi, pp. 3, 10; Yamaguchi, in USSBS, *Interrogations*, p. 178; *Reports of MacArthur*, 2:363;

90. *Put 'em Across*, p. 101; Office of the Chief Engineer, *Engineers*, 6:287–289.

91. *Put 'em Across*, p. 103; Cannon, pp. 67–72; Stanley L. Falk, *Decision at Leyte* (New York: W. W. Norton and Company, 1966), p. 97. Description of the LST from Spector, *Eagle*, p. 230.

92. Brigadier General Samuel D. Sturgis Jr., "Engineer Operations in the Leyte Campaign, Part 1," *Miltary Engineer* 39 (Nov. 1947): 461.

93. Ibid.; Casey, pp. 224–226; Dod, pp. 576–577.

94. Sturgis, "Engineer Operations, Part 1," p. 462; Dod, p. 577; Cannon, p. 82; *Put 'em Across*, p. 263.

95. Sturgis, "Engineer Operations, Part 1," p. 462; Dod, p. 578.

96. Kenney, *Reports*, p. 450.

97. Kenney diary, October 23, 1944, KP; Kenney, *Reports*, pp. 450, 454.

98. Kenney diary, October 24, 1944, KP; Kenney, *Reports*, p. 455; Office of the Chief Engineer, *Engineers*, 6:290–291.

99. Kenney diary, October 23, 1944, KP.

100. Major W. G. Caples, "Airfield Construction on Leyte," *Aviation Engineer Notes* 33 (March 1945): 8–9, COE V, 25, 17; Sturgis, "Engineer Operations, Part 1" p. 462.

101. Classic accounts of the battle are Samuel Eliot Morison, *History of United States Naval Operations in World War II*, vol. 12, *Leyte* (Boston: Little, Brown and

Company, 1958), and C. Vann Woodward, *The Battle for Leyte Gulf* (New York: MacMillan Company, 1947). The most recent study is Thomas J. Cutler, *The Battle of Leyte Gulf, 23–26 October 1944* (New York: Harper Collins Publishers, 1994). A Japanese reconstruction is in *MacArthur Reports,* 2:382–401.

102. *MacArthur Reports,* 2:365–369, 384–386.

103. *MacArthur Reports,* 2:371; Drea, *MacArthur's ULTRA,* pp. 162–163.

104. *MacArthur Reports,* 2:377–378, 387, n. 71.

105. *MacArthur Reports,* 2:400, 404, n. 130, 405, n. 132, 561–563, 566, 569; Hattori Syohgo, "Kamikaze: Japan's Glorious Failure," *Air Power History* 43 (Spring 1996): 16–19.

106. Kenney diary, October 25, 1944, KP.

107. Sturgis, "Engineer Operations, Part 1" p. 463; James M. Farris, "Tacloban," *The Friends Journal,* Spring 1997, pp. 29–32.

108. Casey, pp. 231–232; Sturgis, "Engineer Operations, Part 2," p. 515.

109. Sturgis, "Engineer Operations, Part 2," p. 514.

110. Craven and Cate, 5:368–369; Wheeler, p. 403; Woodward, p. 215.

111. Message, CTF 77 [Kinkaid] to CinC SWPA, October 25, 1944, in USSBS, *Fifth Air Force,* figure 18.

112. Message, Halsey to MacArthur, October 26, 1944, quoted in Morison, 12:340–341.

113. Halsey, p. 228.

114. Kenney diary, October 25, 26, 1944, KP; Wheeler, p. 401; GHQ SWPA, "Standard Operating Procedure Instructions Number 162 Cooperative Action Land-Based and Carrier-Based Aircraft in Support of Landing Operations," September 26, 1944, p. 1, file 710.301A, HRA.

115. Kenney diary, October 26, 1944, KP.

116. Kenney diary, October 27, 1944, KP; Letter, Kenney to Arnold, December 28, 1944, Wilson papers, LOC.

117. Craven and Cate, 5:370–371; Bleakley, pp. 171–173.

118. Letter, Whitehead to Kenney, October 30, 1944, Whitehead papers. On October 31 4th Air Army had 148 planes and the 1st Combined Base Air Force (the combined headquarters for 1st and 2nd Air Flotilla) had 149, *MacArthur Reports,* 2:405, n. 131.

119. Sturgis, "Engineer Operations, Part 2," pp. 515, 517; Casey, p. 228. The 30-year mean rainfall for Leyte in November was 11.86 inches; in 1944, 20.82 inches fell. Although only 4 inches of rain fell in October, all of it was after October 24. Sturgis, "Engineer Operations, Part 2," p. 517.

120. Casey, pp. 231–232; Dod, p. 584; Brigadier General Samuel D. Sturgis Jr., "Engineer Operations in the Leyte Campaign, Part 3," *Military Engineer* 40 (Jan. 1948), p. 15.

121. 5th Air Force Engineers, "Leyte Report," pp. 8–10; AEB, Southwest Pacific, "Leyte Based Air Activity, A-Day to A plus 41," December 13, 1944, file 730.306-5, HRA; Sixth Army, p. 233; Sturgis, "Engineer Operations, Part 3," p. 17.

122. Sturgis, "Engineer Operations, Part 3," p. 18.

123. Message, Kenney to Arnold, November 24, 1944, KP; Letters, Whitehead to Kenney, November 15, 1944; November 18, 1944, file 730.161-3, HRA; Kenney,

interview with Green, p. 31; Letter, Kenney to Arnold, December 28, 1944, Wilson papers, LOC; Falk, *Decision*, p. 223.

124. USSBS, *Fifth Air Force*, p. 63; Colonel Matsumae, 4th Air Army, quoted in Morison, 12:166, n.12; Drea, *MacArthur's ULTRA*, pp. 163–164.

125. Spector, *Eagle*, p. 440. Perhaps taking advantage of literary license, Kenney claimed to witness a kamikaze attack on October 20 against the cruiser *Honolulu*. This cruiser was hit on that day and had to be withdrawn, but it was struck by a torpedo from a torpedo bomber, not a kamikaze. Although the first large-scale attacks did not occur until October 25, the HMAS *Australia* was hit by a suicide bomber on October 21. Kenney, *Reports*, p. 449; Morison, 12:145–146, 148.

126. Kenney diary, November 26, 30, 1944, KP; Boggs, pp. 29–32, 45.

127. Letter, Whitehead to Kenney, October 30, 1944, p. 1, Whitehead papers; *Reports of MacArthur*, 2:378; Drea, *MacArthur's ULTRA*, p. 163.

128. November 5, 24, 1944, KP; AEB, "Leyte," p. 2.

129. Kenney diary, October 30, 1944, November 2, 3, 1944, KP; Halsey, pp. 230, 242; Morison, 12:341–343, 345–360.

130. Halsey, p. 242.

131. For other examples, see Halsey, pp. 160, 183; E. B. Potter, *Bull Halsey* (Annapolis, Maryland: Naval Institute Press, 1985), pp. 308–310, 312.

132. *MacArthur Reports*, 2:369–370; Drea, *MacArthur's ULTRA*, p. 168.

133. *MacArthur Reports*, 2:380–381, 405; Drea, *MacArthur's ULTRA*, pp. 167–168.

134. Drea, *MacArthur's ULTRA*, pp. 175–176; Bleakley, pp. 186–187.

135. Lieutenant Commander Yatsui Noriteru, 7th Escort Convoy, Imperial Japanese Navy, October 26, 1945, in USSBS, *Interrogations*, 1:163; Craven and Cate, 5:377; *MacArthur Reports*, 2:408; Drea, *MacArthur's ULTRA*, p. 169. Kenney relied on reports by the P-38 pilots and gave more impressive results. He claimed that the attacks accounted for three ships being sunk during this period, Kenney, *Reports*, pp. 473–474.

136. Kenney, *Reports*, p. 473; AEB, "Leyte," p. 2; Sixth Army, "Report of the Leyte Operation," p. 43, COE X, 54, 6; Drea, *MacArthur's ULTRA*, pp. 174–178.

137. Kenney diary, November 10, 1944, KP.

138. Yatsui, in USSBS, *Interrogations*, 1:163; Kenney diary, November 11, 1944, KP. In his memoir Kenney stressed the weather considerations, not the distance from the airfields to the targets, as the reason Halsey hit the convoy. Kenney, *Reports*, p. 476.

139. 10th Information and Historical Service, p. 9; Cannon, p. 26. The numbers for how many troops landed vary. The official histories all use 45,000, Craven and Cate, 5:377; Cannon, p. 102; Morison, 12:351. Drea, *MacArthur's ULTRA*, p. 178, states that 38,000 left for Leyte, but 3,250 were lost en route, likewise Falk, *Decision*, p. 224, uses 35,000.

140. *MacArthur Reports*, 2:408; Sixth Army, p. 41, quoted in Drea, *MacArthur's ULTRA*, p. 169.

141. Krueger, pp. 194–195; Spector, *Eagle*, pp. 511, 517; Stanley L. Falk, "Douglas MacArthur and the War Against Japan," in Leary, p. 17; Weinberg, p. 849.

142. Carol Morris Petillo, *Douglas MacArthur, The Philippine Years* (Bloomington, Ind.: Indiana University Press, 1981), pp. 68–69; Colonel Ray T. Elsmore, "Report on Philippine Island Airfields," February 2, 1942, file 730.934-1, HRA; Allied Geo-

graphical Section, GHQ SWPA, "Terrain Study Number 84 Leyte Province," August 17, 1944, p. 51, Willoughby papers, MHI.

143. "Terrain Study 84," p. 51; Allied Geographical Section, GHQ SWPA, "Special Report Number 55, Airfields, Landing Beaches, and Roads, Samar, Leyte, and Dinagat Groups," July 10, 1944, file 706.610H-55, HRA; idem, "Terrain Handbook 34, Tacloban" (Philippine Series), September 25, 1944, Sutherland papers, box 25, NA.

144. Office of the Chief Engineer, *Engineers*, 3:93, n. 16; 6:286.

145. Ibid., p. 97.

146. Ind, p. 115–241, for the activities of agents in the Philippines. *MacArthur Reports*, 2: 311–312.

147. Fifth Air Force Aviation Engineers, "Leyte Report," p. 2, file 730.935-6, HRA.

148. Sturgis, "Engineer Operations, Part 3," p. 19; Canon, pp. 35–37; Leary, p. 72.

149. Spector, *Eagle*, pp. 513–514.

150. Drea, *MacArthur's ULTRA*, pp. 169–172; Cannon, pp. 209–210.

151. William M. Leary, "Walter Krueger, MacArthur's Fighting General," in Leary, p. 74; Drea, *MacArthur's ULTRA*, p. 171; Falk, *Decision*, pp. 244–246.

152. Kenney diary, November 30, 1944, KP; Craven and Cate, 5:384; Boggs, p. 32.

153. Letter, Kenney to Arnold, November 14, 1944, KP.

154. Letter, Barbey to Admiral Jacobs, quoted in Barbey, p. 279.

155. For differences in ground fighting, see Weinberg, p. 647. A thorough accounting of ground combat during the fighting in New Guinea is in Eric Bergerund, *Touched With Fire: The Land War in the South Pacific* (New York: Viking, 1996).

156. Letter, Kenney to Arnold, October 24, 1942, quoted in Craven and Cate, 4:119.

157. USSBS, *Japanese Air Power*, p. 17; Prados, p. 602.

158. Sturgis, "Engineer Operations, Part 2," p. 514; Office of the Chief Engineer, *Engineers*, 6:291.

159. *Put 'em Across*, p. 109; Office of the Chief Engineer, *Engineers*, 6:283–287; Casey, pp. 224–226.

160. Sixth Army, p. 43; Casey, p. 228; Office of the Chief Engineer, *Engineers*, 3:142.

161. Barbey, p. 279; Luvaas, *Dear Miss Em*, pp. 166–167.

162. Letter, Kenney to Arnold, November 14, 1944, p. 4, KP.

163. GHQ SWPA, Operations Instructions Number 70, September 21, 1944, reprinted in Cannon, appendix A.

164. Boggs, p. 32.

165. Morison, 12:190–191.

166. Goldstein, "Pioneer," pp. 221–223.

167. Craven and Cate, 5:366–368; Morison, 12:238–239, 311.

168. Commander Central Philippines Attack Force (Commander Task Force 77, Commander Seventh Fleet), to Commander-in-Chief, United States Fleet, "Report of Operation for the Capture of Leyte Island and Action Report of Engagements in Surigao Strait and off Samar Island on October 25, 1944 (King Two Operation)," January 31, 1945, p. 55, Kinkaid papers, box 8, NHC.

169. Letter, John S. McCain to Kinkaid, November 27, 1944, Kinkaid papers, box 17, NHC.

170. Ibid.

171. Kenney diary, November 27, 28, 1944, KP; Morison, 12:366.
172. Morison, 12:367.
173. Kenney diary, November 29, 30, 1944, KP.
174. *MacArthur Reports*, 2:418; USSBS, *Fifth Air Force*, p. 63.
175. Kenney diary, November 30, 1944, KP.
176. Letter, Commander Allied Naval Forces SWPA, to Commander Allied Air Forces SWPA, "Information Concerning air attacks on surface ships in Leyte Gulf," November 27 and 29, 1944, December 9, 1944, Kinkaid papers, box 8, NHC.
177. Falk, *Decision*, pp. 271–285.
178. Cannon, pp. 275–293; USSBS, *Fifth Air Force*, p. 63.
179. Letter, Kenney to Arnold, November 14, 1944, p. 1, KP.
180. Ibid.
181. Ibid., p. 6.
182. Ibid., p. 7.

10. Luzon and Beyond

Epigraph: Kenney diary, October 29, 1944, KP.
1. Kenney diary, October 29, 1944. Also Letter, Kenney to Arnold, November 14, 1944, KP; Letter, Kenney to Arnold, December 28, 1944, Wilson papers, LOC.
2. Kenney diary, October 29, 1944, KP.
3. Kenney diary, November 2, 1944, KP.
4. Ibid.
5. Kenney diary, November 10, 1944, KP. Kenney almost totally ignores the discussions about plans for the invasions after Leyte in his book; see Kenney, *Reports*, ch. 22.
6. Robert Ross Smith, *United States Army in World War II: The Pacific: Triumph in the Philippines* (Washington, D.C.: Office of the Chief of Military History, 1963), pp. 23–25.
7. Letter, Whitehead to Kenney, November 18, 1944, p. 2, Whitehead papers.
8. Wheeler, pp. 408–409.
9. Kenney diary, November 24, 1944, KP.
10. Kenney diary, November 26, 1944, KP.
11. Kenney diary, November 26, 1944, KP; Wheeler, p. 410.
12. Wheeler, pp. 410–411.
13. Morison, 12:366-367.
14. Kenney diary, November 29, 30, 1944, KP.
15. Kenney diary, November 30, 1944, KP.
16. Wheeler, pp. 412–413; Kenney diary, November 30, 1944, KP; Craven and Cate, 5:395; Morison, 12:6–9; Smith, *Triumph*, p. 25.
17. Office of the Chief Engineer, *Engineers*, 6:303.
18. Kenney diary, November 18, 1944, KP; Craven and Cate, 5:393–394; Morison, 12:21–22.
19. *Reports of MacArthur*, 2:441–442; Morison, 12:14–15.
20. USSBS, *Fifth Air Force*, p. 63.
21. *Reports of MacArthur*, 2:434; Craven and Cate, 5:394; Morison, 12:21.

22. Kenney diary, December 14, 15, 1944, KP; Craven and Cate, 5:396; Smith, *Triumph,* p. 46.

23. *Reports of MacArthur,* 2:443–444; Craven and Cate, 5:397; Smith, *Triumph,* pp. 47–48.

24. *Reports of MacArthur,* 2:449, n. 46.

25. Smith, *Triumph,* pp. 48–49; Office of the Chief Engineer, *Engineers,* 6:315–316.

26. Letter, Kenney to Arnold, December 28, 1944, KP.

27. Office of the Chief Engineer, *Engineers,* 6:314.

28. Letter, Kenney to Arnold, December 28, 1944, KP; Kenney, *Reports,* p. 521.

29. Kenney, *Reports,* p. 497; Smith, *Triumph,* pp. 48–49; Office of the Chief Engineer, *Engineers,* 6:315–316.

30. Prados, pp. 695–695; Craven and Cate, 5:399; *Reports of MacArthur,* 2:449; Morison, 13:37–43; Smith, *Triumph,* pp. 49–51. Morison reports that the destroyer was actually sunk by a torpedo from a PT boat, but it had already been heavily damaged by the air attacks. Kenney, *Reports,* p. 499.

31. Smith, *Triumph,* pp. 51–52.

32. Smith, *Triumph,* p. 52.

33. Kenney diary, January 1, 1945, KP.

34. Message, Kenney to Arnold, December 22, 1944, RG 4, MMMA.

35. Clyde D. Eddleman, "The Lingayen Operation," lecture presented at the Army and Navy Staff College, Washington, D.C., February 4, 1946, Eddleman papers, MHI; Craven and Cate, 5:402–403, 405.

36. Spector, *Eagle,* pp. 518–519; Smith, *Triumph,* pp. 94–95; *Reports of MacArthur,* 2:450.

37. Spector, *Eagle,* p. 519; Smith, *Triumph,* pp. 58–59, 95–97.

38. Kenney diary, November 25, 1944, KP.

39. Kenney diary, November 25, 1944, KP; G-3, GHQ SWPA, Conference Report, Subject: Coordination of Operations, November 5, 1944, Chamberlin papers, MHI; USSBS, *Fifth Air Force,* pp. 36–37; Smith, *Triumph,* pp. 34–38. Kenney thought he had been assured that one of his officers would control air operations over the invasion area, but his proposal was never incorporated into the operational directive. Kenney diary, November 18, 1944, KP.

40. Office of the Chief Engineer, *Engineers,* 6:325.

41. Kenney diary, December 19, 1944, KP; Dod, p. 599.

42. *Reports of MacArthur,* 2:463, n. 75; Morison, 13:98–106; Craven and Cate, 5:409; Smith, *Triumph,* p. 59.

43. Morison, 13:104–106; Craven and Cate, 5:409; Smith, *Triumph,* pp. 60–61.

44. *Reports of MacArthur,* 2:465, n. 79.

45. Craven and Cate, 5:411–412; Morison, 13:106–107; Kenney, *Reports,* p. 501.

46. Smith, *Triumph,* p. 678.

47. *Reports of MacArthur,* 2:466, n. 86, gives January 9 as the date of the last mission. Morison, 13:152, uses January 13.

48. Headquarters Allied Air Forces, SWPA, Intelligence Summary Number 254, January 13, 1945, in Air Evaluation Board, "Southwest Pacific Area, Luzon Campaign Exhibits," p. 22, file 168.7103-59, HRA.

49. Hattori, p. 18.

50. The exact figures for total missions and ships sunk vary considerably. Hattori states that the Japanese army flew 338 missions. His article has no figure for the total number of Japanese navy missions, but he claims they lost 285 on kamikaze missions. *Reports of MacArthur*, 2:569-572, based on Japanese sources, used 400 missions for the Japanese army and 436 for the Japanese navy. The USSBS report, which used many of the same sources, used 650 for the total kamikaze missions and 19 ships sunk, USSBS, *Japanese Air Power*, p. 64. Smith, *Triumph*, p. 66, listed 24 ships sunk. I have relied on Hattori because it is the most recent data and he is a Japanese historian who had access to the extant records as well as to previous research.

51. For overall accuracy problems, see McFarland, pp. 192–194, 284–285, n. 3. Accuracy for the kamikaze missions was computed using 638 missions and 174 hits/damaging near misses, for a 27 percent effective rate. USSBS, *Japanese Air Power*, p. 76, arrived at approximately the same percentage, but used slightly different figures.

52. Kenney, *Reports*, p. 469.

53. Ibid., p. 509.

54. Hattori, p. 17.

55. For a detailed description see Smith, *Triumph*, Chapter 4.

56. Office of the Chief Engineer, *Engineers*, 6:342–343; Craven and Cate, 5:417–418; Boggs, p. 65.

57. Letter, Colonel David W. Hutchinson, 308 Bomb Wing Commander, to Commanding Officer First Marine Air Wing, Subject: Commendation for Colonel Jerome, March 28, 1945, Clayton C. Jerome Papers, United States Marine Corps Historical Center, Washington, D.C.; Office of the Chief Engineer, *Engineers*, 6:342–343; Craven and Cate, 5:418; Boggs, pp. 56–60, 68–73.

58. Krueger, p. 214.

59. Smith, *Triumph*, pp. 129–131.

60. Letter, Whitehead to Kenney, Subject: Percentage of Effort in Support of Ground Troops, March 24, 1945, KP. 24,373 of the 26,250 fighter and bomber sorties were spent on ground support mission; Boggs, 97–98; Craven and Cate, 5:441; Krueger, p. 217.

61. Smith, *Triumph*, pp. 211–213; Spector, *Eagle*, p. 521.

62. Krueger, p. 241; Boggs, pp. 74–80; Smith, *Triumph*, pp. 235–236.

63. Message, Kenney to Whitehead, January 31, 1945, KP. Smith, *Triumph*, pp. 235–236.

64. Message, Kenney to Krueger, February 5, 1945, KP; Craven and Cate, 5:442.

65. Kenney diary, February 5, 1945, KP; Craven and Cate, 5:442.

66. Spector, *Eagle*, p. 526-527.

67. Kenney diary, February 18, 1945, KP.

68. Letter, Paul B. Wurtsmith, Commanding General 13th Air Force, to Commanding General 1st Marine Air Wing, Subject: Statement of Service—Colonel Clayton C. Jerome, August 8, 1945, Jerome papers; Craven and Cate, 5:450–452, 457, 461–462; Boggs, pp. 108–117, 119–135. For details on the various operations, see Smith, *Triumph*, chs. 30–33.

69. Kenney diary, February 17, 18, 21, March 2,6, 1945, KP.

70. Kenney diary, February 8, 23, 1945, KP.

71. Kenney diary, January 27, 1944, KP; Letter, Kenney to Arnold, February 19, 1944, pp. 1–2, 4, box 46, Green Collection; Hayes, p. 547.

72. Quote in Letter, Hansell to Major James M. Boyle, December 1964, file 168.7004–64, HRA, quoted in Grynkewich, p. 63; Letter, Kenney to Arnold, February 19, 1944, p. 4, box 46, Green Collection.

73. General Frederic H. Smith, interview with Murray Green, Washington, D.C., April 24, 1970, p. 11, Green Collection.

74. "Notes to discuss with General Arnold," September 1942; Message, Kenney to Arnold, December 25, 1942, KP.

75. Kenney diary, February 19, 1945, KP.

76. Weinberg, p. 919.

77. Major General John H. McCormick, interview with Murray Green, San Antonio, Texas, May 3, 1970, pp. 12–13, box 71, Green Collection.

78. Message, Kenney to Arnold, March 6, 1944, KP.

79. Kenney, *Reports,* p. 365.

80. Kenney diary, March 17, 1945, KP.

81. For reasons that remain unexplained, a minority of pilots account for a large share of the aircraft shot down. Historically about 5 percent of fighter pilots account for about half of the enemy aircraft shot down, making them extremely valuable combat assets. See Mike Spick, *The Ace Factor* (Annapolis, Md.: Naval Institute Press, 1988).

82. Letter, Arnold to Kenney, March 21, 1944, Arnold papers, LOC, quoted in Grynkewich, p. 34; Perret, pp. 388–389.

83. Letter, Arnold to Kenney, October 19, 1944, Arnold papers, LOC. In his memoir Kenney downplayed Arnold's concern. Kenney, *Reports,* p. 470.

84. Kenney, *Reports,* pp. 495–496, 498. Ironically, Bong was killed on August 6, 1945, test flying a new American jet fighter, the P-80. Kenney, *Reports,* p. 569.

85. Kenney, interview with James, p. 25.

86. Kenney, interview with Hasdorff, p. 54.

87. Kenney, interview with Hasdorff, p. 57.

88. Kenney diary, March 15, 16, 1945, KP.

89. Kenney diary, March 15, 1945, KP.

90. Kenney diary, March 16, 20, 1945, KP.

91. USSBS, *Air Campaigns of the Pacific War, Japanese Air Power* (Washington, D.C.: Government Printing Office, 1946), pp. 69–71; Edward J. Drea, *MacArthur's Ultra: Codebreaking and the War Against Japan, 1942–1945* (Lawrence: University Press of Kansas, 1992), pp. 211–212: Thomas B. Allen and Norman Polmar, *Code- Name Downfall: The Secret Plan to Invade Japan and Why Truman Dropped the Bomb* (New York: Simon & Schuster, 1995), pp. 226–227; John Ray Skates, *The Invasion of Japan: Alternative to the Bomb* (Columbia: University of South Carolina Press, 1994), p. 109.

92. Kenney diary, March 17, 1945, KP.

93. Kenney diary, March 16, 17, 20, 1945, KP; Craven and Cate, 7:332; William T. Y'Blood, "Unwanted and Unloved: The Consolidated B-32," *Air Power History* 42 (Fall 1995): 60–61, 64–65.

94. Kenney diary, March 20, 1945, KP.

95. Ibid.

96. Message, MacArthur to Marshall, January 17, 1945, RG 4, MMMA; Messages, MacArthur to Kenney, January 18, 1945, March 29, 1945, KP.

97. Kenney diary, January 17, 18, 22, 1945, KP; Craven and Cate, 5:473–474, 476–477.

98. Craven and Cate, 5:445–447.

99. Spector, *Eagle,* pp. 532–540.

100. Hattori, p. 20; USSBS, *Japanese Air Power,* pp. 23, 65–68; Spector, *Eagle,* p. 536.

101. Hattori, p. 20; USSBS, *Japanese Air Power,* pp. 23, 66.

102. Quoted in Spector, *Eagle,* p. 539; also Allen and Polmar, pp. 98–106.

103. Craven and Cate, 5:483–484.

104. Halsey, p. 253; Spector, *Eagle,* p. 539.

105. USSBS, *Japanese Air Power,* p. 38; Craven and Cate, 5:479–480.

106. USSBS, *Japanese Air Power,* pp. 23, 38; Craven and Cate, 5:479.

107. Spector, *Eagle,* pp. 541–542; Craven and Cate, 5:686.

108. Allen and Polmar, pp. 137–138; Skates, pp. 57–58.

109. Kenney diary, April 11, 13, 14, 15, 1945; Advanced Headquarters of the Commander in Chief, United States Fleet and Pacific Ocean Areas, Memorandum for Commanders in Chief, Army Forces in the Pacific and U.S. Pacific Fleet, April 15, 1945, KP; Allen and Polmar, pp. 138–139; Skates, pp. 154–155.

110. Kenney diary, April 11, 1945, KP.

111. Kenney diary, May 15, 16, 17, 25, 26, 31, June 1, 1945, KP; Dod, pp. 657–660.

112. Letter, Kenney to Arnold, February 19, 1944, p. 3, Green Collection.

113. Ibid.

114. Letter, Whitehead to Kenney, April 8, 1945, file 730.161-3, HRA; Kenney diary, June 17, 1945, KP.

115. Letter, Whitehead to Kenney, April 8, 1945; Letter, Headquarters Fifth Air Force to Commanding General Far East Air Forces, Subject: Air Plan for Operation Olympic, June 26, 1945, file 730.322-3, HRA; Skates, pp. 175–176.

116. Kenney diary, June 17, 1945, KP.

117. Kenney, *Reports,* p. 545.

118. Kenney diary, June 10, 16, 17, 1945; Craven and Cate, 5:684–688.

119. Kenney diary, July 5, 1945, KP; Letter, Brigadier General Richard C. Lindsay to Norstad, August 6, 1945, quoted in Craven and Cate, 5:701.

120. Kenney diary, July 5, 1945, KP.

121. Kenney diary, June 2, 1945, quote from July 5, 1945, KP.

122. Ibid.

123. Ibid.

124. Memo for Record: Staff Conference by Representatives of CINCAFPAC-CINCPAC-COMGENUSASTAF, August 1, 1945, Subject: Coordination of Air Operations Prior to and during the conduct of Olympic, August 1, 1945; General Coordination of Air Forces, Maps, Air Plan for Operation OLYMPIC, Chamberlin papers, MHI.

125. Ibid.

126. Craven and Cate, 5:693–695.

127. Drea, *MacArthur's ULTRA,* pp. 211–212; Allen and Polmar, pp. 226–227; Skates, p. 109.

128. Drea, *MacArthur's ULTRA,* pp. 215–217.

129. For discussion of the failure to go after railroads and roads, see USSBS, pp. 10–11; Craven and Cate, 5:699; Skates, pp. 141–142. A postwar study about the potential of the kamikaze planes is mentioned in Weinberg, p. 883.

130. Kenney diary, July 5, 1945, August 2, 1945; Kenney, *Reports,* p. 568.

131. Messages, COMGENUSASTAF [Spaatz] to COMGENUSAFPAC [MacArthur], August 2, 1945, August 4, 1945, box 61, Sutherland papers, NA.

132. Kenney, *Reports,* pp. 570–571; Craven and Cate, 5:699; Y'Blood, pp. 67–69.

11. Conclusion

Epigraph: Message, Arnold to Kenney, August 19, 1945, KP.

1. Kenney, "Modern Warfare," pp. 17–18.

2. Letter, Kenney to Arnold, October 21, 1943, p.1, KP.

3. Ibid., p. 4.

4. "Notes to discuss with General Arnold," September 24, 1942; Kenney diary, December 16, 1942, KP; Letter, Kenney to Arnold, October 24, 1942, quoted in Craven and Cate, 4:119.

5. Letter, Arnold to Kenney, September 23, 1943, p. 1, KP.

6. Kenney, interview with James, p. 3.

7. MacArthur's adherence to Kenney's advice closely parallels MacArthur's use of ULTRA. According to Edward Drea, "MacArthur consistently dismissed ULTRA evidence that failed to accord with his preconceived strategic vision." Drea, *MacArthur's ULTRA,* p. 230.

8. Kenney diary, January 27, 1944, KP; Letter, Kenney to Arnold, February 19, 1944, pp. 1–2, 4, box 46, Green Collection.

9. Drea, *MacArthur's ULTRA,* p. 231.

10. USSBS, *Fifth Air Force,* pp. 11, 13–14.

11. Prados, pp. 73, 387–390, 592–594, 734; Weinberg, pp. 551–553.

12. USSBS, *Japanese Air Power,* pp. 14–15, 18–19; Prados, p. 339.

13. Kenney, interview with Hasdorff, pp. 55–56.

BIBLIOGRAPHY

Manuscript Collections

Center for Air Force History, Washington, D.C.: General Kenney's wartime papers are located at the Center for Air Force History, Bolling Air Force, Washington, D.C. The papers are held in eleven binders and consist of a daily record of activities from December 8, 1941, until September 3, 1945, that formed the basis for his book *General Kenney Reports*. The notebooks were apparently prepared by General Kenney sometime after the war, probably in 1945 and 1946, but are based on notes he made during the war. Because some of the entries and comments were obviously made after the fact the notebooks must be used with care. This collection also contains correspondence and reports complied during the war.

Duke University Special Collections Library, Durham, North Carolina: Papers of Robert L. Eichelberger; John J. McSwain.

Library of Congress, Washington, D.C.: Papers of H. H. Arnold; Frank M. Andrews; Muir S. Fairchild; Hugh J. Kneer; Donald Wilson.

MacArthur Memorial Museum and Archives, Norfolk, Virginia: Records of Headquarters, U.S. Army Forces in the Far East, 1941–1942; Records of Headquarters, Southwest Pacific Area, 1942–1945; Records of General Headquarters, U.S. Army Forces Pacific, 1942–1945; D. Clayton James Collection; Douglas MacArthur's Private Correspondence; Richard J. Marshall Papers; Charles A. Willoughby Papers.

National Archives, Washington, D.C.: RG 200 (Richard K. Sutherland Papers); RG 18 (Army Air Forces Headquarters).

Naval Historical Center, Navy Yard, Washington, D.C.: Vice Admiral Daniel Barbey Papers; Vice Admiral Carpender Papers; Admiral Thomas C. Kincaid Papers; 7th Fleet Records.

United States Air Force Academy Library, Special Collections Branch, United States Air Force Academy, Colorado: Murray Green Collection; Emmett O'Donnell Jr. Papers.

United States Air Force Historical Research Agency, Maxwell AFB, Montgomery, Alabama: Records of Headquarters Allied Air Force, Southwest Pacific Area; Records of Air Corps Tactical School; Records of Far East Air Forces Headquarters; Records of Fifth Air Force Headquarters; Records of General Headquarters Air Force; George C. Kenney Papers—This collection primarily contains Kenney's papers for the period after World War II. There is material from the war scattered throughout the collection, mostly unit histories presented to Kenney as gifts.

United States Army Corps of Engineers, History Division, Fort Belvoir, Virginia: Office of the Chief Engineer, General Headquarters, Southwest Pacific Area; Hugh J. Casey Papers; Samuel D. Sturgis Papers.

United States Army Military History Institute, Carlisle, Pennsylvania: Curricular Archives of the U.S. Army War College; Andrew D. Bruce Papers; Steven J. Chamberlin Papers and oral history; John B. Coulter Papers; George H. Decker Papers; Clyde D. Eddleman Papers; Millard F. Harmon Papers; William W. Jenna Papers; Quintin S. Landers Papers; Richard J. Marshall Papers; Truman and Katherine Smith Papers; Lester J. Whitlock Papers; Charles A. Willoughby Papers; Senior Officer Debriefing Program—Conversations between General George H. Decker and Lieutenant Colonel Dan H. Ralls; Senior Officer Debriefing Program—Conversations between General Clyde D. Eddleman and Lieutenant Colonels L. G. Smith and Murray G. Swindler.
United States Marine Corps Historical Center, Washington, D.C.: Clayton A. Jerome Papers.

Unpublished Sources

Angella, Salvatore A. "A Prototype JFACC: General George C. Kenney." Thesis, School of Advanced Airpower Studies, Maxwell Air Force Base, Ala., 1994.
Claussen, Martin P. "Material Research and Development in the Army Air Arm 1914–1945." Headquarters Army Air Forces Historical Office, Army Air Forces Historical Study Number 50, November 1946.
Crabb, J. V. "Fifth Air Force Air War Against Japan, September 1942–August 1945." Manuscript, February 4, 1946. Air University Library.
Dexter, H. P. "Report on Air Support in Southwest Pacific Area During the Period 1 November 1943 to 1 February 1944," April 10, 1944. File 706.4501, HRA.
Goldstein, Donald M. "Ennis C. Whitehead, Aerospace Commander and Pioneer." Ph.D. dissertation, University of Denver, 1970.
Grynkewich, Alexus Gregory. "'Advisable in the National Interest?' The Relief of General George C. Kenney." Thesis, University of Georgia, 1994.
Headquarters Army Air Forces, Office of Statistical Control. "Army Air Forces Statistical Digest of World War II." December 1945. Air University Library.
Kenney, George C. "The Proper Composition of the Air Force." Paper. Army War College, April 29, 1933. File 248.211-62K, HRA.
Kenney, Roland W. "General George C. Kenney, USAF." Manuscript. Copy in author's possession.
———. "The Kenney Family Tree." Farmington, Conn., 1973. Allen County Public Library, Fort Wayne, Indiana.
Kuter, Laurence S. "Growth of Air Power." Manuscript. USAF Academy Library Special Collections Branch.
Watson, Richard L. "Air Action in the Papuan Campaign 21 July 1942 to 23 January 1943." Army Air Forces Historical Studies no. 17, Assistant Chief of Air Staff, Intelligence, Historical Division, August 1944. Center for Air Force History.
Williams, Kathleen. "The AAF in Australia to the Summer of 1942." Army Air Forces Historical Studies no. 9, Assistant Chief of Air Staff, Intelligence, Historical Division, July 1944. Center for Air Force History.

Published Sources—Books

Alcorn, John S. *The Jolly Rogers: History of the 90th Bomb Group during World War II.* Temple City, Calif.: Historical Aviation Album, 1981.

Allen, Thomas B., and Norman Polmar. *Code-Name Downfall: The Secret Plan to Invade Japan and Why Truman Dropped the Bomb.* New York: Simon & Schuster, 1995.

Anders, Curt. *Fighting Airmen.* New York: G.P. Putnam's Sons, 1966.

Archibald, Norman. *Heaven High, Hell Deep, 1917–1918.* New York: Albert & Charles Boni, 1935; reprint, New York: Arno Press, 1980.

Arnold, H. H. *Global Mission.* New York: Harper & Brothers, 1949.

Baker, Nicola. *More Than Little Heroes: Australian Army Air Liaison Officers in the Second World War.* Canberra Papers on Strategy and Defence no. 106. Canberra: Strategic and Defence Studies Centre, 1994.

Ball, Harry P. *Of Responsible Command: A History of the U.S. Army War College.* Carlisle Barracks, Penn.: Alumni Association of the Army War College, 1983.

Ballard, Geoffrey. *On ULTRA Active Service.* Richmond, Australia: Spectrum Publications, 1991.

Barbey, Daniel E. *MacArthur's Amphibious Navy.* Annapolis, Md.: United States Naval Institute, 1969.

Bartsch, William H. *Doomed At the Start: American Pursuit Pilots in the Philippines, 1941–1942.* College Station: Texas A&M University Press, 1992.

Bergerud, Eric. *Touched with Fire: The Land War in the South Pacific.* New York: Viking, 1996.

Beverley, George H. *Pioneer in the U.S. Air Corps: The Memoirs of Brigadier General George H. Beverley.* Manhattan, Kans.: Sunflower University Press, 1982.

Bidwell, Shelford, and Graham Dominick. *Fire-Power: British Army Weapons and Theories of War 1904–1945.* London: George Allen & Unwin, 1985.

Bingham, Hiram. *An Explorer in the Air Service.* New Haven, Conn.: Yale University Press, 1920.

Birdsall, Steve. *Flying Buccaneers: The Illustrated History of Kenney's Fifth Air Force.* Garden City, N.Y.: Doubleday and Company, 1977.

Bland, Larry I., ed. *The Papers of George Catlett Marshall.* 3 vols. to date. Baltimore: Johns Hopkins University Press, 1991– .

Bleakley, Jack. *The Eavesdroppers.* Canberra: Australian Government Publishing Service, 1991.

Boggs, Charles W. Jr. *Marine Aviation in the Philippines.* Washington, D.C.: Historical Division, Headquarters United States Marine Corps, 1951.

Boothe, Clare. *Europe in the Spring.* New York: Alfred A. Knopf, 1941.

Brebner, John Bartlett. *The Neutral Yankees of Nova Scotia.* New York: Columbia University Press, 1937.

Brereton, Lewis H. *The Brereton Diaries.* New York: William Morrow and Company, 1946.

Brown, Jerold E. *Where Eagles Land: Planning and Development of U.S. Army Airfields, 1910–1941.* Westport, Conn.: Greenwood Press, 1990.

Brownstein, Herbert S. *The Swoose: Odyssey of a B-17*. Washington, D.C.: Smithsonian Institution Press, 1993.

Byrd, Martha. *Kenneth N. Walker: Air Power's Untempered Crusader*. Maxwell Air Force Base, Ala.: Air University Press, 1997.

Caidin, Martin. *The Ragged, Rugged Warriors*. New York: E. P. Dutton and Co., 1966.

Cannon, M. Hamlin. *United States Army in World War II: The Pacific: Leyte: The Return to the Philippines*. Washington, D.C.: Office of the Chief of Military History, 1954.

Caro, Robert A. *The Years of Lyndon Johnson*. Vol. 2: *Means of Ascent*. New York: Alfred A. Knopf, 1990.

Casey, Hugh J. *Engineer Memoirs Major General Hugh J. Casey, U.S. Army*. Washington, D.C.: U.S. Army Corps of Engineers, 1993.

Chandler, Alfred D. Jr. *The Papers of Dwight David Eisenhower: The War Years II*. Baltimore, Md.: Johns Hopkins Press, 1970.

Chwialkowski, Paul. *In Caesar's Shadow: The Life of General Robert Eichelberger*. Westport, Conn.: Greenwood Press, 1993.

Cimbala, Stephen J. *Conflict Termination and Military Strategy: Coercion, Persuasion, and War*. Boulder: Westview Press, 1987.

Clausewitz, Carl von. *On War*. Ed. trans. Michael Howard and Peter Paret. Princeton: Princeton University Press, 1976.

Clendenen, Clarence C. *Blood on the Border: The United States Army and the Mexican Irregulars*. New York: Macmillan Company, 1969.

Coffey, Thomas M. *Hap: The Story of the U.S. Army Air Force and the Man Who Built It, General Henry H. "Hap" Arnold*. New York: Viking Press, 1982.

Coffman, Edward M. *The War to End All Wars: The American Military Experience in World War I*. New York: Oxford University Press, 1968; reprint, Madison: University of Wisconsin Press, 1986.

Coll, Blanche D., Jean E. Keith, and Herbert H. Rosenthal. *United States Army in World War II: The Corps of Engineers: Troops and Equipment*. Washington, D.C.: Office of the Chief of Military History, 1958.

Cook, Haruko Taya, and Theodore F. Cook. *Japan at War: An Oral History*. New York: New Press, 1992.

Cooling, Benjamin Franklin, ed. *Case Studies in the Development of Close Air Support*. Washington, D.C.: Office of Air Force History, 1990.

Copp, DeWitt S. *A Few Great Captains*. Garden City, N.Y.: Doubleday and Company, 1980.

_____. *Forged in Fire*. Garden City, N.Y.: Doubleday and Company, 1982.

Corn, Joseph J. *The Winged Gospel: America's Romance with Aviation, 1900–1950*. New York: Oxford University Press, 1983.

Cox, Gary C. *Beyond the Battle Line: U.S. Air Attack Theory and Doctrine, 1919–1941*. Maxwell Air Force Base, Ala.: Air University Press, 1996.

Cozzens, James Gould. *A Time of War: Air Force Diaries and Pentagon Memos, 1943–45*. Edited by Matthew J. Bruccoli. Columbia, S.C.: Bruccoli Clark, 1984.

Craig, Howard R. *Sunward I've Climbed: A Personal Narrative of Peace and War*. El Paso: Texas Western Press, 1975.

Craven, Wesley Frank, and James L. Cate, eds. *The Army Air Forces in World War*

II. Vol. 1: *Plans and Early Operations, January 1939 to August 1942*. Chicago: University of Chicago Press, 1948.

_____. Vol. 4: *The Pacific: Guadalcanal to Saipan, August 1942 to July 1944*. Chicago: University of Chicago Press, 1950.

_____. Vol. 5: *The Pacific: Matterhorn to Nagasaki, June 1944 to August 1945*. Chicago: University of Chicago Press, 1953.

_____. Vol. 6: *Men and Planes*. Chicago: University of Chicago Press, 1955.

_____. Vol. 7: *Services Around the World*. Chicago: University of Chicago Press, 1958.

Croswell, D. K. R. *The Chief of Staff: The Military Career of General Walter Bedell Smith*. Westport, Conn.: Greenwood Press, 1991.

Crowell, Edwin. *History of Barrington Township*. Yarmouth, Nova Scotia: n.p., 1923; reprint, Belleville, Ontario: Mika Publishing, 1973.

Cutler, Thomas J. *The Battle of Leyte Gulf 23–26 October 1944*. New York: Harper Collins Publishers, 1994.

Daft, Richard L. *Organization Theory and Design*. 4th ed. St. Paul, Minn.: West Publishing Company, 1992.

Dastrup, Boyd L. *The U.S. Army Command and General Staff College: A Centennial History*. Manhattan, Kans.: Sunflower University Press, 1982.

Davis, Richard G. *Carl A. Spaatz and the Air War in Europe*. Washington, D.C.: Center for Air Force History, 1993.

Detwiler, Donald S., and Charles B. Burdick, eds. *The War in Asia and the Pacific, 1937–1949: Japanese and Chinese Studies and Documents*. 15 vols. New York: Garland Publishing Company, 1980.

Dod, Karl C. *United States Army in World War II: The Corps of Engineers: The War Against Japan*. Washington, D.C.: Office of the Chief of Military History, 1966.

Dower, John W. *War Without Mercy: Race and Power in the Pacific War*. New York: Pantheon Books, 1986.

Drea, Edward J. *MacArthur's ULTRA: Codebreaking and the War Against Japan, 1942–1945*. Lawrence: University Press of Kansas, 1992.

_____. "Ultra Intelligence and General Douglas MacArthur's Leap to Hollandia, January–April 1944." In *Intelligence and Military Operations*, ed. Michael I. Handel, pp. 323–349. London: Frank Cass, 1990.

Edmonds, Walter D. *They Fought with What They Had: The Story of the Army Air Forces in the Southwest Pacific, 1941–1942*. Boston: Little, Brown, 1951; reprint, Washington, D.C.: Center for Air Force History, 1992.

Edwards, John Carver. *Airmen without Portfolio: U.S. Mercanaries in Civil War Spain*. Westport, Conn.: Praeger, 1997.

Eichelberger, Robert L., with Milton MacKaye. *Our Jungle Road to Tokyo*. New York: Viking Press, 1950.

Faber, Peter R. "Interwar U.S. Army Aviation and the Air Corps Tactical School: Incubators of American Airpower." In *The Paths of Heaven: The Evolution of Airpower Theory*, ed. Philip Meilinger, pp. 195–226. Maxwell Air Force Base, Ala.: Air University Press, 1997.

Falk, Stanley L. *Decision at Leyte*. New York: W. W. Norton and Company, 1966.

Feldt, Eric A. *The Coastwatchers*. New York: Oxford University Press, 1946.

Fine, Lenore, and Jesse A. Remington. *United States Army in World War II: The*

Corps of Engineers: Construction in the United States. Washington, D.C.: Office of the Chief of Military History, 1972.

Finney, Robert T. *History of the Air Corps Tactical School, 1920–1940.* Maxwell Air Force Base, Ala.: Air University, 1955; reprint, Washington, D.C.: Center for Air Force History, 1992.

Fishcher, Michael E. *Mission-Type Orders in Joint Air Operations.* Maxwell Air Force Base, Ala.: Air University Press, 1995.

Franzwa, Gregory M., and William J. Ely. *Lief Sverdrup.* Gerald, Mo.: Patrice Press, 1980.

Futrell, Robert Frank. *Ideas, Concepts, and Doctrines: Basic Thinking in the United States Air Force 1907–1960.* Maxwell Air Force Base, Ala.: Air University Press, 1971.

Gann, Timothy D. *Fifth Air Force Light and Medium Bomber Operations during 1942 and 1943.* Maxwell Air Force Base, Ala.: Air University Press, 1993.

Gilbert, James L., and John P. Finnegan, eds. *U.S. Army Signals Intelligence in World War II: A Documentary History.* Washington, D.C.: Center for Military History, 1993.

Gillison, Douglas. *Royal Australian Air Force, 1939–1942.* Canberra: Australian War Memorial, 1962.

Glasebrook, Millie, ed. *American Aviators in the Great War 1914–1918.* Carson City, Nev.: Glasebrook Foundation, 1984.

Greenfield, Kent Roberts, ed. *Command Decisions.* New York: Harcourt, Brace and Company, 1959.

Greer, Thomas H. *The Development of Air Doctrine in the Army Air Arm, 1917–1941.* Maxwell Air Force Base, Ala.: Air University Press, 1955.

Hallion, Richard P. *Strike From the Sky: The History of Battlefield Air Attack, 1911–1945.* Washington, D.C.: Smithsonian Institution Press, 1989.

Halsey, William F., and J. Bryan III. *Admiral Halsey's Story.* New York: McGraw-Hill Book Company, 1947.

Hansell, Haywood S. Jr. *The Air Plan that Defeated Hitler.* Atlanta: Higgins-McArthur/Longino & Porter, 1972.

_____. *The Strategic Air War against Germany and Japan: A Memoir.* Washington, D.C.: Office of Air Force History, 1986.

Hansen, Marcus Lee, and John Bartlett Brebner. *The Mingling of the Canadian and American Peoples.* New Haven, Conn.: Yale University Press for the Carnegie Endowment for International Peace, 1940.

Harvey, David D. *Americans in Canada: Migration and Settlement Since 1840.* Lewiston, N.Y.: The Edwin Mellen Press, 1991.

Haugland, Vern. *The AAF against Japan.* New York: Harper & Brothers Publishers, 1948.

Hayes, Grace P. *The History of the Joint Chiefs of Staff in World War II: The War against Japan.* Washington: Naval Institute Press, 1982.

Herring, Robert P., ed. *History of the 308th Bombardment Wing.* San Angelo, Texas: Newsfoto Publishing Company, 1945.

Hewitt, J. E. *Adversity in Success.* Victoria, Australia: Langate Publishing, 1980.

Hinkle, Stacy C. *Wings over the Border: The Army Air Service Armed Patrol of the*

United States–Mexican Border 1919–1921. Southwestern Studies no. 26. El Paso: Texas Western Press, 1970.

History of the 91st Aero Squadron. Coblenz, Germany: Gebruder Breuer, 1919.

Holley, I. B. Jr. *Buying Aircraft: Matériel Procurement for the Army Air Forces.* Washington, D.C.: Center for Military History, 1989.

————. *Ideas and Weapons.* New Haven, Conn.: Yale University Press, 1953; reprint, Washington, D.C.: Office of Air Force History, 1983.

Horner, David M. *The Commanders.* Sydney: George Allen & Unwin, 1984.

————. *Crisis of Command.* Canberra: Australian National University Press, 1987.

————. *High Command: Australia and Allied Strategy, 1939–1945.* Sydney: George Allen & Unwin, 1982.

Hudson, James J. *Hostile Skies: A Combat History of the American Air Service in World War I.* Syracuse, N.Y.: Syracuse University Press, 1968.

Hughes, Thomas Alexander. *Over Lord: General Pete Quesada and the Triumph of Tactical Air Power in World War II.* New York: Free Press, 1995.

Hurley, Alfred F. *Billy Mitchell: Crusader for Air Power.* Bloomington: Indiana University Press, 1975.

Ikle, Fred C. *Every War Must End.* New York: Columbia University Press, 1971.

Ind, Allison. *Allied Intelligence Bureau.* New York: David McKay Company, 1958.

Iriye, Akira. *Power and Culture: The Japanese-American War, 1941–1945.* Cambridge, Mass.: Harvard University Press, 1981.

James, D. Clayton. *A Time for Giants: The Politics of the American High Command in World War II.* New York: Franklin Watts, 1987.

————. *The Years of MacArthur.* 3 vols. Boston: Houghton Mifflin, 1970–1985.

Kennett, Lee. *The First Air War, 1914–1918.* New York: Free Press, 1981.

Kenney, George C. *General Kenney Reports.* New York: Duell, Sloan and Pearce, 1949; reprint, Washington: Office of Air Force History, 1987.

————. *The MacArthur I Know.* New York: Duell, Sloan and Pearce, 1951.

————. *The Saga of Pappy Gunn.* New York: Duell, Sloan and Pearce, 1959.

Kohn, Richard H., and Joseph P. Harahan, eds. *Air Superiority in World War II and Korea.* Washington, D.C.: Office of Air Force History, 1983.

Kreis, John F. *Air Warfare and Air Base Air Defense, 1914–1973.* Washington, D.C.: Office of Air Force History, 1988.

————, ed. *Piercing the Fog: Intelligence and Army Air Forces Operations in World War II.* Washington, D.C.: Air Force History and Museums Program, 1996.

Krueger, Walter. *From Down Under to Nippon.* Washington, D.C.: Combat Forces Press, 1953.

Leary, William M., ed. *We Shall Return!* Lexington: University Press of Kentucky, 1988.

Levine, Alan J. *The Pacific War: Japan versus the Allies.* Westport, Conn.: Praeger, 1995.

Lewin, Ronald. *The American Magic.* New York: Farrar, Straus, Giroux, 1982.

Lines, Kenneth. *British and Canadian Immigration to the United States Since 1920.* San Francisco: R & E Research Associates, 1978.

Long, Galvin. *MacArthur as Military Commander.* New York: Norstrand Reinhold Company, 1969.

Lundstrom, John B. *The First Team and the Guadalcanal Campaign*. Annapolis, Md.: Naval Institute Press, 1994.

Luvaas, Jay, ed. *Dear Miss Em: General Eichelberger's War in the Pacific, 1942–1945*. Westport, Conn.: Greenwood Press, 1972.

MacArthur, Douglas. *Reminiscences*. New York: McGraw-Hill Book Company, 1964.

MacIssac, David. *Strategic Bombing in World War Two*. New York: Garland Publishing, 1976.

———. "Leadership in the Old Air Force: A Postgraduate Assignment." In *The Harmon Memorial Lectures in Military History, 1959–1987*, ed. Harry R. Borowski, pp. 89–106. Washington, D.C.: Office of Air Force History, 1988.

Manchester, William. *American Caesar: Douglas MacArthur, 1880–1964*. Boston: Little, Brown and Company, 1978.

Masland, John W., and Laurence I. Radway. *Soldiers and Scholars: Military Education and National Policy*. Princeton, N.J.: Princeton University Press, 1957.

Matloff, Maurice. *United States Army in World War II: Strategic Planning for Coalition Warfare, 1943–1944*. Washington, D.C.: Office of the Chief of Military History, 1959.

Matloff, Maurice, and Edwin M. Snell. *United States Army in World War II: Strategic Planning for Coalition Warfare, 1941–1942*. Washington, D.C.: Office of the Chief of Military History, 1953.

Maurer, Maurer. *Aviation in the US Army, 1919–1939*. Washington, D.C.: Office of Air Force History, 1987.

———. *The U. S. Air Service in World War I*. 4 vols. Washington, D.C.: Office of Air Force History, 1979.

McAulay, Lex. *Battle of the Bismarck Sea*. New York: St. Martins Press, 1991.

———. *Into the Dragon's Jaws: The Fifth Air Force over Rabaul*. Mesa, Ariz.: Champlin Fighter Museum Press, 1986.

McCarthy, Dudley. *South-West Pacific Area: First Year*. Canberra: Australian War Memorial, 1961.

McClosky, Paul. "Storytelling in Economics." In *Narrative in Culture: The Uses of Storytelling in the Sciences, Philosophy, and Literature*, ed. Cristopher Nash, pp. 5–21. London: Routledge, 1990.

McFarland, Stephen L. *America's Pursuit of Precision Bombing, 1910–1945*. Washington, D.C.: Smithsonian Institution Press, 1995.

McFarland, Stephen L., and Wesley Phillips Newton. *To Command the Sky: The Battle for Air Superiority Over Germany, 1942–1944*. Washington, D.C.: Smithsonian Institution Press, 1991.

Meilinger, Philip S. *American Airpower Biography: A Survey of the Field*. Maxwell Air Force Base, Ala.: Air University Press, 1995.

Mets, David R. *Master of Airpower: General Carl A. Spaatz*. Novato, Calif.: Presidio Press, 1988.

Miller, John Jr. *United States Army in World War II: The Pacific: Cartwheel: The Reduction of Rabaul*. Washington, D.C.: Office of the Chief of Military History, 1959.

Millett, Allan R., and Peter Maslowski. *For the Common Defense: A Military History of the United States of America*, rev. and expanded ed. New York: Free Press, 1994.

Milner, Samuel. *United States Army in World War II: The Pacific: Victory in Papua*. Washington, D.C.: Office of the Chief of Military History, 1957.

Moore, John Hammond. *Over-Sexed, Over-Paid, Over-Here: Americans in Australia 1941–1945*. St. Lucia: University of Queensland Press, 1981.

Morison, Samuel Eliot. *History of United States Naval Operations in World War II*. Vol. 6, *Breaking the Bismarcks Barrier*. Boston: Little, Brown and Company, 1950.

_____. Vol. 8, *New Guinea and the Marianas*. Boston: Little, Brown and Company, 1953.

_____. Vol. 12, *Leyte*. Boston: Little, Brown and Company, 1958.

_____. Vol. 13, *The Liberation of the Philippines*. Boston: Little, Brown and Company, 1959.

Morrow, John H. Jr. *The Great War in the Air: Military Aviation From 1909 to 1921*. Washington, D.C.: Smithsonian Institution Press, 1993.

Mortensen, Daniel R. *Close Air Support Operations: North Africa*. Research and Analysis Division Special Studies Series. Washington, D.C.: U.S. Army Center of Military History, 1987.

Morton, Louis. *The United States Army in World War II: The Pacific: The Fall of the Philippines*. Washington, D.C.: Office of the Chief of Military History, 1953.

_____. *United States Army in World War II: Strategy and Command: The First Two Years*. Washington, D.C.: Office of the Chief of Military History, 1962.

Murphy, James T., with A. B. Feuer. *Skip Bombing*. Westport, Conn.: Praeger, 1993.

Newton, Wesley Phillips. "Acosta, Bertram Blanchard." In *Dictionary of American Biography, Supplement Five*, ed. John A. Garraty, pp. 2–3. New York: Charles Scribner's Sons, 1977.

Odgers, George. *Air War against Japan, 1943–1945*. Canberra: Australian War Memorial, 1957; reprint, 1968.

Office of the Chief Engineer, General Headquarters Army Forces, Pacific. *Engineers of the Southwest Pacific, 1941–1945*. Vol. 3, *Engineer Intelligence*. Washington, D.C.: Government Printing Office, 1950.

_____. Vol. 6, *Airfield and Air Base Development*. Washington, D.C.: Government Printing Office, 1951.

The Official World War II Guide to the Army Air Forces. New York: Bonanza Books, 1988; reprint of *The Official Guide to the Army Air Forces*, New York: Simon and Schuster, 1944.

O'Neil, Paul. *Barnstormers and Speed Kings*. Alexandria, Va.: Time-Life Books, 1981.

Orange, Vincent. *Coningham: A Biography of Air Marshal Sir Arthur Coningham*. London: Methuen, 1990; reprint, Washington, D.C.: Center for Air Force History, 1992.

Overy, R. J. *The Air War, 1939–1945*. New York: Stein and Day, 1980.

Parks, Edward. *Nanette*. New York: W. W. Norton and Company, 1977.

Parrish, Noel F. "The Influence of Air Power upon Historians." In *The Harmon Memorial Lectures in Military History, 1959–1987*, ed. Harry R. Borowski, pp. 25–42. Washington, D.C.: Office of Air Force History, 1988.

Perret, Geoffrey. *Winged Victory: The Army Air Forces in World War II*. New York: Random House, 1993.

Petillo, Carol Morris. *Douglas MacArthur, The Philippine Years*. Bloomington: Indiana University Press, 1981.

Potter, E. B. *Bull Halsey*. Annapolis, Md.: Naval Institute Press, 1985.

Potts, E. Daniel, and Annette Potts. *Yanks Down Under, 1941–1945*. Melbourne: Oxford University Press, 1985.

Prados, John. *Combined Fleet Decoded: The Secret History of American Intelligence and the Japanese Navy in World War II*. New York: Random House, 1995.

Prescott, Samuel C. *When M.I.T. Was "Boston Tech" 1861–1916*. Cambridge, Mass.: Technology Press, 1954.

Put 'Em Across: A History of the Second Engineer Special Brigade. Harrisburg, Penn.: Telegraph Press, 1946; reprint, Washington, D.C.: Office of History Corps of Engineers, 1988.

The RAAF in the Southwest Pacific Area 1942–1945. Canberra: RAAF Air Power Studies Centre, 1993.

Rawlyk, George A. *Nova Scotia's Massachusetts: A Study of Massachusetts–Nova Scotia Relations, 1630–1784*. Montreal: McGill-Queen's University Press, 1973.

Rayner, Harry. *Scherger*. Canberra: Australian War Memorial, 1984.

The Reports of General MacArthur. 2 vols. Washington, D.C.: Government Printing Office, 1966.

Rickenbacker, Edward V. *Rickenbacker*. Englewood Cliffs, N.J.: Prentice-Hall, 1967.

Robertson, Florance L. K. "Keeney, Keny, Family of Milton, Mass., and Nova Scotia, Canada." In *Genealogies of Mayflower Families*, selected and introduced by Gary Boyd Roberts, pp. 413–434. Baltimore: Genealogical Publishing Co., 1985.

Rogers, Paul P. *The Bitter Years: MacArthur and Sutherland*. New York: Praeger Publishers, 1990.

———. *The Good Years: MacArthur and Sutherland*. New York: Praeger Publishers, 1990.

Rosen, Stephen Peter. *Winning the Next War: Innovation and the Modern Military*. Ithaca, N.Y.: Cornell University Press, 1991.

Rothgeb, Wayne P. *New Guinea Skies: A Fighter Pilot's View of World War II*. Ames: Iowa State University Press, 1992.

Sakai, Saburo, with Martin Caidin and Fred Saito. *Samurai!* Garden City, N.Y.: Nelson Doubleday, 1978.

Schaller, Michael. *Douglas MacArthur: The Far Eastern General*. New York: Oxford University Press, 1989.

Shiner, John F. *Foulois and the US Army Air Corps*. Washington, D.C.: Office of Air Force History, 1983.

Shortal, John F. *Forged by Fire: General Robert L. Eichelberger and the Pacific War*. Columbia: University of South Carolina Press, 1987.

Skates, John Ray. *The Invasion of Japan: Alternative to the Bomb*. Columbia: University of South Carolina Press, 1994.

Smith, Dean C. *By the Seat of My Pants*. Boston: Little, Brown and Company, 1961.

Smith, Robert Ross. *United States Army in World War II: The Pacific: The Approach to the Philippines*. Washington, D.C.: Office of the Chief of Military History, 1953.

———. *United States Army in World War II: The Pacific: Triumph in the Philippines*. Washington, D.C.: Office of the Chief of Military History, 1963.

Spector, Ronald H. *Eagle against the Sun*. New York: Free Press, 1984; reprint, New York: Vintage Books, 1985.

———, ed. *Listening to the Enemy*. Wilmington, Del.: Scholarly Resources, 1988.

Spick, Mike. *Milestones of Manned Flight.* New York: Smithmark Publishers, 1994.
_____. *The Ace Factor.* Annapolis, Md.: Naval Institute Press, 1988.

Stanaway, John. *Possum, Clover & Hades: The 475th Fighter Group in World War II.* Atglen, Penn.: Schiffer Military/Aviation History, 1993.

Steele, Ian K. *Warpaths: Invasions of North America.* New York: Oxford University Press, 1994.

Stephens, Alan. *Power Plus Attitude: Ideas, Strategy and Doctrine in the Royal Australian Air Force, 1921–1991.* Canberra: Australian Government Printing Service, 1992.

Stevenson, Clare, and Honor Darling, eds. *The WAAAF Book.* Sydney: Hale and Iremonger, 1984.

Taafe, Stephen R. *MacArthur's Jungle War: The 1944 New Guinea Campaign.* Lawrence: University Press of Kansas, 1998.

Thayer, Lucien H. *America's First Eagles: The Official History of the U.S. Air Service, A. E. F.* Edited by Donald Joseph McGee and James Bender. San Jose, Calif.: R. James Bender, and Mesa, Ariz.: Champlin Fighter Museum Press, 1983.

Thompson, George Raynor, and Dixie R. Harris. *United States Army in World War II: The Signal Corps: The Outcome.* Washington, D.C.: Office of the Chief of Military History, 1966.

Thompson, George Raynor, Dixie R. Harris, Pauline M. Oakes, and Dulany Terrett. *United States Army in World War II: The Signal Corps: The Test.* Washington, D.C.: Office of the Chief of Military History, 1957.

Ticknor, Caroline, ed. *New England Aviators, 1914–1918.* 2 vols. Boston: Houghton Mifflin Company, 1919.

Underwood, Jeffery S. *The Wings of Democracy: The Influence of Air Power on the Roosevelt Administration, 1933–1941.* College Station: Texas A&M University Press, 1991.

United States Strategic Bombing Survey (USSBS). *Air Campaigns of the Pacific War.* Washington, D.C.: Government Printing Office, 1947.
_____. *Air Forces Allied with the United States in the War against Japan.* Washington, D.C.: Government Printing Office, 1947.
_____. *The Allied Campaign against Rabaul.* Washington, D.C.: Government Printing Office, 1946.
_____. *The Effect of Air Action on Japanese Ground Army Logisitics.* Washington, D.C.: Government Printing Office, 1947.
_____. *The Fifth Air Force in the War against Japan.* Washington, D.C.: Government Printing Office, 1947.
_____. *Interrogations of Japanese Officals.* 2 vols. Washington, D.C.: Government Printing Office, n.d.
_____. *Japanese Air Power.* Washington, D.C.: Government Printing Office, 1946.
_____. *Oil in Japan's War.* Washington, D.C.: Government Printing Office, 1946.
_____. *Oil in Japan's War, Appendix.* Washington, D.C.: Government Printing Office, 1946.
_____. *Summary Report (Pacific War).* Washington, D.C.: Government Printing Office, 1946.
_____. *The War against Japanese Transportation, 1941–1945.* Washington, D.C.: Government Printing Office, 1947.

Vandenberg, Arthur H. Jr., with the collaboration of Joe Alex Morris. *The Private Papers of Senator Vandenberg.* Boston: Houghton Mifflin Co., 1952.

Wallace, Graham. *Claude Grahame-White A Biography.* London: Putnam, 1960.

Watts, Berry D. *The Foundations of U.S. Air Doctrine: The Problem of Friction in War.* Maxwell Air Force Base, Ala.: Air University Press, 1984.

Weinberg, Gerhard L. *A World At Arms: A Global History of World War II.* Cambridge: Cambridge University Press, 1994.

Werrell, Kenneth P. *Archie, Flak, AAA, and SAM: A Short Operational History of Ground-Based Air Defense.* Maxwell Air Force Base, Ala.: Air University Press, 1988.

———. *Blankets of Fire: U.S. Bombers Over Japan during World War II.* Washington, D.C.: Smithsonian Institution Press, 1996.

Wheeler, Gerald E. *Kinkaid of the Seventh Fleet.* Washington, D.C.: Naval Historical Center, 1995.

Willoughby, Charles A., and John Chamberlin. *MacArthur, 1941–1951.* New York: McGraw-Hill, 1954.

Winnefeld, James A., and Dana J. Johnson. *Command and Control of Joint Air Operations.* RAND Report R-4045. Santa Monica, Calif.: RAND Corporation, 1991.

———. *Joint Air Operations: Pursuit of Unity in Command and Control, 1942–1991.* Annapolis, Md.: Naval Institute Press, 1993.

Wilson, Donald. *Wooing Peponi.* Monterey, Calif.: Angel Press, 1974.

Wohl, Robert. *A Passion for Wings: Aviation and the Western Imagination, 1908–1918.* New Haven, Conn.: Yale University Press, 1994.

Wolk, Herman S. "George C. Kenney: MacArthur's Premier Airman." In *We Shall Return!* ed. William M. Leary, pp. 88–114. Lexington: University Press of Kentucky, 1988.

———. "George C. Kenney: The Great Innovator." In *Makers of the United States Air Force,* ed. John L. Frisbee, pp. 127–150. Washington, D.C.: Office of Air Force History, 1987.

Woodward, C. Vann. *The Battle for Leyte Gulf.* New York: MacMillian Company, 1947.

Yoshino, Ronald. *Lightning Strikes: The 475th Fighter Group in the Pacific War, 1943–1945.* Manhattan, Kans: Sunflower University Press, 1988.

Published Sources—Articles

Alcorn, John. "The Grim Reapers: 3rd Bomb Group." *American Aviation Historical Society Journal* 20 (Spring 1975): 6–15.

———. "The Grim Reapers, Part 2." *American Aviation Historical Society Journal* 20 (Fall 1975): 187–193.

Anderson, Orvil A. "Air War in the Pacific." *Air Power Historian* 4 (Oct. 1957): 216–227.

Andrews, Frank M. "Our Use of Air Power: The GHQ AF as an Instrument of Defense." *Army Ordnance* 18 (Nov.–Dec. 1937): 137–142.

Arnold, Henry H. "The Air Force and Military Engineers." *The Military Engineer* 33 (Dec. 1941): 545–548.

Baldwin, William C. "Engineers in the Southwest Pacific, 1941–1944." *Military Engineer* 83 (March–April 1993): 76.

Ball, Desmond J. "Allied Intelligence Cooperation Involving Australia During World War II." *Australian Outlook* 32 (Dec. 1978): 299–309.

Bartlett, K. S. "Brookline's Gen. Kenney Raining Armies on Japs in Southern Pacific." *Boston Globe,* January 31, 1943, p. 1.

Bartsh, William H. "Was MacArthur Ill-Served by his Air Force Commanders in the Philippines?" *Air Power History* 44 (Summer 1997): 44–63.

Berlin, Robert H. "United States Army World War II Corps Commanders: A Composite Biography." *Journal of Military History* 53 (April 1989): 147–167.

Bernstein, Barton J. "Understanding the Bomb and the Japanese Surrender: Missed Opportunities, Little-Known Disasters, and Modern Memory." *Diplomatic History* 19 (Spring 1995): 227–273.

Birnn, Roland R. "A War Diary." *Air Power Historian* 3 (Oct. 1956): 195–200; (Jan. 1957): 40–45; 4 (April 1957): 98–103.

Brett, George H., with Jack Kofoed. "The MacArthur I Knew." *True,* October 1947, pp. 25–27, 139–148.

Briggs, Phillip J. "General MacArthur and the Presidential Election of 1944." *Presidential Studies Quarterly* 22 (Winter 1992): 33–40.

Callahan, William R. "Brookline Boy Takes Command of our Air Force in Pacific." *Boston Globe,* September 16, 1942, p. 1.

Cooper, Dennis Glen. "Tales of Gallantry in the Southwest Pacific." *Aerospace Historian* 32 (June 1985): 107–116.

Cromie, Robert. "Kenney of the Fifth!" *Chicago Sunday Tribune,* November 14, 1943, p. 1.

Dame, Lawrence. "A Flying General." *Boston Herald,* September 8, 1945, p. 1.

Downs, Eldon W. "Army and the Airmail—1934." *The Airpower Historian* 9 (Jan. 1962): 35–51.

Drea, Edward J. "'Great Patience is Necessary': America Encounters Australia, 1942." *War & Society* 2 (May 1993): 21–51.

Falk, Stanley L. "Gaps in the Published History of the Air Force: Challenge for Historians." *The Historian* 44 (Aug. 1982): 453–465.

———. "General Kenney, The Indirect Approach and the B-29s." *Aerospace Historian* 27 (Sept. 1981): 147–155.

Farris, James M. "Tacloban." *The Friends Journal* (Spring 1997): 29–32.

Finney, Robert T. "Early Air Corps Training and Tactics." *Military Affairs* 20 (Fall 1956): 154–161.

Fox, William T. R., ed. *Annals of the American Academy of Political and Social Science* 392 (Nov. 1970).

Futrell, Robert F. "Air Hostilities in the Philippines, 8 December 1941." *Air University Review* 16 (Jan.–Feb. 1965): 33–45.

Godfrey, Stuart C. "Engineers with the Army Air Forces." *The Military Engineer* 33 (Nov. 1941): 487–491.

Handel, Michael. "The Study of War Termination." *The Journal of Strategic Studies* 1 (May 1978): 51–75.

Hansell, Haywood S. Jr. "General Laurence S. Kuter 1905–1979." *Aerospace Historian* 27 (June 1980): 91–94.

Hattori, Syohgo. "Kamikaze, Japan's Glorious Failure." *Air Power History* 43 (Spring 1996): 14–27.

Holley, I. B. Jr. "An Air Force General: Laurence Sherman Kuter." *Aerospace Historian* 27 (June 1980): 88–90.

_____. "RAF/USAAF Land/Air Operations: Mediterranean & Northwest Europe." *Air Power History* 38 (Winter 1991): 30–34.

Horner, David M. "Special Intelligence in the South-West Pacific Area in World War II." *Australian Outlook* 32 (Dec. 1978): 310–327.

Howell, Jane M., and Christopher A. Higgins. "Champions of Change: Identifying, Understanding, and Supporting Champions of Technological Innovation." *Organizational Dynamics* (Summer 1990): 52–58.

James, D. Clayton. "The Other Pearl Harbor." *MHQ: The Quarterly Journal of Military History* 7 (Winter 1995): 23–29.

Johansen, Herbert O. "Our Air Task Force." *Air Force* 27 (Dec. 1944): 4–7, 40.

Kenney, George C. "Air Power in the Southwest Pacific." *Air Force* 27 (June 1944): 6–10, 59–61.

_____. "The Airplane in Modern Warfare." *Air Services,* July 1938, pp. 17–22, 36.

Krauskopf, Robert W. "The Army and the Strategic Bomber, 1930–1939, Part II." *Military Affairs* 22 (Summer 1958): 208–215.

Lear, Kirk A. "American Parachute Assaults in the Southwest Pacific: Lessons for Today's Joint Airdrop Doctrine." *Air Power History* 42 (Fall 1995): 4–15.

Nenninger, Timothy K. "Creating Officers: The Leavenworth Experience, 1920–1940." *Military Review* 69 (Nov. 1989): 58–68.

_____. "Leavenworth and Its Critics: The US Army Command and General Staff School, 1920–1940." *Journal of Military History* 58 (April 1994): 199–231.

Newton, Lowell W. "Jungle Airfields." *Air Power History* 42 (Fall 1995): 16–23.

Norberg, Carl A. "In the Southwest Pacific with the Army's Navy." *Aerospace Historian* 27 (Fall 1980): 163–168.

Nunn, Jack H. "MIT: A University's Contributions to National Defense." *Military Affairs* 43 (Oct. 1979): 120–125.

O'Sullivan, Charles P. "Sully's Saga." *Air Power History* 41 (Winter 1994): 4–17.

Paris, Michael. "The Rise of the Airmen: The Origins of Air Force Elitism: c. 1890–1918." *Journal of Contemporary History* 28 (Jan. 1993): 123–141.

Parnell, N. M. "Reminiscences of a Radio Operator." *American Aviation Historical Society Journal* 32 (Winter 1987): 254–265.

Pierce, Robert. "Hardships." *American Heritage* 42 (Dec. 1991): 110–116.

Powers, John J. "Founding of the Air Force Institute of Technology." *Air University Review* 15 (Sept.–Oct. 1964): 36–50.

Saunders, Oswald H. "The Army War College." *Military Engineer* 26 (March–April 1934): 101–104.

Shiner, John F. "Birth of the GHQ Air Force." *Military Affairs* 42 (Oct. 1978): 113–120.

_____. "The Air Corps, the Navy, and Coast Defense, 191–1941." *Military Affairs* 45 (Oct. 1981): 113–120.

Smyser, R. E. Jr. "Airdromes for War." *The Military Engineer* 33 (Dec. 1941): 562–566.

Sturgis, Samuel D. "Air Power as Affected by Airdrome Construction." *The Military Engineer* 40 (Sept. 1948): 413–422.

_____. "Engineer Operations in the Leyte Campaign, Part I." *The Military Engineer* 39 (Nov. 1947): 457–463.

_____. "Engineer Operations in the Leyte Campaign, Part II." *The Military Engineer* 39 (Dec. 1947): 513–518.

_____. "Engineer Operations in the Leyte Campaign, Part III." *The Military Engineer* 40 (Jan. 1948): 15–19.

Wohl, Robert. "The Bards of Aviation: Flight and French Culture 1090–1939." *Michigan Quarterly Review* 29 (Summer 1990): 303–327.

Westenhoff, Charles M. "Aggressive Vision." *Airpower Journal* 3 (Fall 1989): 34–49.

Wilson, Donald. "Origins of a Theory for Air Strategy." *Aerospace Historian* 18 (March 1971): 19–25.

Y'Blood, William T. "Unwanted and Unloved: The Consolidated B-32." *Air Power History* 42 (Fall 1995): 58–71.

Interviews and Oral Histories

Adair, Charles. Interview by John T. Mason Jr., February 26, 1975, Washington, D.C. U.S. Naval Institute Oral History Program. NHC.

Anderson, Samuel E. Interview by Hugh N. Ahmann, June 28–July 1, 1976, Santa Monica, California. File K239.0512-905, HRA.

Badham, William. Interview by George W. Goodard, May 20, 1966. File K2239.0512-989, HRA.

Crabb, Jarred V. Interview by LTC Julian and Major Goldstein, April 17, 28, 1970, USAF Academy. File K239.0512-622, HRA.

Decker, George H. Interview by Dan H. Ralls, November 3, 9, December 8, 18, 1972, Washington, D.C. Military History Institute.

Dodson, Dorothy. Interview by Thomas E. Griffith Jr., May 22, 1995, Arlington, Virginia.

Eddleman, Clyde D. Interview by Lowell G. Smith and Murray G. Swindler, January 28, February 11, April 15, 1945, Arlington, Virginia, and Carlisle Barracks, Pennsylvania. Military History Institute.

Ellis, Richard H. Interview by Maurice Maryanow, August 17–21, 1987, Washington, D.C. File K239.0512-740, HRA.

Gideon, Francis C. Interview by Mark C. Cleary, July 7, 1982, Larkspur, Colorado. File K239.0512-1338, HRA.

Giles, Barney M. Interview by James C. Hasdorff and Noel Parrish, November 20–21, 1974, San Antonio, Texas. File K239.0512-814, HRA.

Hipps, William G. Interview by Walton S. Moody, George M. Watson Jr., November 28, 1984, Washington, D.C. File K239.0512-1732, HRA.

Kenney, George C. Interview by Assistant Chief of Air Staff, Intelligence, Army Air Forces Headquarters, April 24, 1943, Washington, D.C. File 142.034-2, HRA.

_____. Interview by George W. Goodard, May 6, 1966. File K239.0512-1011, HRA.

_____. Interview by James C. Hasdorff, August 10–21, 1974, Bay Harbor Islands, Florida. File K239.0512-806, HRA.

_____. Interview by D. Clayton James, July 16, 1971, New York. File 168.7103-24, HRA.

_____. Interview by Marvin Stanley, n.d., Washington, D.C. File K239.0512-747, HRA.

Partridge, Earle E. Interview by Tom Strum and Hugh N. Ahmann, April 23–24, 1974, Colorado Springs, Colorado. File K239.0512-610, HRA.

Porter, Edith. Interview by James Kenney, 1982, Yarmouth, Nova Scotia.

Smith, Frederic H. Jr. Interview by James C. Hasdorff and Noel F. Parrish, June 6–8, 1976, San Antonio, Texas. File K239.0512-903, HRA.

Street, St. Clair. Interview by Beverly Moore, September 19, 1945. File 706.201, HRA.

Wilson, Donald. Interview by Hugh N. Ahmann, December 10–11, 1975, Carmel, California. File K239.0512-878, HRA.

_____. Interview by Beverly Moore, September 22, 1945. File 706.201, HRA.

INDEX

A-20s, 75, 82, 99, 106, 132, 135, 212
A-29s, 42
Acosta, Bert, 9
Adachi Hatazo, 98, 104, 136, 155
Admiralty Islands (Admiralties), 151–155, 161, 238
Advanced Echelon. *See* 5th Advon
AIB. *See* Allied Intelligence Bureau
Air Blitz Unit, 44, 124
Air Corps, 23–24, 27–29, 31, 33–39, 40–43, 45, 58–59, 67, 74, 81, 90, 233, 242
Air Corps Tactical School (ACTS), 28, 35, 43, 44, 58–59, 75, 99, 134, 233, 236. *See also* Air Service Tactical School
Airfield construction, 88–91, 114, 124–125, 127–129, 138–140, 158, 163, 165–169, 174, 192, 196, 199–201, 202–203, 208, 210–211, 214, 217, 223, 226, 247
  Japanese, 155–157, 205, 247
  See also Aviation engineers
Air Freight Forwarding Units, 127
Air mail crisis, 34, 36
Air Service, 7, 10–12, 14, 18–19, 20–24, 35, 59
Air Service Command. *See* 5th Air Service Command
Air Service Engineering School, 20, 21, 42–43, 58, 99, 257n13
Air Service Tactical School, 21–22. *See also* Air Corps Tactical School
Air superiority, xi, 15–16, 74–75, 81, 94, 120, 122, 129, 144, 198, 200, 201, 233–236, 238, 240–241, 247
Air Support Command, 117–118
Air transport, 44, 64–65, 124, 127–128, 135, 138–139, 234–235, 237

Japanese use of, 205
  in New Guinea, 86–89, 93–94
Air Transport Command, 86, 127
Aitape, 159–160, 164, 166
Alamo Force, 119
Allied Air Forces, ix, 46, 49, 52, 53, 59, 61–63, 68, 117–118, 141, 159, 165, 175, 187, 231–232
Allied Intelligence Bureau (AIB), 78, 84. *See also* Coastwatchers
Allied Land Forces, 49, 53, 87, 122, 136
Allied Naval Forces, 49, 146, 159, 187, 191
Anderson, Samuel, 56
Andrews, Frank, 28–29, 35–39, 56
Antiaircraft fire, 12, 27–28, 106, 131, 146, 204
Arafua Sea, 160, 170
Arawe, 145
Army Air Forces, ix, 23, 47–48, 58, 68, 80, 82–83, 87, 130–131, 148, 175, 219–220, 228, 230, 233, 243–244
Army Air Service. *See* Air Service
Army War College (AWC), 22, 29–35, 43, 67, 242
Arnold, Henry H., 40–42, 47–48, 55–59, 66, 68, 94–95, 109–110, 113, 116, 123–126, 134, 147, 179, 182, 197, 202, 226–227, 230, 236, 264n150
  and B-29s, 148, 149, 150, 181, 186, 243–244
  at CGSS, 23
  on flexibility, 83
  on Kenney, 89, 142–143, 219–222, 244
  perspective on war, 130–132, 220–221
  about skip bombing, 82